Inside Reagan's Navy

Inside Reagan's Navy

The Pentagon Journals

Chase Untermeyer

TEXAS A&M UNIVERSITY PRESS · COLLEGE STATION

This paper meets the requirements of ANSI/NISO z39.48-1992 (Permanence of Paper).
Binding materials have been chosen for durability.
∞ ♻

Library of Congress Cataloging-in-Publication Data
Untermeyer, Chase, 1946– author.
Inside Reagan's navy: the Pentagon journals / Chase Untermeyer. — First edition.
pages cm
"When Things Went Right (Texas A&M University Press, 2013), predecessor to this
volume in telling the story of my years in the Reagan Administration." — Preface.
Includes bibliographical references and index.
ISBN 978-1-62349-212-0 (cloth: alk. paper) — ISBN 978-1-62349-216-8 (ebook)
1. Untermeyer, Chase, 1946—Diaries. 2. United States. Department of the Navy—
Officials and employees—Diaries. 3. United States—Politics and government—1981–1989.
4. Lehman, John F. 5. Webb, James H. I. Untermeyer, Chase, 1946- When things
went right. Preceded by (work): II. Title.
E876.U846 2015
973.927—dc23
2014016903

The author is directing any royalties he may receive from this
book to the George W. Bush Presidential Center.

★ ★ ★

*To the men and women of the
United States Navy and Marine Corps
—past, present, and future.*

★ ★ ★

"Who could fail to work for such a service?"

WINSTON CHURCHILL, EX–FIRST LORD OF THE ADMIRALTY (1923)

––––––

"Remember that from 1913 to 1921, I personally was fairly close to world events, and in that period, while I learned much of what to do, I also learned much of what not to do."

FRANKLIN D. ROOSEVELT,
EX–ASSISTANT SECRETARY OF THE NAVY (1937)

––––––

"To change anything in the Na-a-vy is like punching a feather bed. You punch it with your right and you punch it with your left until you are finally exhausted, and then you find the damn bed just as it was before you started punching."

FDR (1940)

––––––

"Some of the Army-Navy troubles [during World War II] . . . grew mainly from the peculiar psychology of the Navy Department, which frequently seemed to retire from the realm of logic into a dim religious world in which Neptune was God, Mahan his prophet, and the United States Navy the only true Church."

HENRY L. STIMSON, EX–SECRETARY OF WAR,
WITH MCGEORGE BUNDY (1947)

––––––

Contents

Preface

Third Time in the Fleet

During the two rich and important years that I served as executive assistant to then–Vice President George Bush (1981–83), I had occasion to go places and do things that had existed only in my dream life as a newspaper reporter and state legislator back in Texas. With my base a tiny cubbyhole in the West Wing of the White House, a mere 15-second walk from the Oval Office, I traveled with Bush all over America and to every continent except Antarctica. Through him I was able to have dinner with Margaret Thatcher at Number 10 Downing Street, lunch with Emperor Hirohito in the Imperial Palace in Tokyo, and a private audience with Pope John Paul II at the Vatican.

But, as glamorous as this was and as grateful as I was, my job held little substance. I became increasingly and painfully aware that others were governing the United States and I was not. With mounting intensity I resolved to leave the VP's office after the 1982 midterm elections for a spot elsewhere in the executive branch, one that would give me responsibility for policies and programs and provide me with practical instruction in how to advance the Administration's agenda through the bureaucracy and the Congress.

There was never any question in my mind where I wanted to go: the Navy Department.[1] It was a major scene of action in the Reagan Administration under the brilliant, dynamic, and crafty young secretary John Lehman, who was scoring triumph after triumph in his drive to achieve the President's goal of a 600-ship fleet. How I got to Navy forms the climax of *When Things Went Right* (Texas A&M University Press, 2013), predecessor to this volume in telling the story of my years in the Reagan Administration. What I did when I got there is the story of this volume.

My mother always liked to say that this was my third time in the fleet.

---

1. Once an independent Cabinet agency, the Navy Department has been a subunit of the Department of Defense since 1947. Like the Army and Air Force departments, it has no operational role (which belongs to the secretary of Defense, the Joint Chiefs of Staff, and combatant commands around the world) but is instead responsible for recruiting, training, and equipping the force. The Navy Department contains two services, the Navy and the Marine Corps.

The second was when I served (1968–70) during the Vietnam War as a division officer and navigator aboard an aged destroyer, USS *Benner* (DD-807) in the Western Pacific and then as flag lieutenant (aide) to the commander of US Naval Forces in the Philippines. The first time I was in the fleet, she would point out, was in utero, for she was one of the first women line officers in the Navy, serving as a communicator in "Old Main Navy" in Washington. In the capital she met my father, an Army officer working on Lend-Lease. They were married in 1944, and I came along in March 1946, about seven months after VJ Day.

As the son of two veterans of World War II, I quite naturally looked upon service during Vietnam as a duty. I also saw it as a necessary and valuable first step in what I hoped would be a career in public life. Therefore, during the winter of 1966 I signed up for the Naval Reserve Officer Training Program at Harvard, where I was an undergraduate. This was not the most popular student activity at the time, when opposition to the war in Vietnam roiled campuses all over the country and my contemporaries agonized over how to maintain student exemptions from the draft. Naval ROTC resolved my immediate postgraduate future and gave me the exciting prospect of travel and adventure. I was therefore among few men graduating from Ivy League institutions in June 1968 who were eager to leave campus life behind and put on the uniform of their country.

Just two years later, President Nixon announced the "Vietnamization" of the war, leading to a significant reduction in troop levels and the officer corps. We reserve officers with no desire to remain on active duty were given a reduction in our obligated service. Exercising this option, I mustered out at the small naval air station at Sangley Point on Manila Bay and embarked on a 16-month trek through Asia and Africa. I left the Navy without rancor and with only fondness for it. Indeed, I wanted to return to the Navy one day—not as an officer but as an appointed panjandrum. I correctly guessed that I had a better chance of rising to importance in the Navy through the workings of politics than through steady progress up through the ranks.

Having been in uniform, even for only two years, proved a great advantage when I rejoined the Navy as a civilian some 12½ years later. Pentagon appointees need not have served in the Armed Forces, and starting in the 1980s a decreasing number of senior civilian officials have been veterans. But those with prior military experience bring to their jobs an immediate understanding of military people and their proud culture. The lack of such service only means that nonveterans need more time to grasp the new world (and new jargon) they suddenly encounter within the five walls of the Pentagon. Veterans also bring a certain credibility with professional military people. Often during my civilian service at Navy an admiral would stop an explanation of some nautical matter to interject, "But you know: you've been at sea." The mere thought that one day a flag officer would say this to me would have greatly amused—and I suspect gratified—lowly Ensign Untermeyer as he stood the mid watch on the bridge of *Benner* in the Tonkin Gulf.

When the political personnel system granted my wish to go to Navy in March 1983, it was as deputy assistant secretary for Installations & Facilities. This position, for which I devised the proper naval acronym DASNIF, gave me charge of the Navy Department's bases and buildings, occupational safety, and environmental affairs. In addition, I was "executive agent" for the entire Department of Defense (DOD) on matters involving the Outer Continental Shelf. During the one year I served as DASNIF, sympathetic career civil servants and military officers helped me learn how to get things done in the loftier levels of the Navy and Marine Corps and with the mandarins of DOD.

My second, longer, and more significant post was as assistant secretary for Manpower & Reserve Affairs, to which President Reagan appointed me in August 1984. As "AsstSecNav" for four years, I had responsibility for all policy affecting Navy and Marine personnel: pay, housing, health care, recruitment, education (including the US Naval Academy at Annapolis), training, family issues, women's issues, minority issues, and the justice system. In those years at the climax of the Cold War, the two services were approximately twice the size they are today, with 600,000 sailors and 200,000 Marines on active duty. I also had responsibility for the roughly one-third million civilian employees of the Navy Department, most especially its senior civil servants.

In both of these jobs, I strove not to be the DOD political appointee of legend: a prosperous businessman or attorney who served in uniform during "the war," gave or raised a lot of money for the president, and then received appointment as a service secretary or assistant secretary. Once appointed, such folk would relive the glory days of their youth by putting on all manner of military getups and "visiting the troops"—an excuse to fly in high-performance jets or ride around in tanks. What they didn't do was attend to the paperwork, the personnel assignments, and the budget-making back in the Pentagon. These boring things they happily left with impressive and beribboned staff officers who would generate more junkets by regularly telling them "the men really enjoyed your visit, sir" and "we've got to get you out to a carrier in the Med."

During the five years I served in the Navy Department, my duty station was not at large but at my desk. What travel I did was for basic orientation and knowledge. I did like going to sea, but such trips were all taken off the East Coast and typically confined to weekends. After observing the fleet and Fleet Marine Force, picking up manpower-related problems, I could then be back in the Pentagon before the Secretary asked where the hell I was. Prior to visiting a ship or a base, I had my staff tell the local commander that I did not want to ride in something or shoot something but to talk to chaplains, visit a brig, and share meals with sailors, Marines, and their petty officers.

Not travel, but countless and endless meetings dominated my life in the Pentagon. These were on such subjects as recruitment, housing, dental policy, physical standards for aviators, the organization of naval education and training, retirement, special pays for doctors, and above all the budget. The reader is spared the vast majority of these important but benumbing sessions. Instead, this book aims to give a sense of practical naval administration by concentrating on just a few major topics, such as the selection of new homeports, the reform of the Naval Academy, increasing fleet assignments for women, and DOD's response to the terrifying new disease called AIDS.

Yet a book of this nature and length cannot go into much detail on even these few issues. For example, I only touch on what were extensive labors on the Naval Academy—its leadership, curriculum, and disciplinary cases—involving innumerable sessions in my Pentagon office and treks to Annapolis. To provide this detail would drag down the narrative. So in my picking and choosing I describe the secretary of the Navy's highly intellectual approach to Academy matters, relate how I as his agent worked to achieve and sustain his reforms over staunch resistance by the nuclear Navy, and examine just one incendiary case, that of a midshipman accused of using cocaine.

Likewise, this book only marginally discusses one of the signal achievements of the Reagan years, the procurement of new ships, subs, planes, and weapons systems for the Navy and Marine Corps. Others had the responsibility to build such things; my responsibility was to find, train, and care for the sailors and Marines required to fight them. Neither does this book chart the period's naval operations throughout the world nor the development of a bold new maritime strategy to confront the Soviet Navy in its home waters in time of war. What it does seek to do above all is to highlight two remarkable men who served Ronald Reagan as secretary of the Navy.

The first was John H. Lehman Jr. (1981–87), who was not only the most effective service secretary since World War II but truly one of the most adept and successful political executives in modern US history. Born in 1943, Lehman earned a doctorate in international relations and acquired a detailed knowledge of how American government works while on the staff of the National Security Council and an appointee at the Arms Control & Disarmament Agency during the Nixon-Ford years. After Reagan's election in 1980, Lehman won an intense internal struggle to become "SecNav." In this political battle royal, his principal supporter was Vice President–elect Bush. Once in office, Lehman surged forward to fulfill the promise made in the 1980 Republican Party platform—a plank he himself wrote—to build the US Navy up to a fighting strength of 600 ships. To achieve this goal, Lehman summoned all his technical mastery of ships, aircraft, and weaponry, his unmatched skill at congressional relations, and his ability to outfox bureaucratic foes. Today's much-reduced if still capable US Navy is at heart the one that John Lehman built in the 1980s.

James H. (Jim) Webb Jr. succeeded Lehman in 1987 after serving as the first assistant secretary of Defense for Reserve Affairs. His story began as a fierce boxer at the US Naval Academy and, following his graduation in 1968, in the Marine Corps. The inheritor of a proud family military tradition, Webb was a platoon commander in the so-called Arizona Valley, one of the toughest sectors in one of the toughest periods of the Vietnam War. In a firefight he threw himself on a grenade to save the life of one of his Marines. For this act of unhesitating heroism, he received the Navy Cross, the highest award for valor that the Department of the Navy can bestow. Yet his wounds forced him to leave the Corps he loved and to pursue a civilian career as a lawyer and congressional staffer. Webb's experience in Vietnam led him to write a novel, *Fields of Fire* (1978), considered the finest and most realistic work of fiction to come out of the war. His service as SecNav ended after only ten months when he did something quite rare in American politics: he resigned in a dispute over policy. Always viewing himself as a writer and not as a public official, Webb published two more novels and an excellent history of the Scots-Irish in America, *Born Fighting* (2004). He then served a single term (2007–13) as United States senator from Virginia.

In quite different ways, both Lehman and Webb were admirable and impressive, but like all leaders they were not without flaws. Beyond question, both men had talents far superior to mine, which is why they achieved what they did and I less. Any criticism I made at the time of their management styles and means of dealing with people is not repeated here to make them look bad and me look good but to shade proper portraits of them and give leadership lessons for anyone who may read this book.

These pages do not hesitate to mention times when my own service was flawed and when I richly deserved the secretarial correction or castigation that followed. But they also tell of times when I got things right, justifying Ronald Reagan's decision to put me in charge of Navy and Marine manpower. In any event, the experience at Navy formed my concepts of political leadership over a proud and skilled career force that I put to use when I headed an agency of my own, the Voice of America, at the end of the first Bush Administration. They are also offered here to guide subsequent generations of appointees, whether at the Navy Department or anywhere else.

★   ★   ★

What appears in the following pages are selected, edited, and annotated entries from twenty-four volumes of a journal kept since the age of nine. They represent a mere fraction of all I wrote during a five-year period. The selections were made to give an impression of my service, of the personalities with whom I came in contact, and of the very thrilling era of Ronald Reagan. Editing was done for brevity and clarity's sake in telling the story. Where required I add explanatory material in brackets: that which is in ordinary type reflects knowledge I had when I wrote the entry, and that in italics reflects facts or views from a later time.

In *Nicholas Nickleby* (1838–39), Charles Dickens spluttered:

> Some of the craftiest scoundrels that ever walked this earth, or rather—for walking implies, at least, an upright position and the bearing of a man— that ever crawled or crept through life by its dirtiest and narrowest ways, will gravely jot down in diaries the events of every day and keep a regular debtor and creditor account with Heaven, which shall always show a floating balance in their own favour.

Perhaps John Lehman, Jim Webb, and others may find cause in these pages to make a similar spluttering. In defense I reply that they *did* it; I only recorded it. And, while it may be of only slight comfort to them, I have omitted a great deal of other material that they might find even more disagreeable. Again, my purpose was not to defame them but to describe them and their achievements, which definitely show balances in *their* favor. In the words of Plutarch:

> The most glorious exploits do not always furnish us with the clearest discoveries of virtue or vice in men. Sometimes a matter of less moment, an expression or a jest, informs us better of their character and inclinations than the most famous sieges, the greatest armaments, or the bloodiest battles.

*   *   *

This book would be nonexistent were it not for the people who, more than thirty years ago, gave me the chance to serve at the senior levels of American government. This list of course begins with President Reagan and then–Vice President Bush. But on the very next rung is the Honorable John S. Herrington, who as director of Presidential Personnel in 1983–85 championed my going to Navy and later promoted me for assistant secretary for Manpower & Reserve Affairs, a post he had occupied briefly but with distinction. To them all go my sincerest thanks.

I am also grateful to many people who made this book physically possible, primarily Dr. Mary Lenn Dixon, Charles Backus, and Thom Lemmons at Texas A&M University Press, which contracted for this volume even while its predecessor, *When Things Went Right,* was still being reviewed by scholars for possible publication. I greatly appreciate the entire staff at the Press, the Naval Historical Center, and a former colleague at the Navy Department of the 1980s, Seth Cropsey, who read the manuscript and gave me his valued thoughts.

Whatever service I provided the men and women of the Navy and Marine Corps during 1983–88 was directly due to the help and guidance of a sterling cast of characters that begins chronologically with the Honorable Everett Pyatt; the Honorable George Sawyer; the Honorable Chapman B. Cox; the late Captain Eugene Peltier, (CEC) USN; my personal assistant, Betty Thompson; the late Lt. Gen. Lew Buehl, USMC; the late Vice Adm. Bill Lawrence, USN; Lt. Gen. Bill Maloney, USMC; the late Brig. Gen. Don Hittle, USMC; Col. Gerald H. (Gerry) Turley, USMC; my civilian deputies Tony DiTrapani, Alice Stratton, the late Leonard McRoskey, and above all Dick Elster; my (Navy) executive assistants Capt. Kelsey Stewart, Rear Adm. Sam Yow, Capt. Joe Harford, and Rear Adm. Louise Wilmot; my (Marine) military assistants Col. William H. (Doc) White, Brig. Gen. George Walls, and Col. Manfred Rietsch; my special and staff assistants; innumerable Navy and Marine officers and senior enlisted, ashore and afloat; and career civil servants like Frank Swofford, Jim Colvard, Dottie Meletske, Charlie Nemfakos, and Doc Cooke, who taught me much and helped me do my job, expecting in return only clear guidance and a cooperative spirit.

Inside Reagan's Navy

Chapter 1

The Education of a DASNIF

My first Pentagon job wasn't in the Pentagon at all but in a nondescript office building in Crystal City, a complex of squat towers adjoining National Airport. There the Navy Department rented space for its logistical functions, and there, the Monday after leaving the Vice President's suite in the West Wing of the White House, I reported for duty as a deputy assistant secretary of the Navy.

Monday, 14 March 1983

Today commenced my new life in Washington. The Metro ride out to Crystal City from Northwest Washington took about half an hour, an ideal amount of time to read the newspaper or a book. There's a tunnel from the Metro station straight to Crystal Plaza 5, where Navy S&L (Shipbuilding & Logistics) is located.

My first stop in S&L was the office of Ev Pyatt, the principal deputy assistant secretary.[1] The first thing Ev told me is I won't have [my predecessor] Chapman Cox's old office around the corner from Assistant Secretary George Sawyer nor Chapman's responsibility for logistics. Someone more concerned than I with bureaucratic face might object to having his office, duties, and staff juggled even before he is on the payroll. But I recognize that I'm on probation with Sawyer and Pyatt and if I do well they'll gladly give me more to do.

I was taken to my new office and introduced to staff director Capt. Eugene Peltier, a tall, monastic-looking fellow with a matter-of-fact manner. One of the Seabees (a naval civil engineer), Gene briefed me on the biggest issues I'm likely to face, in particular the $2 billion budget for naval military construction, or "milcon."

At noon I went to S&L's attractive mess [dining room] for lunch. I sat next to George Sawyer, who engaged in detailed shop talk with his chief assis-

---

1. Everett (Ev) Pyatt was a Navy career civil servant. A big, ungainly fellow with a chuckle-some sense of humor, he was loyal, smart, and candid, the ideal mentor for a fresh-caught political appointee.

tants during the meal. This is contrary to the etiquette of a ship's wardroom, though I never knew a ship whose officers were lively enough conversationalists to avoid the subject of work. Sawyer is an affable soul, though his reputation for temper makes me wary.

Karl Rove is in town, and after dinner in the White House Mess I showed him around the West Wing [*a place he would know extremely well twenty years later*]. His direct-mail business is doing well; most recently he handled Congressman Phil Gramm's special election campaign. We had a good talk about Texas politics, the Bush staff, and Untermeyer's future.

Wednesday, 16 March 1983

Today I attended the staff breakfast that George Sawyer holds promptly at 7:30 every Wednesday to hear each honcho report on his area of responsibility. When my turn came, I admitted, "I haven't understood anything of what's been said here. It's like being an exchange officer with the Thai navy." The acronyms, weapon systems, and abbreviations were so baffling that the only words I understood were verbs and prepositions. George good-naturedly assured me that I'll learn it all in time. At least I am getting the full-on exposure to "the bureaucracy" I yearned to join.

This evening, I gathered my old gear in the White House before heading home. This was the fabled moment of leaving the West Wing for the "last time" that I vowed always to keep in mind. That determination proved successful, and tonight I left without tears. I am grateful for what I've done, and I'm grateful for what I'm going to do.

Friday, 18 March 1983

One of the prime responsibilities in my new job at Navy was to be "executive agent" for the Department of Defense on all matters affecting the Outer Continental Shelf.

At 9:30, environmental staffer Mary Margaret Goodwin[2] and I boarded a Navy motor pool car for a quick rainy ride to the Pentagon. Deep within the building, appropriately far from the surface, lurks the Submarine Force. Waiting there was a Commodore[3] Eytchison and several four-stripers [naval

---

2. Mary Margaret's brother, Dennis Revell, was married to President Reagan's daughter Maureen.

3. This was during the brief period when one-star Navy officers were again called commodores. I liked the historic tang to the title, but the one-stars wailed, "My mother thinks I'm

captains]. It was my first exposure to high-ranking naval officers in my new role, and it is not easy to shift into being the dignitary after trailing behind one for so long.

The submariners wanted to brief me on their concerns regarding the planned sale of oil leases in Narragansett Bay before I go see people at Interior. A captain said that oil rigs in sub transit lanes would pose a threat to navigation, since underwater cruising isn't precise, and the noise generated by the platforms would prevent the quiet listening required to track enemy subs. The commodore compared this sound to "a jackhammer in the concert hall."

In the car heading back to Crystal City, I told Mary Margaret, "When I rejoined the Navy in this job, I thought the enemy was the Soviets. Now I learn it's the Interior Department." For my sake I hope we are successful in this confrontation. My early reputation as a political fixer may be made on it.

Monday, 21 March 1983

Today the Navy landed on the shores of the Interior Department and advanced to the suite of the Minerals Management Service (MMS). There I met with Dave Russell, a young man of stocky build, thinning red hair, and a permanent smirk. I affirmed my support of Administration policy on mineral development, which promotes national security through energy independence. But, I said, Navy's concerns in Narragansett Bay reflect a more concrete aspect of national security, for while there may or may not be oil under the waves, we know for sure that Soviet subs are.

My arguments failed to move Russell, who was quietly unyielding on our request. I suspect he is trying to out-Watt Jim Watt[4] in promoting oil and gas exploration on the Outer Continental Shelf. I shall have to wage the battle on a higher plane. Going one-on-one with Jim Watt is a daunting prospect, but I'm confident enough in our case and friendly enough with the Secretary to welcome it.

Thursday, 24 March 1983

Today the ranking Marine officers responsible for installations briefed me on the effort by Oceanside, California, to annex Camp Pendleton [the big opera-

---

an admiral!" Their whining ultimately led to the restoration of the clunky rank of "rear admiral, lower half."

4. Secretary of the Interior, 1981–83.

tional Marine base between San Diego and Los Angeles]. On 8 April, I will meet with Larry Bagley, the mayor of Oceanside. One of the briefers said, "Mr. Untermeyer, you are unique right now, because you are the only official in the Navy Department that Mayor Bagley hasn't insulted."

Steve Shipley, Secretary Watt's executive assistant, called to say his boss "thinks we ought to place obstacles on the Outer Continental Shelf so our submarines can practice their navigation." After this side-splitter, I said I'm concerned that Interior looks on Navy "as just another anti-drilling group, like the Georges Bank fishermen or the Commonwealth of Massachusetts."

Friday, 25 March 1983

Today Capt. Gene Peltier and I went to the headquarters of the Naval Facilities Engineering Command (NAVFAC), where for my sole benefit its top officers conducted a full formal briefing. There was a published agenda, slides, and coffee served by the aide to "the chief" (of naval engineers). One striking statistic: Navy owns four million acres of land, equivalent in size to New Jersey.

At lunch with the Seabees, I asked a captain who worked for both Chapman Cox and his Democratic predecessor what advice he might give me. He said simply, "Trust your people." My going-in attitude toward career folk springs from what George Bush learned as director of the CIA. Like me, he was a political outsider among professionals. GB said he started off presuming competence and loyalty and let his underlings disprove this notion, rather than start off presuming incompetence and disloyalty and make them prove themselves trustworthy.

Monday, 28 March 1983

I received a call from Paul Thayer, the deputy secretary of Defense, asking what to tell Jim Watt about the Narragansett Bay lease sale. Thayer is a rough-and-ready test pilot-turned-corporate executive, very similar to his friend and predecessor Bill Clements,[5] also of Dallas. But this afternoon he was low-key and respectful, perhaps out of contrition for flunking an earlier phone call from Watt. "I don't envy what you are about to do," I told Thayer, "but I'm grateful."

---

5. Clements, the wealthy owner of an oil drilling company, had served as DepSecDef from 1973–77. Even after becoming the first Republican governor of Texas in modern times, Clements always spoke most proudly of the time "when I ran the Pentygun."

Friday, 1 April 1983

Today I chaired a meeting to develop Navy's position on the bid by the city of Portsmouth (Virginia) to lease a 40-acre landfill from us. In a one-hour discussion over a dumpsite, I had more job satisfaction than in a week of work for the Vice President.

Saturday, 2 April 1983

At a party tonight I met Tidal (Ty) McCoy, the assistant secretary of the Air Force for Manpower, Reserve Affairs & Installations. A West Point grad, Ty speaks very fast, punctuating his conversation with a soldier's mindless obscenities. He had an interesting characterization of the different services. The Navy is very hierarchical, he said, with the CNO [chief of naval operations] the supreme boss for four years. The Air Force by contrast, operates as a board of directors, with the chief of staff merely a presiding officer. And the Army is run by the chief of staff and a kitchen cabinet of cronies from West Point, one or two of whom may have retired. Ty said nothing about the Marines.

Tuesday, 5 April 1983

Today, shortly after arriving at Crystal Plaza 5, I was summoned to "the front office." There George Sawyer raised the request by Congressman Jack Edwards (R-Alabama) for joint civilian-military use of Barin Field near Mobile. Gene Peltier had given me a number of decent arguments why Edwards's request didn't make sense. I signed this over to Sawyer, who signed it over to SecNav Lehman—only to have Lehman overrule S&L on the grounds that Edwards deserves a plum now and then. Though he had been a participant in this episode, George used it as an object lesson for me. "Don't trust these guys," he said bluntly.

Wednesday, 6 April 1983

Today brought the weekly S&L breakfast. It always feels as if the week is over the hump after these breakfasts, even though chronologically that's not true.

At the Pentagon, I met with counterparts from Air Force and Army to devise a joint position in response to the "installations management" initiative by Assistant Secretary of Defense Larry Korb and his deputy Bob Stone. My colleagues, both career civil servants, see this as a power grab by the Office of the Secretary of Defense (OSD) and want to counter-propose a tri-service committee. When I asked the aim of such a panel, the two men chuckled, so obvious was the answer to them: the aim of the tri-service committee is to kill the OSD scheme.

Thursday, 7 April 1983

In a meeting with my predecessor, Chapman Cox, awaiting confirmation as assistant secretary for Manpower & Reserve Affairs, I mentioned George Sawyer's "object lesson" a couple of days ago on distrusting uniformed officers. Chapman said he doesn't distrust them but that I should always be skeptical when they say something *can't* be done.

Friday, 8 April 1983

I did some final reading on the Camp Pendleton annexation issue before my meeting with Mayor Larry Bagley of Oceanside, a scowling terrier of a man. With him was Congressman Ron Packard (R-California), a dentist and former mayor of neighboring Carlsbad in northern San Diego County. There are many base-related conflicts with Oceanside, a blighted honky-tonk town dependent on what Packard's aide called "young oversexed Marines."

During the 90-minute session I listened sympathetically to my visitors' tale of Navy Department double-crosses. I kept the tone even rather than confrontational. Packard asked what it will take for Navy to drop its opposition to Oceanside's annexing the base. I offered to find out the answer—a chore that could take weeks. Delay is important because San Diego County will decide the Oceanside–Camp Pendleton issue in early May.

Thursday, 14 April 1983

At lunch today, George Sawyer declared, "I'll bet there are not ten members of Congress who can tell you what DOD's [Department of Defense's] budget request is, within 10 percent." To test his hunch, he began to poll those of us around the table, starting with me. I blinked and a number came to me: 274 billion dollars. George blinked back; I was absolutely right. I had read the figure a couple of weeks ago, and it stayed with me, thanks to a local politician's simple mnemonic: my voting precinct in Houston is number 274. Of course, I didn't tell George this.

Wednesday, 20 April 1983

At the Kennedy Center tonight, I sat next to Barbara Bush, whose stage whispers and delicious commentary so attracted a fellow sitting in the next box that he practically leaned over me to listen to her. Out came the 67-year-old Frank Sinatra, in show business for over 40 years, to deliver such numbers as "I Get a Kick Out of You," "My Kind of Town (Chicago Is)," and his 1970s signature song, "New York, New York." Sinatra's voice often disappeared into a rasp or a conversation, but it was still good to see the great Frankie in person. Afterwards we were ushered down to the green room to meet him. Sinatra called me "sir."

Monday, 2 May 1983

The best news of the day was the rejection of Oceanside's petition to annex Camp Pendleton. Under state law, the city can't try again for another year. I notified the EA [executive assistant] to the under secretary, who said, "It's a good thing for you to win your first battle." Of course the Marines did the real lobbying, but I don't mind getting the credit.

Tuesday, 3 May 1983

Thirty-nine people applied to be my secretary, and the reviewing committee screened out only twenty-one of them. Under the rules, if I interview one, I must interview all eighteen. The two highest-scoring candidates are a current S&L secretary and one who works for Army. So, to avoid interviewing everyone or creating a problem for a colleague, I will simply hire the woman at Army, Mrs. Betty Thompson.

This sight-unseen personnel action was one of the wisest I would make in a dozen years in Washington. Betty Thompson proved a wonderful assistant and faithful friend who would go with me from S&L to the E-Ring of the Pentagon to the West Wing of the White House and finally to the Voice of America—a ten-year run.

I was at the Pentagon for a 2:00 meeting of JIMFOG, the Joint Installations Management Flag Officer Group, the tri-service committee created to keep the OSD nose out of the services' installations tent. OSD's Bob Stone, with quavering voice, urged us to "start small." He left the room, and for the balance of three hours we proceeded to be as small as possible. Men of one- and two-star rank haggled over whether to use "foster" rather than "promote" or "review" versus "examine." A colleague called the session "government at its worst."

Tuesday, 10 May 1983

At the Pentagon, Chapman Cox and I greeted our guest for lunch: Liche Castaño, mayor of Vieques, the small island just east of Puerto Rico that the Navy has used for target practice and ammunitions storage for years. Despite this, Castaño is very pro-Navy. Built like a barrel, the mayor is a cocky and well-humored political operator. "Do you know what my opponents said before the last election?" he demanded. "They said I got $25,000 from the CIA! Can you imagine that?" Chapman replied, "Liche, you're right. You'd never take anything less than $100,000."

This afternoon I met with Sen. John Warner (R-Virginia) in the doughty Russell Senate Office Building to talk about the future of the Washington Navy Yard. Warner doesn't mind if we move a few Navy offices to save on rent; he just doesn't want us to depopulate Crystal City until after his re-election in 1984.

Monday, 23 May 1983

The under secretary, Jim Goodrich, invited me to brief him before our 2:00 meeting with Gov. Ricardo Bordallo (D-Guam). Goodrich, an enormously pleasant older man who headed the Bath Iron Works shipyard, yearned to have his *Encyclopedia Britannica* back home in Maine so he could read up on the island.

Bordallo came in with his entourage, including a huge Chinese-Chamorro senator who kept dozing off during the meeting. The governor was not unlike the typical labor leader, with a necktie that was too short and a belly that was too big. He went down his laundry list of requests for the Navy, everything from wanting scrubbers on the power plant's smokestacks to our blasting through some coral to create a cruise ship pier. UnSecNav sat like a red-cheeked Buddha, saying, "Yes, yes." I hope the Guamanians didn't think he was agreeing with them instead of merely acknowledging their words. I rather like having responsibility for two exotic isles: Guam to the west and Vieques to the east.

Thursday, 26 May 1983

Andy Card called from Massachusetts to say he's still getting nowhere in his search for a federal job. At least he's earning an income from a company based in Vienna, Virginia, that wants him to move here. But Andy, eyeing another race for governor in 1986, doesn't want to move to DC except for a government job. I connected him with Jane Kenny [who has taken over my political personnel duties] in the VP's office.

A former state legislator, Andy was a key organizer in the Bay State for George Bush in 1979–80. At the time of this call, he was still recovering from a loss in the 1982 Republican primary for governor.

From this low point, Andy Card would rocket into the stratosphere of American government. With the help of VP Bush and Jim Baker, he would soon become White House liaison to the governors. When Bush became president, Andy became deputy chief of staff and then (in 1992) secretary of Transportation. During the Clinton era, he headed the Washington-based trade association for the "Big Three" automakers and served on the board of the Union Pacific Railroad. And when George W. Bush was elected president in 2000, the family stalwart returned to the White House as chief of staff.

Thursday, 2 June 1983

Ev Pyatt and I talked about the opposition by Bob Stone of OSD to building military housing in urban areas. "It'll be fun to roll Bob Stone again," he said gleefully. So far I haven't learned how to do that, but Ev always knows the way.

Ev then raised "another subject." George Sawyer resigned today as assistant secretary for Shipbuilding & Logistics after days of absences and rumors, and John Lehman told Ev that he wants him to succeed George. Reagan Administration policy is not to give major political appointments to career civil servants, but Ev is truly the wisest choice. He knows the programs, he has the experience of getting things done in the Pentagon, and above all he is committed to the Reagan-Lehman expansion of the Navy. Probably no politically certifiable person has that combination of talents, and if such a person exists, it would take months to find and confirm him.

Friday, 3 June 1983

I had a memorable meeting with Rear Adm. John Bulkeley, a fellow in his seventies recalled to active duty as president of the Board of Inspection & Survey. An energetic nub of a man with pale blue eyes and a crew cut, Bulkeley is at once lovable and fearsome. He is a tiger on the subject of health and safety conditions aboard our ships, each of which he personally visits every three years.

Bulkeley has only a single row of ribbons topped by a solitary one—for the Medal of Honor, which he received for evacuating Gen. Douglas MacArthur and his family from Corregidor by PT boat in 1942. On the wall was a poster that speaks to his fame during World War II: it shows PT boats destroying a Japanese battleship, overlain with a facsimile "US Navy Dispatch." Addressed to "Production Lines, USA," it urged them to "beat your schedule so we can beat the enemy. [signed] LCdr John Bulkeley, CO, Torpedo Squadron 3."

Monday, 6 June 1983

At 7:30 this evening, I attended the gala dinner-dance in honor of Helene von Damm,[6] the new ambassador to Austria. It was given at the Mayflower Hotel by Roy Pfautch, a pixyish fellow with a great deal of money who's been a camp follower of the Reagan inner circle for years. The event brought out Cabinet officers and numerous other Administration appointees.

I sat at the Franz Liszt table, presided over by a subdued Mike Deaver. The meal was rather good, finished with a Sachertorte. [*In Vienna, Helene would marry a member of the Sacher family, owners of the hotel that introduced the famous dessert.*] Roy had a stageful of performers sing Viennese melodies and a special song for Helene: a parody of "I'm the Hostess with the Mostes" from *Call Me Madam* called "The Chieftainess of White House Personnel." Lastly, the company sang "Auf Wiedersehen," with coloratura piano playing by Mike.

After Helene said a few gracious words, the band struck up a waltz and the performers surged into the crowd. I was talking to my dinner partner when a young woman in red satin held a long-gloved hand out to me. I

---

6. Helene, a native of Austria, had been Ronald Reagan's personal secretary in California and the White House before becoming director of Presidential Personnel.

shook it, thinking it was someone I ought to know. But she was inviting me to dance. Soon we were twirling to Sigmund Romberg.

This was the first of a long and glorious series of "pfabulous Pfautch pfunctions" that I was fortunate to attend during the Reagan-Bush Administrations. The irrepressible and generous Roy was the unsung hero of the era, throwing parties that brought together members of the Administration, great and small, boosting morale and building esprit de corps.

Tuesday, 7 June 1983

At noon I entered the office of Ellison C. (E. C.) Grayson, the deputy assistant secretary of the Navy (DASN) for Manpower. We chatted beneath signed color photos of recent CNOs and other four-stars. They, like so many people whose names E. C. dropped today, are all "very dear friends." He comes from a wealthy San Francisco family, and the thing he liked talking about, second only to himself, was "the [Bohemian] Grove." This year he's taking SecNav, CNO, and other flag officers as his guests.

Wednesday, 8 June 1983

Gene Peltier and I met with Joe Taussig, DASN for Civilian Personnel Policy. The son and grandson of admirals, Joe lost a leg at Pearl Harbor, pictures of which—the harbor, not the leg—are all over his cluttered office. He is even more of an egotist than his colleague E.C. Grayson, referring several times to "my sailors," meaning the entire USN. When Gene and I finally broke away, I said how pleased I am to deal with inanimate objects like wharves and acreage, not manpower.

Wednesday, 15 June 1983

Rick Cornelius, the Navy environmental lawyer, called with word of a potential goat crisis. A few years ago, environmental groups sued the Navy to control the goat population on San Clemente Island (off Los Angeles and San Diego), to halt their eating an endangered species of plant that harbors an endangered species of lizard. We consented, but once we began killing the critters, the Friends of Animals sued us to stop. Eventually, a deal was worked out by which we agreed to catch goats and deliver them to the Friends, who removed them to a farm they have in Texas [*where they promptly died of diseases unknown on San Clemente*].

Everyone agreed that the wily goats that escaped capture could and would be shot by marksmen in helos. But, not surprisingly, it took Navy a very long time to sign the contract with the marksmen. This, combined with a higher-than-predicted number of escaped goats, led to a new population boom on the island. By the time the Friends of Animals got a federal restraining order last week, we had shot only 642 goats.

Rick said something has to be worked out because this matter has SecDef's personal interest: the head of the Friends, Cleveland Amory,[7] is Caspar Weinberger's Harvard classmate ('38) and *Crimson* colleague.

Wednesday, 22 June 1983

At his final staff breakfast, George Sawyer said, "As a parting shot, gentlemen, I'll say that when I came to this town my impression was, 'My God: if the people only knew how they are governed.' After two years, I'd put that in caps. This is the most confused and corrupt town I've ever been in." Someone chimed in, "Coming from a man who was in the Middle East, that's saying a lot!" George's Irish face retained its smile as he clenched his pipe and said, "The only difference is here it's cheaper. You can buy a guy for a $500 honorarium."

SecDef Weinberger has sent Jim Watt a letter naming me negotiator on a memorandum of understanding (MOU) between Defense and Interior on the Outer Continental Shelf. A lot is riding on this negotiation. If it's successful, I'll have my first major accomplishment as DASNIF. When I told Ev Pyatt, my tutor in working the great DOD bureaucracy, how I got SecDef to write Watt so fast (by using general counsel Will Taft's office), he said, "You're catching on!"

Monday, 27 June 1983

Today I steeled myself to read the draft of the Portsmouth landfill lease agreement. One passage seemed the work of William S. Gilbert rather than of [Navy lawyer] Jerry Depken:

---

7. Author of the classic mid-century books on the American upper class *The Proper Bostonians, The Last Resorts*, and *Who Killed Society?*

(T)he term of easement,
it shall be appurtenant
and servient
to the dominant tenement.

Thursday, 30 June 1983

Rick Cornelius reported that the Friends of Animals has agreed to make a
final goat-capture effort on San Clemente Island during the next two weeks.
This is a "window" during which bombardment will cease and Marines will
clear the roadways of unexploded ordnance. Then we can resume shooting
the goats. This tale has served me well in social settings over the past two
weeks.

Wednesday, 6 July 1983

Today brought the final round of negotiations with Dave Russell at Interior.
When he picked up the draft MOU that I had sent him, I expected Dave to
say they had some problems with it. Instead, he announced, "I kind of like
this." Our only tiffs were over word choice. "Where do we sign?" asked one of
Dave's staffers. The reason Interior is so eager to reach agreement with DOD
is because they want the Senate to remove some anti-leasing language placed
on their appropriation by the House, and the MOU would be a handy tool.
Were it not for this fortuitous circumstance, our negotiations would have
been much more contentious.

    Tonight I washed dishes to the triumphal strains of Handel's *Music for
the Royal Fireworks,* as suitable for the Defense-Interior MOU as for the
Treaty of Aix-la-Chapelle.

Thursday, 7 July 1983

This afternoon Senator Warner called me to say he is attacking the proposed
relocation of Navy Department offices to the Washington Navy Yard purely
for reelection reasons. "I don't want you all to get in the clutches of those landlords," he said. "Of course, I wouldn't know one of 'em if he walked into my
office now." Somewhat surprised (and dubious), I asked if he knows Charles E.
Smith, who owns Crystal City and collects $20 million a year in rent from
Navy. "Oh, Charlie? Is he involved over there?" Warner asked ingenuously.

Wednesday, 20 July 1983

Today Chapman Cox and I met with Secretary Lehman on the strategic homeporting initiative. It was my first time to deal with the Secretary on a policy matter since becoming DASNIF over four months ago. After congratulating me on the "treaty" with Interior, Lehman turned to where on the East Coast to place the battleship *Iowa*, a cruiser, and three destroyers. Lehman has long favored a homeport in the New York area to engender more congressional support there for the Navy. When Chapman suggested we give Rhode Island some Naval Reserve vessels as a sop, Lehman interjected, "Bullshit! We aren't giving them anything till they change their senators."

Lehman, an impressive fellow, was ready with a decision: Stapleton on Staten Island, but first we have to get its cost below that of Rhode Island. He suggested "someone talk to [Staten Island congressman] Guy Molinari in the dead of night, saying we want a sweetener from David Rockefeller and the New York Partnership, such as family housing."

Monday, 1 August 1983

Today I attended the "reclama" session on internal Navy Department "marks" (cuts) in family housing programs. *Reclama* is a strange, purely Pentagonian word meaning an appeal. But I picture it as something out of *The Travels of Marco Polo*: "After a journey of two weeks, during which all but one of our camels died, we finally reached the palace of the Great Reclama."

Wednesday, 3 August 1983

Diane Morales[8] put me to work pouring drinks while she went downstairs to greet her special guests: Interior Secretary Jim Watt and his wife Leilani (Lani). It was an evening Diane had been organizing for months, and it was for me a chance to see up close the most controversial Cabinet officer of modern times.

Right away, Watt started asking me questions: What did I do before working for Vice President Bush? Do I speak Spanish? Do I have political

---

8. Diane Morales was a highly attractive and able young Houstonian whose mother Helen was personal secretary to (and later wife of) one of the city's greatest mayors, Louie Welch. Originally a political appointee at Interior, Diane at this time was a Reagan-appointed member of the Civil Aeronautics Board, which regulated the airline industry.

ambitions? He asked specifically about my running for Congress, into which he wants to promote several protégés, including Diane. I said Congress would appeal to me only as an avenue into executive positions. In his grace before dinner, which came right in the middle of the Untermeyer discussion, Watt thanked the Lord "for the plan you have for each one of us."

Watt and I both believe that GB's problem isn't philosophy but style, of not saying what he feels. It's the difference between being an Episcopalian and an evangelical. The Secretary pushed Diane to ban all smoking from all airlines. Highly sensitive to cigarette smoke, Jim in this case *wants* government regulation. He repeated the advice given him by ex–Treasury Secretary Bill Simon: "Be bold, and avoid your counselors of caution."

Tuesday, 9 August 1983

The following week, I traveled to Alaska for a meeting of the Outer Continental Shelf Policy Committee, on which I represented Defense. The panel made field trips to Prudhoe Bay on the North Slope and to an Amoco oil platform in the Cook Inlet.

Our guide around the platform was Butch Andersen, a great guy (missing a few fingers) who loves being in Alaska and working offshore. While we stood on the equipment deck after the tour, waiting for the chopper to pick us up, Butch talked about hunting moose. With great enthusiasm he described tracking the wily moose through the bush and finally drawing a bead on it. Then his face lost its smile. "But once you pull the trigger," he said grimly, "the fun's over, 'cause then you gotta haul the son-of-a-gun outta the woods."

This story soon became part of my answer when people like Jim Watt asked if I wanted to be a congressman. Yes, I'd like to be elected to Congress, I would reply, since that means one has truly arrived in American politics. But election night would be the peak, the veritable pulling of the trigger. After that would come years of heavy moose hauling in Washington.

USS *Iowa* firing a full salvo of her nine 16-inch guns. Along with three other battleships of her class built during World War II, *Iowa* was recommissioned for active service during the Reagan Administration.

Assistant Secretary of the Navy Chase Untermeyer is rendered honors as he comes aboard the destroyer *Peterson* at the Norfolk naval base, October 1985.

Chase Untermeyer, the newly minted DASNIF, with his boss, Assistant Secretary of the Navy George Sawyer (left), in Sawyer's Crystal City office, June 1983.

Untermeyer gets the scuttlebutt from members of the air wing at the Marine Corps Air Station Beaufort (SC), July 1984.

Secretary of the Navy John F. Lehman Jr. administers the oath of office as assistant secretary of the Navy to Chase Untermeyer in the secretary's Pentagon office, 7 August 1984. Holding the Bible at right is Fred Davidson III, deputy assistant secretary for Reserve Affairs.

Lt. Gen. Alfred M. (Al) Gray, commanding general of the Second Marine Division, hosts Untermeyer at Camp Lejeune (NC), August 1984. Gray would serve as commandant of the Marine Corps from 1987–91.

Charles Francis Adams IV (right) visits Untermeyer's office to see the official portrait of his father, Charles Francis Adams III, secretary of the Navy under President Hoover. At left is Under Secretary of the Navy James F. (Jim) Goodrich.

President Reagan shakes hands with Untermeyer after an event in the White House Rose Garden, October 1984.

Assistant Secretary of the Navy Chase Untermeyer at his desk on the E-Ring of the Pentagon, January 1985. Next to the US flag are those for the Marine Corps and the Navy.

The (nominal) head of the search for new Navy homeports besieged by reporters at the Naval Air Station Corpus Christi (Texas), February 1985.

Special blessing: Untermeyer with Vice Adm. William (Bill) Lawrence, chief of Naval Personnel, in the assistant secretary's office, 1985. A former prisoner of war in Vietnam, Lawrence was one of the most highly revered naval officers of his day.

Special challenges: at left, Vice Adm. Lewis A. Seaton, surgeon general of the Navy; at right, Vice Adm. Dudley Carlson, who succeeded Lawrence as chief of Naval Personnel.

Secretary of Defense Caspar W. Weinberger (far left) introduces British Prime Minister Margaret Thatcher to Untermeyer after a ceremony in her honor in the Pentagon courtyard, 26 July 1986. At rear is a still-stunned Secretary of the Army Jack Marsh.

At the launching of the frigate *Kauffman* in Bath, Maine, on 29 March 1986, Untermeyer confesses being "an aide who needed an aide." On the front row, from left: Sen. William Cohen, Vice President George Bush, Gov. Joseph Brennan, Untermeyer, Bill Hargett (president of Bath Iron Works, the shipbuilder), Beth Kauffman Bush, and Cary Kauffman.

Secretary Lehman (center) with his top assistants at their farewell luncheon for him at a Washington club, 7 April 1987. From left: Everett (Ev) Pyatt, assistant secretary for Shipbuilding & Logistics; Untermeyer; Under Secretary James (Jim) Goodrich; Melvyn (Mel) Paisley, assistant secretary for Research, Engineering & Systems; Robert (Bob) Conn, assistant secretary for Financial Management; and Walter Skallerup, general counsel of the Navy.

Mrs. Connie Rietsch and Untermeyer jointly "frock" his military assistant, Manfred Rietsch, with the eagles of a full colonel in the Marine Corps, in the assistant secretary's office, 20 November 1987. Over Col. Rietsch's left shoulder are four-strand aiguillettes denoting he is an aide to someone of four-star rank. Aides to the president and vice president wear these cords over their right shoulder.

Secretary of the Navy James (Jim) Webb, seated left, and Under Secretary Larry Garrett, seated right, with their top assistants, in the secretary's office, 9 February 1988. Standing from left: Ev Pyatt; Bob Conn; Untermeyer; Tom Faught, assistant secretary for Research, Engineering & Systems; and Harvey Wilcox, acting general counsel of the Navy.

Untermeyer talks with the most celebrated member of his staff, Fawn Hall, who had been secretary to Lt. Col. Oliver North in the White House before the exposure in late 1986 of the Iran/Contra affair.

Chapter 2

Incautious Snakes and an Irritated Princess

Friday, 26 August 1983

At 10:00, NAVFAC briefed me on the troubles of the Guam Power Authority, with which Navy shares responsibility for electric generation on the island. We own the transmission lines, and chiefly for reasons of pride Guam wants them. But neither we nor Air Force wants to jeopardize the steady supply of juice to our installations on the island by handing the lines over to the fiscally shaky Authority. We keep one plant "spinning" (i.e., running without any output) just to pick up the load whenever the system fails—as it frequently does when incautious snakes crawl out onto the lines, killing both the system and themselves.[1]

Later I had an appointment with DepSecDef Thayer. I walked past the Marine sentry at the door and was greeted by Brigadier General Lary, Thayer's military assistant. Lary checked on his boss by using the spyglass peephole so popular in the Pentagon and Alcatraz and then opened the door to announce me. The DepSec turned in his swivel chair in a spacious, overdecorated office. Facing him in a straight chair, I gave a quick report on Port Hueneme. Thayer acted as if I had his complete attention, and indeed I may have been the only briefer he's had in the Pentagon who just sat and talked with him, without using notes, brochures, chart overlays, or multi-screen slides.

Port Hueneme was a Navy facility, used mainly by the Seabees, whose docks were coveted by the port of Oxnard, California. The port hired ex-Congressman Bob Wilson, a popular former member of the House Armed Services Committee, to force Navy to give up the docks. Occurring right when I became DASNIF and before I had learned how to counter such gambits, the "loss" of Port Hueneme was my biggest regret during an otherwise successful tenure.

---

1. These are the infamous brown tree snakes, which destroyed all birdlife on the island and continue to pop up everywhere, indoors and outdoors, making Guam a very creepy place indeed.

While DASNIF, I joked that Navy had made a major mistake by locating its bases on the ocean, where the bulk of the population lived. The Army and Air Force, by contrast, had wisely put their bases in isolated places like Kansas and the Dakotas, free from encroachment by local authorities and developers.

Monday, 29 August 1983

I received a note typed by GB in Maine: "The other day I had a visit from John Lehman, [who was] high, very high, in his praises for your work— unsolicited by me, I might add." This was good to see and good for GB to believe. But as little as I know him, I view Lehman as a crafty young pol who *of course* would tell the Vice President that his boy Untermeyer is doing great. After all, the chief reason I got this job was because Lehman calculated that it would be another useful link to the potential president.

Tonight Congressman Guy Molinari and members of the Staten Island business community gave a dinner in a Georgetown restaurant to thank the Navy for choosing Stapleton for the *Iowa* surface action group. Senator Al D'Amato was Molinari's sidekick and joshing partner. The jolly, smoky, well-fed evening was filled with old-time New York *gemütlichkeit,* or whatever the Italian term for it is. I loved the occasion for its crackling political and ethnic flavor. And how fine it is to be an honoree at such affairs and no longer just an attendee!

Wednesday, 7 September 1983

In mid-afternoon I swung by the grand old apartment house at 2101 Connecticut Avenue to pick up Roberta McCain. She is the widow of Adm. Jack McCain (CINCPAC in 1968–72) and mother of freshman Congressman John McCain III (R-Arizona). I gave her a lift to Annapolis for today's memorial service for Peggy Kauffman.[2] A lovely lady and lively conversationalist, Mrs. McCain kept me fully entertained all the way to Annapolis.

The service, held in the un–air-conditioned yet always magnificent Naval Academy Chapel, was simple and brief. By Mrs. K's own wish, there was no eulogy, though the Very Rev. Francis B. Sayre Jr. (Woodrow Wilson's grand-

---

2. The spectacular "Mrs. K" was the widow of Rear Adm. Draper Kauffman, for whom I was aide in the Philippines in 1969–70. Both couples were close, and I got to know the McCains on their frequent visits to our small naval station on Manila Bay. At the time, their son the future lawmaker and presidential candidate was a prisoner of war in North Vietnam.

son) expanded upon the lesson to say a few gracious words about her. The Navy Hymn was sung most poignantly at the service's close.

Thursday, 22 September 1983

At Interior this afternoon, Dave Russell was clearly worried that Secretary Watt might not survive his latest gaffe. Yesterday, Watt told a chamber of commerce group that a special commission to study coal leasing was well balanced: "We have every kind of mix you can have. I have a black, I have a woman, two Jews, and a cripple. And we have talent." For Watt loyalists to despair over his knack for creating unnecessary controversy shows how serious this incident is. Watt apologized to the President, but four Republican senators have called for his removal.

Saturday, 24 September 1983

Throughout the 1980s, the Navy under John Lehman's stewardship kept growing toward President Reagan's 600-ship goal. This meant numerous launches of numerous types of vessels. In Beaumont, in my Texas backyard, I got to witness one of the oddest.

In the VIP transit lounge at the naval air facility at Andrews were Ev Pyatt; Gen. P. X. Kelley, the new commandant of the Marine Corps and a Boston Irishman of great political charm; Vice Adm. W. H. Rowden, commander of the Military Sealift Command; and the star of the flight, Congressman Jack Brooks of Beaumont, chairman of the House Government Operations Committee. Today Jack was in supreme puckish spirits. During the flight, Rowden's aide showed me a note that his boss, sitting next to Brooks, had slipped him. "Who am I talking to?" it asked. My reply mentioned, among other things, that Brooks is prominently featured in the famous photograph taken aboard another government plane on 22 November 1963, observing his old friend Lyndon Johnson being sworn in as president.

The C9 came in over the vast refinery- and tank-filled plain of southeast Texas to land at 10:30. At the Bethlehem Steel shipyard, located on a bend of the Neches River, we boarded the ex-tanker *Eleo Maersk,* which workers in Galveston soon will slice in two. Then they will insert the "midbody" constructed in Beaumont and launched today, weld her up, and eventually produce the *PFC William B. Baugh,* the first of the Marines' "pre-positioned" supply ships.

I climbed up to the pilot house with General Kelley, who said he conceived the idea of such a ship four years ago and found the money to make his dream a reality. The new class of ships will be stationed in "benign" ports, each vessel holding enough petrol, food, water, equipment, and ammo to supply a Marine brigade in time of need.

The ceremony began with the blast of the noon whistle. General Kelley declared, "It is a special honor for me to be in a state where, as in the Marine Corps, patriotism, guts, and determination are a way of life." His wife Barbara was supposed to conduct the launching, but she is ill, and the Commandant performed in her stead. "Is everybody ready?" he yelled to the crowd. Then, with a thumbs-up gesture, he turned a switch. Nothing happened for five aching minutes as yard workers fiddled with something at the base of the hull. Then, with a hypnotic slowness and a silence that belied its gargantuan size, the midbody slid sideways down a ramp. It hit the Neches, creating an enormous (and also strangely noiseless) wave that bashed into the subtropical growth on the other side of the channel. Lines held the hull, though their protective wrappings whipped open, and big red tugs moved in to hold it in place.

Monday, 26 September 1983

SecNav cut one of his deals with Joe Addabbo (D-New York), chairman of the House subcommittee on defense appropriations. Trying once again to stir up some business for the former Brooklyn Navy Yard, ole Joe wants to move *Iowa* there [from Norfolk] till the Staten Island homeport is built. Lehman agreed, not knowing (or not saying) that the battlewagon is thirty-five feet too tall to pass under the Brooklyn Bridge.

Wednesday, 5 October 1983

In black tie I went through rain-washed streets to the VP's house.[3] The Bushes came downstairs, and we chatted for a few moments before boarding the motorcade. We drove the short distance down Massachusetts Avenue to Anderson House and the dinner given by President Karl Carstens of West

---

3. Chiefs of Naval Operations lived in the house, located on the grounds of the Naval Observatory, until 1974. It was then made available to vice presidents, who previously had no official residence. CNOs now live in Tingey House in the Washington Navy Yard, a place full of history but without the park-like seclusion that makes the Naval Observatory a better spot to live than the White House.

Germany. He and his wife greeted the Bushes at the entrance, and as German military officers saluted and a brass fanfare sounded, we all mounted the marble staircase. There followed an excellent and substantial dinner prepared by Carstens's own chef.

The perfect end to the evening came back at the Observatory when I was walking to my car. I encountered BPB, taking the air with C. Fred [the cocker spaniel]. "We miss you terribly," she said. She asked if I'm enjoying the job and whether it is satisfying. I said I am and it is, whereupon she said, "Our job is just as frustrating as it was on the first day; you can't do anything."

Monday, 10 October 1983

Jim Watt has announced his resignation, telling the President that he has served out his "usefulness" to the Administration. In a telling phrase, he said he "leaves a legacy of people and programs"—a way of saying his successor will inherit political appointees Watt personally selected, cultivated, and motivated.

Friday, 21 October 1983

At a wedding reception, I spoke with John Herrington, the director of Presidential Personnel, who suddenly said, "We're going to promote you. I don't know what, so keep your eyes open. You know politics, and you know the policies of the President and Vice President." It's precisely what John told me last March when I went to Navy. It means he hasn't forgotten me and may be thinking of me in connection with S&L, although I consider that unlikely.

Sunday, 23 October 1983

Today, along with the rest of America, I awoke to the ghastly news of a suicide terrorist's having driven a truck filled with explosives into the Marine barracks in Beirut. The load went off, killing at least 147 Marines,[4] most of them asleep in their bunks. The carnage represented almost 10% of the USMC peacekeeping force in Lebanon. The President immediately flew home from Augusta for meetings with the NSC [National Security Council]. He vowed that the Marines would stay. That conforms to our policy of supporting the weak central government of President Amin Gemayel, but it also means the

---

4. The final death toll was 241.

Corps will continue to be passive targets for more terrorists and snipers. I think they will have to be withdrawn before the 1984 election to prevent a terrific backlash from a public that has never been enthusiastic about having the Marines in Beirut in the first place. The backlash may start now.[5]

Monday, 24 October 1983

I represented Navy at a meeting of the Defense Government Property Council. Such matters are not my normal responsibility, but neither are they anyone else's, so I was designated to attend. I rationalized it as a way of learning about some of the unglamorous things that make up a defense department. It was a depressing, drizzly day with flags at half-mast for the killing of all those fine sleeping Marines yesterday in Lebanon. To see someone in a Marine uniform today was to feel instantly sad.

Tuesday, 25 October 1983

In another part of the world, the US today scored a military success. With some 300 troops from half a dozen Lesser Antillean countries as compatriots and cover, we invaded the Marxist island of Grenada to restore a parliamentary democracy. The first thing we seized was the long runway being built by the Cubans and Soviets—and several Cubans and Soviets along with it. The action isn't exactly RR's Falklands, but at least he has taken a piece off the board, the first time we have ever done so against the communists.

Thursday, 27 October 1983

I called Peter Robinson, [formerly VP Bush's speechwriter and now] of the President's speechwriting staff, to suggest with mock seriousness an insert for RR's speech tonight on Grenada. The line is from Hilaire Belloc's *The Modern Traveller* (1898), which Peter had me read last year:

> Whatever happens we have got
> The Maxim gun and they have not.

---

5. The Marines would be withdrawn in February 1984.

Saturday, 29 October 1983

Tonight I attended a conservative affair—conservative with a royal *c*. Paul and Laura Dietrich gave a cocktail party in honor of young Prince Vincenz von Liechtenstein, nephew of both the reigning prince of Liechtenstein and of Archduke Otto von Hapsburg. He is tall and sandy haired, with a trace of the family's famous lower lip seen in the portraits of Velázquez. Vincenz leads a conservative youth organization promoted by Uncle Otto to counter the left's hold on European students. With him was his wife, the Princess Hélène, a roly-poly, rosy-cheeked member of the French branch of the Bourbons. When I asked if she were also involved in politics, the princess replied with some irritation, "My family has been involved in politics for 500 years."

Tuesday, 8 November 1983

In early November, I visited Marine installations in Southern California.

We left Camp Pendleton aboard a two-engine C12 for El Toro in Orange County, the Marines' main jet base on the west coast. In the command briefing I was told of terrible encroachment problems. Incredibly, the Irvine Company (the great local landowner) wants to build a hospital and an office/hotel complex right in the jets' flight path. This sort of thing may eventually force us to abandon the base.[6]

The nearby Marine helicopter base at Tustin is a fascinating place, dominated by two huge World War II blimp hangars with wooden rafters (now classified as historical structures). Outside, helos fly around as thick as dragonflies in a summer field, many carrying deadweights of three to six tons.

The colonel escorting me around Tustin asked if I would like to see advance preparations for Thursday night's Marine Birthday Ball, notably the construction of the traditional cake.[7] He also asked if I would present a medal to the departing head of the mess hall, a sergeant. I entered the galley to find the honoree standing at rigid attention in front of about 50 of his white-aproned mess cooks. An officer read the citation, and another extended

---

6. El Toro would be closed in 1999.

7. Marines observe the anniversary of their founding, on 10 November 1775, in places large and small around the world, in peace or war. The proper greeting to all Marines on that date is "Happy birthday!" The birthday cake is practically an object of veneration.

toward me the box containing the medal. Not having done this before, I took the whole box rather than the medal alone. Whispered the proper procedure, I stood holding the medal until the reading ended. Then I stepped forward to pin the award on the sergeant's blouse [as military shirts are called], warning him that he was my first victim. Despite the suddenness of all this, I managed to carry it off with only minor embarrassment.

Wednesday, 9 November 1983

I have concluded that Marine officers come in just three types. Type 1 is stern and physical, like former Commandant [Robert] Barrow. Type 2 is outgoing, like the current commandant, P.X. Kelley. And Type 3 is quiet and cerebral, like Maj. Gen. Tony Lukeman [commander of Camp Pendleton].

The absolute validity of this early observation has been borne out in my experience ever since. Type 1 Marines tend to be excellent leaders in combat and on the parade ground. Type 2 Marines tend to rise to flag ranks. And Type 3 Marines, the smallest subset, make diligent staff officers. This phenomenon arises from the fact that the Marine Corps is a strict orthodoxy, with the commandant its supreme and unerring pontiff. In the other services, numerous personality types are tolerated. A naval officer, for example, may be ironic or shy or cynical, but never a Marine.

Tuesday, 29 November 1983

This evening I went to the State Department for the dinner the Bushes gave the new Israeli prime minister, Yitzhak Shamir. I was seated at the same table as Deputy Secretary of State Kenneth Dam, Chief of Protocol Selwa (Lucky) Roosevelt, and her husband, Archibald Roosevelt Jr., grandson of TR. The meal was poor and the toasts standard, but the entertainment was excellent: The Singing Sergeants of the US Air Force Band. Their most beautiful selection was the spiritual "Soon I Will Be Through with the Troubles of the World," whose refrain was, "Goin' home to meet my Jesus! Goin' home to meet my Jesus!" Whatever diplomatic faux pas this committed was soon corrected with some numbers from *Fiddler on the Roof.*

Thursday, 8 December 1983

When I was on the vice presidential staff, despairing over a lack of substantive work, I listened with envy at staff meetings as the VP's national security advisor reported on meetings she attended of interagency groups (IGs) and special interagency groups (SIGs). This led to my conclusion that to be a genuine Washington policymaker, "You gotta be on IGs and SIGs." This day, I finally got to be on one.

With [John Lehman's friend and counselor] Hugh O'Neill, I went to the State Department for a meeting of the Interagency Group on the London Dumping Convention, which would forbid sub-seabed disposal of nuclear wastes. This was of concern to Navy because we plan to dispose of decommissioned nuclear submarines by removing their radioactive cores, cutting up the hulls, and dropping the pieces into very deep crevices in the ocean floor.

Speaking in favor of the convention were EPA and State's legal staff, who worry that the US might appear a bad guy, "isolated" in world councils, if we don't sign on. This worries me not a bit, and I took the floor to say, among other things, that such a policy would discourage the private sector from financing disposal efforts. This caused a flutter in certain parts of the room. Apparently, mentioning the private sector in such a gathering just isn't done, especially among those who must have been dozing when the 1980 election was held.

Monday, 12 December 1983

Tonight the Folger Shakespeare Library was the scene of an informal but gala "Father Christmas" party given by Roy Pfautch. What makes a Pfautch party so special and fun is that it knows no class distinction; there were secretaries of both types—clerical and Cabinet—in profusion. We all had to bring a toy for the USMC's Toys for Tots program. Inside the library's paneled and banner-hung great hall, a brass ensemble played Christmas airs, waiters took drink orders, and there was a huge chafing dish filled with chestnuts.

Among those I saw was John Herrington, who grimly asked, "Are you involved in any of the shipbuilding programs?" When I said I'm not, he said, "Good. Stay away from them and the people working on them."

After a dinner of roast beef, Yorkshire pudding, and plum pudding with hard sauce, we all returned to the great hall for caroling. Mike Deaver was at the keyboard. Charlie Wick, director of the USIA [US Information Agency] recited "A Visit from St Nicholas" wearing a red bathrobe and long cap. Then there was a visit from Santa Claus—Ed Meese! Assisted by elves (wives of Cabinet secretaries), Santa gave out gag gifts to Cabinet officers and other VIPs. Among these was Gen. P. X. Kelley. "It's not nice to have a more impressive uniform than Santa Claus," Ed said. He gave the Commandant a stuffed elephant, a gift from the President to Toys for Tots. "Semper fi,"[8] responded the general, who has taken a lot of criticism for saying that security in Beirut was "adequate."

The evening ended as it was lived, in good cheer. A prime underlying reason is a growing confidence that we'll all get a terrific present in 1984: The reelection of RR. This is in dramatic contrast to the glum mood of last Christmas.

Sunday, 18 December 1983

The *New York Times* carried a page-one story headlined "Ex-Navy Aide Gave No-Bid Work to His Past and Future Employers." The story alleged that George Sawyer issued a noncompetitive contract to John J. McMullen Associates of New York [his former firm] to do design work on refitting [the battleship] *New Jersey*. The story also said George spoke up for General Dynamics (GD) when John Lehman and Adm. Hyman Rickover were feuding with GD over cost overruns on Trident subs. George now works for GD's tank division. I can't believe that George Sawyer would do anything noncompetitive.

At John and Lois Herrington's annual Christmas party this evening in McLean, John asked (à propos of the story in the *Times*), "Have you heard? It's true. *Get ready for a rapid promotion.*" There was no possible interpretation of these words other than that I'm in line to become assistant secretary for Shipbuilding & Logistics.

AsstSecNav! It has been a dream for years, the sort of job I yearned to have after the 1980 election but knew I could not get just yet. Therefore, I gratefully and happily became GB's executive assistant. Both Theodore and Franklin Roosevelt were assistant secretaries of the Navy, though that was when it was the number-two job in a Cabinet department. Still, in the mythology of government and the establishment, being an assistant secretary of the Navy is a very choice job, more so than assistant secretaryships in OSD and in the domestic departments. It is, after all, the *Navy*, than which there is nothing grander.

Tuesday, 20 December 1983

At 12:30, I was at the Pentagon for a luncheon SecNav hosted for his personal staff and all political appointees. He was 45 minutes late, having been

---

8. The casual way Marines give their motto, Semper Fidelis, Always Faithful.

"downstairs" in SecDef's office wrangling over the budget. (This is perhaps the only sanctioned use of the word *downstairs* in Navy parlance. Normally it's "below.") When Lehman arrived, we feasted on beef Wellington, with Irish coffee and cigars to follow. It was all very WASP (except for Fred Davidson, DASN for Reserve Affairs, who is black), very male, very clubby, and very Navy.

To conclude the lunch, the Secretary offered a toast to Christmas, saying, "It's been a great year." He left immediately, without greeting any of us. He's a very strange man. If I become an AsstSecNav, I'll see a lot of Lehman and can then form a better idea of him. For now he strikes me as brilliant, ambitious, self-centered, and immature.

Sunday, 1 January 1984

Nineteen eighty-three brought me what I asked for: a deputy assistant secretaryship at Navy, and I performed well in the new job. Being DASNIF gave me exactly what I wanted by way of responsibility over a substantive area. I solidly enjoy dealing with the Navy Department's "lands and estates" and have found plenty of satisfaction. Handling Outer Continental Shelf issues was a bonus, with the memorandum of understanding between Defense and Interior a major achievement.

I haven't "missed the White House," as people constantly ask. One important reason is that I still see the place from time to time and participate in grand events like the Bushes' dinner for the Israeli prime minister. I also have fresh memories of how insignificant I was in the *real* White House and of all those people I saw going into [Chief of Staff] Jim Baker's office to govern America as I composed yet another fruitless memo.

If I have a request of 1984, it is to gain a presidential appointment in the Defense Department, such as assistant secretary of the Navy for either S&L or Manpower if Chapman Cox moves up. Each week I read Chapman's reports to SecNav, and they are mostly heavy eyelid stuff like recruiting, health benefits, educational benefits, pay scales, etc. Despite this, I would welcome that job and could possibly handle it better than S&L, which is so steeped in the esoterica of ship and aircraft design, contracts, and civilian maritime affairs. Surely I couldn't hope to finish out a Reagan Administration any better than having been executive assistant to the vice president and an AsstSecNav.

Chapter 3

The Call from Across the River

Wednesday, 4 January 1984

Marybel Batjer [in charge of political appointments at DOD] gave me the news that DepSecDef Paul Thayer has just resigned to devote himself to his defense in an SEC [Securities & Exchange Commission] complaint that he gave inside information to friends in Dallas before coming to DOD. A lesson for anyone aspiring to high office is to keep personal finances simple and preferably to be poor.

Friday, 6 January 1984

Today the papers announced the quick and predictable appointment of [DOD general counsel] William Howard Taft IV as DepSecDef. Even if he didn't bear a distinguished GOP name, Will would have gotten ahead, for he is almost a son to Cap Weinberger.

Wednesday, 18 January 1984

Gene Peltier passed on a water-cooler rumor that Ev Pyatt's name has finally cleared the White House and will soon be sent to the Senate. If this is true, it means that John Lehman won his arm-wrestling match with John Herrington over naming a civil servant to the AsstSecNav (S&L) job. This would explain why I have heard nothing from John H. in the month since he alerted me to "get ready for a rapid promotion." Of course, all along I've recognized that Ev *should* have the job because of his superior qualifications and my lack of the same. Still, it was my chance to become an AsstSecNav.

Friday, 20 January 1984

With considerable kidding from careerists at a Pentagon meeting, I left for a political appointees–only event: the third annual "executive forum" on the anniversary of RR's inauguration, held at the DAR Constitution Hall. The Marine Band was there, playing "Hail to the Redskins," the fight song of the local pro football team, who go into their second Super Bowl in a row on Sunday. I find it especially hard to be enthusiastic for the 'Skins, or the Hogs as they are also known for some reason. After all, who can take seriously a team whose anthem contains the line "Fight for old DC"? [Jim Watt once observed that it's a bad sign when political appointees from elsewhere in America begin to think of the Washington Redskins as their team.]

The welcome was given by secretary-to-the-cabinet Craig Fuller, who announced that "the next gathering of this group next January will be *outdoors*." On a day with temperatures in the teens, the audience had to think a horrified moment before bursting into applause.

An offstage voice announced the President, who strode onstage wearing his California brown suit. What can compare to seeing a president (but especially *this* president) as the Marine Band plays "Hail to the Chief"? RR paid tribute to the musicians by saying, "I'll never criticize an organization as old as the Marine Corps." Later he made another joke about his age (73 next month). He noted that HHS [the Department of Health & Human Services] recently announced that life expectancy in the US had increased. "I've already lived about 20 years longer than my life expectancy when I was born," the President said. "This is a source of irritation to some people."

He then recounted the achievements of his three years in office: lowering inflation and interest rates, reviving employment, spurring economic growth, boosting the stock market, and rebuilding the nation's defenses. Reagan told us: "We'll do what's best for the people and let the politics take care of themselves. And won't some people in this town be surprised when they find out that doing what's good for the people also turns out to be good politics?"

Wednesday, 25 January 1984

Today I went to the Hill to inform Congresswoman Bobbi Fiedler (R-California) that we will ask the Oxnard Harbor District to pay 100% of the wharfage and dockage fees collected from commercial vessels using our piers and tugs at Port Hueneme. The meeting was necessary because Oxnard wants 40% of the take, and I had to cushion the blow.

Fiedler's suite is 1607 Longworth, which was formed out of the annex to then-Congressman Bush's office (1608, which exists no more) that I occupied as an intern in 1967. A pharmacist who led anti-busing efforts while a member of the Los Angeles school board, Fiedler has a long face and straight, severe, black hair. She almost never cracked a smile and tried every minute to show how tough she is. At one point, for example, she said, "I don't want to get into a pissing match with the Navy." My face betrayed no reaction to this, though the mental image of such a contest proved quite distracting: Bobbi versus the whole Navy or just the Navy champ?

Tuesday, 7 February 1984

Chapman Cox called me into his office to talk about homeporting a 15-ship carrier task group in Puget Sound. While I was there, Hugh O'Neill called, and I heard Chapman say, "Yeah, I'm waiting for my interview with Cap. . . . I bet you do!"

We junior CIA agents are good at deducing big things from very little. My interpretation of this half-conversation is that Chapman is under consideration for general counsel of the Defense Department, succeeding Will Taft. And it also means there could be an opening for assistant secretary for Manpower & Reserve Affairs [Cox's current job], which O'Neill may covet. That's the only assistant secretaryship I could ever hope to get, now that S&L is definitely going to Ev Pyatt. Maybe John Herrington will think of me for his old position.

Wednesday, 8 February 1984

I was meeting with a staffer when (at 4:50) Betty buzzed to say, "John Herrington is on the line and says he has to talk with you." I asked the staffer to step out for a few minutes, which he quickly and graciously did. What John then told me was almost word for word what I had longed to hear.

"Some things are working over here, personnel-wise," John said. "Cap Weinberger has been looking carefully for a general counsel, and he and I have settled on Chapman Cox. Cap and I discussed his replacement, and I told him I would very much like to have you. You'd be perfect for this job, and it's the right thing to do; you've toiled in the [political] vineyards and deserve it. Weinberger said he knows you and knows you worked for the VP, and he likes a quick turnover. We want to do a package deal—Cox and Untermeyer—before anybody knows what hit 'em."

The only problem, as I correctly deduced yesterday, is that John Lehman wants the job for Hugh O'Neill. "We need to neutralize Lehman," John said in an interesting choice of words. He said he would put in an immediate call to the VP "and tell him he needs to weigh in on this." So excited that I got my right hand spattered in ink from scribbling notes fast and furiously, I asked John whether our being successful in this gambit would cause any problems for me in working with Lehman. "No problem," he said flatly. "These are presidential appointments, not secretarial appointments."

I immediately fetched back the staffer so no one would think anything extraordinary was afoot. But as he talked, I processed a brainful of excited, exultant thoughts: assistant secretary for Manpower & Reserve Affairs makes excellent sense. It's the job for a generalist/politician. . . . If I get it, I will have achieved the apex of what I could want from a Reagan Administration, and I'd be content to remain in Washington through 1988 without desiring any other post. . . . One non-personal reason for GB to want me as ASN is that I'm his only clearly identified loyalist at Defense. I've had that distinction at the mere DASN level, though the January issue of *Conservative Digest* unveiled "the Bush Network" in Washington and didn't mention me at all.

When a job change at the top causes a string of openings farther down, Navy people say "the daisy chain started moving." In my case, the chain started with the SEC discovery of Paul Thayer's second and not very secret life, riding around on a high-powered motorcycle with a young woman named Sandy Rhyno on the back seat. In addition to the rides, Thayer gave her stock tips. His subsequent resignation as DepSecDef opened that job for Will Taft, whose job as DOD general counsel was taken by Chapman Cox. So in later years when people asked me how I became an AsstSecNav, I would answer, "I owe it all to Sandy Rhyno."

Thursday, 9 February 1984

Hugh O'Neill called, ostensibly about Outer Continental Shelf issues. That done, he asked, "What else is going on?" Obviously he knows that I know we're both contenders for Chapman Cox's job, but in fine oriental fashion I said nothing and he didn't raise the sticky matter himself. Hugh is a good fellow I would want to get and keep on my side should I indeed take up residence on the E-Ring [of the Pentagon].

Following John Herrington's direction, I phoned the VP, who called back at 9:30 this evening. "What's happening?" he asked breezily. When I inquired whether John Herrington had spoken with him "about our plot," GB said he had, and then he gave me the best news of the day: traveling with him tomorrow to Europe on Air Force 2 will be none other than John Lehman, "and I thought I'd mention it to him." Of course this also means Lehman will be out of town, leaving Herrington free to proceed on the Cox-Untermeyer package deal. The only thing I could think to ask GB beyond this was to speak with SecDef and shore up his support, and GB said he would be seeing Weinberger prior to departure tomorrow. "I just hope like hell it works out," he said in closing. "Good luck, Chahlie!"

Friday, 10 February 1984

Today I awoke to the news that Soviet president Yuri Andropov was dead. He hadn't been seen in public for six months, the official reason being a bad cold. With RR vacationing on the ranch at Santa Barbara, GB postponed his trip to Europe to tend to National Security Council affairs. Yuri, how could you do this to me?

Monday, 13 February 1984

When John Herrington returned my call, I asked if GB had spoken to Lehman about me. John said slowly, "He did, and he got a positive response." Then he said, "I find it very interesting that none of this has reached you. I can't believe Lehman hasn't called you on this." If, as it now appears, SecNav lost out on naming Chapman Cox's successor, I can understand why he would be less than eager to call me. With an ominousness that suggests Lehman reneged on some promise, John said, "If you don't hear anything from him, I'll call him." I told John I'd like to sit down with him and get the benefit of his experience as AsstSecNav (M&RA). "Just be loyal to Ronald Reagan and George Bush!" he said, to which I replied, "That's the easy part."

Wednesday, 15 February 1984

My appointment with SecNav was for 10:45, and I left a JIMFOG meeting early to be there on time. His EA [executive assistant], Captain/Commodore-selectee Paul David Miller, motioned me in. John Lehman got out from behind his desk to welcome me and escort me over to the same place where we sat almost exactly a year ago: I on a couch and he slumped so low in an armchair that his arms practically protruded straight out from his shoulders. He wore a dark three-piece suit but also scuffed black shoes and a green tie. He looked straight at me with unblinking blue eyes.

Lehman said Chapman Cox has been selected as the new DOD general counsel, which of course I already knew. But I was surprised to hear him say that the first person to tell him this news was George Bush, when he called to plug me. "He put in a strong word for you," Lehman said without much trace of emotion, "and I told him I thought you'd be a good choice. . . . You've done an excellent job over there [as DASNIF]. Ev Pyatt tells me how you grab on to each issue and take care of it so it doesn't become a problem. So I'd like to offer the job [of ASN] to you." It was laconically offered, but I was no less glad to hear it or eager to accept.

The clearance and confirmation process can take months, Lehman warned, "even for Mother Theresa." He then talked about the job that needs to be done in Manpower. The biggest problem, he said bluntly, is that "it's the weakest bureau I have in the way of deputies": E. C. Grayson, the San Francisco socialite, as principal deputy; Joe Taussig as DASN for civilian personnel; and Fred Davidson as DASN for reserve affairs. SecNav said that those who fought him (and failed) to prevent the build up of the Navy now will try to deny the fleet manning levels and civilian "end strength."[1] In addition to fending this off, I am to lead the homeporting initiative and to correct the Rickover-induced bias for the hard sciences (versus the humanities) in naval education.

The ship's clock rang eight bells, for noon. I told SecNav that I look forward "to being *here,* to working with you, and being in the middle of things." Seeing me to the door, he said that "as fast as they pull Chapman in [as general counsel], I want you pulled in behind him." Another handshake and I was off, down the E-Ring corridor that soon will be my stomping grounds.

And that's how things get done, how a succulent job like AsstSecNav is obtained while few people even know there's a vacancy. One has friends in critical positions—an assistant to the president for Presidential Personnel, a vice president of the US—and inside sources of information. A quick use of both, and a political appointment is snapped up before (as in this case) the supposed boss has a chance to do anything to the contrary. Less than 14 years after leaving active duty, at an age when at best I would be a commander, I am about to achieve four-star rank.

Thursday, 16 February 1984

Fran Melideo [Gene Peltier's secretary] buzzed to say excitedly, "Vice President Bush is coming on the line!" In a moment I heard, "Chahlie! I got back

---

1. This phrase refers to the number of people (uniformed and civilian) a military service has at the end of a fiscal year, although it would more appropriately describe the ability of Pentagonians to sit through the interminable meetings of outfits like JIMFOG.

[from Moscow] to find everything's under control. Can we start bragging on you at staff meetings and all?" I said I don't know whether my name has yet gone to senior [White House] staff. Regardless of this technicality, GB said, "Congratulations, it's just wonderful. We're very proud of you. So get those flags flying!"

Jane Kenny [the VP's staffer for Presidential Personnel] later called to say, "You can be officially congratulated: the President signed off on your selection at 4:13 this afternoon." From this point on, my fate is wholly bureaucratic and constitutional. But at that precise moment Ronald Reagan personally gave me his approval. When he officially nominates me [to the Senate], and when he officially appoints me [after confirmation], those will be administrative acts done for him by clerks. So it is today, not then, that is the day to hallow.

Friday, 17 February 1984

For the first time in 11 months as DASNIF, I was tabbed with representing S&L at SecNav's thrice-weekly "lineup" or staff meeting. Cdr. Dan Murphy[2] described the seating: SecNav at his desk, from whose right sit "the Under" [Under Secretary Goodrich] and the flag officers in charge of legislation, information, and policy. Then comes Hugh O'Neil, the AsstSecNavs, the general counsel, and those Dan called "horse holders" — various uniformed aides and specialists like lawyer Capt. Ted Gordon and PAO [public affairs officer] Capt. Jim Finkelstein. Looming over the scene is Capt. Paul David Miller, alongside a stand-up desk.

My spot, on the couch, directly faced Lehman, which prompted him to announce that Untermeyer is "my nominee" to succeed Chapman Cox in M&RA. This said, SecNav went around the room for reports. It was a wonderful *tour d'horizon* of matters of which I was only dimly aware in far-off Crystal City: congressional moves, press inquiries, budget issues, OpNav[3] politics, and more. Chapman gave a report he later said was premature. "I should have kept my mouth shut. Those sessions are a chance for the Sec-

---

2. SecNav's staff secretary and the son of Bush's chief of staff, retired Adm. Dan Murphy. The younger man also became an admiral and in time commanded the Sixth Fleet, as had his father.

3. OpNav is the staff of the Chief of Naval Operations. The staff of the commandant of the Marine Corps is known as HQMC (for Headquarters Marine Corps), and that of the secretary of the Navy is called the Secretariat.

retary to show he knows more about the thing you're talking about than you do."

Afterward, Chapman invited me to his office to talk. He said that being assistant secretary for Manpower is "one to savor," and he leaves the job with great regret, though becoming DOD general counsel is a definite promotion. Earlier when I had said that presidential nominees are not "just names on a piece of paper but human souls," Chapman said, "That's precisely the attitude to have in this job. There are a million souls out there in the fleet that are *your* responsibility."

Thursday, 23 February 1984

Today the *Washington Post* reported Chapman Cox's selection for DOD general counsel, followed by this single sentence: "Cox would be replaced by Chase Untermeyer, deputy assistant secretary for Installations & Facilities, [Administration] officials said." The story was headlined "Much-Decorated War Novelist Chosen for Pentagon Position." This referred to Jim Webb, who will be assistant secretary of Defense for Reserve Affairs. I rejoice that through the medium of my new job I'll finally be able to meet Webb, whose books *Fields of Fire* and *A Sense of Honor* I read this past year.

The great party-giver Roy Pfautch called with a last-minute invitation to a dinner he was throwing tonight for the new secretary of the Interior, Bill Clark. "It's small, not like one of my big do's," he explained. This meant only about 100 guests. The theme was "South of the Border." I wore jeans and boots but dispensed with the cowboy hat. I arrived at the posh Madison Hotel simultaneously with Secretary and Mrs. Weinberger. His security man looked askance at my attire and said a polite but almost premonitory "Good evening, sir" as we all stepped into the elevator. Fortunately, Weinberger said to his wife, "Chase will be joining us soon." A few moments later, he asked, "Is there anything I can do to help?"

Sen. [John] Tower [chairman of the Armed Services Committee] was at the party, and he was an important stop to make. Tower had already heard my news, and when I said I'd be honored to have him introduce me at the hearing on my nomination, he laughed. "I will," he said, "and then I'll leave, turning the chair over to Carl Levin," the anti-DOD [Democratic] senator from Michigan. At the reception, Attorney General–designate Ed Meese saw me pass and immediately offered his congratulations, which I returned. John Herrington was dressed in a Border Patrol uniform, prompting Secretary Clark to joke later that "Marshall Coyne [owner of the Madison] just lost six of his waiters." Secretary Weinberger gave a toast that made a passing reference to "the many things we in the Defense Department do despite our meager budget."

I was the only "Bush person" present tonight among original Reaganites. Of course I was a fill-in, and yet I have been accepted as a friend and a trusted member of the Administration. All this can be distilled in my friendship with John and Lois Herrington. That, perhaps more than being a protégé of GB, is the reason I have copped a prize appointment from the President in the fourth year of his term.

Chapter 4

Breaking My Flag

Wednesday, 29 February 1984

Chapman Cox welcomed me into his office for a couple of meetings. Before they began, he spoke to me confidentially about his military assistant, Col. W. H. (Doc) White, USMC. "Doc was killed in Vietnam," Chapman said to my astonishment, going on to explain what he meant: Doc took a round of machine gun fire to his head and was pronounced dead by a corpsman, who immediately left him to tend to other wounded Marines. All the while, Doc was perfectly conscious of what was happening and felt a marvelous, euphoric peacefulness.

When the communists counter-attacked, another Marine leapt into Doc's foxhole and started to return fire, not realizing that he was standing on Doc. The vibration of the Marine's automatic weapon, passing through his body and boots, acted as a heart massage and revived Doc. The only trace of this encounter with death is a nasal quality to Doc's speech, which is masked somewhat by a [North] Carolina accent.

Chapman told me all this to show his admiration for Doc, adding that he should be a commander of troops, not a Pentagon staffer. Chapman would like Doc to return to the FMF [Fleet Marine Force] but doesn't want to make people think Doc was fired or otherwise didn't work out.[1]

Sunday, 4 March 1984

In a secondhand book shop I bought the two-volume set *The Wilson Years*, written by Josephus Daniels, SecNav from 1913–21. In it, Daniels recounts how on the morning of Wilson's inauguration (71 years ago today) he ran into the young Franklin Roosevelt in the lobby of the Willard Hotel and asked if he would like to become his assistant secretary. FDR's words could (and

---

1. In my taxonomy of the Corps, Doc was very much a Type 1 Marine.

maybe should) have been my own when John Lehman made a similar offer to me last month: "How would I like it? I'd like it bully well. It would please me better than anything in the world. All my life I have loved ships and have been a student of the Navy, and the assistant secretaryship is the one place, above all others, I would love to hold."

Tuesday, 6 March 1984

To fulfill Lehman's desire that I backfill Chapman Cox's duties as soon as possible, I was given a nondescript office across the E-Ring corridor from the assistant secretary's suite. There I spent a good part of each day reading, receiving briefings, and attending a lot of meetings.

I got to the Pentagon in time for a meeting in SecNav's office on this year's 2500 Naval ROTC scholarship recipients. Just as Japanese rooms are measured by the number of tatami mats they contain, Pentagon offices are judged by their number of windows. Both Lehman and Chapman have three.[2] Yet Lehman's office seems smaller because the Pentagon's pillars (a modest bow toward classicism) sprout just outside, making things gloomy.

The briefing was given by Vice Adm. Bill Lawrence, chief of Naval Personnel, whom I met in the outer office. Actually, this was our second time to shake hands: he was superintendent of the Naval Academy at the time of Rear Admiral Kauffman's funeral in August 1979. Lawrence was a POW [prisoner of war] in Vietnam, and he is universally acclaimed for his sensitivity and straight dealing. I am fortunate to have him as a counterpart.

Capt. Ted Gordon later took me to his office to talk about general matters. I have not lost my Crystal City–based view that the Lehman operation is a secretive club of close-in aides—Ted, Hugh O'Neill, Paul David Miller, and Dan Murphy—in which toughness is worshipped and the toughest of all is John Lehman. Ted gave me what in that crowd is considered a bouquet: he said that whereas he has heard moans of despair about E. C. Grayson and Fred Davidson, he never has about me. As compliments go, this seemed one of the "for a fat lady, you don't sweat much" variety.

Ted advised me to travel, even overseas, without fear of being slapped down for what he called "boondoggling." (The real word is junketeering. I

---

2. Even-numbered offices on the Pentagon's prestigious E-Ring have actual views, unlike all other offices in the massive building, which look out only at other windows set within concrete walls, a bleak, prison-like prospect.

suppose the confusion for military folk comes from "boondocks," the word they use for a remote location. But junkets are to such non-boondocky places as Paris and Hong Kong.) I told him how taking 99 trips in two years with GB inoculated me against official travel, adding that my policy as DASNIF has been to go only on trips that had a particular substantive reason. This noble attitude didn't impress Ted, and I am grimly willing to bet that the one time I do get in trouble over a trip is the time I actually take one. Ted is too slippery a fellow, crocodile smile and all, to be a friend or even trustworthy. But an open relationship with him is essential. As AsstSecNav I shall aim to perform ably, at best winning John Lehman's lifelong respect and at worst not receiving any more compliments from Ted Gordon.

Friday, 9 March 1984

The highlight of the day came when Jim Webb called on Chapman Cox, and I sat in. Selected for the newly created position of assistant secretary of Defense for Reserve Affairs, Webb entered dressed in a sports jacket and carrying a well-worn briefcase. He stands a bit taller than I do, with piercing green eyes and a full head of tight curls. I introduced myself as "one of your admirers and readers," which I am and which would have been fine had I stopped there. But I went on to say, "I'm looking forward to reading your third book when it appears." Webb looked blank for a moment and said it was published last October![3] It was the typical witless conversation that authors have with foolish fans.

Webb is considered controversial because he has made some strong statements against women in combat, for which he's become a marked man for feminists. Among these, unfortunately for him, is Marybel Batjer. Jim quoted John Herrington as chortling that he managed to get the three of us "around Marybel." This was a horrifying notion inasmuch as I consider her a friend and sensed that she felt I had indeed worked my own deal to become assistant secretary. Webb proclaimed AsstSecNav (M&RA) "the best job in this whole building."

The call ended with Webb's describing his battle against the antiwar types who promoted the Vietnam Veterans Memorial, which he opposed as concentrating too much on those who died rather than those who served. I very much want to get to know Jim better. When I mentioned we have a

---

3. This was *A Country Such as This*.

mutual friend in Chris Buckley, he said the two of them concluded they are "the only two tattooed Republicans in Washington."

Sunday, 11 March 1984

Today I hibernated, staying indoors to read through an entire attaché case of folders from the Board for Correction of Naval Records, which will report to me. BCNR processes 8000 cases annually, some 1400 of which come to M&RA for examination. I also read a few folders arising from the amalgam of appeals bodies known as the Naval Council of Personnel Boards, which I shall also oversee. I read of lesbians in the Marine Corps, [male] homosexuals on [the carrier] *Kitty Hawk,* a disbursing officer on [the Indian Ocean base of] Diego Garcia who couldn't balance his checkbook, and a midshipman at the Naval Academy who failed to return a book to the library for several months.

Wednesday, 14 March 1984

I went to Crystal Plaza 5 for my "last lunch" with the staff, exactly one year after arriving at S&L. I told the group I couldn't be taking on my new duties without this past year of "finishing school," and I joked that whereas then I couldn't understand anything that was said around the table, "it's now up to 18%."

Back in the Pentagon, Capt. Kelsey Stewart and Col. Doc White met with me on such procedural matters as how I want to handle the schedule. Kel's official title is executive assistant and naval aide, and Doc's is military assistant and Marine aide, but I do not look on them as aides in the sense that I once was. "Because I've been there," I said, "I will never put demands on you," horrified at the notion of two senior officers doing menial tasks for me.

There's some risk, I suppose, in smearing too many ashes on myself. But I don't view myself as important, needing to be pampered and honored throughout the fleet. Mine is an 18th century American view of public office in which the honor of serving is the greatest reward and the service itself is characterized by austerity, principle, hard work, and dedication to a larger cause. I intend to show leadership by personal intensity and rigor. I shall be tremendously humbled and thrilled to be AsstSecNav. Maybe never again in my life will I hold an office as high. But even if so, I want to be pleased with *how* I served, not just that I served.

Thursday, 15 March 1984

The highlight of the day was SecNav's luncheon for members of the Blue Ribbon Panel he appointed to examine the Naval Academy's emphasis on technology over the humanities and to recommend changes in the admissions standards, the curriculum, or both. Among the members are Vice Adm. James Stockdale (ret.), the ranking POW in Vietnam, now an author and a research fellow at Stanford's Hoover Institution, and columnist George Will.

When we sat down to a succulent meal in the secretary's private dining room, Lehman expressed his concern that Annapolis is turning out technically proficient managers but not leaders—officers who in wartime will depend on machines rather than their own intuition, judgment, and intellect. This heavy reliance on technology also means that no one in our modern armed forces is ever held accountable for things that go wrong. "It's always the *system* that was wrong," he said.

Lehman is a passionate believer that a study of the humanities will prepare naval officers for the complex world in which they will operate. "I'll bet that most people in this building, if you used the phrase 'crossing the Rubicon' or spoke of the Analogy of the Cave, would just give you a blank stare." (Er, let's see: the Analogy of the Cave: Plato? Aristotle?)[4]

Friday, 16 March 1984

Midshipmen were crisscrossing the Yard [at Annapolis] when Chapman and I entered the campus, proceeding to Rickover Hall, a new classroom building. Chapman noted the irony that the Blue Ribbon Panel named by SecNav to excise Rickoverian influence over the Academy's curriculum and admissions policy should be meeting there.

We were greeted by the superintendent, Rear Adm. Charles (Chuck) Larson.[5] Chapman later said that Larson represents everything that John Lehman dislikes about the modern, post-Rickover Navy: a handsome, poised

---

4. Plato spoke of men chained inside a cave, facing a wall, in which all they knew of life was formed by shadows cast upon it.

5. Larson rose to four-star rank and the helm of the Pacific Command. He had a second tour as superintendent of the Academy after a cheating scandal in the mid-1990s. Although a Democrat who made an unsuccessful race for lieutenant governor of Maryland in 2002, Larson likely would have received a major post had his Academy classmate and close friend John McCain been elected president six years later.

submariner who speaks the language of technology perfectly but is not "a whole person."

Tuesday, 20 March 1984

At the White House, I met with John Herrington to talk about the job he has given me and that he himself held in 1981–83. John urged me to develop a personal relationship with John Lehman. It was sound advice, but I may become an expert in naval manpower and reserve affairs long before I can hope to be a Lehman intimate.

Back at the Pentagon, E. C. Grayson came in for his weekly meeting. He carries the title principal deputy assistant secretary of the Navy, and on his agenda was "PDASN Utilization." This made for a perfect opener for me. I said that as an ex-DASN and ex-staffer I fully understand the importance of having direct access to the boss. And that is exactly why, I said, "as a management principle, blind to personality," the principal deputy's job should be abolished, eliminating a layer between me and the DASNs. E. C. quietly said, almost to himself, "I guess that means I will leave." He is a gentleman, and with luck he'll take this cue and depart gracefully.

Wednesday, 21 March 1984

I interviewed Capt. Sam Yow, commander of a VP [anti-submarine patrol aircraft] wing in Jacksonville and Kel Stewart's choice to succeed him as executive assistant. I can ask for more names, but Yow proved impressive. A native of North Carolina, where his mother still has a tobacco farm, Yow is confident without being arrogant. There's no question he will do well "working the corridor," especially with Paul David Miller. I want an EA who is a rising star in the Navy, and Yow is certainly flag-rank material.

A budget session in the afternoon was quite a show, with John Lehman testing wits, words, and will with Adm. Jim Watkins, the CNO. It was a fascinating verbal joust between two men who have risen "to the top of the tree" through a combination of ability and guile and who must work together, which they do without any apparent pleasure.

At issue was a proposed $150 million cut in steaming time for the fleet. Lehman said "the navy we tell the Congress is better than ours [i.e., the Soviets'] steams only a third as much as we do," going on to ask why we keep every available ship at sea as much as possible. Using British slang probably acquired at Cambridge, Lehman asked, "What difference does it make to the wogs if our carrier battle groups have one cruiser instead of two?" Lehman's line of inquiry illustrated his irritation with flag officers such as Watkins who define their mission in steaming days and flying hours.

CNO couldn't let this assertion go unchallenged. He stoutly maintained that steaming time means readiness and the maintenance of equipment. Ah, but it also means wearing it out, Lehman rejoined, and family separation is historically the number-one cause for sailors' and officers' complaints. Yes, CNO said, but reenlistment rates are way up.

During this battle (in which the participants seldom looked at each other), P. X. Kelley leaned back in his chair with a South Boston look of gritty defiance, holding a long unlit cigar between his fingers. The VCNO [vice chief of Naval Operations], Ron Hays, said nothing, so that when CNO called on him, his splendid voice attracted 100% attention. Como. Paul Miller chewed the end of his necktie.

The contestants eventually adopted "the Hidalgo solution," a reference to Jimmy Carter's last secretary of the Navy: splitting the difference, in which CNO accepted a cut of $75 million. Observed Lehman: "Policy follows the dollars."

Friday, 23 March 1984

At the end of the day, I went down to talk with Ted Gordon about my staff personnel decisions. He endorsed them all but warned that Lehman will be reluctant to appear complicit in the firing of E. C. Grayson. I am perfectly willing to be the bad guy. As for [Lehman's friend] Seth Cropsey, I shall of course be glad to hire him. "I've been the bride at a couple of shotgun weddings around here," I told Ted. "I guess it's time for me to be the groom."[6]

Tuesday, 10 April 1984

In the afternoon, I drafted a memo for the Secretary to send E. C. Grayson, officially notifying him that his job is being abolished but saying that he can remain a DASN until 20 January 1985. Then I called in E. C. and showed him the memo. It was a rather mechanical way to break the news, but given E. C.'s bent to hear only what he wants to hear and to interpret wildly from that, I saw no alternative but to let him see in print precisely what the deal is.

---

6. Seth, who became a grand friend of mine as well, would be given the title deputy under secretary of the Navy and work directly for Lehman on special projects.

I don't want to build my reputation on the corpses of others, and all would have been easier had E. C. taken the hint weeks ago and left. But SecNav has given him more than nine months of grace (and me more than nine months of Grayson), so we aren't being cruel to anyone except the taxpayers.

Wednesday, 11 April 1984

Col. Doc White escorted me up to the ex–World War II warehouse that is Headquarters Marine Corps for lunch with Lt. Gen. Bill Maloney [deputy chief of staff for manpower] and his ranking staff. The lunch, like the Corps itself, was informal with a heavy overlay of formality: the linen napkins, the place cards, and the waiter in the whitest possible jacket emblazoned with the "globe and anchor" emblem. The menu matched what was noted that I ate back in February at Chapman Cox's luncheon for the same group: a cup of soup, a chef's salad, and iced tea, followed by vanilla ice cream and coffee.

The generals briefly described their responsibilities. The most interesting comment came from Brig. Gen. Carl Mundy, the recruiter.[7] He said that the J. Walter Thompson advertising agency has had the USMC advertising contract since 1947 and has thus shaped the image of the Corps that practically all non-Marines have had of the institution ever since.

The pre-war Marine Corps was made up of some pretty low characters, many of whom joined as troubled youths, given a choice by judges between enlistment and incarceration. Audiences watching the 1932 film version of Somerset Maugham's great short story "Rain" knew that Joan Crawford's character, Sadie Thompson, was a scarlet woman because she socialized with Marines stationed on Samoa. Maugham thought it sufficiently sleazy for Sadie just to enjoy the company of sailors, but for Hollywood true depravity required Marines.

The complete turnaround in the Corps' image was to some degree the handiwork of the J. Walter Thompson agency ("The few, the proud, the Marines"), but it came chiefly from the "uncommon valor" demonstrated on Guadalcanal, Peleliu, Iwo Jima, Okinawa, the Chosen Reservoir, Hue City, and many other battlegrounds known and unknown. By the 1980s, the USMC enlisted only high school graduates

---

7. Because it passes on the traditions of the Corps to new generations, recruiting has always been honored duty in the USMC. Only high-flying officers and enlisted are chosen for these assignments, and being recruiter-in-chief was an important milestone on Mundy's way to becoming commandant, which he was from 1991–95.

with clean records, young men with whom parents would want their daughters to be seen in public—and be an outfit many thousands more were eager to join.

When day was done, Ted Gordon came to my office to say that SecNav had second thoughts after reading my memo on E. C. Grayson, seeing in harsh black and white exactly what we agreed. Lehman had Ted call E. C. last night for fear "he would take strychnine" and say that SecNav will let him remain a DASN for as long as he wants to stay. A guy who should have been gone in nine hours and was given nine months now will be with us forever. This is a side of John Lehman, notorious ball-cutter, I never would have imagined. If he becomes SecDef, would he retain his foes Larry Korb and Dick DeLauer so as not to hurt their feelings?

Friday, 13 April 1984

The quarterly report of the Navy Federal Credit Union has me as its cover boy, with a story inside on my speech to its annual meeting last month. The cover itself did not identify my photo; all it said was "protect your credit cards."

Monday, 16 April 1984

At 11:00, Chapman Cox, Vice Adm. Tom Hughes [deputy CNO for Logistics], and I met on Gulf Coast homeporting. We all agreed it's risky placing a carrier in waters that Cuba and its Soviet ally can bottle up. CNO, however, is willing to consider putting a battleship in the Gulf. This, I imagine, would be *Wisconsin,* the fourth and final battleship to be recommissioned.[8]

A battleship in the Gulf! In a flash I saw the outline of a glorious personal project: getting the Navy into Galveston Bay. Pulling this off would be in the great tradition of Texans in both the legislative and executive branches of national government who, while laboring loyally for the United States, made sure that Texas also came out all right in the deal. In my later years I would love nothing more than to gaze at gray hulls tied up at Pelican Island [in Galveston] and know that, as an assistant secretary of the Navy way back in the Reagan Administration, I helped bring them there.

---

8. The four Iowa-class battleships, built toward the end of World War II and hefting 16-inch guns, were *Missouri, Wisconsin, New Jersey,* and *Iowa* herself.

Tuesday, 17 April 1984

After all the other assistant secretaries had drifted away from SecNav's lunch, I remained to go over some matters with him, in particular the draft CNO memo on homeporting. Lehman opposes putting *New Jersey* in Pearl Harbor, but he likes the idea of placing a battleship in the Gulf. "Compete it," he said, and we shall. I don't doubt a moment that the Houston-Galveston area and the whole state of Texas will come forward with an offer that none of our poorer kin on the Gulf can match.

Wednesday, 2 May 1984

The best part of the day was when Betty [Thompson] and I went to the Naval Historical Center in the Navy Yard to look for a portrait to hang in my E-Ring office-to-be. We found some twenty portraits of 20th century secretaries of the Navy lining the passageway, far from public view. The curator was eager for me to borrow one or more from this group, and I was interested in three Charles's, each from a famous family: Charles Bonaparte, Charles Francis Adams III, and Charles Edison, son of Tom.[9]

The oversized portrait of Adams was propped up against some filing cabinets. "I'll take it!" I said without hesitation. Adams is special to me because it was in his name that his son, Charles Francis IV (board chairman of Raytheon), presented me an officer's sword at Harvard sixteen years ago as the graduating midshipman with "the most aptitude and motivation for service to the nation."

Thursday, 3 May 1984

There was a three-hour-long meeting on ship overhauls. SecNav declared that naval shipyards, pushed by fleet commanders, have a "damn the cost, full-speed ahead" attitude on moving ships out of the dry docks. In this argument, he was up against crusty old Vice Adm. Earl Fowler, commander of the Naval Sea Systems Command (NavSea), which runs the naval shipyards. Fowler condemned "the E-Ring mentality" and warned that if pushed to save

---

9. Bonaparte, who served Theodore Roosevelt from 1905–1906, was Napoleon's great-nephew. Adams, direct descendant of the presidents Adams, served Herbert Hoover from 1929–33. And Edison served Franklin Roosevelt in 1940 before resigning to campaign successfully for governor of New Jersey.

money, "I might have to put out some RIF [reductions-in-force] notices. I understand that doesn't go over too good in an election year." Calm in the face of this counter-assault, Lehman grinned and said, "The stiletto flashes."

Monday, 7 May 1984

Today I had a much-delayed private chat with Lehman on various issues. When I mentioned how hard it is to see him, Lehman repeated what Henry Kissinger said to him 15 years ago [when he was the National Security Council's congressional liaison]: "If you feel you need an appointment to see me, you'll always need an appointment to see me." This meant that in order to talk to him I need to hang around his office and await my turn.

Lehman gave me firm but gentle correction on a couple of matters. Cal Thomas of Moral Majority had recommended a Vietnamese refugee for admission to the Naval Academy. USNA prepared a reply in the negative, saying the kid's test scores were too low, and I had forwarded this letter to Lehman for signature. But SecNav said the kid has had a remarkable life story, is devoted to the United States, and is "the kind of guy we want as a naval officer. Your job is not to take the school solution." I must be "the compassionate angel" when the Navy or Marine staff say no, and I must be "the hanging judge" when they try to cover up some wrongdoing.

This was an interesting insight into Lehman, a conservative icon who is also a genuine Eastern establishment humanist, distrustful of the military, sympathetic to minorities, and willing to err on the little guy's side against "the System."

In the other chiding I received, Lehman said I ought not to have sent him a certain memo "because it will leak to the *Washington Post*." If I have to write him anything, it should be unsigned and on plain white paper. This, too, is very Kissingerian.

Tuesday, 8 May 1984

I asked E. C. Grayson to "represent the President" at the Spokane Lilac Festival, an invitation passed from the White House to SecDef to SecNav to me. Predictably (and pathetically), E. C. was thrilled beyond description. It's a tragedy that many working stiffs labor every day and pay their taxes so that E. C. Grayson can have a federal job and attend lilac festivals.

Friday, 11 May 1984

Vice Adm. James Stockdale (ret.) was in the office all morning to talk about the USNA Blue Ribbon Panel. He had several flights of verbal fancy, at one point recollecting officers in prison camp in North Vietnam who collaborated with the enemy. One extraordinarily handsome and successful officer, sure to make flag, was the first to break—because he craved attention and approval, which the North Vietnamese were quick and clever to realize and to exploit.

Tuesday, 22 May 1984

Today E. C. Grayson and I had lunch with David McLaughlin, the president of Dartmouth, who wants Naval ROTC back in Hanover. So does John Lehman, eager for more humanists in uniform. This we discussed when E. C. wasn't talking "The Grove." After lunch, E. C. had his regular weekly meeting with me. He had a predictably marvelous time "representing the President" at the Lilac Festival in Spokane. Everybody loved him, he said—all except "a fundamentalist minister" who objected to a sea story E. C. told about a helicopter crewman's "mooning" a Soviet intelligence-gathering ship. Egad.

Friday, 25 May 1984

After a meeting in the Old Executive Office Building, I went two decks below to the Vice President's office, where [chief of staff] Adm. Dan Murphy was still at work. The Admiral welcomed me warmly and expressed his delight that I have gotten such a responsible position at Navy. I said one of the reasons I went over to the Pentagon was to try to break into "the national security club" that rather snootily considers itself uniquely capable of dealing with international and defense issues. (This is true whether club members are liberal or conservative, Democrat or Republican.) I cannot gain entrance simply by being employed by the gigantic DOD. But what I have gained—and what I'm convinced is far more useful than being a member of the club—is a knowledge of how the Pentagon works: how budgets are prepared and pushed, how policies are created and blocked, and how high-ranking military officers think and act.

Monday, 28 May 1984

Today, Memorial Day, Col. Doc White and I took one of the buses that ferried most of the 4000 invited guests to Arlington National Cemetery for the state funeral and interment of the Unknown Serviceman from the Vietnam War. Upon arriving, we walked the remaining block to the classical amphitheater, arriving with a stream of dignitaries, families of MIAs (those missing in action), heads of veterans groups, and some ordinary-looking men — ordinary save for the pale blue constellation of stars around their necks that denotes the Medal of Honor.

The Marine Band played dirges until, promptly at 2:00, the President and Secretary of Defense walked into the apse. An announcer said that the Unknown Serviceman had arrived at the West Entrance. I could hear the clip-clop of horses' hooves as the caisson drew up to the amphitheater, having made the journey from the Capitol. As the Band played "God of Our Fathers," the pallbearers (an enlisted man from each of the services), preceded by an honor guard, moved slowly around the colonnade and entered the apse. There the flag-draped silver casket was placed on a black platform directly in front of the President. The National Anthem was played (not sung), and a rabbi offered a prayer.

SecDef stepped forward and in a single sentence introduced "our commander-in-chief." With some hesitation, the audience applauded. RR gave a short but moving eulogy. (As he spoke, rain began to fall, causing some people to get into raincoats or raise their umbrellas. But I sat stoically listening to the President, and the cloud soon passed.) He didn't dwell on the Vietnam War itself, though he proudly referred to it as "a noble cause," the same phrase that so horrified the liberals when he spoke it in 1980. Rather, he talked of those who served in Vietnam, and he won a special standing ovation from the MIA families when he demanded a complete accounting from Vietnam of all the missing. His voice cracking, so unusual for him, RR turned to the casket and hailed the lad inside. An aide stepped up holding a square of black velvet on which rested the Medal of Honor. The President took it and placed it on a special stand in front of the casket, walked back a pace or two, and then returned to his seat.

As the Marine Band played "A Mighty Fortress," Hugh O'Neill and I left our marble box to proceed to the terrace of the Unknowns. Stereophonically, the Army Band, on the terrace, picked up the melody as we arrived there. Ushers motioned for us to walk down the steps, which for Hugh and me meant literally the front row, directly in front of the band and just over from the Joint Chiefs of Staff.

The casket was borne to its place between the graves of the Unknowns of World War II and Korea and in front of the sarcophagus of the Unknown Soldier of World War I, dedicated 63 years ago with President Harding the principal mourner. There were full honors for the serviceman: four "Ruffles and Flourishes" and a 21-gun salute. Chaplains pronounced "prayers of commitment," after which the President placed a wreath before the casket. He then stepped back and saluted—the picture of the day. With impressive precision, the honor guard folded the flag and presented it to the President, who in turn gave it to the civilian administrator of the cemetery. There was no lowering of the coffin during the ceremony. The President departed, and soon the rest of us filed out, ending a memorable event.

Fourteen years after this stirring ceremony, the remains in the tomb were identified as those of an Air Force pilot shot down over South Vietnam in 1972. They were disinterred and delivered to his family for private burial. Because modern DNA testing may eventually identify all other remains from that conflict, it was decided not to inter other bones but to rededicate the tomb to all missing service members.

Thursday, 31 May 1984

A high point of the week was having Jim Webb over for a get-acquainted lunch. The new assistant secretary of Defense for Reserve Affairs is a feisty fellow who likes to portray himself as controversial—a Tennessee Irishman.[10] Our conversation began somewhat rockily as he asserted that in my function as "appeals judge" of the Navy Department I ought to give the benefit of the doubt to the command structure rather than to the person involved. This reflects the fact that in Jim Webb's life, having been a Marine platoon leader matters more than being a civilian lawyer. And when we talked about the curriculum and admissions standards for USNA, Webb (Class of '68) objected strongly to my (and Bill Lawrence's) opinion that the very fact it is a military institution deters traditional liberal arts types. Perhaps Webb was thinking of himself. We ended the meal on the road to a friendship that I hope in time develops.

---

10. "Few things in life have come as naturally to me as combat," Webb wrote in *Born Fighting* (2004).

Thursday, 7 June 1984

The gracious Congressman Jack Edwards of Mobile, ranking Republican on the defense subcommittee of the House Appropriations Committee, hosted a dinner tonight, effectively in my honor, at Mr. K's Chinese restaurant on K Street. The other guests included both senators from Alabama, Howell Heflin (D) and Jeremiah Denton (R); Bill Nichols (D), a powerful member of the House Armed Services Committee; Bob Hope, director of the Alabama State Docks (the port of Mobile); and Bill Roy, shipyard owner and chief booster for bringing the Navy to Mobile.

Heflin is a classic Deep South senator of the old school, rotund, jowly, with thick brows and a graying cowlick. He speaks a patois that once dominated the Senate, for example pronouncing "issue" as EE-shuh. I sat next to Denton, a retired rear admiral and Christian Right leader who was a POW in Vietnam. Decrying the "lack of support for our commander-in-chief," his voice rose to a disturbing, almost manic level as if he had forgotten he was addressing colleagues in a small dining room instead of a convention of evangelicals. (He didn't quite approve of my drinking Tsingtao beer—till he tasted it.)

Roy and others gave the hardline on getting a battleship into Mobile: "We want it, and we'll do whatever it takes to get it." The congressmen said unnecessarily that the Alabama delegation is extremely influential on defense issues. For this reason I imagine that Mobile will be a contender right down to the last and could very well win. I didn't forget for a moment that I was popular tonight only because of the homeporting issue, and yet I did make some important congressional contacts. Will they survive a SecNav decision to put the ships someplace other than Mobile?

Tuesday, 12 June 1984

The late Congressman F. Edward Hébert of New Orleans used his power as chairman of the House Armed Services Committee to move the headquarters of the Navy and Marine Corps Reserve to his hometown. This gave me a regular reason to get down to the beautiful and exciting Crescent City.

[In the evening] I returned to the boat landing, where gathered the Navy and Marine Corps flag officers of New Orleans in their dress white uniforms. We crossed the Mississippi to the Chalmette Battleground, the scene of Andrew Jackson's victory over the British. It is a great grassy field between the river and a line of trees, with earthen works on a third side and a cemetery on the other. A squat obelisk rises, as does a fine antebellum home once owned by the son of General Beauregard. It was a splendid place to stage a change of command for the Marine Reserve. When honors were rendered for the departing and arriving generals, a 13-gun salute sent strange reports ringing off the Beauregard mansion and floated white smoke over Chalmette, much as it must have been in 1815.

In the reception after the ceremony, I met Tommy Lupo, a dapper little man with a thin mustache, a long cigar, and a Key West tan. He is a tremendous supporter of the Navy and Marines. When the task force that had been off Beirut touched Key West en route home, Tommy paid for all the food ashore for all hands on all ships.

Tommy invited me to dine with him and others (including a defense contractor) at the fabled Commander's Palace in the Garden District. We were greeted at the door of the restaurant by its owner, John Brennan, and seated in the Garden Room upstairs, with beautifully lighted oak branches just outside the windows. I dined on an appetizer of sautéed crawfish on vermicelli; redfish meunière topped with lump crabmeat; and Celebration, which is a mound of vanilla ice cream encased in chocolate mousse and topped with hot raspberry sauce. There was a tussle for the check, which I'm glad Tommy won, for I couldn't have let the contractor pay for my meal.

Thursday, 14 June 1984

I met with my staff lawyers, Lt. Col. Woody Bond and Cdr. Biff LeGrand,[11] on some personnel cases. One concerned a homosexual tossed out in 1949 who now wants his discharge upgraded to honorable. Homosexuality between consenting adults (who are equal in rank) is no longer a criminal offense, but people will be discharged for engaging in it. Such a discharge can have a nonpunitive characterization such as honorable or general if the person has a good record. In this case I ruled against the ex-sailor because he conducted his liaisons in a naval hospital [which was contrary to "good order and discipline"]. Biff, who had taken the man's side, jokingly said he represented the ACLU in the case.

---

11. Carlson "Biff" LeGrand later became a rear admiral and deputy judge advocate general of the Navy.

Tuesday, 19 June 1984

E. C. Grayson announced at the end of our weekly meeting that he would like to leave Navy in mid-August to work in the President's reelection campaign. He was clearly pained to hear those words from his own mouth. Apparently he will be no more than a volunteer with Reagan-Bush '84, but it's an ample fig leaf. I didn't pretend to regret his decision; I simply hailed it as a good move in building "credit" toward a better job in government after the election.

Wednesday, 20 June 1984

Today I went to the Navy Annex to meet with Vice Adm. Bill Lawrence and his top staff. Next to Bill stood his EA, Capt. Mike Boorda. A little fellow with a round tummy, Boorda looks like a grad student in a captain's uniform. His ambition and reputed ruthlessness are so well known and so coldly apparent that my visceral reaction to him was one of caution. During the Carter-to-Reagan transition and into the Lehman era, Mike was the de facto head of M&RA.[12]

Friday, 22 June 1984

Doc White, Lt. Gen. Bill Maloney, and I were driven in a green USMC car to "the Marine Corps Academy" at Quantico [Virginia]. Once inside the beautiful, rolling 60,000 acres of Quantico, we went to The Basic School.[13] It is where all Marine officers come upon commissioning, whether they be infantrymen, aviators, lawyers, or whatnot. It is a tenet in the Corps that all Marine officers are the same and all will lead troops in combat if called upon.

The 16 weeks at TBS are an indelible experience in the lives of Marines; Doc said he can still remember every man in his Basic class from 23 years ago. It is also part of what Bill Maloney likes to call "bonding," a psychologist's term for the deep, emotional ties of respect and loyalty that men can develop

---

12. Mike Boorda was a fascinating, tragic figure who rose from seaman to four-star admiral without higher education of any kind. He was serving as chief of Naval Operations in 1996 when he took his own life, reportedly out of anguish over allegations that he wore an unauthorized decoration.

13. Known by the initials TBS, never "the BS."

in conditions of mutual danger or discomfort. These bonds extend up and down ranks and ages: a three-star like Bill can look upon a second lieutenant he's never met with almost fatherly pride, and that second lieutenant can see a lieutenant general and know that the older man has gone through the identical experience he has.

The making of a Marine, officer or enlisted, is the most beautiful thing in the world to another Marine, the closest thing to childbirth that a man can experience—only in this case it's the newborn who suffers all the pain. For this reason, commands like Quantico are among the most prized in the Corps.

We observed a panel discussion, part of the Combat Leadership Course that concludes TBS. A sergeant major and two lieutenant colonels, both of whom received the Navy Cross[14] in Vietnam, answered questions about leadership under fire. A lieutenant asked how the course will be conducted ten years from now when there are no officers around who fought in Vietnam. He was told that what they learned at TBS was born of experience in combat. All they have to do is have faith in it.

Our final stop was the Marine Security Guard School for US embassy and consulate guards around the world. We saw the fully realistic "Post One," identical to the reception point at every major embassy, especially those beset by terrorism or other political unrest. It is a brick emplacement with bullet-resistant glass and the latest radio, TV, and sensor equipment.

For my instruction and entertainment, a "reaction drill" was staged. A group of off-duty Marines in burnooses pretended to be an angry mob, throwing muddy sponges and other debris at Post One while the sentry, in dress blues, calmly put on his flak jacket and helmet. When the screaming "Arabs" rushed the embassy, a squad of Marines in riot gear charged back. We watched the clash through a picture window alongside the foyer. A canister of "tear gas" (talc) dropped from the ceiling, and the embassy was saved. Afterwards, the defenders lined up for me to meet them. The Arabs were never seen again.

---

14. The Navy Cross is the highest medal for valor that the Navy and Marine Corps may bestow. Ranking just below the Medal of Honor, it was awarded to Jim Webb and to the admiral for whom I was aide, Draper Kauffman.

Tuesday, 26 June 1984

Today I met with Mel Paisley[15] on SecNav's desire to create a corps of managers, both military and civilian, who specialize in acquisition. Music played in Mel's office, not because the hard-of-hearing Paisley forgot to turn it off but to baffle Soviet listening devices trained on us from their new embassy in clear line of sight across the river.[16]

Mel was a vice president at Boeing before joining "my friend John." He said I'd be employable by industry, perhaps put in charge of a product line. The trick is knowing how to work with and motivate people, he said. That's of course the politician's skill, but a prospective employer probably would choke if I declared my aim "to bring sound government practices into business."

Wednesday, 27 June 1984

Today Joe Hagin[17] was already in the parking lot when I arrived at the Naval Air Facility at Andrews AFB. He, in his "Vice President George Bush" polo short, spied me in my suit and exclaimed that he was underdressed. He was fine, I assured him; after some deliberation I decided to dress up so as not to look like a typical turista on an aircraft carrier. Once on board ship, I put on khaki trou but retained a short-sleeved shirt and striped necktie. There was therefore no mistaking the assistant secretary, and no one was going to tell me to remove the tie.

Inside the DV (Distinguished Visitor) Lounge was my other guest, Richard Breeden, the VP's deputy counsel.[18] Out on the pad was a Navy T39 [a Sabreliner twin-engine jet trainer] that took off smartly at 8:00. Less than an hour later, we approached NAS Norfolk from the sea. A public affairs officer greeted us on the tarmac and took us into the DV Lounge for a short wait till the COD [carrier on-board delivery aircraft] arrived. The officer said that a total of 14,000 people visited carriers out of Norfolk last year. I've been reluc-

---

15. Assistant secretary of the Navy for Research, Engineering & Systems from 1981–87. A decorated Army Air Corps fighter pilot during World War II, Paisley was John Lehman's closest friend and compatriot.

16. My office, which also looked straight at the USSR embassy, lacked such a musical "burble," and so the Russians may have eavesdropped on my conversations. But as I told visitors, "It's what I do to fight the Soviets: I'm boring them to death."

17. Then legislative assistant to the Vice President, Joe would have senior positions in the White House under both Presidents Bush, most notably as deputy chief of staff from 2001–2008.

18. Chairman of the Securities & Exchange Commission from 1989–93.

tant to be one more potentate dropping out of the sky to interrupt shipboard routine. But I really needed to see a carrier and to learn about naval aviation, and going aboard *Eisenhower* (CVN-69) was a fine way to do so.

The COD, a Grumman C1, looks like an ugly bug. A crewman came into the lounge with white life vests, which we put on before boarding the plane. Once inside, we put on crash helmets with ear protectors and were strapped in, facing aft. This reduces the impact of "catching the hook" upon landing on the deck of the carrier. We took off and flew down the Virginia–North Carolina coast before heading about 100 miles out to sea, where *Ike* is operating.

Once we reached the carrier, we circled in front of the 95,000-ton, nuclear-powered behemoth before making our final approach. Out my window I caught sight of the gray deck an instant before the *ka-thwack!* and sudden stop of an arrested landing. The COD was promptly moved to one side so that regular flight operations could resume.

Still in flight gear, I stepped out of the plane to be greeted by the ship's executive officer, who indicated above the roar that the official greeters waited on the other end of the sideboys. How grand it is to step through the double line, smiling for the camera as the bosn's pipe sounds and sailors salute, to be greeted by a two-star admiral. I now know exactly how AsstSecNav FDR must have felt.

Right away we sat down to a film about carrier operations. Its dramatic, colorful footage and Wagnerian music made carrier pilots seem like gods, which is of course exactly how they view themselves. My visceral bias against pilots was born at the Sangley Point BOQ [bachelor officers' quarters], and those guys just flew pokey P3s. Jet pilots are even more obnoxious, and it has always concerned me that many of them later wind up flying commercial airliners. I have to keep these feelings to myself because aviators not only predominate in upper naval ranks, they are highly self-protective, and John Lehman is one.[19]

Our first stop after lunch was the "pri fly," the compartment atop the island where the "air boss" controls the 4½-acre fight deck and everything that lands on it or takes off from it. A spotter announced each jet as it circled to land and whether the deck's arresting gear was ready to stop that particular kind of aircraft. Landing looks so effortless, and yet pilots say they are tense every time they do it. At the other end of the flight deck, steam catapults

---

19. My prejudice against pilots softened into bemused respect as I got to know more of them.

were launching planes. It was a sight I could have watched for hours, yet we had to keep moving.

While we toured sickbay, a nuclear weapons alert was staged by the MarDet (Marine Detachment). This happens whenever anyone so much as approaches or talks to a Marine guarding *Eisenhower*'s cache of neither-confirmed-nor-denied nuclear weapons. All I could hear were unintelligible bellows. "They don't treat it as a drill," a corpsman told me. Richard said a Marine pointed a rifle at him when he peeked around a corner. I met the studious-looking captain in charge of the detachment and thanked him for the show.[20]

Later I met with about 35 chief petty officers and *Eisenhower*'s master chief. They were mostly interested in shorter sea time, contending that long deployments discourage reenlistments. This is an old story, and it's hard to have a "forward-deployed" navy without sending ships like *Eisenhower* far from home for long periods.

Thursday, 28 June 1984

Today I awoke after a night's sleep undisturbed by the continuous slam-dragging noise of aircraft hitting the deck and catching the wire. After breakfast, Joe, Richard, and I were taken to the "bow bubble," a glassed-in compartment where two of the ship's four catapults are controlled. We had an ideal view of the ballet performed by *Eisenhower*'s deck crew as they scrambled to attach the variety of planes to the "cats" (careful of the air intakes and the wings and tails of the aircraft), working on their backs and then rolling aside when time comes to launch. Our escort said, "You can never really explain all this; you've gotta see it."

Friday, 29 June 1984

At 10:30 there was a meeting on homeporting in SecNav's office. The uniformed Navy wants to assign *Missouri* to Pearl Harbor, halfway to potential trouble spots, despite the Secretary's strong preference for vote-rich Califor-

---

20. In the days of sail, Marines acted as snipers in the rigging and enforcers below decks. "What standing armies are to nations [and] what turnkeys are to jails, these Marines are to the seamen in all large men-of-war," wrote Herman Melville in *White Jacket*, his semiautobiographical novel of the mid-nineteenth-century Navy. In the late twentieth century, Marine detachments were only to be found aboard carriers and, briefly, battleships.

nia. By now well used to the effrontery of "the System," Lehman exploded. "This is bullshit! They've already *got* a battleship in Pearl Harbor!" He referred to *Arizona*.

Later, calmed down, Lehman mused that "the Navy made a great mistake in the early 1970s, abandoning the Northeast and losing liberal congressional support. They haven't forgiven us yet for costing all those jobs. Joe Addabbo [chairman of the defense subcommittee of the HAC (House Appropriations Committee)] never fails to remind me of that every time I visit him. After all, the Navy is the liberal establishment's service of choice, the service of Franklin Roosevelt and of John Kennedy."

SecNav dictated a memo to CNO accepting his recommendation that *Wisconsin* go to the Gulf and that Long Beach, San Francisco, and Pearl compete for *Missouri*. I gave the news to a smiling VCNO when we walked in for lunch in CNO's Mess. Four deputy CNO's (all vice admirals) joined us. Unlike poor E. C. Grayson, I don't hold every flag officer in awe. They all deserve praise indeed for having advanced so far in a highly competitive and demanding field. Yet my very valuable experience as a flag lieutenant in 1969–70 taught me that admirals are not demigods; they are pols, just like I am.

Monday, 2 July 1984

At 3:00, Capt. Sam Yow and I had his welcome-aboard conversation. My new executive assistant is so pleasant and so competent that already I rejoice he is on duty. With an easy-going North Carolinian style coupled with an impressive career in aviation and manpower issues, Sam will be good for the office, good for the Navy, and good for me.

Friday, 6 July 1984

Recently the Congress, reacting to genuine national revulsion at drunk driving, passed legislation denying federal highway funds to any state that doesn't set a minimum drinking age of 21. This naturally raises the question of what we, a major employer of 18-, 19-, and 20-year olds, ought to do. Asked about this by SecNav at today's line-up, I said the [negative] impact on morale would be tremendous and added that the Marines worry that their enlisted clubs will go broke. John Lehman sees the matter in philosophical terms: "It's the age-old Manichean heresy that the object causes sin, not the individual—that liquor causes drunkenness and bombs cause war."

Later, I found and sent to Lehman sections in the memoirs of Josephus

Daniels in which the World War I secretary proudly wrote of "protecting our youths" by banning alcohol and contraceptives from the fleet.

Tuesday, 10 July 1984

I had lunch with retired Brig. Gen. Don Hittle, USMC, who was the second AsstSecNav (M&RA) in 1969–71 and today is a close confidant of SecNav. Right now, he's doing the brainwork on Lehman's solitary fight against strengthening the role of the chairman of the JCS. SecNav believes that this will not only endanger Navy and USMC's interests whenever Army or Air Force has the chairmanship; it will increase the military's role in national security decision making—a matter of some concern to would-be SecDef John F. Lehman Jr.

Thursday, 12 July 1984

I participated in a little ceremony inaugurating PRIMUS (Physician Reservists in Medical Universities), a plan to sign up doctors in critically short specialties like surgery. I quoted Swift: "'The best doctors in the world are Dr. Diet, Dr. Quiet, and Dr. Merryman.' After 250 years, that is still pretty good medical advice. But today, speaking for the Navy Department, I say the best doctors in the world are Dr. Padilla, Dr. Givens, Dr. Rogers, and Dr. Mulhern"—the young men in blazers (and, in one case, a white lab coat) ranged in front of us. After they were sworn in, I chatted with this bright bunch and was amused that when I asked their new rank, they had to look on their commissions to answer. I'm not sure they knew even then what a lieutenant commander is.

Saturday, 14 July 1984

[In Memphis, I addressed a dinner of the National Naval Officers Association, composed of black Navy and Marine officers.] I began by saying that I had "shaky knees at being with so many senior officers. I'm not talking about General Maloney or Admiral Austin. You have to remember that I am a retired JG [lieutenant (junior grade)], so I'm talking about all you *lieutenants* out there." This got a big laugh. The closest I came to anything political was when I said, "the difference between this administration and the previous one—or a possible subsequent administration—is that they look at the country and see *groups;* we look at the country and see *individuals*." I said that goals are important as targets and as measurements, but we in the Navy Department look upon black officers as *officers* and that the best goal is "more, ever more, and ever better."

I closed by noting the presence in the room of one of the last of the "Golden Thirteen," the first black naval aviators, commissioned in World War II against the will of an all-white officer corps. "What kept them together and brought them together again tonight after years of discrimination, discouragement, and hurt?" I asked. The answer is love of the Navy—"a Navy that is stronger because of them, stronger because of you, and which will be stronger yet when there are more like you."

Tuesday, 17 July 1984

I was the reviewing official at tonight's "sunset parade" at the Marine ("Iwo Jima") Memorial at Arlington National Cemetery. I sat between Maj. Gen. Joe Went, in charge of the USMC Reserve, and Col. R. D. Weede, the CO of the Marine Barracks at 8th and I [Streets in Southeast Washington]. The colonel gave me fascinating insights into the mechanics of the event: the troops practiced twice today, critiquing each other; when they go up or down the steps of the memorial, six covers (hats) should be perfectly aligned, right and left; the right biceps of the Silent Drill Team are larger than their left by about an inch for tossing a ten-pound rifle around so much; the gloves used by the two men selected for "inspection" during the drill are made of doeskin and last only for a couple of weeks of heavy-duty use; and an occupational hazard is breaking tiny bones in the hand if the butt of a swung rifle hits the wrong place.

Colonel Weede indicated that time had come to rise and proceed to the edge of the grass. At the flash of a saluting saber, the band struck up four "Ruffles and Flourishes," one for each star, the maximum possible for anyone, including a president. This was followed by a short, spirited portion of "Stars and Stripes Forever" [the musical honors for a civilian official]. Behind me, the flag of an AsstSecNav was "broken" on the flagpole.[21] The parade then formed and passed in review, the band playing the "Marine's Hymn," all smart and perfectly paced. The ceremony concluded with the firing of three volleys and the playing of "Anchors Aweigh."

---

21. The flag is tightly bound with string and pre-positioned at the peak of the mast or flagpole. At the appropriate instant, the string is yanked and the flag is "broken." When a naval potentate arrives on board a ship, it is said that he has "broken his flag."

As I was taking the salute this evening, the thought shot through my head that my whole life had prepared me for that moment: Naval ROTC, aide duty in the Navy, public office in Texas, service in the White House and around the world. I gave a little prayer of thanks.

Friday, 20 July 1984

In this afternoon's budget meeting, Rear Admiral Frank Kelso[22] reported that Sen. Ted Stevens (R-Alaska), under pressure from home state landlords, has reversed his pro-Navy position on housing. Lehman laughed: "Landlords have PACs; renters have only liberals."

Saturday, 21 July 1984

I arrived at the Naval Observatory after noon for lunch with the Bushes. They were sitting on the verandah despite the drippy skies. It was a real family gathering, with [son] Marvin and [his wife] Margaret and good old Don Rhodes.[23] GB quizzed me on my job, and when I told him how I ensured that my executive assistant didn't try to act like the boss, the VP smiled knowingly and said, "I taught you something, Chahlie."

Conversation inevitably shifted to the Democratic Convention and [Walter Mondale's choice of Queens congresswoman] Geraldine Ferraro [for vice president]. GB doesn't want to debate her but can't escape it. "You can't win," he said. "If you're tough—'See here, Mrs. Zaccaro'[24]—then they call you overbearing and ungentlemanly. But if you're polite—'Oh well, I can surely see your point on that'—then you're a wimp."

Tuesday, 24 July 1984

Around 9:45 we came in over the beautiful green coastal plains of South Carolina, laced with twisting rivers. When Lt. Gen. Bill Maloney and I landed at MCAS [Marine Corps Air Station] Beaufort (pronounced *Byew*-fort), we

---

22. Kelso was a hulking Tennessean with flaring eyebrows and an outgoing personality. A former commander of the Sixth Fleet, Frank was both a warrior and a budgeteer and consequently a Lehman favorite. He would be CNO from 1990–94.

23. Don Rhodes was for almost fifty years the Bush family's indispensable helper and beloved friend.

24. Ferraro, married to John Zaccaro, ran under her maiden name for Congress in 1978, most likely because her cousin was the Queens district attorney.

were met by a large delegation of officers headed by Major Gen. Steve Olm-stead, commanding general of the Marine Corps Recruiting Depot at Parris Island for all of two weeks. Before that, he was deputy chief of staff for the Marine Reserve.

Steve, by nature a tightly-wound man, was *almost* relaxed, and he certainly was expansive, overjoyed to have one of the prize commands in the Marine Corps. As I have noted here before, the making of Marines is thrilling for any other Marine, with the deepest sense of pride and accomplishment a man can feel. (The slogan of P.I. [Parris Island] is, "We don't train recruits; we make Marines.") For this reason, Maj. Gen. Tony Lukeman's taking command of the recruiting depot at San Diego (or "Brand X," as Bill laughingly calls it) helped curb the pain of giving up Camp Pendleton.

We crossed a broad marsh on a dike bridge to enter Parris Island. Spaciously laid out at the confluence of two blue tidal rivers, it was named for its British grantee in the early 18th century and has been a USMC training base since World War I.

Our first stop was the Drill Instructor School, where the famed DIs [drill instructors] are screened and trained. They are sergeants on their first or second enlistment who volunteer for the tough but career-enhancing duty of being the creator of 60 Marines in 11 weeks. Because of much-publicized boot camp deaths that scarred the Corps — one in 1956 in which a DI marched six men to their deaths in a swamp is remembered as if it occurred last month — DIs are carefully chosen and trained. They have to handle recruits without touching them or using abusive language. "Abusive language" includes calling them something unflattering but non-scatological like a pig, and DIs can't even use profanity in conversation with another DI if it's within earshot of their recruits. Wearing the famous "campaign cover" (better known as the Smokey Bear hat), DIs live in the same squadbay as their men (or women) and must be in good enough shape to demonstrate each act of training and to be able to fall behind and catch up with their platoon on its five-mile runs.

I had lunch with ten mortified recruits with shaved heads and green utility (camouflage) uniforms. In my attempt to stir conversation, I might get a one-word answer to a question but not much more than that. Recruits are denied the pronoun "I;" the men speak of themselves only as "this recruit." Their chief motivator is to survive 77 days of hell on P.I. and be reborn as Marines who can say "I" again. Afterward, at the chapel, I was briefed by a chaplain who was so egotistical that he must have swept up all of those thousands of "I's" the recruits can't use.

All women recruits in the USMC are trained at Parris Island. We entered a squadbay where recruits were cleaning their M16 rifles. (Although women cannot serve in infantry units or even ceremonial units with a rifle, they learn how to use and care for the M16.) To say they were prepared for my visit is an understatement. When we entered, the platoon leader leapt to her feet, called the women to full attention, and yelled, "Platoon Seven proudly welcomes and will now give a totally dedicated and thoroughly motivated greeting to the Honorable Mr. Untermeyer." With that, the recruits yelled, "Platoon Seven wishes the Honorable Mr. Untermeyer a good afternoon, *sir!*" It was so funny that all I could do was say good afternoon in reply.

Later, I met with about 20 DIs, men and women, who poured out their feelings about their jobs and the recruits they train. The DIs disputed the notion, now almost a Navy Department mantra, that today's recruits are the best ever. They may be smarter, but they're also more independent, asking what the sergeants called "why" questions. The DIs said they live in fear that one of their charges will write home with a complaint that Mama will send a congressman. As the most outspoken young sergeant put it, "You leave here with well-developed neck muscles from looking over your shoulder so much."

When I later reported this exchange to Steve Olmstead, he got flush-faced and pursed-lipped the way he always did when the subject of Fred Davidson came up. He said he and his staff must closely supervise the DIs because of the abuses of the past and because of the godlike, macho role each man plays in the lives of his recruits. ("Ole Sergeant Jones was the toughest man I ever knew.") That the DIs think Marines were better a dozen years ago struck both Steve and Bill Maloney as laughable, for in the '70s the Corps was filled with discipline cases. "We felt on Okinawa like we were judges and prosecutors," Steve said. "And wardens!" Bill added. The generals summed up the complaints I heard as the age-old lament for "the old Corps."

Asked to say a few words after dinner tonight in the officers club, I said that "I heard today, for not the last time, a yearning for 'the old Corps.' I'm confident that the *new* Corps that begins tonight with the arrival of those recruit buses is in good hands."

Wednesday, 25 July 1984

Today began at 6:00 sharp, with the first purple rays of dawn tinting the still Beaufort River, seen through Spanish moss. The only creatures that seemed to be stirring at that hour were scores of rabbits grazing on the edge of the marsh. But over at the Recruit Receiving Building, things were also hopping.

All yesterday, a new crop of recruits was being flown commercially from around the eastern US to Charleston, where they were given a steak dinner and put on buses for the long silent ride to Parris Island. Though the Marines deny it, buses always arrive late at night (here and in San Diego) for the shock of first exposure if nothing else.

The recruits were stony-faced guys in blue jeans, T-shirts bearing product names, and long, haphazardly-groomed hair. Three local barbers arrived and began reducing each lad to a plucked turkey. One of the barbers told me that the first swath is the trickiest, after which the strokes become easier.

Following breakfast there were morning colors at Steve's headquarters. I stood with his staff on the steps of the colonial-style building, facing a company of graduating WMs (women Marines). Beyond them was the Parris Island band and a tall flagpole. At the exact instant of 8:00, a Marine rang eight bells, the large flag rose smartly, and the band played "The Star-Spangled Banner." Then, honors were rendered to me: four "Ruffles and Flourishes," a section of "The Stars and Stripes Forever," and, for the first time, a 17-gun salute.[25]

A tiny female lieutenant announced that her recruits were ready to be inspected. Accompanied by Steve, I "trooped the line," another first. The sight would have appalled the gunnies [Marine gunnery sergeants] who taught our platoon of Ivy Leaguers how to march at Purdue eighteen years ago right now, for my right foot hit the deck in time with the music, not my left. Oh, well: one definite advantage of being an assistant secretary of the Navy is that truly everyone can be out of step but me.

I was given a final and very unexpected honor: a little concert comprised of "The Eyes of Texas," "The Yellow Rose of Texas," and, most amazing, "Ten Thousand Men of Harvard." How the Marine Band at P.I. acquired the sheet music to the Harvard fight song is something I'd like to know—but won't ask. If I did, the Marines in their fashion would drop everything they were doing to comply with "the Secretary's" request.

Thursday, 26 July 1984

Leafing through the backup on a personnel case, a name leapt up at me: Cdr. Dale Bosley, CO of SEAL Team 5 in California. I saw this in celebration,

---

25. Gun salutes in the United States are always odd numbered, with twenty-one rendered for the president, nineteen for the vice president or an ambassador, seventeen for governors and ranking DOD officials, and so on down to five for a vice-consul. The shots are fired at three-second intervals, the amount of time required to say, "If I wasn't a gunner I wouldn't be here. Fire number one! If I wasn't a gunner I wouldn't be here. Fire number two!" and so forth.

for Dale is one of the most impressive men I have ever known. A Princetonian, he was in my squad at Purdue in 1966 and the next summer was also assigned to *Walworth County* for our NROTC first-class cruise.[26] Dale was a combination of poet and athlete, the first person I ever knew who ran for pleasure. That he is now a SEAL is no surprise; in fact, I think it was during that summer of intense boredom that he took the SEALs swim test. As with other people I knew through the Navy in 1966–70, I have wondered how and when to get back in touch with Dale, and today's paperwork made that possible. I'm delighted Dale remained on active duty and now has a command. I wrote him a letter, curious how an AsstSecNav letterhead will hit his unit.[27]

---

26. Walworth County was an LST, or landing ship tank, used in amphibious assaults. Throughout our time on board, engine trouble kept the ship from ever leaving the dock at Little Creek, Virginia. Our "cruise" was first-class only in that we held the rank of first-class (college senior) midshipmen.

27. Because he needed Washington duty for promotion, I gladly put Dale on my staff the following year. He would go on to serve Secretary Weinberger, during which time he studied nights at Georgetown Law School. After his retirement, Dale was made marshal of the US Supreme Court.

Chapter 5

Secret Mission to Dallas

Tuesday, 31 July 1984

The *Washington Post* listed only one item of business coming before the Senate Armed Services Committee (SASC) today: a resolution in support of a US Army museum. But of course today was when the SASC would also meet on my nomination to be AsstSecNav.

The elegant hearing room in the Russell Building[1] was packed, no trick given the few seats available for spectators. Senator Tower, the chairman, wasn't present due to intense negotiations with the House over the Defense authorization bill. This was disappointing, but in the chair was a historic figure, Sen. Barry Goldwater (R-Arizona), looking and sounding very good today. At one time or another, Senators John Stennis (D-Mississippi), Strom Thurmond (R-South Carolina), Sam Nunn (D-Georgia), James Exon (D-Nebraska), John Warner (R-Virginia), and Carl Levin (D-Michigan)[2] attended the hearing.

First to be heard was a panel of nominees for OSD assistant secretaryships. Each made very brief statements of the "great honor . . . important job" variety. Finally, it was Ev Pyatt's and my time to take the witness table. Senator Warner, a member of the committee [and SecNav in 1972–75], introduced both of us. He read sonorously from a prepared statement that gave greater praise to Ev, who not only deserved the tribute but is also Warner's constituent. The senator then obtained permission for a non-senatorial witness to testify for Ev. This was former SecNav Edward Hidalgo, for whom Ev worked during the Carter Administration. There were a few questions, chiefly

---

1. This is the handsome original (or "old") Senate office building nearest the Capitol. It was renamed in honor of Senate titan Richard B. Russell (D-Georgia) after inmates complained of receiving mail addressed to them as "Senator ____, Old SOB."

2. Stennis was former chairman of the SASC; Goldwater, Levin, Nunn, Thurmond, and Warner were future chairmen.

from Senator Levin, the SASC's most active liberal. These mostly centered on recent disclosures of wrongdoing by General Dynamics on some submarine contracts. The contracts were signed while Hidalgo was secretary, so Ed's appearance today squelched Levin's obvious intent to embarrass the Reagan Administration.

Then came my turn. I had no prepared statement, but yesterday I had scribbled down some points in my pocket notebook, which I studied during the OSD nominees' testimony. Then, in the way I like to appear before congressional committees, I was able to sit with my hands neatly folded in front of the microphone and just talk. This had its effect, so much so that I was almost unnerved by the committee's complete attention. First, I thanked Senator Warner for his introduction, noting that "He may be a senior and respected member of this body, but across the river we still think of him when he was 'SecNav' in a difficult and challenging period." Warner bowed in courtly gratitude. Then I said that since being nominated in May, I have traveled to see "our sailors and Marines" on *Eisenhower,* at Quantico, on Parris Island, and in Memphis and how impressed I have been by them. "They are motivated by sincere patriotism and also by the fact that theirs is a good job, an honorable job." The task for me, I said, is "to keep a good thing going." I remembered — by the expedient of jotting "Res." on the water glass napkin — to throw in hearty words about the reserves, a favorite cause on the Hill.

Senator Levin asked me a couple of questions his staff had prepared. In one, he tried to make a political point: Why does the Administration want to buy nine P3C aircraft when the uniformed Navy only wants five? The answer is that the P3s are built close by Joe Addabbo's district. I wasn't going to get into *that,* so I exercised the nominee's right of ignorance. Then Levin asked if I would make it my "highest priority" to replace the old C-118s with C9s [for the Naval Reserve]. We're already doing it, I replied. "But will you make it your *highest* priority?" Levin continued. Only when we both agreed on "a high priority" did I say, "Yes, sir."

When I was able to go, I discovered the small hearing room held a number of friends, including Judge Malcolm and Emma Wilkey. I joked that the Judge "is trying to watch this process from beginning to end," since he will also swear me in. Nancy Carey [*a friend who worked for a telecommunications firm*] sent a note that was waiting when I got home: "You were terrific — elegantly eloquent — and an obvious hit with Warner and Goldwater. Treatment of Levin was masterful — just the right amount of firmness and deference. VERY well done."

Wednesday, 1 August 1984

At today's lineup, SecNav said of the current internal DOD budget sessions, "Thing are going well. That means we're winning." His staff has drafted language to give to Senator D'Amato to add $2 million to a pending supplemental appropriations bill to open a Navy reserve center and a recruiting station aboard *Intrepid*. The World War II carrier, now a museum, is moored at one of the Hudson River piers in New York. Lehman said, "Chase, both of these are your dogs. See that they're done."

So I have acquired another project, a wacky and tricky one. *Intrepid* still belongs to Navy, but attorneys Hugh O'Neill and Ted Gordon say that we can pay the museum to house the two centers on board our own ship. Why do we want to do this? Because the father of the museum is a wealthy New Yorker named Zack Fisher, and his charities include Joe Addabbo. SecNav is right to say that *Intrepid* is a great recruiting tool and we ought to take advantage of it. The reserve center idea is shakier, inasmuch as Addabbo has just had a brand-new one built in Brooklyn. My concern is that if we establish the two centers on board ship, Fisher might then push Navy to bail out the ship, in a manner of speaking, due to our great investment in it. For this reason, I told my staff that the two centers should be "light" so that we won't lose much if *Intrepid* goes bust.

Thursday, 2 August 1984

While waiting for a meeting with SecNav, I was told by his receptionist that Como. Dudley Carlson, chief of legislative affairs, was on the phone. When I picked it up, Dudley said only, "Mr. Secretary." It took a moment of silence on the other end of the line for me to realize that this was Dudley's way of saying that the Senate, earlier than expected, had just voted to confirm me. "Is that all advised and consented?" I asked Dudley, and he said yes.

At that moment, I was announced into SecNav's office. "Slipped through!" was all he said in response to the news. Then, surprising me more than the Senate's early vote, Lehman said, "I want you to go to Dallas and represent us at the Republican convention." He wants me to watch the platform deliberations, a role akin to the one he played at the 1980 convention, when he actually sat on the platform committee and produced the plank calling for a 600-ship navy. "It's made all the difference to us the way that plank read," he said, adding, "The fact I wrote it has helped."

Friday, 3 August 1984

My breakfast guest, retired Adm. Elmo (Bud) Zumwalt, was already in the SecNav mess, reading the paper, when I got there. Zumwalt is now about 60, and his famous flaring eyebrows have whitened. I had invited him back to the Pentagon to get to know him, since as CNO (1970–74) he was renowned for his concern for people, flooding the fleet with "Z-grams" that struck down nettlesome "Mickey Mouse" personnel policies. As we ate, Zumwalt mostly asked *me* questions, keen to know the state of naval manpower. He was particularly pleased with our progress on retention and race relations. "Those of us who had a more difficult situation to contend with can only stand back and applaud," Zumwalt said.

Tuesday, 7 August 1984

This morning it was my turn at the SecNav lineup to get a secretarial scolding. Lehman had read something in *Navy Times* that aroused his ire. This was all the worse for me, since I hadn't seen this week's issue. An article said CNO had "adopted guidelines" on fraternization. Lehman asked if these are as tough as in the USMC, which bans all forms of fraternization, and whether we were consulted. I had to say no. "I don't like to see policy guidance on something as sensitive as this done without our involvement," he said sternly.

Still stung by this admonishment, I was nervous when I returned to SecNav's office at 3:00 for my official swearing-in. (This was so I can start being paid and sign papers; a ceremonial swearing-in will be held later in the month.) All Lehman said in his remarks before administering the oath was how I "blanched" back in February at his prediction that my confirmation would take months. He then asked who would be holding the Bible. I was perfectly prepared to hold it next to me like a preacher, but that wouldn't do for SecNav. He looked at Fred Davidson and said, "Fred, get up here!" John then read off the entire oath, such that I only needed to say "I do." This eliminated the risk of the verbal stumbles which nervous appointees and bridegrooms make at such times. That was all.

It's sad but must be noted that my mood was sour on what ought to have been a major day in my life. This was due to several things: the Secretary's lecture, quite deserved, at the lineup this morning; today's gray, muggy weather; and especially the abysmally long period of time—a single day short of six

months—for the oath-taking finally to occur. And this was in the absence
of any serious competitor for the job, of any problem in my background or
financial statement, or of any controversy on the Hill.

The way things are going now, I may never attain what I want, which is
to be perfectly in control of my situation, undertaking initiatives of my own
instead of just acting on John Lehman's. The only cure is longevity, and as
in everything I've done in life, I am confident that *eventually* I shall succeed.

Wednesday, 8 August 1984

Word came that SecNav wanted to see me. Only hours away from taking off
for France, Pakistan, and China, Lehman was ready to talk about my mission
to Dallas next week. "You have to have your antennae up," he warned. "The
danger [in the writing of the GOP platform] is several fold." The libs will
want to expunge "naval superiority," and other service proponents may try to
enshrine their own ambitions in the document. Conservatives, in the person
of [ex-Reagan press secretary and political aide] Lyn Nofziger, now a lobbyist
for maritime interests, will seek subsidies for commercial shipbuilding, to be
paid out of Navy's budgetary hide.

John's advice is to get close to the Platform Committee's top staffers,
John Carbaugh and Margo Carlisle, who will control everything that goes
into the document. With a smile, Lehman said, "Go drinking with them. For
this exercise you can't be an effete, Gucci-loafered Bushite."

This Young Republican game-playing is the sort of thing John Lehman
loves and I detest. I am no good at it (witness my four years of not drinking
with the boys in Austin), and I know I have better things to do back in DC.
Worse, the platform process is beyond my control, and even if I am diligent
the defense plank can be jiggered (or Nofziggered) away from Navy at the
final moment. As a result, I don't welcome this coming week and fear its
consequences.

Thursday, 9 August 1984

At 9:15, I left the building with Col. Doc White, dressed in his tree suit, or
camouflage "utilities." We proceeded to Andrews, where waited a 25-year-old
C-131, a twin-engine prop plane with an extremely comfortable interior—
tribute to its service as LBJ's post-presidential aircraft. In the DV lounge I
placed a call to Congressman Trent Lott (R-Mississippi), chairman of the
GOP Platform Committee. John Lehman had pre-introduced me, so Lott

was extremely accommodating. He arranged for credentials and affirmed his support of Navy shipbuilding, to the greater glory of Ingalls Shipyard at Pascagoula. Getting acquainted with Lott will be a potential gain this next week, for he is probably the next Republican leader of the House.[3]

I also received a call from John Carbaugh, chief staffer for the Platform Committee. A hearty and friendly North Carolinian, Carbaugh was a long-time aide to Sen. Jesse Helms who first got to know John Lehman in the Nixon White House. We discussed some language in the draft plank on defense, agreeing to follow up in Dallas. Carbaugh vowed all support for Navy out of admiration for John, "the only guy in the Administration who's done anything." Treachery may lie ahead, but it looks as if I'm well set with the platform folks.

The plane lifted off smoothly, but just as we hit 13,000 feet, the windshield shattered. It didn't break, but we had to fly slower and lower. On board was Brig. Gen. Jim Mead, the director of Manpower Plans & Policy at Headquarters Marine Corps. A gigantic Boston Irishman of great energy and humor [a classic Type 2 Marine], he is known not as Big Jim but as Large James. He spoke enthusiastically about the close cooperation of Navy and Marine Corps in amphibious operations [which we were en route to observe]. Mead was even more rhapsodic about Maj. Gen. Al Gray (a.k.a. "The Tasmanian Devil"), the CO [commanding officer] of the 2d Marine Division, soon to be a three-star and commander of Fleet Marine Force Atlantic.

Gray and several of his general officers greeted our plane when we landed at sprawling Cherry Point, NC, the principal East Coast Marine air base, counterpart to El Toro in California. Short, red-headed, and bug-eyed, Al is, in Jim Mead's admiring phrase, "not pretty." But he is a fighter's fighter.

Friday, 10 August 1984

Skies were low, cancelling a half-hour helo ride to Camp Lejeune and requiring an hour-long trip by van. This was fine, as I got to see coastal North Carolina and work on some folders brought from DC. The East Coast equivalent of Camp Pendleton, Lejeune is named for John A. Lejeune, renowned early 20th century commandant of the Marine Corps. His name is typically pronounced "Lejoon," but "Lezhern" is correct. General Lejeune was from

---

3. No doubt Lott would have risen to the top spot had he stayed in the House, but in 1988 he was elected to the Senate, succeeding John Stennis. There he also advanced up the ranks, serving as majority leader from 1996–2001.

Louisiana, and last November 10 at Camp Pendleton, Mrs. Lemuel Shepard [whose husband was commandant from 1952–56] told me she knew Lejeune and that he pronounced his name the French way.

The crusty but endearing Al Gray loves tanks, so our first stop was the brand-new, first-class repair bays for all large vehicles. We were photographed in front of a Beirut vet still bearing shrapnel scars. Later, after lunch with men of the 10th Marine Regiment, I visited an M-198 Howitzer "gun park." Everything was Marine-like, with the troops at attention, their sergeants forward, and their equipment carefully laid on a piece of cloth for inspection. I played my role, shaking hands with each man and asking questions, right down the line. It was all something of a show, but if I tried to forestall such performances for my benefit, someone like Doc White would tell me that Marines *like* doing things like that and *really* appreciate the ten-minute visit of an assistant secretary of the Navy. The odd thing is that might actually be true.

A helo flew me through thick mist over coastal marshes to a point about five miles offshore where *USS Saipan* was anchored. She is an LHA, an amphibious assault ship that resembles a World War II aircraft carrier but is equipped with Marine helos and landing craft. I was briefed on tomorrow's assault, a simulated landing in Denmark to blunt a Soviet thrust out of East Germany. A piece of North Carolina in the approximate size and shape of Denmark will be the exercise area. There will be some opposition from "Orange" forces.

Jim Webb, dressed in utilities with a red "ASD Webb" nametag, arrived in the flag wardroom just after I did, loving the whole scene. We then proceeded into dinner, hosted by the commander of Naval Amphibious Group II. I sensed that the admiral would be a whole lot happier about tomorrow's exercise if he didn't have so many VIPs around. After dinner he took me to the flag bridge, where he pointed out the Soviet AGI (intelligence-gathering ship) that is shadowing *Saipan*. Meanwhile, a staff captain was aligning all the ships of the task force in a column behind us: *Raleigh, Portland, Harlan County,* and *Spartanburg County.* Also on the bridge were some Marine Reserve officers from San Diego. We talked for an hour as the sun set.

It had been a fine day with wonderful people, ending aboard a ship at sea. But when I got too happy I reminded myself that in only 48 hours I have to be in Dallas to mix it up with GOP platform writers, and the glow vanished.

Saturday, 11 August 1984

Doc rapped on the cabin door at 0500, and we went to the flag mess for some predawn coffee, juice, and doughnuts. Just inside the island we awaited the arrival of P. X. Kelley. He was late, which commandants have an option of being, and when his helo landed the bosn of the watch announced, "Marine Corps, arriving!"[4] P. X., in utilities with a row of four shiny stars on each shoulder, strode in with the commanding general of the 4th Division (the reserves). The Commandant has a grand way of greeting his comrades-in-arms: reaching out to shake their hands, he yanks them in close to clap them on the shoulder. With assistant secretaries of the Navy, however, a simple handshake suffices.

While P. X. went below for breakfast and a pep talk to the troops, Al Gray, Jim Mead, Doc, and I climbed into the commandant's helo for the flight to the beach. The morn was misty and gray, so *Saipan* looked menacing as we pulled away. We landed near the 10th Reconnaissance Battalion's buildings and were taken to a recreational pier on Onslow Beach, where stands were erected for members of the Reserve Forces Policy Board to watch today's landing exercise. At 7:30, Operation Phalanx Sound II got underway with landing craft leaving the amphibs anchored within sight offshore. A4s "strafed" the beach, on which preset charges exploded with a lot of gratifying smoke and flame. A tape played the soundtrack from *Victory at Sea*.[5]

First to hit the beach were LVTs, troop-carrying armor, followed by LCUs [landing craft utilities] with tanks aboard. In a real landing, the armor would have kept on charging as far and as fast as they could till meeting resistance. Today there was mock resistance—riflemen in the dunes firing pop guns—but because of environmental and geographic constraints (such as the Intracoastal Canal), all the armor stopped on the beach. The troops eventually got inland. It was all a good show. Major General Gray said goodbye to me at the pier, after which Doc and I proceeded across the canal bridge. It

---

4. When officials board a naval vessel, a bell is rung with two quick bongs for every star they merit. After being "bonged aboard," the official is then announced with grand abbreviation. With the president or vice president, it is "United States, arriving!" With civilian Navy Department officials, it is "Navy, arriving!" And an admiral in command might get, "Sixth Fleet, arriving!" This recalls the histories of Shakespeare, in which dukes are referred to as "Gloucester" or "York."

5. Composed by Richard Rodgers and arranged by Robert Russell Bennett for a 1952 series on NBC television, the score was for many years every Navy guy's favorite piece of music.

was patrolled by Marines in battle paint, probably to the consternation of some sail boaters about to pass through.

Monday, 13 August 1984

After breakfast I was off for the Dallas Convention Center. Attendance at the platform hearings is strictly controlled, and I was politely passed from hand to hand till I met John Bolton,[6] executive director of the Platform Committee. He arranged for me to get tickets for the rest of the week. In the relatively small room I sat next to David Broder[7] of the *Washington Post*, who said that when he interviewed GB recently "he spent the first five minutes bragging about how well you're doing over there [in Defense]. Of course we didn't use a word of it."

The day the committee met, the Post *carried a story about how White House chief of staff Jim Baker had dispatched staffers to ensure nothing got in the platform contrary to Administration policy. Dave naturally assumed I was one of these agents. I let him continue in that misimpression, since it would have been a much juicier story that the secretary of the Navy sent a top aide to Dallas to lobby for his shipbuilding budget. At no point during this week did I ever run across envoys of the secretaries of the Army and Air Force. Not being Lehmans, it never occurred to them to get their spending priorities into the document being hammered out in Dallas.*

Senator Tower was the first witness, and there was a colloquy between him and Senator Warner in which both said that naval superiority [over the Soviets] is a necessary and desirable thing.[8] Warner spoke the holy writ: "We are an island nation heavily dependent on our sea lanes of control." For my mission this week, this was highly encouraging, and I wrote down a possible amendment embodying RR's statement at the recommissioning of [the battleship] *New Jersey*: "Maritime superiority for us is a necessity."

---

6. Bolton would serve as an assistant attorney general from 1985–89, assistant secretary of State for International Organization Affairs from 1989–93, and ambassador to the United Nations from 2005–2006. Brilliant and able, Bolton has been caricatured as a right-wing firebrand, perhaps the fault of a fearsome mustache. But in private John is supremely affable, and I have been happy to know him since this meeting.

7. David was until his death in 2011 the dean of American political reporters, writing from his perch at the *Washington Post*. He, his wife Ann, and I had been on the 1977 Bush trip to China.

8. Warner's state of Virginia was home to Newport News Shipbuilding Corp., which made nuclear submarines and aircraft carriers.

When the committee broke for lunch, I fell in step with Senator Warner to encourage him on inserting "naval superiority" into the platform, which would make my whole week. Warner stared straight ahead and said, "We'll get it in there."

Tuesday, 14 August 1984

David Broder, jokingly outside the room and then more seriously inside, asked if I would take notes on the proceedings and pass them to his colleague Bill Petersen. I never fully functioned in this assignment, yet how many appointees of the Reagan Administration are stringers for the *Washington Post?* (On reflection, there's an entire corps of leakers to the paper inside the White House.[9])

I boldly went up to the committee table to suggest to Senator Warner the section in which to insert his "naval superiority" amendment. As I returned to my seat, John Carbaugh inquired, "Chase, are we all right?" His question had a note of suspicion and warning in it, for he considers Warner the weak sister of the committee.

Warner offered an amendment calling for "technological superiority" [in overall US armed forces] and "qualitative superiority in other areas, such as our maritime forces." This passed, and a form of "naval superiority" is in the platform. "John [Lehman] owes me one," Warner said to me upon adjournment.

Wednesday, 15 August 1984

Copies of the draft platform were available in a cardboard box inside the convention center, where the full Platform Committee met at 10:30. I quickly flipped through the document and was relieved to find there all the language from the national security subcommittee. Moreover, the maritime policy section in the transportation plank looked vanilla enough. Andy Wahlquist of Senator Warner's staff said they had been searching for me to see if the shipbuilding section was all right, and Warner himself asked me the same thing when I saw him later.

Committee chairman Trent Lott, a man of admirable smoothness and

---

9. I was a paid stringer for the *Post*, reporting to Dave, while I was a political reporter for the *Houston Chronicle* in 1974. Everyone, including George Bush, knew that the chief leaker in the Reagan White House was James A. Baker III.

good nature, had each of the subcommittee "chairs" report on their planks. Jack Kemp used two sections (on the economy and foreign policy) to orate, and he was a frequent participant in every debate. He makes an excellent advocate, except that he talks too much and too fast. Does he really expect to be run for president on a platform of changing US monetary policy? Just to say the words causes eyelids to droop.

Thursday, 16 August 1984

Sitting beside me when the Platform Committee convened at 9:00, David Broder leafed through the draft document and noted that it didn't contain a single mention of the Vice President. He was right.[10] Sensing a Broder story in the making, I slipped away to speak with Elsie Hillman, GB's good friend [and distant relation] who is national committeewoman from Pennsylvania. She suggested I find a place in the draft where she could slip in the VP's name. I selected the section on crime, in which the drug-interdiction program, a major vice-presidential project, likewise bore no tribute to him.

I removed the crime plank from my copy of the platform, scratched in the proposed amendment ("Under the leadership of Vice President Bush . . . ."), and gave it to Elsie. She was headed toward the stage to give it to her ally, State Rep. Carmel Sirianni, when she fortunately thought to ask me for a description of the interdiction program and the VP's involvement in it. I dictated a couple of lines which Elsie wrote on the reverse of the sheet and then took to Sirianni. At the right moment, the Pennsylvania legislator obtained recognition and introduced the amendment. A startled Lott asked her to explain it, whereupon she flipped over the sheet and read my rationale word for word. This prompted laudatory words [on Bush's role in drug interdiction] from Congressmen Tom Loeffler of Texas and Bill McCollum of Florida. The Sirianni amendment was adopted by a voice vote, and the platform was no longer Bushless.

Dave Broder perked up and asked me, "Did you put her up to this?" I smiled and said, "No comment," but Elsie and I shook hands. It was a neat bit of fast action for GB, and frankly I'm glad Dave noticed. Much later in the day—in fact, only minutes before adjournment—there was a motion to say "Reagan-Bush Administration" everyplace "Reagan Administration"

---

10. This probably was no oversight. Kemp was aiming at the 1988 presidential nomination, in which he would face Vice President Bush, and Lott was his ally.

stood. The person who moved the amendment received a round of applause. He was Jack Kemp of New York.

Back in Washington, I reported to Lehman that "I managed to get the 600-ship navy mentioned in the platform three times, which is the same as one mention of an 1800-ship navy."

Chapter 6

Fleet Week

Monday, 27 August 1984

Huskies had removed all the chairs, pushed the conference table against the wall, and otherwise created more standing room for my formal swearing-in ceremony this afternoon. We got word that SecNav would not be coming. This was his first day back from a two-week trip, and his staff said he had a meeting out of the building.

Malcolm Wilkey arrived with Emma and a suit bag containing his robes.[1] In the ceremony, he talked about knowing me since I was a boy and then administered the oath. In repeating the words after him, I managed to avoid the standard tongue-twister, "without any mental reservation or purpose of evasion."

The deed done, I praised Judge Wilkey as a respected conservative jurist; I noted the presence of Cary Kauffman and said how much I wished her [deceased] parents were with us; and I announced that we had "a figure of naval history" present: MAGU,[2] who had been among the first women officers in the Navy. "My mother says this is the third time I've been in the Navy," I said. "The second was on active duty in 1968–70, and the first was in utero in 1945–46."

Sunday, 2 September 1984

Today brought the "shoot-down" ceremony in Norfolk, a Lehman-inspired event commemorating the 40th anniversary of Ensign George Bush's being shot down in the Pacific. I put on an anchor-print tie and drove to the Naval

---

1. Because of longstanding family ties—he had been my parents' lawyer in Houston in the early 1950s—Judge Wilkey consented to giving me this oath of office. Normally he resisted performing at such ceremonies, since (as in my case) the appointee typically takes the actual oath much earlier in order to get on the federal payroll. Malcolm called this "one for the money and two for the show."

2. My mother, Marguerite Alonza Graves Untermeyer, liked to be called by her initials.

Observatory, as on so many other Sundays in 1981–83. On the helo, the VP said Elsie Hillman reported seeing me in Dallas, and I related our gambit to get his name in the platform. Later, Bush asked whether I like John Lehman. I praised the boss's brains and energy but noted "he has some personality quirks that I haven't decided are of genius or of madness."

At NAS Norfolk, Admiral Dan Murphy and I were assigned to the same car. With grand good nature, Dan barked that I should sit on the right. This proved the only honor rendered me as an AsstSecNav, not that I insisted on any. Today was George Bush's and John Lehman's day, and my aim was to be a simple member of the VP's entourage, in which I've had a lot of experience. If my ego ever needs refurbishing, I can always visit another Marine base.

Tuesday, 4 September 1984

At 2:30, I had a welcome meeting with Wayne Arny, Ev Pyatt's new principal deputy and former SASC specialist on shipbuilding. Wayne is 42, comes from Philadelphia, graduated from the Academy (Class of '64), and is a former fighter pilot. He is bright and smoothly articulate, with a sleek blond handsomeness. We had a lively 75-minute, nonstop conversation about homeporting and the *Intrepid* reserve center, projects SecNav has given me but that really are in Wayne's area. We both agree it makes supreme political sense to homeport ships in Texas in order to create interest in the Navy among land-oriented Texans.

Rear Adm. Cec Kempf, chief of Naval Reserve, came by at 5:00 on the *Intrepid* reserve center. I don't like this project any more than does OpNav, but I am the unapologetic executor of SecNav's wishes. I said we *will* do it, recognizing that it will be a month-long struggle to beat OpNav into submission. I emphasized, however, that our purpose is just to create a reserve center on board *Intrepid,* not to bail out the debt-ridden museum. When he discovers we're only talking about a modest rent, Zack Fisher (the increasingly less-wealthy underwriter of the museum) might well mobilize Sen. D'Amato and Congressman Addabbo to inspire SecNav to cave in. I already have enough experience with John Lehman to know this has a good chance of happening.

Thursday, 6 September 1984

Today Doc White took me across the footbridge over Highway 50 to the Pentagon Officers Athletic Center, better known as the POAC [pronounced "po-ack"]. It is an extremely popular gym whose facilities are good but worn, with an atmosphere on the sunny side of a dank sweat sock. My principal interest in joining is to use the heated indoor pool. Membership costs only $108 per year.

In my subsequent years in the Pentagon, the POAC would prove an important psychological as well as physical resource, a welcome way each evening to pound out the stresses and struggles of the day.

The guest speaker at my staff luncheon was Como. Dudley Carlson, Navy's chief of legislative affairs. He spoke with enthusiasm and a high degree of comedy. "Can you imagine what it's like for the Army to show congressmen and staff what they're doing?" he asked. "'Here is a trench. It's a new one. Here is a truck. What do you think of our truck?' But the Navy—we've got *aircraft carriers! Planes that land on ships! Nuclear submarines!*"

Tuesday, 11 September 1984

I saw UnSec Goodrich at 10:00 for our weekly meeting. I briefed him on *Intrepid* and then sought his "fatherly advice" on the seeming impossibility for me to meet with Lehman and get guidance on the issues I face. The Under chuckled and said, "First of all: you're not alone!" Everyone—including, he inferred, himself—has trouble seeing SecNav, unless they stay behind at line-ups or use some other means to capture him. My Anglo-Germanic way of doing business considers this foolish, yet my grumpiness won't cause Lehman to change his ways (or his staff).

I have another idea, which I exposed to the Under: to take action on my own on the things on which I now seek secretarial guidance, recognizing that sometimes I'll do something he doesn't like. The Under agreed but counseled that when this happens I ought to be able to tell Lehman I *tried* to see him.[3] Back in the office, I told Rear Adm. Kempf to proceed with the plan on *Intrepid* he outlined yesterday.

I ran into Paul Miller [SecNav's EA] later today, and he went into his county-commissioner routine of draping his arm around me—a gesture of enormous condescension, not of friendship. He promised to reset a can-

---

3. This bureaucratic wisdom is best expressed as, "It is easier to seek forgiveness than permission." A standard naval practice is to send one's superior a so-called UNODIR message, saying "unless otherwise directed" by the superior, the officer will take a certain specified action.

celled meeting with the Secretary, which he did. But of course it, too, was later cancelled.

At 4:00, I welcomed Charlie Dougherty (pronounced the Philly way, "Dockerty"), the square-shaped, square-headed former Republican congressman from Philadelphia whom John Lehman wants sometime and somehow to succeed Fred Davidson as DASN (Reserve Affairs). I advised Charlie [first met while working for VP Bush] not to tell this to anyone. If word leaks out, Fred could mobilize the reserve associations to keep him.

Thursday, 13 September 1984

Warren Lee Smith[4] sent a clipping from last Sunday's *Houston Chronicle* headlined "High Ally for Navy Base." The story said: "The Houston-Galveston area may have an ally in the right place when the Navy finally decides where it will place a major new installation for warships. The boon to the Houston-Galveston chances could prove to be Chase Untermeyer, a former Texas state representative and aide to Vice President George Bush, who was recently sworn in as assistant secretary of the Navy."

Of such notions are reputations made, and, in the best tradition of Lyndon Johnson, I would love to be known as the man who brought the Navy to Texas and specifically to Galveston Bay. But to protect SecNav from complaints against me by representatives of other coastal states, I may recuse myself from the selection process. I don't plan to be silent, however. If in the end Texas/Galveston wins and someone wants to hail me as the guy who did it, I can smile and shrug.

Monday, 17 September 1984

Today brought an event to which I'd been looking forward for some time: a brief visit to my office by Charles Francis Adams IV of Boston, retired board chairman of Raytheon. Escorted by UnSec Jim Goodrich (on whose Bath Iron Works board he once served), Adams had come at my invitation to view the portrait of his father hanging in my office. While we talked, a photographer snapped away—a bit forward with an Adams, perhaps, but Mr. A was animated and charming. I also showed him the officer's sword that he pre-

---

4. A devoted friend since I first campaigned for the Texas Legislature, Warren Lee regularly sent me clippings from the Houston papers, which I read, culled, and passed on to Vice President Bush.

sented to me in May 1968; he thinks it was the last one he gave before the
Harvard NROTC unit was disbanded.

The mail brought a delightful letter from Gov. Mark White (D-Texas):
"It has come to my attention that you have reenlisted in the federal bureaucracy as assistant secretary of the Navy. I find it difficult to believe that the
bright lights of Washington hold more of a fascination than the warmth of
your home state, but then I must confess the Republican mind has always
mystified me. I can only offer my congratulations and best wishes for success
in Washington and a speedy return to Texas following the November elections."

Thursday, 20 September 1984

*Seven weeks before the presidential election, the former maritime reporter for the
Houston Chronicle was guest speaker at a luncheon of the Propeller Club of
Houston.*

I closed with a story about "the $49 cruise" that Uncle George [Sands] told
me: two prospective passengers paid their money, after which they were hit
on the head by the agent and tossed in a little rubber boat. When they came
to out in the ocean, the first man asked, "Do they serve breakfast on this
cruise?" The second man replied, "They didn't last year."

When the chuckles died down, I said: "In 1976, America took the $49
cruise, trying to buy its defense on the cheap, believing that love and human
kindness would soften the hearts of the Soviets and Cubans. For the past four
years, with a different steamship line and a different skipper, we have made
immeasurable progress. We took the $49 cruise before, and shame on us. But
eternal shame on us if we sign up once again for that cruise to nowhere."

Wednesday, 26 September 1984

At this morning's lineup, the first in a while, SecNav said he must answer a
letter from Sen. [William] Proxmire (D-Wisconsin) challenging the propri-
ety of George Sawyer's going to work for General Dynamics after leaving
the Navy Department. Hugh O'Neill cautioned Lehman that what he writes
could come back to haunt him if he himself is ever hired by a defense contractor. "Not me!" said SecNav. "I'm going to work for the Little Sisters of
the Poor."

I stayed behind to tell SecNav I want to request an opinion from the

Judge Advocate General as to whether it would violate the law against women in combat to have them serve on MLSF (Mobile Logistics Support Force) ships. Lehman fears anything sensitive on paper, and this one is certainly sensitive. DACOWITS[5] will ask us about it in November. I let Lehman know that I favor the proposal, pointing out that women already serve on Military Sealift Command (MSC) ships. "This is exactly the sort of issue that I, you, and the Administration shouldn't be caught in the middle of," he said. For one thing, he has maintained all along that logistics ships are combatants — to prevent contracting-out and labor problems, as in MSC. "If we let the ladies on the MLSF, the unions will be right behind," Lehman said.

There was more: Lehman further opposes putting women on ships on long deployments so as not to exacerbate family separation problems. "Every Navy wife in Norfolk will wonder what's going on at sea," he said, now playing Father Lehman rather than Lehman the Libertarian. Obviously, we can't say anything like that to DACOWITS, but can we explain the MLSF-MSC distinction? SecNav replied that my task is to "smother the issue" with studies and assertions of our commitment to finding ever-greater roles for women in the Navy.

As soon as I could, I departed for Annapolis with Dick Elster.[6] Our mission was to find out from Rear Adm. Chuck Larson, the superintendent, what he's doing to comply with SecNav's July edicts reforming the curriculum and admissions procedures at the Naval Academy. I invited along Chuck Hirsch, an apple-cheeked White House fellow assigned to SecNav.

The aggressive, intense Larson took us immediately to a conference room where, with view graphs, he proceeded to answer nearly all my questions. The real friction began when I, not Larson, noted that they are advertising for a new dean of admissions in addition to an academic dean. I had found out about this from a retired admiral, and Lehman this morning said he will choose *both* deans. Larson looked incredulous, as if I were telling him that John Lehman wants to choose his orderly. An admissions dean is a "low-level" appointment, just like one of the faculty, Larson tried to argue.

[Later, after a couple of other stops at the Academy, I returned to the superintendent's office.] Larson had something to say; he was as emotional as

---

5. The Defense Advisory Committee on Women in the Services. Its ability to get senior Pentagon leaders to pay attention to women's issues has made DACOWITS one of the most influential of all federal advisory committees.

6. Both previously and subsequently an instructor and administrator at the Naval Postgraduate School in Monterey, California, Dick served ably and tirelessly as deputy assistant secretary for Manpower, succeeding E. C. Grayson.

his Great Plains good-naturedness permitted. "I do my best thinking while running, and I ran at lunch," he told us. "And I am upset at the feeling I get that Some People think I am trying to sneak around and do things behind their back." But if he meant the admissions dean gambit, he's guilty as charged. Chuck Hirsch exclaimed as we left Annapolis that the encounter with Larson was a fascinating example of the war between the civilian and "blue suit" navies of which Lehman has told him.

Friday, 28 September 1984

Today was rainy and chilly, so the retirement ceremony for Lt. Gen. Harold (Hal) Hatch was held inside the Band Hall at the Marine Barracks. The room is done in high Georgian style, with a great proscenium arch, an emblazoned globe and anchor, and a recessed ceiling in blue and white. A company of Marines was paraded at the front, and behind them the band played marches, every note of which was perfectly heard.

As I sat there, surrounded by Sousa, I thought that these may well be glory days for the United States and for me. As Franklin Roosevelt dominated another generation, so might Ronald Reagan crown this age, a time of national renewal. In years to come, people will look back on these days and speak with admiration and longing for what was going on in Washington. In such a time, it will be with pride that I will say I served at Navy during the Reagan Administration, and a younger generation may hear me with envy.

To have a crack at the Secretary, I later attended a reporting-out by a couple of selection boards. He was enthusiastic about stories in the Houston papers reporting my speech last week to the Propeller Club. "It helps a lot," he said. I took the opportunity to say I shall send him a letter of recusal on Gulf Coast homeporting. "What for?" he asked, adding without hesitation that I should do no such thing; that he doesn't worry if ports that lose the competition allege a conflict of interest. "I want your best analysis and opinion," SecNav said. I was pleased by this vote of confidence. It was also a license to lobby for Galveston.

Sunday, 30 September 1984

In my office I concentrated on the backlog of Article 138 complaints against superior officers. I have told Cdr. Biff LeGrand that I want to see all Article 138s, calling them "a peephole into the fleet." Although such complaints are usually dismissed, the process allows for serious wrongs to be brought to my attention, and I don't want my staff rubberstamping a System reply.

Under Article 138 of the Uniform Code of Military Justice, anyone in the Armed Forces "who believes himself wronged by his commanding officer [and] refused redress" has the right to complain to anyone superior to that officer. Eventually, the complaint must be forwarded to the service secretary or the secretary's designee for final disposition, which may include granting full relief. Lehman had delegated this authority to me, and I took it very seriously.

My attitude was endorsed by no less a personage than Herman Melville. Needing a free trip home after his well-known bouts of whale hunting and beachcombing in the South Pacific, Melville signed on as an ordinary seaman aboard a naval frigate and spent a year sailing from Hawaii to Massachusetts. This grim experience inspired White Jacket (1849), a semi-fictionalized portrait of the US Navy of the day. In the book, Melville wrote: "While we deferentially and cheerfully leave to Navy officers the sole conduct of making or shortening sail, tacking ship, and performing other nautical maneuvers as may seem to them best, let us be aware of abandoning to their discretion those general municipal regulations touching the well-being of the great body of men before the mast; let us beware of being too much influenced by their opinions in matters where it is but natural to suppose that their long-established prejudices are enlisted."

Tuesday, 2 October 1984

Today SecNav hosted a luncheon in his private dining room for all four of us assistant secretaries (Paisley, Pyatt, Conn, and Untermeyer) plus general counsel Walt Skallerup. Lehman began by saying, "Last week, Cap [Weinberger] had a similar luncheon with us service secretaries. There was a general laying-on of hands, at which he said he planned to stay on during a second term, and he hoped all of us would do the same. I am making the same statement to you all. I am very pleased with everything you've done. You can't argue with success. So I hope all of you will agree to stay."

I don't think it was required, but there was an answer from each of us. Bob Conn[7] agreed to remain "but with *you,* not anybody else." Mel Paisley noted he has lost about $1 million since 1980 by leaving Boeing to work in Navy. As for me, I said jokingly but quite factually, "Of course I'll stay. This is more

---

7. Assistant secretary of the Navy for Financial Management, 1981–88.

money than I've ever made in my life." Lehman said he will remain SecNav for at least two more years "and, who knows, maybe the whole four years."

Lehman also said we should be thinking about changes we want to make to our own staffs. He looked directly at me as he talked, and we both knew he was thinking about Fred Davidson. I lament that Fred is so devious, cunning, and hostile to flag officers. He is exceedingly smart and could do a fine job if only he didn't poison his own effectiveness.

Thursday, 4 October 1984

A while ago, I had retired Admiral Zumwalt as my guest for breakfast. Today I had his successor as CNO, Adm. James Holloway Jr., in for lunch. Holloway is a short, square fellow with an exuberant personality and the genial, crafty manner of a rural state senator. Holloway was CNO in 1974–78 and still keeps his hand in the family business (his father also having been an admiral) as president of the Association of Naval Aviation and chairman of the USNA Academic Advisory Board.

Holloway supports SecNav's reforms at Annapolis even though as CNO he instituted the 80/20 math-science/humanities split in majors that Lehman has now undone. But he cautioned, "We gotta have some dumb kids so we can have Marine officers and people stupid enough to fly F14s off the decks of carriers at night."

Tuesday, 9 October 1984

The prime topic at breakfast with my Army and Air Force counterparts was last Sunday's presidential debate. There is general gloom among Republicans, not only because RR did poorly against Walter Mondale but because his performance raises the hitherto silent question of whether at 73 he is mentally up to the job. Mondale is not going to be elected, but the next four weeks will be a lot scarier now.

The day before yesterday, Barbara Bush was talking to a couple of reporters, and in her feisty way she denounced Geraldine Ferraro's attacks on the Bushes for being well-off by noting she [Ferraro] is "a $4 million—I can't say it, but it rhymes with 'rich.'" Distraught at the hooting reaction, BPB called Ferraro to apologize and told the press, "I did not mean to call Ms. Ferraro a witch."

This evening I took a Navy car to the Agriculture Department, whose marble indoor patio was the scene for VP Bush's dinner for the new prime minister of Israel, Shimon Peres. In the receiving line, GB smiled warmly and introduced me to Peres by my title. BPB and I embraced and kissed, and before I could say anything she said, "If you need someone to handle public relations, I'm it!" I said, "I'm only sorry you felt you had to apologize." Obviously the "rich-witch-bitch" incident has deeply hurt her.

Thursday, 11 October 1984

The stakes and the risk for GB in tonight's vice presidential debate were enormous. Not only was he carrying Republican hopes for a rebound from RR's disappointing performance last Sunday, but he himself would be under scrutiny for 1988.

Ferraro was ready to pounce when, during the second half of the debate devoted to foreign affairs, GB corrected something she said. "I almost resent the patronizing attitude that you have to teach me about foreign affairs," she lashed back. GB had some good moments, but his problems, alas, were his boyish enthusiasms and his casual, semi-frivolous word choices, speaking of "you know, the civil disobedience thing" or a statistic that is "way, *way* up." Happily, the TV gurus called the debate a draw.

Friday, 12 October 1984

Today I toured the Navy boot camp in San Diego, which processes some 34,000 sailors a year. My only comparison was with what the Marines do. The training at Parris Island is of course more physical, but it's also geared in the clever, single-minded USMC way toward "making a Marine." In San Diego, both the pressure and the motivation are less, with no one coming to earn the title "sailor." In Doc White's view, Marines are trained to act and fight automatically, without thinking. Sailors, he holds, are maintenance personnel who look after a ship's equipment. Another difference between the two training facilities is leadership. The Marine drill instructor is a god to his troops and is with them 100% of the time. The Navy "company commander" is a less celestial figure who is encouraged to go home and be with his family as much as possible.

Perhaps as a result of these differences, I didn't sense today something I had noticed at Parris Island and in the prisons I visited as a state legislator in Texas: the prehistoric scent of fear.

Saturday, 13 October 1984

From San Diego I went to San Francisco to represent the Navy Secretariat at Fleet Week. This was an old municipal celebration revived by Mayor Dianne Feinstein, who wanted her city by the bay to take pride in its naval heritage, to the consternation of local peace activists. In 1992, she would be elected US senator as a Democrat from California.

The clouds were vanishing fast as Doc and I crossed the Bay Bridge into San Francisco, always beautiful despite covering up its famous hills with high-rise office buildings. In the officers club at the Presidio, an old Army post by the Golden Gate, Navy moguls gathered for the opening event of Fleet Week. Prime among these was Adm. Sylvester R. (Bob) Foley, mighty CINCPACFLT [commander in chief of the Pacific Fleet, pronounced "sink pack fleet"]. Foley is a funny-tough aviator with a florid face, pointed ears, and steel-framed glasses. With an alteration in costume, he could easily pass as Archbishop Foley.

We got in our cars and proceeded down the steep, winding, forested slope of the Presidio to the Municipal Pier, where were sideboys, arrival honors, and a reviewing platform for military and civilian dignitaries. With rising excitement in the crowd, a black sedan passed by the stands, and Mayor Dianne Feinstein jumped out to wave a gloved hand at us. To a Navy band's jaunty rendition of "San Francisco (Open Your Golden Gate)," she strode with the swivel-hipped hurry of a chorus girl through the saluting sailors to start shaking hands with platform guests. Mayor Feinstein is a stunningly successful politician who has breached the wide gaps in San Francisco's exotic populations and won the overt affection of the city. She is constantly having fun, yet she can be selectively tough (as with municipal workers). Her third husband is Dick Blum, a tall, mop-haired investment banker of about 40 who climbs Mt. Everest as a hobby.

Promptly at 11, a spectacular parade of ships began entering the harbor, led by the nuclear sub *San Francisco*. There followed the cruiser *Long Beach,* the carrier *Constellation,* and a line of destroyers, ending with a high-endurance Coast Guard cutter and a fleet oiler. The Bay sparkled splendidly, and the Golden Gate Bridge, all orange, looked closer than it actually is. The climax to the "Fleet Pass in Review" was a performance by the Navy's Blue Angels, five old A4F Skyhawks that do their aerial acrobatics all over the country. "The Blues" flew back and forth, in front and over us, in a variety of breath-taking maneuvers.

At lunch aboard *Constellation,* I discussed the problems of Navy families with the wives of senior officers. This made me resolve to propose to SecNav the creation of a DASN position to handle such matters, as well as drug and alcohol abuse.

At 6:15, Doc and I left for the St. Francis [hotel] and the Mayor's formal dinner in honor of Fleet Week. I sat between Mayor Feinstein and her protocol aide Charlotte Mailliard, a native of the Panhandle who married into a venerable San Francisco family.[8] When I looked at the program I was surprised to see that I was to give a toast. All day I was more than pleased to let Admiral Foley speak for the Navy, not only because he is senior to me[9] but because a four-star admiral means the Navy in a way no fellow from Washington in a business suit ever can. The Mayor spoke enthusiastically about Fleet Week. ("How about those Blue Angels?") Admiral Foley replied in like spirit, praising the new Navy and the new sailor.

That was all anyone needed to say, but I was still called forward. I gave a more sober tribute to San Francisco, borrowing Conrad's words about England at the beginning of "Youth" to say it is a place "where men and sea interpenetrate." I recalled seeing some sailboats today with PEACE banners and said, "There are no greater peace activists than the men and women in uniform who have known war's consequences." Then I toasted "peace—and the future of the United States Navy."

It was all well received, Dick Blum asking his wife rhetorically, "Why is it that these Republicans are so good on the stump?" I did try to be Reaganesque, speaking slowly and with feeling.

Monday, 15 October 1984

Doc and I were driven to the San Francisco City Hall, a grand turn-of-the-century capitol, for the concluding event of Fleet Week. There were some protesters outside, apparently angry about the Navy in Puerto Rico. In the elegant paneled outer office of the mayor, there was a cocktail reception for all Navy guests, especially including the COs of the visiting ships. I spoke to as many of these as I could; some were about my age.

We moved to the Mayor's private office (in which George Moscone

---

8. In 1997, she would marry George Shultz, Reagan's second secretary of State.

9. An assistant secretary of the Navy has four-star rank but for protocol purposes is ranked "with and below" a serving Navy full admiral or Marine full general. The under secretary has equivalent rank with the four-stars, and the secretary outranks everyone.

was shot in 1978, leading to Dianne Feinstein's ascendance) for a briefing by Charlotte Mailliard, producer of tonight's extravaganza. We lined up by seniority and were led to the top of a grand staircase. Behind us was a giant American flag in balloons. A Marine honor guard lined the steps, on which was a sky-blue carpet that matched Her Honor's gown. And at the bottom of the steps was a huge sheet cake showing a submarine coming through the Golden Gate.

I was announced and descended the staircase, carefully watching my steps to avoid a Gerald Ford–like tumble. As I neared the landing where CNO and CINCPACFLT stood, I noticed a young man in black tie on the last step, his back to me, holding out his arms as if to lead a chorus. But I couldn't pay any attention to him, since I needed to take my exact place. Just as I did, the crowd erupted in a loud gasp. I looked, and the Navy birthday cake lay in ruins. The fellow had done a swan dive onto the cake and with his arms and legs was destroying as much of it as he could. Police rushed forward to peel the gooey guy off and haul him away. Then waiters covered the ruins of the cake with a tablecloth. We dignitaries pretended not to notice any of this. Later, the four-stars, Mayor Feinstein, and I took hold of a Navy sword and cut the unvandalized portion of the cake, smiling for cameras as if nothing at all had happened.

In early 1993, soon after she became a senator, I saw Dianne Feinstein for the first time since Fleet Week 1984 and recalled the cake incident. She had absolutely no memory of it. Apparently, it was just one of countless acts of "guerrilla theater" in her colorful hometown that she had had to endure.

The Mayor's dinner was held across the street in the lobby of the elegant old Opera House, site of the 1945 United Nations conference, lit by candles, banked by plants, and serenaded by violins. We dined rather well on duck with hoisin sauce.

Dianne beckoned me over to ask what I thought about Hunters Point as a possible base for the battleship *Missouri*. We spoke as one politician to another. Later, talking across Jim Watkins, she asked if I were married, and when I said no, her eyes lit up. "I know all kinds of single *Republican* women!" she said and started buzzing with Charlotte. Across the table, Dick Blum said I had made a fatal mistake. Mayor as yenta.[10]

---

10. As pointed out in a National Public Radio broadcast (Chana Joffe-Walt, "What's a Yenta," 13 June 2012), the proper name for a Jewish matchmaker is shadchanit. A yenta is a gossipy

The real fun began after the toasts. Dianne passed the hand-held microphone to CNO and called for a mass a capella singing of "Anchors Aweigh." This was followed by "God Bless America" led by me at the Mayor's request, perhaps because it is the Reaganite anthem. I acquitted myself well enough to be asked to lead in "The Battle Hymn of the Republic." What can possibly top Mrs. Howe's grand march? Why, "I Left My Heart in San Francisco," of course, sung by a major donor to the dinner.

Back on [the naval station on Treasure Island], I walked down to the Bay for a final look at the skyline on a starry, still night and chuckle over the evening's events.

---

old hag. In any event, I managed to find a wife without benefit of the San Francisco city government.

Chapter 7

SecNav Car #2

Tuesday, 16 October 1984

Tonight, SecNav gave a dinner in honor of Chapman and Jeannette Cox aboard CNO's borrowed barge.[1] We got underway from the Navy Yard and cruised past the lights of Washington as SecNav Mess stewards served dinner on the fantail. I had a long talk after dinner with my former boss, George Sawyer. A member of the USNA Academic Advisory Board, he thinks Lehman's curriculum and admissions reforms may be too radical. "The Academy is a trade school and always will be," George said.

We passed close by *Sequoia,* which once served as (and was called) the presidential yacht even though it was officially assigned to the secretary of the Navy. Jimmy Carter sold it in 1977 in an empty gesture of thrift. Now in private hands, *Sequoia* looks beautiful, and Lehman is intent on getting her back. I suggested a boarding party tonight, and Lehman semi-seriously asked his general counsel if he can still issue letters of marque and reprisal.

Thursday, 18 October 1984

At noon I hosted Jennifer Fitzgerald and Thad Garrett[2] for lunch. As expected, they were impressed with my grand Pentagon estate. Thadd gaped at the office and asked, "Is this something you use every day?" We three are all disappointed with GB's performance in his debate with Ferraro. He was ultra-Bush, enthusiastic beyond normal limits, and not "vice-presidential."

---

1. In naval usage, a barge is a cabin cruiser assigned to an admiral in command.

2. Jennifer was scheduling assistant to Vice President Bush. Thadd was a Washington lobbyist and African Methodist Episcopal minister who had been Bush's domestic policy advisor.

Saturday, 20 October 1984

After changing a tire on my car, I returned to the apartment to wash up. That's when the phone rang, and a familiar voice, that of the vice president of the United States, said, "Chahlie! I was wondering if you could drop by at 6:30. Bar[3] is off, and I thought of having you and Thadd and Jennifer— people who haven't been on the road [i.e., campaign trail]—to talk a little politics. Wear old, *old* clothes." I knew that Jennifer had urged him to do this following our Thursday lunch. It was an opportunity not to be missed, barely two weeks before the election, to speak the minds we unburdened on each other that day.

At dusk, I left for the Naval Observatory. A Filipino steward took me upstairs where GB was watching the evening news with Thadd and John Walker[4]; Jennifer came later. When John left, we three felt freer to tell the VP (slouched down on a couch, feet on the coffee table) what we felt. Thadd, in his preacher's role, said GB should not have remarked after his debate with Ferraro (within the hearing of a TV mike) "we tried to kick a little ass." It was 100% Bush, which is why he's defensive on the point. He likes the "macho man" reaction to the line and thinks it may have helped him with redneck conservatives. My point, picking up from Thadd, was that he should do nothing to "trivialize" his reputation as a statesman.

GB listened quietly but obviously was not pleased with anything we said. His focus is on the election of 1984 when, true enough, such incidents won't much matter. Our focus is on the election of 1988 and how he comes across to voters. I drew things to a close by suggesting, "We'd better be going, or someone is going to kick our asses out of here." GB followed us downstairs and out of the house to stand on the porch as we departed—not so much to say goodbye, I suspect, as to see if we did any postgame analysis. He asked Jennifer to walk Fred the cocker spaniel, and Thadd asked if I could give him a lift home.

In the car, Thadd and I complimented each other on what we had said to the VP but doubted it would do much good. I once heard Walter Mondale say that political friends would stop by his office in the West Wing to bemoan how badly President Carter was doing and how people perceived him. But when Mondale all of a sudden would walk them down to the Oval Office to tell Carter himself, the visitors would babble, "You're doing great,

---

3. Barbara Bush.

4. Then an assistant secretary of the Treasury and later a federal judge, the extraordinarily able John Walker was Vice President Bush's first cousin.

Mr. President! The whole country is behind you!" This evening we determined to avoid that foolish practice, and my candor either cinched or lost me my chance to be chief of staff in a Bush White House.

Sunday, 21 October 1984

I called Jennifer to ask how she thought yesterday's heart-to-heart with GB went. "What we said needed to be said," she replied. "He's not being served right. You made the point: you're not serving him if you let him think that everything he's doing is wonderful. On reflection he agreed with what we said. He'll respect us a lot more for saying that—though he wasn't very happy last night. He made me walk the dog!"

Tonight I had a fish-and-chips supper with Marjorie Arsht[5] and her boss and friend, Maurice Barksdale, assistant secretary of HUD, while watching the second and final presidential debate. RR demolished the question of whether he is too old to be an effective president. "I am not going to exploit the age issue," the President said with his trademark twinkle. "I am not going to talk about my opponent's youth and inexperience." Maurice, Marjorie, and I breathed easier; our jobs are safe.

Wednesday, 24 October 1984

In a Pentagon passageway I encountered Don Hittle, who related what he had told SecNav about returning NROTC to Dartmouth: he's ag'in it. Don was in my job [in 1969–71] when all the Ivies threw us out, and he remains bitter. One of Don's arguments to Lehman was that by compromising with Dartmouth to get NROTC back on campus, he may be whipsawn by conservatives.[6]

Sunday, 28 October 1984

Right at the time the Dartmouth issue was coming to a head, I traveled to the campus of Notre Dame in Indiana for the annual conference of the Association of

---

5. Marjorie was present at the creation of the modern Texas Republican Party. As a teenager I had worked in her valiant but losing 1962 race for the Legislature. In after years she became "another mother."

6. Always striving to broaden support for the sea services, especially among the nation's political and business elite, Lehman wanted more Ivy League graduates to have a personal connection to the Navy and Marine Corps.

NROTC Colleges and Universities. It was composed of deans and senior faculty from the 64 institutions with NROTC units.

I was introduced to Father Theodore Hesburgh, president of Notre Dame and a living legend, who (alas) knows and acts like it.[7] He talked on the slightest inquiry about anything, which tonight was on extraterrestrial life and on immigration reform. Asked to address the group, Hesburgh spoke at length on the 40-year relationship between the Navy and Notre Dame, noting that they kept NROTC when Ivy League schools threw us out. As a result, Hesburgh believes, we shouldn't be too eager to let them back in. I ventured to ask, "You mean you don't believe in redemption, Father?"

My talk to the Association was built around a favorite quotation from John Adams, who in a letter to Abigail [from Paris in 1780] wrote: "I must study politics and war that my sons may have liberty to study mathematics and philosophy." These words spoke eloquently and persuasively to me in the winter of 1966, when I decided to join the Harvard NROTC, and I hope I imparted a similar feeling today.

Wednesday, 31 October 1984

Today I represented the Secretariat at a White House ceremony launching a new postage stamp that honors Hispanic Americans. It was the essence of campaigning from the Rose Garden: RR could woo voters in Texas, California, and Arizona just by stepping out of the Oval Office for a few minutes. He spoke briefly in his warm, soft voice with the touch of huskiness that denotes sincerity. Reagan is truly a master, and I am grateful to see him in action (at a distance today of about three paces), just as an earlier generation was to see Franklin Roosevelt. When he finished, RR unveiled a poster of the stamp and descended the platform to shake hands with us military types. "This is all overwhelming for a former second lieutenant," he said.

In mid-afternoon I reached Dave McLaughlin at Dartmouth to discuss their decision to drop active consideration of NROTC. I tried to be both polite and pointed when I asked him to describe the pressures he faces from "antimilitary elements" on the faculty. This caused the normally placid presi-

---

7. Hesburgh constantly traveled the country and the globe as a member of presidential commissions and corporate boards. This gave rise to a campus joke: What is the difference between Father Hesburgh and God? Answer: God is everywhere, and Father Hesburgh is everywhere but Notre Dame.

dent to explode. "It's not 'antimilitary elements.' It's people who believe in the liberal arts." It's now amply clear that we should just shrug off this whole episode. When I reported to Lehman on the death of his project to return NROTC to the Ivy League, he just smiled and said, "Don Hittle will be *ecstatic*."

Tuesday, 6 November 1984

Today, Election Day 1984, held an expectant, holiday mood. I had been invited to the massive GOP gala at the Shoreham and to a private election night party. But after 20 years of watching (or not watching) election returns with others, I resolved to be a recluse and enjoy the drama to the fullest.

Such as the drama was. To no one's surprise, the President swept the country, carrying state after state. As of this hour (midnight) it's not sure whether Mondale even won his home state of Minnesota.[8] So great was the electoral-vote triumph that TV commentators felt obliged to encourage viewers in states where the polls were still open to go out and vote, if only to decide local referenda. Dan Rather of CBS declared, "The old Democratic, New Deal coalition is going, going, gone!"

I watched a near-teary Walter Mondale concede and a still-brittle Geraldine Ferraro claim victory for a liberalism that the American people had just decisively rejected. Then RR addressed a wildly cheering crowd at the Century Plaza in LA. He spoke of "a prairie fire" that he and they began in California in 1966 and which then swept the country. "America's best days lie ahead," he said with his warmest smile and tuck of the chin. "And you ain't seen nothing yet!" A few minutes later, GB and some (but by no means all) of the family appeared in Houston. He spoke well, and the crowd chanted, "'Eighty-eight! 'Eighty-eight!"

It was symbolic that I watched tonight's results in my splendid office in the Pentagon. Now I get to keep it. But my primary emotion tonight was not selfishness. Of course I rejoice at what the past four years have brought me, but I rejoice more for our country and the things RR has done for it. In 1980, it looked as if America was in the process of disintegration, the result of 16 years of decline. But the nation has indeed been brought back, economically and militarily but most of all spiritually. I can't help but speculate on the gloom that must pervade the Kremlin tonight.

---

8. He did, barely.

Saturday, 10 November 1984   –

Right after the election, I flew to Texas for, among other events, the Marine birthday ball in Houston. It was held in the storied Shamrock Hilton two years before the hotel's tragic demolition. The ball would provide the second misadventure involving a cake in a month.

At 9:00 p.m., Maj. Gen. Hugh Hardy and I got into position for the march-on of the cake. Whoever handled arrangements tonight must have been a commie agent. When we stepped off from the mark on the floor to take our places for the ceremony, the PA began playing the National Anthem, and the colors weren't even in the room. The "Marines' Hymn" was played before the cake was even in sight. Ordinary souls might not have thought anything amiss, but the Marines *knew.*

In my little talk, I spoke of last Tuesday's election as a reaffirmation of peace through strength, as epitomized by the Marine Corps. It was twice interrupted by applause and calls of "oorah!" The evening's glitches were not over. As Hugh executed a crisp military slicing of the cake with a saber, the waiter with the plates and forks stood frozen at the wall of the ballroom. Undeterred by adversity, in the great Marine tradition, Hugh used his white gloves to place cake slices in the hands of the youngest Marine present, his own (as the oldest), and mine. He then yanked off the gooey gloves with his teeth, and we three proceeded to eat with our fingers, as if that is what Corps doctrine prescribes for birthday balls. My high station merited me the sole napkin, just used for wiping the sword. Our nibbling completed, we marched out to "Semper Fidelis."

Twenty years later, as ambassador to Qatar, I mirthfully related this story to the gunnery sergeant commanding the embassy's Marine Security Guard detachment just before the cake ceremony at their annual birthday ball. The "gunny" blanched. "The plates!" he said, rushing off to forestall an identical incident.

Thursday, 15 November 1984

Don Hittle and I talked about bringing civilian personnel ("civpers") policy back under the Secretariat, where it was when Don was assistant secretary. Since then, civpers has been under OpNav. "It's an entirely different thing than military personnel," he said, "and yet it's fascinating. There are 350,000 civilian employees in the Navy Department, one of the biggest single work-forces in the country."

Friday, 16 November 1984

At the SecNav lineup, Hugh O'Neill told of plans to begin the final goat shoot on San Clemente Island, an issue close to my affections. John Lehman, who fearlessness takes on entire congressional committees, is extremely wary when it comes to goaticide. "Cap [Weinberger] goes ballistic on this," he told Hugh.[9] "I don't want to do anything till someone gives me a piece of paper saying, 'Shoot the fucking goats.'"

Later I returned to Lehman's office for the reporting-out of the selection board for commodore. I leaned over the board president's shoulder to look at the list, finding Sam Yow's name there. It was no surprise given how great a guy he is and how successful a career he's had, but it was grand news nonetheless. Other E-Ring executive assistants were also on the list.

I couldn't tell Sam right away because at noon I hosted a luncheon in the private dining room for the key staffers from the Manpower Subcommittee of the HASC. When the staffers returned to the Capitol, I was finally able to tell Sam, "I saw the list for commodore, and you're on it." I congratulated him and said how proud I am of him and how proud the entire staff will be when the news is announced. I hope I'm around long enough and do a good enough job of picking staff such that officers like Lt. Col. George Walls and Cdr. Jay Foley will also make flag rank.[10]

Wednesday, 21 November 1984

Today at the office I wrote a two-page letter of unsolicited advice to GB on what he should do to prepare for 1988. Among other things, it urged him to "cease and desist immediately" from hinting he may not run for president that year. I'll be very interested in how the VP responds.

Nancy Ellis [the Vice President's sister] wrote, proposing lunch Tuesday in Boston: "The Ritz? My party—or maybe the Chilton Club, where the food is *delish*. We *must* talk—I can't bear all GB's press."

---

9. Weinberger's Harvard classmate, the author and animal advocate Cleveland Amory, pronounced the anathema, "If the Navy gets to heaven, I hope they find that God is a goat."

10. George indeed became a brigadier general and Jay a rear admiral.

Monday, 26 November 1984

Before leaving for Boston, I had an 8:00 A.M. meeting with Congresswoman Sala Burton (D-San Francisco), widow of the super-liberal Phil Burton,[11] to discuss the homeporting of *Missouri*. The meeting was also attended by Como. Dudley Carlson, the Navy's chief lobbyist on the Hill. Though he is quite smart and effective in his job, Dudley has little respect for politicians, and I don't think he likes what he's doing one bit.[12]

The motherly Mrs. Burton's concern over *Missouri* is that it probably will carry nuclear weapons, something we "neither confirm nor deny." There are nuclear weapons aplenty aboard ships already in San Francisco Bay, but she doesn't want any more. "I am antinuclear to the point of *hysteria*," she said. "We love the Navy, and we want ships, but we don't want those nuclear weapons. I mean, enough's enough!"

Dudley and I wound up playing bad cop/good cop, with him speaking loudly and insistently against points the congresswoman raised and me speaking with sweet reasonableness as one pol to another. Dudley didn't even try to be soothing, saying that San Francisco would be a nuclear target regardless of where we homeport *Missouri*. I sought to take the edge off Mrs. Burton's anxiety by noting that OpNav favors Pearl Harbor for the ship. Fearful that this divulged an in-house secret, Dudley leapt in to say, "Secretary Untermeyer is confiding with you, Mrs. Burton. That's not to leave this room." Mrs. Burton has other worries, among them the "threat" to our sailors by the 150,000 of her constituents who are gay. That one *she* said wasn't to leave the room.

Tuesday, 27 November 1984

[In Boston] I walked through the Back Bay to 287 Dartmouth Street, unmarked except for the street number and an insignia in the doorway. It is the Chilton Club, the *ne plus ultra* of women's clubs in Boston. Waiting for me there was Nancy Ellis, who stood and saluted as I approached. We had drinks before going in for a buffet lunch in the relatively small dining room,

---

11. Phil Burton was in the House from 1963 until his death in 1983. Sala, a native of Bialystok, Poland, was chosen in a special election to succeed him, serving until her own death in 1987.

12. A master of the quip, Dudley once said that to work with Congress "you have to have your gag reflex under control."

at whose tables were other handsome-looking ladies. Boston women become their most attractive past the age of 50.

Our central interest was of course Nancy's brother. Loyal though she is, she asked almost rhetorically whether GB "can ever connect with the man on the street the way Reagan can." I said that RR and Jack Kemp benefit from having a firm and limited set of principles that they constantly repeat. "It's hard to see what George *does* stand for, really," Nan said. "He's the ultimate pragmatist." We agreed that he has to emphasize his strength in foreign affairs and national security and "do all the right things" in 1985 and afterward to recapture undisputed frontrunner status for 1988.

Saturday, 1 December 1984

Today I drove to Union Station for today's outing by train for the Army-Navy game in Philadelphia. I really preferred staying home this weekend, especially after being away for a week. But in my first year as an AsstSecNav I felt obligated to make an appearance and show team spirit.

The long train began with cars assigned to Army, followed by those assigned to CNO and SecNav, and ending with a modern observation car used by W. Graham Claytor, SecNav in 1977–79 and now board chairman of Amtrak. My assignment was in "SecNav Car #2," which is to say *not* with the other assistant secretaries. Preferring to ignore this childish slight, I was glad to keep my distance from John Lehman & Co. all day.

Monday, 3 December 1984

The 1984 edition of Roy Pfautch's Christmas party brought together practically the entire administration, short of the President and VP. It was held in the Departmental Auditorium with its soaring ceilings, gigantic columns, and gold-embossed crests and domes. Music was provided by Mike Deaver, playing "Memories" from *Cats*. Onto the stage came Santa's Helpers, a cluster of Cabinet wives, and Santa himself. This year's mystery Santa was hard to discern through the false whiskers, and he didn't speak, which would have given him away. It took P. X. Kelley to "blow Santa's cover": CIA director Bill Casey.[13]

---

13. Casey's old-fashioned Brooklyn brogue was so thick and unintelligible that agents at Langley joked that the director didn't need a voice scrambler on his office telephone.

Saturday, 8 December 1984

I entered the magnificent, byzantine St. Matthew's Cathedral for the wedding of Chris Buckley to Lucy Gregg [daughter of the VP's national security advisor, Donald Gregg]. *Le tout conservateur* was there: in addition to Chris's famous father Bill, there were his uncle, ex-Sen. Jim Buckley, New York Conservative Party chairman Dan Mahoney, columnist James J. Kilpatrick, and the great Clare Boothe Luce. An ideological opposite but family friend was tall, tall John Kenneth Galbraith. The service was conducted by an elegantly-accented priest who spoke to the literal meaning of the couple's names ("light" and "Christ-bearer").

The reception, held in the Woodrow Wilson House on S Street, bore the lavish imprint of Chris's mother Pat. From the receiving line guests proceeded out to the garden, its two terraces completely enclosed and heated. On the first level was a bar, oysters and shrimp, and on the main level were more bars, hot hors d'oeuvres, and a Peter Duchin combo playing lively dance music. The best moments for me were spent with Mrs. Luce, who invited me to sit with her and others as they talked about the press. To make the point that in 1855 the British national press was unpopular, too, I plucked from my pocket a copy of Trollope's *The Warden,* which I had for reading on the Metro. Mrs. Luce, a Trollope fan, was delighted at the sudden appearance of the book, with its clever characterization of "The Jupiter" (a take-off on *The Times* of London).

The Bushes arrived; an item in yesterday's *Post* said they would be out of town, but this was probably a feint. I shook hands with GB, and Shirley Green and I waved at BPB as we danced. GB has yet to acknowledge my long letter of political advice. That might suggest displeasure, for he never fails to respond to someone's letter.

Monday, 10 December 1984

Dick Elster, Sam Yow, and I met in CNO's conference room with Rear Adm. Chuck Larson for the superintendent's first briefing on a "core curriculum" in the humanities at Annapolis. Afterward, I asked about "personnel matters," and Larson said he'll have recommendations for academic dean next week for SecNav's selection. The choice of an admissions director will take a little longer, he said. When I reminded him that Lehman wants to be consulted before a selection is made for the second job, Larson said, oh no: the two of them had met a month ago, at which time SecNav gave the unilateral decision to him. This was somewhat embarrassing to learn, especially from Chuck. Lehman hadn't told me of their meeting or of his change of mind regarding the admissions director.

Tuesday, 11 December 1984

Ted Gordon came to tell me SecNav can't bring himself to fire Fred Davidson, even though he has more or less promised the job of DASN (Reserve Affairs) to Charlie Dougherty. It's another manifestation of the soft, warm heart of one of the Reagan Administration's toughest guys. So, I shall have to maunder along with the staff I've got, and Ted will have to break the word to Charlie.

Wednesday, 12 December 1984

On the Hill, I visited with Congressman Charles ("Good Time Charlie") Wilson (D-Texas). His sexual, alcoholic, and probable drug involvements have become his fame, but somehow the people of East Texas keep reelecting him. The sad thing is that Wilson is a talented and likeable fellow who could be a power in Congress if his interests were more like Sam Rayburn's and less like Charlie Wilson's. He is serious, however, about bringing two Reserve frigates to Orange, which is suffering from 30% unemployment due to the decline of the oil industry.

From Wilson's office I went to that of Johnny Breaux (D-Louisiana), a fine fellow who still looks like the 28 year-old elected to Congress in 1970.[14] He said Louisiana will match the offer of any other state or port in getting ships. I didn't say so, but I can't imagine our choosing his hometown, Lake Charles, which lies 20-plus miles up a muddy channel.

Thursday, 13 December 1984

Beginning in 1983, the senior civilian and uniformed officials in the Navy Department participated in an annual series of "management retreats" held at the American Security Council's conference facility in Boston, Virginia. In his memoir, Command of the Seas *(1988), Lehman wrote that the Boston conferences were "crucial to our reforms of the Navy."*

---

14. Breaux would serve as senator from Louisiana from 1987–2005.

After an hour and a half ride deep into Virginia, Ev Pyatt and I reached a rolling estate dominated by a great stone house with tall red-brick chimneys resembling nightshades. It was "Longlea," the house described in Robert Caro's biography of Lyndon Johnson[15] where LBJ conducted his affair with Alice Glass.

The other participants, representing the peak of the Navy and Marine Corps, began arriving. The first was John Lehman, dressed casually. The CNO and Commandant, in sports jackets and ties, arrived by helo, landing in a pasture with no one to greet them but cows. We first gathered in the living room, pulling armchairs into a great circle. But on this remarkably warm day we eventually moved out to the famous long, broad terrace, where Alice Glass presided over gatherings of the Washington liberal elite of her day. I sat next to P. X. Kelley, downwind of a cigar he claimed was "a rare pre-Castro Cuban."

There was a heated wrangle over how project management should be structured. The intellectual and turf battle this sparked was intense but served to clear the air, making the tone of all that followed more cooperative and conciliatory. At one point Lehman, sounding like a 1960s campus radical, declared, "The military is organized for its primary mission, which is to kill people. It is not set up to deal with politics or with business." I'm sure the uniformed potentates present disagreed powerfully with him, but they kept their chins tucked down and said nothing, not wanting to spoil the mood of the day or, worse, prolong it.

The conference ended with Seth Cropsey's briefing on the proposed reform of the Joint Chiefs of Staff. SecNav, who has made this fight his crusade, said, "It's life or death for us. No other issue poses greater danger to the Navy and Marine Corps." This is because a strengthened JCS and Joint Staff is presumed to mean a strengthened Army and Air Force. Lehman interrupted the discussion to command us all to look over our shoulders and see an orange sun sink behind the Blue Ridge.

Monday, 17 December 1984

SecNav's lineup had an unusual amount of manpower issues, not least of which was beards. CNO recently announced a ban on chin whiskers [revoking a Vietnam-era privilege granted by Bud Zumwalt]. Lehman heard

---

15. *The Path to Power*, 1982.

some grumbling about this in Norfolk last week, and today he said "intelligence was lacking"—which meant from me. True, I had heard nothing, but I have operated on the notion that uniforms and grooming are a purely military matter in which the Secretariat should wisely stay out. When I said as much this morning, Lehman replied, "They will always *say* that. But you shouldn't consider anything as outside your purview." It was an embarrassing scene that I deserved, if only for an idiotic choice of words.

I had lunch at the Metropolitan Club with Jim Holloway, the former CNO. We talked about "command responsibility," the ancient precept that the senior man must be punished for anything that goes wrong in his realm, even if he were truly blameless. Holloway (and I) believe this cannot be absolute, especially if it means the loss of a good man. "The truth is, there aren't many flag officers who are worth a damn," Holloway said, "and if the time comes when you have to fire one of these, it hurts."

Thursday, 20 December 1984

There was a meeting on reserve affairs in Jim Webb's office, which is on the opposite side of the building from me. "The good news is that we're on the E-Ring," Jim said. "The bad news is that we look out over the GSA trash dump." The room is a veritable museum, decorated with much Webbilia: black and white photos of him in Vietnam, framed appointment certificates, laminated covers of magazines in which his writings have appeared, some old bottles (one of which contains sand from Iwo Jima), and a pair of his USNA shoulder boards—all with a "Please Do Not Touch" sign.

Sunday, 23 December 1984

At noon I arrived at the Naval Observatory for the Bushes' Christmas party for family and friends. I took the opportunity to ask GB what he thought of my "unsolicited memo of political advice," and he said he hadn't seen it. Somewhere the missive was mislaid (or waylaid), so I'll pass him another copy in Houston.

Thursday, 27 December 1984

In the Brazosport area south of Houston, I received the pitch from the local navigation district on why it should be the Navy homeport for the Gulf. After a lunch of red beans and rice we went to the proposed site, a long spit of land now leased to Phillips Petroleum. A 650-foot tanker was tied up when our mob arrived there, and we walked to the end of a long, thin steel pier, preceded by cameramen adept at filming as they hurtle backwards. This resulted in the action shot of Assistant Secretary Untermeyer striding forward in the company of men in hard hats and visored caps reading "Port of Freeport." (JFK-like, I held my cap in my hand.) There was an impromptu interview at the tip of the pier. When the cameras were off, I said, "I'd also like to announce that I am standing in a pool of water." Thus ended a fun visit with everything I enjoy: good friends, the Texas coast, ships, Cajun food, and playing the role of local boy returned as Washington potentate.

Friday, 28 December 1984

I returned a call from GB, who had phoned when I was en route to Freeport. "Unter!" he said. "Star of stage and television!" The VP thanked me for my memo of 21 November. "It was just great," he said, promising that in 1985 "a shift [to making all decisions with an eye to '88] will take place. We're doing it very subtly. Already there are some changes that reflect the Untermeyer viewpoint." He hinted that his new chief of staff [succeeding Admiral Murphy] "will have political savvy." [*This would be Craig Fuller, the secretary to the Cabinet.*] The only major part of my memo with which he disagreed was the admittedly bold assertion that he should try to place "Bush people" in various departments, agencies, and the White House staff, building a cadre on whom he could call one day. (Mondale did this.) "I am disinclined to fight that fight," he said, not wanting to rattle the Reaganites in 1985 any more than in 1981.

On the first day of the new year, I wrote the traditional essay on the year just past, which read in part:

1984: A Toff[16] at Last

The year which ended yesterday brought me what I asked of it: an assistant secretaryship of the Navy. To get this before the age of 40 is a major achievement and the satisfaction of all I hoped to gain in the Reagan Administration.

Working for John Lehman offers the rare chance to see a modern governmental genius in action. But after two years of working for George Bush,

---

16. British slang for an important person.

it was a rude change to serve someone as self-centered and petty as the kid from Philadelphia.

I greet 1985 eagerly: freed of *climbing*, I can now concentrate on the almost limitless opportunities my new job offers. I want to visit bases, take on special projects, and earn John Lehman's respect and possible friendship. Logic demands that I stay where I am, doing good for sailors and Marines and amassing experience that the 41st president of the United States will value and need. Even if GB follows precedent and doesn't become president,[17] I can be grateful for the chance to be assistant secretary of the Navy in the days of Ronald Reagan. It is a wonderful job, and if ever it gets boring or no longer fun or challenging, then I should just quit and go home.

---

17. No serving vice president had been elected president since Martin Van Buren in 1836.

Chapter 8

Jus' Give Us Dat Port

Tuesday, 1 January 1985

I drove to the Marine Barracks at 8th and I [Streets] for the traditional New Year's Day reception and "surprise concert" at the Commandant's House. It was a big affair, drawing all of the Corps's general officers in the DC area plus selected DOD civilian officials, diplomats, congressmen, and journalists. Toward 1330, we went outside to watch the approach of the Marine Band. One January 1st long ago, the Band (under John Philip Sousa) honestly surprised the Commandant, but now it's as surprising as the end to *Casablanca*. General and Mrs. Kelley stepped out onto the landing of the house, right above the red-jacketed musicians, the rest of us off to one side. The generals in their dress blues came to attention as the Band struck up the "Marines' Hymn." The Band then played a couple of Sousa marches, and the bully baritone, Sgt. Mike Ryan, sang a beautiful blessing for the house. P. X. thanked the Band "for this wonderful surprise" and read a selection from the Bible. Then he invited the bandsmen in for food and drink, as the rest of us filed away.

Wednesday, 2 January 1985

When Lt. Gen. Bill Maloney came in for his weekly meeting, I asked about the search for "the new Doc," meaning my next Marine aide. I told him that if I could be assigned a "hard-charging and upwardly-mobile" lieutenant colonel with the potential to be "another Bill Maloney or P. X. Kelley," I would be happy. "He doesn't have to be Irish, but it helps." This factor notwithstanding, we both thought of an excellent possibility: Lt. Col. George Walls, already my special assistant for (minority) officer programs and a likely pickup for colonel.

Friday, 4 January 1985

The Madison Hotel was the scene of a luncheon given by a 90-member delegation from Lake Charles that flew up this morning just for the event. The man I called "the Louisianan-in-chief of the US Navy," Adm. Ron Hays, and I were the well-fed quarry for the roomful of people eager to get the *Wisconsin* surface action group. We were warmly welcomed by Congressman Johnny Breaux and Sen. Bennett Johnston. Lunch began with crawfish etouffée accompanied by a videotape on the glories of southwest Louisiana.

Eventually I was called up to respond. With the experience of addressing countless Kiwanis Club luncheons as a state rep, I made my remarks informative but also funny in the relaxed, half-mocking style Cajuns (and Texans) like. I was extremely impressed by the Lake Charles homeporting proposal, I said: "It has everything. It's got the complete lyrics to 'Jolie Blonde.' It's got the playbook for [the local football team] the McNeese Cowboys. It's got a detailed environmental impact study on the effect of taking nutria into the intake valves of our ships. But the most impressive thing of all was the cover, made from recycled boudin [sausage]." Then I told the delegation facts about the homeport selection process. Sam Yow and I left in a Navy car with gift letter openers and clocks, each bearing the slogan "Sailors Make Good Neighbors."

Monday, 7 January 1985

The following week, I visited several personnel-related activities at the gigantic naval agglomeration in the Hampton Roads area of Virginia.

Outside the gate [of the Norfolk naval station] is the brand-new child care center. It's not unusual for a child to spend the first five years of its life there while his/her single parent goes through a succession of Norfolk assignments. As excellent as it is, I found the center terrifically sad, much more affecting than the brig. The kids are lucky to have a big beautiful place with lots of attention, toys, and outdoor equipment, but they don't have Mommy or Daddy, and their searching eyes were heartrending.

My final couple of hours were spent at the brig, the only long-term correctional facility in the Navy. It was built in 1972, about the same time as the famous old "red-line" brig in Portsmouth, NH, was closed.[1] There are about

---

1. It was so-named because prisoners had to keep within lines painted on the deck in red.

250 prisoners (not "inmates") serving sentences of up to life. The supervisory personnel wear no weapons and are forbidden to touch the prisoners. Marines are called in at times of disturbance. "I tell the men they are here *as* punishment and not *for* punishment," the CO told me. We walked around the various spaces, including the chapel, library, woodshop, metal shop, and a cell block containing two men incarcerated for murder. One kills when told to do so by voices only he can hear; fortunately they were mum this afternoon.

I have been interested in corrections ever since my days in county and state government. There isn't much that's pretty in the whole business. Yet I believe that, in taking very seriously my job as appeals judge of the Navy Department, I can provide an enormous service to society, in this case naval society, and the civilian world to which we eventually release our prisoners.

Night had fallen by the time we left the brig. I could only vaguely discern the silhouettes of ships tied up at the piers, and yet they were magical, as was the pair of masts I saw this morning sliding over the roof of a building. Some 75 ships are in port right now, about one-seventh of the entire US fleet, which is why we must disperse our assets in new homeports. The grandest sight of all was the battleship *Iowa*. Nothing, not even a super-carrier, is more awe-inspiring. "That's a *ship*," said Capt. Kelsey Stewart [my ex-aide who commands the naval station], and even after seeing six dozen ships I could only agree.

At dinner tonight with Kel and Jean [Stewart] were Col. Tim Geraghty, CO of the Marine Barracks, and his wife Karen. Geraghty is an affable and alert fellow with a strong square Irish face. It's easy to see how he was marked out for greater things by P. X. Kelley and the rest of the general staff. ("We're all cosmetic," Bill Maloney admitted recently.) He was indeed given the choicest assignment for an upward-bound colonel: as CO of the mobile assault unit in Lebanon. It was his dire fate to be in command there when the Beirut barracks were blown up in October 1983. The inescapable memory of that awful Sunday morning hovered over our table, as it must hover over the Geraghtys always.

Thursday, 10 January 1985

Vice Adm. Tom Hughes [deputy CNO for logistics] began his update on homeporting by telling Lehman, "Mr. Secretary, we can play any damn tune you want. You just tell us if we're on key or off." SecNav, cheerful throughout the 75-minute meeting, was quite candid: "Tom, I've got to depend on you to keep straight the two sets of books [on homeporting]. The real reason isn't military but for the economic and political base [in Congress] we must get back if we're going to stay healthy for a long time. Dispersal is a valid consideration, but it isn't driving this."

Several more times during the briefing, Lehman underscored his message. Seeing that a group of minesweepers is available for homeporting, he fairly smacked his lips: "Minesweeps [*sic*] are useful little goodies. We should put some in New Hampshire because [Sen.] Warren Rudman (R-New Hampshire) may be our most important guy on Appropriations and [Sen.] Bill Cohen (R-Maine) is going to be our most important friend on Armed Services. We've got to give them something." Of course minesweepers are not the only available currency: "A carrier is big wampum politically," he said.

Friday, 11 January 1985

Vice Adm. Lew Seaton, the surgeon general, horrified the Under and me with the preliminary results of an investigation into a cardiovascular surgeon at Bethesda who had been decertified by a hospital in New Jersey before he joined the Navy. His recruiter told him not to put that unpleasant fact on his application! Even more astounding was that the man's colleagues at Bethesda didn't notice anything wrong until six of his patients had died.

The medical community, in and out of uniform, looks upon itself as the essence of skill, unable to accept the idea that a mortal (i.e., a non-physician) could ever understand their business. In truth the docs don't know how to manage their affairs any better than anyone else. I told [Vice Adm.] Bill Lawrence today that there's no reason he can't run medical manpower the same as he does the rest of the Navy. This probably sounded as radical to him as John Lehman's contention that non–nuclear-trained officers can command nuclear-powered ships and that non-aviators can be air officers aboard carriers. Just as radical, perhaps, but more defensible.

I recently fought the Medical Command over promotion rates for dentists. MedCom wanted a 70% rate for captain, while my staff and I felt it should be only 60%. Lehman explained today that he opted for the higher rate "to stave off a revolt by the dentists," whom he said are still fuming about being placed administratively under the docs. Voilà, another insight he could have given me if only we met regularly to discuss such things. I should stop belaboring this point. John Lehman is who he is because he is unconventional and hates being bound to meetings. If I didn't have to go to meetings all the time, perhaps I could be a freer spirit, too.

Wednesday, 16 January 1985

After lunch I was called on the hotline by Paul Miller to get to the Secretary's office right away on a personnel case. It turned out to be one I'd never seen concerning an NROTC midshipman who, before his commissioning in 1981, confessed to having lied about using drugs four years earlier. Denied his commission on account of fraudulent enlistment, the fellow has been suing us to keep from spending two years as an enlisted man. Lehman thinks "we owe him something for screwing him over for four years." Either not knowing or disregarding the fact that I had never seen the case, Lehman heatedly said, "Your job is to make sure that common sense is applied."

I was knocked a bit off-balance by the blast, but—in part masochistically and the rest opportunistically—told Lehman I tend to be hardline on certain cases (like NROTC "paybacks") out of conviction, not because OpNav or HQMC beguiles me.

Ted Gordon, who had sat in on this session, came to my office shortly afterward to apologize, saying he didn't think the Secretary would react that way. I wonder if Lehman still bridles at the fact that the White House put Untermeyer (and not his choice) into the Manpower job. If so, he fails to realize that I'd become an instant Lehmanite if only he let me into his confidence, if not his circle.

Thursday, 17 January 1985

Today's meeting in Under Secretary Goodrich's office on changing the jobs of Navy senior civil servants every five years (agreed to at the Boston Conference) promised to be contentious, and it proved tumultuous. Mel Paisley's mouth was the first one open, as he has been the prime pusher of the idea "to keep 'em all from becoming goddamn bureaucrats." His plan would put my Manpower shop in charge of rotating all Navy Department members of the SES [Senior Executive Service].

There were cries of protests from the four-stars present, and Mel yelled, "You guys just want to keep it to yourselves!" The VCNO, Adm. Ron Hays, pointed to me and said, "I have no problem with Chase because I know him and I know his background. But I don't know what will happen three or four years from now." Chimed in Adm. Steve White, the chief of Naval Materiel, "The next guy who holds his job may get it because he can write music, for God's sake." (That was probably a reference to Bill Middendorf, who as

SecNav during the Nixon and Ford administrations loved to lead the Navy Band in his own compositions.)

My office is totally unprepared—and I am totally unqualified—to decide the job assignments of 454 senior civil servants; that's 200 more than there are flag officers, and even John Lehman doesn't think up an assignment for every admiral. But I didn't enter into the debate, as I'm probably going to get the authority and I oughtn't appear to Ron and Steve as the villain; *Mel* is their villain.

Friday, 18 January 1985

Mayors Kathy Whitmire of Houston and Jan Coggeshall of Galveston came in to discuss their homeporting proposal. They urged me not to be "too impartial."

Next, Vice Admiral Lawrence arrived for our weekly meeting. As we were talking, SecNav called me on one of his pet peeves: the "second physical" given to aviation candidates in Pensacola after passing one back home. Lehman admires the spunk of those who memorize the eye chart and wants them to become aviators. He sent his personal medical counselor (and courtier), Rear Adm. Bill Narva,[2] right down to see me. The Secretary's edict to do away with the second eye test sounds as screwy to me as to the two admirals, and Bill Lawrence is a pilot. There I go again: seduced by "the System"!

Saturday, 19 January 1985

Bundled up against dropping temperatures brought by the "Alberta Clipper," I stomped to the Washington Hilton for the Texas State Society's "Black Tie and Boots" pre-inaugural gala. Shortly after I arrived, Congressman Tom Loeffler (in a Stetson that curled over his eyes) announced Vice President and Mrs. Bush and three of their kids (George, Neil, and Doro). The curtains then opened, revealing a special gift to the Bushes: a hefty longhorn steer named "Mr. VP." Tom said the steer will be sold back in Texas and the pro-

---

2. Narva was one of the more amusing characters on the fringes of the Reagan Administration. As physician to the Congress, he traveled the world with magnates like the speaker of the House and the chief justice in case they needed medical attention. This was despite the fact that Bill's medical specialty was dermatology. The great and good liked having Bill around because of his silken personality, not because they might develop a worrisome mole. Bill and his wife Rose, who managed a series of fancy Washington hostelries, were solid figures in Washington café society.

ceeds given to the Bushes' favorite charity, the M.D. Anderson Cancer Center in Houston. GB was at a loss for words, and I wished I could have slipped him this line: "You know, there's something that being vice president of the United States has in common with Mr. VP here: you're big enough to get respect, and yet you just can't do things like the other fellers can."

Thursday, 24 January 1985

SecDef Weinberger wants to counterattack those Democrats on the Hill who call for defense cuts by proposing to eliminate bases in their districts—the old "gold watch" ploy but always an attention-getter. I gave Lehman what he nicknamed "the dartboard list" of 20 installations paired with the names of unfavorite congressmen. He quickly ran through this, picking bases in the districts of foes like [California congressmen] Ron Dellums and Pete Stark. Because this base-closure drill is just a game, Lehman enjoyed saying things like, "Definitely put that place on the list! What's he ever done for us? Fuck him! Close it down!"

When this exercise ended, I took a car to Constitution Hall and the fourth annual Presidential Executive Forum for administration appointees. First came some rather dull remarks by Cabinet secretaries. Then the VP entered to "Hail Columbia" and warm applause; clearly he is the appointees' choice for 1988. He gave a good little talk that was frequently interrupted by applause and laughter. Of course the unequaled star was the President, whose arrival was greeted by war whoops and a two-minute ovation. RR wore his brown suit and looked ruddily radiant. He conveyed a sense of sincerity and intimacy when he spoke of his administration as "we." For instance, he said, "In our first four years, we made history. In our next four years, we will change history." The theme song for the second term, he announced, will be "Shake, Rattle, and Roll." When the President finished, the Marine Drum & Bugle Corps invaded the hall, and the familiar crowd-pleasing *coup de théâtre*—the dropping of a huge American flag on a trapeze from the rafters—concluded the rally in fine spirit.

In a second meeting with Lehman after my return from the rally, I made the case for bidding farewell to Fred Davidson, saying, "It's a matter of some pain now or a lot of pain later." I offered to be the bad guy, as I was with E. C. Grayson. "Your method with E. C. was a little brutal," Lehman joked, "but I have to admit it was effective." (I wasn't brutal, but E. C. has a low threshold of hurt and reacted accordingly.) Then Lehman said, twice, "Go ahead and do it." There were several witnesses in the office, and I asked, "Will you all back me up on this?" Lehman and everyone laughed, knowing it is the key question.

Tuesday, 29 January 1985

I went up to the Rayburn Building to call on Congressman Sonny Montgomery (D-Mississippi). I know him through the Bush connection, which made the visit all the friendlier. Montgomery's great passions are the reserves and what he considers his monument, the 1984 G.I. Bill. Last week, Larry Korb tried to get the law's name changed to the CAP, for College Assistance Program—an attempt to flatter the boss ("Cap" Weinberger) of such gross obviousness as to doom itself. I told Montgomery that Navy wants the law to be called the SONNY, for Students Oriented to National Needs and Yearnings.

Thursday, 31 January 1985

In the Dirksen Senate Office Building I represented the Navy Department at the luncheon given by the civic leadership of New Orleans in behalf of their battleship homeporting proposal. The entire Louisiana congressional delegation turned out, led by Senator Bennett Johnston and the inimitable Russell Long. The gracious and popular Congresswoman Lindy Boggs presided, but the real master of ceremonies was Congressman Billy Tauzin (pronounced "toh-san"), a dark-haired beaming lad who looks both shady and a lot of fun. He said that when he came to Congress he was asked if he wanted to go on the Foreign Affairs Committee. "Are you kiddin'?" he quoted himself as replying. "Down my way, foreign affairs are illicit relations you have with women who speak English."

Tauzin invited me to the microphone, and the audience gave me a standing ovation, which was overdoing it. I began in the high-humored spirit of the occasion. Adapting an Aggie joke, I told of two Texas ranch hands who drove their pickup east on I-10 for a weekend in New Orleans. All the way they argued how to pronounce it: Noo Or-leans, N'Orluns, or N'Wallyuns. On the outskirts of the city, they stopped for lunch in a fast-food restaurant and decided to ask the waitress to settle the argument. "Excuse us, ma'am," said one of the cowpokes. "We're from Texas, and we'd like to know how you say the name of this place." The waitress looked sympathetic, smiled sweetly, and said, "Well, because y'all are from Texas, I'll say it real slow: *Bur-ger King*."

Handshaking my way out of the room, I rode on the House subway with Congressmen Tauzin and Bob Livingston (a Republican). Tauzin, still chuckling over the Burger King story, told one on GB: how, right after Reagan came out of the hospital in 1981, he had lunch with several congressmen to stir up support for his budget and tax bills. Tauzin told a Cajun joke that so convulsed the President that RR started coughing badly, his lung not having yet healed. Bush leaned over and whispered, "Billy, tell another one!" It's funny, but I don't believe it.

While on the Hill, I called on Congressman Trent Lott of Mississippi, the House Republican whip. He grilled me courteously but relentlessly on Pascagoula's chances of getting the surface action group. He dismissed other contenders, conceding, "Of course, if Louisiana can steal it, they will, and if Texas can buy it, they will."

Tuesday, 5 February 1985

At the lineup, Dudley Carlson reported that freshman Sen. Phil Gramm (R-Texas), now on Armed Services, has said the only question is *which* Texas port will get *Wisconsin*. SecNav added that Gramm wants on the Seapower Subcommittee, clearly understanding that "if he gets the Navy by the balls, our hearts and ships will follow."

Thursday, 7 February 1985

Today I met with the entire Louisiana congressional delegation and Gov. Edwin Edwards (D) in Senator Long's office. I was impressed that while his outer office is filled with colorful posters about the Pelican State, the inner office is quiet and tasteful, with Audubon prints and only one discreet portrait of his famous father Huey. Governor Edwards repeated his commitment to the Navy for "any amount of money you want," up to $50 million, to homeport ships in his state. I asked if that's an item in his state budget this year, and Edwards (a white-haired smoothie) acted a bit ruffled. He said the money will be there when it's wanted by the Navy, even if he has to call a special session of the legislature to approve it. I made the point that while money is an important consideration for us, the first consideration has to be whether the site makes sense for the Navy. All said they fully understand and accept that.

Then came a painful moment. Several days after what I thought was a boffo speech at the New Orleans luncheon, Hugh O'Neill told me that I had said "Louisiana politicians have no class"—when I meant to say they have no *peer*. I apologized to the delegation, whereupon Billy Tauzin said with his trademark twinkle, "Jus' give us dat port, an' you can say anything about us you want."

Edwards has no peer among governors in fully enjoying all the legal scrapes he gets into. "If y'all come to Looziana, I promise you won't have anybody lookin' into what you do, 'cause all those prosecutors are so busy lookin' into *me*," he said to guffaws.

Saturday, 9 February 1985

At the Pentagon this quiet day I worked on personnel cases. The toughest concerned a Marine lieutenant who had been drinking before he took a sharp turn in his sports car at over 80 mph. The car flew about 500 feet, throwing him out and partially crushing him. He is now 100% disabled. Under the law, he can get Navy disability pay only if his injuries were "in the line of duty" rather than through misconduct. It was obviously the latter, and in a note to SecNav I said that was my conclusion, adding "you may want to grant relief on humanitarian grounds." What will be interesting is whether Ted Gordon keeps Lehman from seeing this. Ted often has to get the boss to follow his head and not his heart. I recently learned that he got Lehman to reverse himself on the case on which he called me down to his office in a rage on 16 January. My best defense is that I spend hours on weekends reading the files and entering a considered judgment on each case.

Monday, 11 February 1985

After some Malaysian pirates robbed a merchant ship under charter to the Navy, Seth Cropsey wrote a memo to SecNav proposing that we go after 'em. This appealed to Lehman's historic impulses. "That's what navies are for," he announced at today's lineup. I don't doubt that if Jim Watkins lent Lehman a frigate he'd go blast the bad guys himself à la Stephen Decatur. OpNav certainly doesn't want the job.

Of much greater import is the ongoing saga of Takis Veliotis, onetime head of the Electric Boat Division of General Dynamics, who fled before the sheriff to Greece. There he has been leaking documents that hint Navy settled its claims on submarine contracts with GD too cheaply back in 1981. Getting tough on GD was one of Lehman's biggest and earliest achievements, and now that is being called into question. "It's worse than his selling secrets to the Soviets," Lehman said, opening a folder and removing a sheath of papers. "He's selling them to the *Washington Post*." The documents, obtained from the *Post* by CIA, deal with extremely sensitive information about our subs and include pictures. All this isn't making John Lehman very happy these days, so I shouldn't think he is singularly mad at me.

Tuesday, 12 February 1985

[At the Marine Corps Air-Ground Combat Center at Twentynine Palms, California] I was about to board a helo when an officer said I needed to call my office. Sam Yow reported that SecNav had called on the hotline in a froth to say that the lease for a Naval Reserve center aboard the old carrier *Intrepid* in New York had not been executed and that the ship museum is in immediate danger of bankruptcy. I suspect a New York hustle at work, but Sam spent the rest of the day getting OpNav to finalize the lease. Who knows what we will pay for it in the end.

This news cast a pall over the day, but I resolved not to let it discourage or depress me. A visit to the LAV (Light Armored Vehicle) unit did much to pound out regrets over the *Intrepid* episode. A couple of junior enlisted men, a driver and a gunner, gave me a fore-and-aft, top-to-bottom tour of an eight-wheeled LAV-25, an all-purpose artillery and troop carrier costing $600,000, before we went for a ride in the desert.

While I didn't ask for the LAV ride, I couldn't say no to it, either. We rode along some dirt roads before trying a steep incline. Then it came my time to take the wheel. I drove competently enough, especially once I got used to the slow response of the engine and learned to let momentum and gravity take us down hills, not using the accelerator. I drove us back to the barn on a surfaced road. Drivers in the other lane had no idea that a total amateur was at the wheel of the big LAV rumbling toward them.

Friday, 15 February 1985

At the Marine Corps Recruit Depot (where recruits from west of the Mississippi are trained; all others go to Parris Island), I was the reviewing official at the graduation parade. Lt. Gen. Tony Lukeman, the commanding general, escorted me forward for honors and the pass in review. The 17-gun salute caused exclamations of surprise throughout the crowd and some frightened children to cry. I was so taken by the whole scene myself that Tony had to prompt me to give the command, "Pass in review!" Then the great mass of green on the field came to life and marched past us.

We returned to the stands for the moment, both poignant and delightful, when the DIs [drill instructors] give the final order for their platoons to dismiss. "Aye, aye, sir!" they yell, about-face, and then erupt in arm waving and backslapping, their 11-week ordeal over. I walked down from the stands to observe the reunion of families with their greatly-changed sons. I paused to congratulate some of the new Marines, especially those who didn't seem to have anyone from home present.

The most memorable encounter was with a DI in his Smokey Bear hat, wandering around looking at the scene with an unmistakable misty eye. His first platoon graduated today, and it was clear that he loved every one of those guys. "I learned from the privates," he readily admitted. "They kept me from falling on my rear." He still regrets that when he himself graduated from boot camp he never thanked his DI. Was he walking about, hoping for one of his progeny to thank him today?

Next door, at the Navy Training Center, I starred in another graduation ceremony. Standing on a red carpet, I received the second 17-gun salute of the day, upsetting more kiddies. Then I inspected the honor guard, stopping to speak briefly with each man, as is the custom.[3] After the recruits went through their drill, a man in charge announced, "Mr. Secretary: the division is formed!" My line was: "Very well. I wish to address the division." A speaker's stand and a microphone were brought forward, and the air was mine.

Sympathetic with the hundreds of troops standing in the sun, I was brief—and even spared them the time it would have taken to say, "I'll be brief." I said: "The Navy is as old as John Paul Jones and as young as the men on the field before us." I added, "These are great days in which to be in the armed forces of our country because the American people want to give you the equipment, the training, the affection, and the respect you deserve."

---

3. John Connally, then SecNav and later governor of Texas, was hit in the head by a recruit's rifle when his greeting was heard by the scared sailor as "Present arms!" Recalling the photo of that awful incident, I always kept a safe distance between me and the armed troops in ranks.

Tuesday, 19 February 1985

I had a very special and very potent guest for lunch: Jim McGovern, staff director of the Senate Armed Services Committee.[4] Actually, I hadn't invited Jim; I invited the chief staffer for the Personnel Subcommittee, Pat Tucker, but he wouldn't come without his boss. The Under, Mel Paisley, and Ted Gordon all dropped by our table to pay court to Jim. Though he holds great power, Jim is a down-to-earth guy, a 1969 Annapolis grad who still looks like the beaming Irish kid sacking groceries to earn pocket money. We discussed manpower issues, dominated by the grim fact that in the current freeze on defense spending, Navy won't get a single additional man for the fleet. (We're asking for 15,000.)

Sen. Paula Hawkins (R-Florida) sent an emergency request for me to meet with a delegation from Tampa that wants *Wisconsin*. She had made an unequivocal statement supporting Pensacola, even though Tampa Bay has 34% of the vote in the state and she may face a tough opponent next year in Gov. Bob Graham. I have known Paula and her AA [administrative assistant] John Mica since my days with the VP and was glad to be an attentive ear to the Tampans. Paula used the occasion (with press present) to blast Graham for not pledging state resources to get the battleship "like every other governor on the Gulf." That's not quite true, but I made a point of mentioning Louisiana's pledge of $50 million (which may all be play money). When time came to leave, John shook my hand and said, "You really helped us."[5]

The biggest event of the day was the much-anticipated meeting in my office at which I was briefed on the OpNav study paring 16 potential homeports down to four. The finalists could have been predicted months ago: Pensacola, Mobile, Corpus Christi, and Galveston. Places like Lake Charles, New Orleans, and Tampa were eliminated simply for having long steaming distances to blue water—an appalling 98 miles in New Orleans's case.

Sen. Phil Gramm called during the meeting, and I phoned him back as soon as we finished. It was my first contact with the new junior senator from my state. "Let's just work together," the crafty Gramm soothingly suggested. "I know this is a two-way street, and I'll be helpful to you if you want me to." When I referred to his being on the SASC, he added "*And* the Seapower Subcommittee *and* the Force Projection Subcommittee. I'm in the Navy now!"

---

4. Secretary of the Air Force, 1988–89.

5. Not enough. Graham defeated Hawkins in 1986, but Mica was elected to Congress in 1992.

Wednesday, 20 February 1985

Receiving the report on Gulf homeporting this afternoon, Lehman quickly concurred with the four recommendations but put Lake Charles and Pascagoula back onto the list for political symmetry (at least one site per state). In a typically Lehmanesque, totally unanticipated addendum, he also said to add Key West. In 1981, he snatched 77 acres of the old naval station out of the hands of real estate developers. Since then, we have done nothing to utilize the land, so Lehman asked OpNav to "look for something we can move out of Norfolk in the dead of night."

Later, the Secretary and I met with a high-level Texas delegation in Phil Gramm's office in the Russell Building. Also present were Sen. Lloyd Bentsen, Gov. Mark White, Speaker of the House Gib Lewis, and Lt. Gov. Bill Hobby (all Democrats). Mark said, "I'm so much for Texas that I'd prefer the ports of Amarillo and Lubbock to those of any other state." Noncommittal to a fault, Lehman heard the bipartisan pitch with nods and hums. But he closed by saying, "I can assure you that the fact I've put a former member of your legislature in charge of this project will have nothing to do with this whatsoever."

Friday, 22 February 1985

My speech to Fred Davidson this afternoon was even to its author a thing of wonderment: so positive, so friendly, and yet so terminal. I had talked with SecNav, I said, and feel that after a year as AsstSecNav it is time to develop my own team. And, I'm sure you agree, four years is about the right amount of time to stay in one of these jobs. I sure don't plan to stay in this one longer than that. It's time for you to move on to something better. . . . I then spelled out the plan whereby after Easter [former Congressman] Charlie Dougherty would become DASN (Reserve Affairs) and Fred would be given a consultancy for a certain period to tie down a new appointment (which won't ever come).

Fred heard all this placidly and even willingly. Without a beat he agreed that it was indeed the right thing for him to do. Later I called Ted Gordon to announce "the deed is done." Marybel Batjer then called me, delighted that "somebody has the guts to fire someone around here." Out of compassion for Fred, I will let it be known that he's leaving on his own motion.

Wednesday, 6 March 1985

I attended the reporting-out for captains in the staff corps (medical, dental, chaplain, etc.) so that I could be all alone with Lehman after everyone else cleared out. I mentioned the coming retirement of Lt. Gen. Bill Maloney as deputy chief of staff for Manpower and asked what role we (*sic*) would play in choosing his successor. Lehman said we (*sic*) would indeed be players, and he asked my thoughts. I expressed concern that a particular general officer whose name Bill had floated is not a "people person." Lehman then did a typically curious thing: he asked me to repeat my words to his Marine aide, Col. Mike Mulqueen. Why? Because Lehman considers Mike a spy for the Commandant and knew that my thinking would be duly reported back to HQMC—that and the fact that SecNav wanted it to be.

Thursday, 7 March 1985

I got to the Secretary's office for the reporting-out of the selection board for Marine colonels just as the board president mentioned George Walls of my staff, emphasizing, "He made it on his own record." I told Lehman that George is my sole choice (already blessed by HQMC) to be my new Marine aide. Lehman looked impressed; has anyone yet had a black aide in the Navy Department?

Friday, 8 March 1985

Today my luncheon guest was Clare Boothe Luce, whom I picked up at Watergate South in a Navy car. At age 82 she is still an exquisitely beautiful woman. Though her eyesight is poor, Clare noticed the bust of James Forrestal[6] at the Mall Entrance as we climbed the steps. "Poor Jim," she sighed.

In the Navy private dining room we were joined by Jim Webb, whom I had invited to meet a fellow author. They took to each other immediately, Mrs. Luce later characterizing Jim as "a doll."[7] They spoke at length on a theme Clare presented: that government service "saps the creative juices from a writer." She never wrote another play after being elected to Congress, and

---

6. The first secretary of Defense, Forrestal committed suicide in 1949.

7. Jim afterward said he told his wife JoAnn, "You should be grateful there's a forty-year difference in our ages."

"poor Archie MacLeish" never recovered from wartime service as a propagandist. Jim said that government executive service requires snap decisions, while good fiction requires "ambiguities." Looking at the menu, Mrs. Luce chuckled over a good example of governmentalese: a listing for an "egg omelet."

Our conversation ranged over both topical and philosophical matters, interspersed with splendid Lucid anecdotes, such as a visit Clare and "Harry" paid to Gertrude Stein's Alpine atelier just before World War II. Stein's friends would give her paintings of young artists they hoped she would endorse, and she hung their canvases in her small barn for a year. If she liked one instantly, she concluded it probably wasn't original, for it obviously evoked a conditioned response. If she disliked one instantly, it might have been because of its stark, bold originality. She could only tell if one were good if she missed it when the friend took it back.

After lunch and Jim's departure, I escorted Mrs. Luce down to the long corridor in which hangs the *Life* collection of World War II art. (Legend has Henry Luce starting the magazine as an amusement for Clare.) At the end of the corridor is the section devoted to Douglas MacArthur, one case containing the copy of *Life* dated 8 December 1941 with the general, hands on hips, filling the cover. "I took that picture in the Philippines!" she announced, adding that she also did the story inside.

Thursday, 14 March 1985

I received a call from one of Earth's mightiest beings, Adm. Kinnaird (Kin) McKee, chief of naval reactors and heir to Admiral Rickover. He had gotten word of a letter I was about to send the chancellor of the State University of New York, saying that we welcome ways our nuclear-trained officers could earn academic credit at SUNY. McKee was practically spluttering in rage: "These are *my* officers! They don't have time to do anything extra. I wish you'd consulted me on this. I'm an old schoolmaster," meaning he was once superintendent at Annapolis. I shall raise this issue with SecNav, who may relish a new battle with the "nukes."

Friday, 15 March 1985

When my time came to report at SecNav's lineup, I told of yesterday's telephonic blast from Admiral McKee. This produced general laughter and calls of "Welcome to the club!" Lehman thinks that giving academic credit to nuclear-trained officers is desirable but instructed me to "work with McKee." That of course means nothing will happen. But Ev Pyatt and Mel Paisley urged me to do it, just so I would distract McKee from battles *they* are having with him.

Saturday, 16 March 1985

[In Miami,] along with AsstSecDef Larry Korb and my counterparts from the other services, I appeared at a hearing by the US House Government Operations Committee on the drug interdiction program. Our bus from the hotel to the Dade County courthouse had a police escort, and Customs agents stood on the steps of the courthouse with concealed automatic weapons and overt radios. They did the Secret Service routine till we were all safely inside. The international cocaine smuggling business is so big and so bloody that Customs deemed it not impossible for someone to attack the government officials most involved with suppressing the trade. There was, however, no danger and few spectators.

Where we really expected crossfire was in the hearing itself. Glenn English (D-Oklahoma), chairman of the Subcommittee on Agriculture, has been pushing the Administration to do more to stop the importation of drugs. An old doctrine called *posse comitatus* forbids the Armed Forces from actually intercepting and arresting the druggies. But under a 1981 amendment to the statute, we can render information and assistance to state and local law enforcement and to the Coast Guard.

Larry made a brief ad lib statement, took a few soft questions, and left, not to be seen again. In my testimony, I said, "There is not a Navy plane flying, a Navy radar sweeping, nor a Navy surface unit sailing in these waters that is not on the lookout [for drugs]." This attracted the attention of the prune-faced, bulbous-nosed old demagogue Claude Pepper (D-Miami).[8] He was dressed in bright St. Patrick's Day attire, prompting one of his colleagues to refer to him as Green Pepper. Others respectfully called him "Mr. Chairman," since he chairs House Rules. Pepper repeated his common tirade against DOD for not doing "all you *could*. . . . You should make it your *business* to stop these people." I smiled and nodded and said nothing. Then Ty

---

8. Pepper, a southern liberal, was US senator from Florida from 1936 until his defeat in the 1950 Democratic primary. He returned to Congress in 1963 as a member of the House and served until his death in 1989.

McCoy [of Air Force] took the microphone to embellish what he had said earlier about DOD drug-interdiction efforts, inspiring Chairman English to give us all a homework assignment: to produce a plan of how much more the services can do. Other than this, all went well, and we were free to go.

Monday, 18 March 1985

Lehman called on the hotline, asking me to step down to his place. When I arrived, he reported word from the White House congressional liaison that Sen. Bennett Johnston of Louisiana will sell his vote on the MX missile in exchange for the battleship surface action group. This won't be the only time such a gambit is tried, and it's no surprise coming from one of the pelicans. SecNav said, "As you have probably guessed, I have a pretty good idea where those ships are going to go, and it isn't Louisiana. So, give me a list of other ships to give Johnston instead." I tasked Tom Hughes with the drill. Later, with the package in hand, I returned to the Secretary's office. In a springy mood, Lehman chose a reserve oiler and two minesweeps for Lake Charles. There's no telling whether Johnston will take the deal.

Tuesday, 19 March 1985

While at the Academy today, I sat in on a class in the humanities to see how they are presently taught. This was a seminar in medieval history led by a pudgy young New Yorker with Medusa-like hair. There were about 20 midshipmen in his class, and they asked some pretty good questions. Afterwards, the teacher said he has found midshipmen better able to understand the societal order of the Middle Ages than his former students at Iowa and Columbia. "This is, after all, a medieval institution," he said with a smile and a shrug. The mids can understand the respect given to the clergy in olden times because officers at the Academy are given the same unquestioned obedience. "The Academy tells them that black is [Navy] blue, and they believe it."

Wednesday, 20 March 1985

Walking with SecNav for a meeting with Chuck Larson in the Blue Room, I noted that Senator Johnston had voted against the MX missile. "Good!" the Secretary exclaimed, for that means we now don't have to give Louisiana any ships at all.

Lehman had a cold, which was appropriate since he often refers to USNA as "the Nasal Cavity." (He also calls his fellow naval aviators "nasal radiators.") He liked Larson's plan for an honors program and told him, "Consider there's no restraint in funding. We'll move the money through a reprogramming." The amount is miniscule by Pentagon standards: only $215,000 this year and $614,000 the next. Chuck, who once headed the Trident [nuclear sub] program, said, "I used to leave that much under the table every night." So, we may finally be reaching a happy ending to the year-long struggle over the Secretary's reform of the Academy.

Although the naval jungle would try to grow back over the land Lehman plowed with his reforms, his emphasis on the humanities took root. The Naval Academy website in 2013, more than a quarter-century after he left office, described the goal of the academic program in words Lehman could have written himself: "Core requirements in engineering, natural sciences, the humanities and social science assure that graduates are able to think critically, solve increasingly technical problems in a dynamic, global environment, and express conclusions clearly."

Thursday, 21 March 1985

In the afternoon I was interviewed by a reporter from National Public Radio probing whether homeporting is driven by genuine strategic concerns or by congressional politics. That is our deep dark secret, so I had to speak vigorously about the need to disperse the fleet. The reporter then quoted Congressman Ted Weiss (D-New York) as saying Navy wants ships in new places in order to seduce the local congressional delegations. Weiss is absolutely right, but I said, "The congressman contradicts his own argument. We are going to be in New York [with *Iowa* on Staten Island], and I'm sure that isn't going to change his views on defense."

Saturday, 23 March 1985

I walked in the rain to Dupont Circle and the *fin de siècle* mansion that houses the Sulgrave Club, Washington's premier ladies' association. There Ambassador Luce gave an elegant yet informal dinner party for a veritable convention of young writers: Chris Buckley and Lucy, Jim Webb and JoAnn, Lloyd Grove of the *Post,* and, most marvelous of all, Edmund Morris and his wife Sylvia. A bearded and wiry South African, Edmund won the Pulitzer

Prize for *The Rise of Theodore Roosevelt*. Sylvia, who wrote a biography of Edith Kermit Roosevelt (Mrs. TR), is writing one now on Clare. Also present was a fellow producer of bureaucratic literature, Ken Cribb, counselor to Attorney General Meese. We enjoy each other's occasional company because of a mutual love of politics and laughter, though I'm never quite sure when Ken constantly calls me "a moderate" if he says it with mirth or malice.

Ambassador Luce was dressed in a long Chinese-style gown set off by a hammered gold necklace and bracelets that clattered as she moved. She told some choice stories about Douglas MacArthur, in particular his debt to a geopolitical strategist named Homer Lea.

I held back from lionizing Edmund, yet he was a patient and fascinating responder to all my questions. For example, he said that TR was a captivating speaker in the way Hitler was: despite an irritating voice and teeth that clicked out syllables, he mesmerized people with the very strangeness of his personality. Edmund despaired over future biographies of this era's public figures, who tell intimacies over the telephone and not in letters or diaries.

Sunday, 24 March 1985

At the VP's house this rainy noontime there was a near-complete reunion of "The Yangtze River Gang" that went to China in September-October 1977, as big an event in George and Barbara Bush's lives as in the rest of ours. Hugh and Betty Liedtke flew up from Houston, and Marianna Thomas (Lowell's widow) came down from New York. From DC and environs came Jim and Susan Baker, Jim and Sally Lilley, Dean and Pat Burch, and David and Ann Broder. But the star guests were our "Chinese friends" who then were our escort-interpreters and now are assigned to the Chinese embassy here. Chief among them is the ambassador's assistant, Tiger Yang,[9] and his wife Le Aime.

We laughed over a continuous slide show of pictures from the trip. (Untermeyer's hoofing during the amateur night as *The East Is Red No. 32* steamed through the Yangtze Gorges will ne'er be forgotten.) Then we partook of a buffet of barbecued chicken drumsticks. I sat with BPB and some others in the alcove formed by the house's famous turret. The VP rang for attention and announced that Messrs. Broder and Untermeyer "by popular

---

9. After the 1977 trip, "Tiger" Yang Jiechi became an English interpreter for the Chinese leadership and a specialist on Sino-American affairs. In 2001, he became Chinese ambassador to the United States, in 2005 foreign minister, and in 2013 state councilor for foreign affairs.

request will *not* sing" but that we would all gather for a reunion photo. I sat on the floor with the Vice President and the Secretary of the Treasury [Baker] as Laurie Firestone (Mrs. B's social secretary) made repeated flashes with a Polaroid camera.

Dean and I compared thoughts on Craig Fuller's reshaping of the VP's staff. BPB stood nearby and asked what we think of his choices. We repeated our concern that "it doesn't look like a *Bush* staff." She agreed absolutely but hasn't shared this with GB. I gather she isn't thrilled with Craig. When I mentioned earlier in the afternoon that I'll see them at the Chinese ambassador's dinner on April 1, she swiftly said, "April Fool's Day: that's when Craig Fuller takes over." I chatted with GB just before leaving, and he hinted that he also has doubts about what Craig has done, especially in sacking loyalists like Steve Rhodes and Joe Hagin. "I did what people said I should do, which was to stay out of it," he said. "Now . . . ." and his voice trailed off with a tone of regret.

Wednesday, 3 April 1985

I put on black tie and walked next door to the Sheraton Washington for tonight's big Navy League banquet. We Pentagon dignitaries were seated randomly inasmuch as every table was bought by a defense contractor, and the random distribution was a feeble attempt to lessen lobbying. Up on the long dais, SecNav sat wearing a piquant red bowtie, smoking a big cigar, and looking up at the ceiling in bored distraction in the English aristocratic/academic manner. All that was missing was a snifter of brandy to slosh.

Introduced by the rollicking P. X. Kelley, Lehman was quite impressive, speaking from just a folded yellow sheet of notes with great articulateness and accuracy. And arrogance: he acted as if he truly believed P. X.'s declaration that he is the greatest secretary of the Navy in US history. He blasted "military reformers," Pentagon bureaucracy, "congressional anarchy," sole-source contracting, the "gold plating" of weapons systems by Navy planners, and "amateurism" by military personnel in procurement. He hailed the recent creation of a separate career path for "materiel professionals" as "the greatest reform in naval officer careers in a century." And he announced the "de-organization" of the Naval Materiel Command. Maybe due to the heavy concentration of contractors in the audience, Lehman received no standing ovation at the conclusion of his remarks, despite a magnificent effort.

Lehman is a fascinating man who can be the smiling Irish altar boy and the disdainful Cambridge don; who can bring forward men of competence to reshape the US Navy and yet prefer the company of shills and toadies; and who can be the darling of the right wing while privately scorning them and acting every bit the "elitist" they detest. Through his attention to detail and his push for greater competition in buying ships, planes, and weapons, he saves the taxpayers hundreds of millions of dollars. He can therefore shrug off the cost of giving disability benefits to sailors and Marines who by the book don't deserve them.

I count myself lucky to know and work for him, and maybe someday I shall figure him out. If I had to decide upon it now, I would simply say that John Lehman is a brilliant, self-centered man who shall either succeed mightily or fall into obscurity.

Wednesday, 17 April 1985

I attended Rear Adm. Chuck and Sally Larson's luncheon for the 25th annual Naval Academy Foreign Affairs Conference. This afternoon's special guest was Sir Oliver Wright, the florid eccentric who is Britain's ambassador to the United States. Also present was the legendary Adm. Arleigh ("31-knot") Burke, the former CNO. During lunch, Burke quoted an old line that "the US Navy learned everything we know from the British, and we still don't know anything." There was nervous laughter.

After lunch we proceeded to stately old Mahan Hall for Sir Oliver's amusing and incisive address on the NATO alliance. Once master of Christ's College at Cambridge, Wright was particularly good at answering students' questions. At one point he said: "My job as ambassador in Washington is to see what the Administration and the Congress are going to do and then inform my government so we can adjust our policy, ex post facto, to what our friendly neighborhood superpower has already decided."

Tuesday, 23 April 1985

Nine-fifteen brought the first lineup since SecNav returned from Israel and Iceland. I used the occasion to respond to a "please see me" note atop a memo I sent him on what's being done to curb minority attrition from flight school. Raising his hands to his head, Lehman exclaimed that "a whole new bureaucracy" was being created to fight a simple problem. He was wrong, and I didn't want to be the foil in a Lehmanic tirade on his favorite subject.

Lineups are atrocious places to discuss complicated issues in the first place, but the presence of such a crowd forced me to stand up for myself. Lehman then dropped the matter, in effect conceding my points, with some basic good humor.

Though Seth Cropsey congratulated me on winning the clash (or what Cdr. Dan Murphy described to Sam Yow as a "joust"), I felt uncomfortable over the incident. My desire is not to win debates with John Lehman but to benefit from his knowledge of the Navy, to correct any misimpressions he may have, and above all to learn his views. By restricting my opportunity to talk in anything other than quick spiels in staff meetings or calls on the hotline, he makes it very hard to have rational exchanges.

Wednesday, 24 April 1985

As I worked at my desk, Sam Yow came in to say three Secret service agents were out front, advancing Barbara Bush's visit here tomorrow for lunch. He correctly described them as "big, bigger, and biggest." They were very friendly, and the prime question was where a ladies restroom might be. Answer: SecNav will provide his head [bathroom] for the occasion.

Lt. Gen. Bill Maloney disclosed that there would be a message tonight announcing his retirement and the selection of Lt. Gen. Ernie Cheatham to succeed him as deputy chief of staff for Manpower. Twice I asked Bill to describe Cheatham and twice he declined, except to say Cheatham played for the Baltimore Colts before entering the USMC. That might be a hint that Cheatham is a tough guy. I can at least thank HQMC for assigning one of my favorite folks in green, Maj. Gen. Lou Buehl, as head of Reserve Forces.

Thursday, 25 April 1985

At 11:45 I went to the Mall Entrance to await Mrs. Bush's arrival in a two-car motorcade. In the excitement of her coming, I neglected to mention that before lunch we'd have a brief visit with John Lehman. She was thus mildly startled to enter a suite and find herself being kissed by the secretary of the Navy. We talked a few minutes there before she and I crossed the E-Ring corridor to SecNav's private dining room and a Mexican plate lunch.

BPB began by talking about her efforts on literacy, but soon we were discussing the almost total turnover in the VP's office. We both think it could have been handled with greater kindness and consideration for the old-timers. As for one of these, Jennifer Fitzgerald, we both agree she is far better off in the Senate office. "I used to think she was terrible," BPB said. "Now I just feel sorry for her."

After the plates were cleared, I took Mrs. B to my office to meet my staff.[10] They were all lined up as if to be inspected. She shook everyone's hand and said, "Take care of him!" After exacting a promise that I wouldn't see her back downstairs, she (and agents and uniformed Pentagon policemen) then left.

I returned a call from Congressman Jack Brooks (D) of Beaumont. Normally tempestuous, Brooks was effusively warm and friendly, reporting that the Texas Legislature has appropriated $25 million for homeporting *Wisconsin* in Texas. When Lt. Gov. Bill Hobby spoke with me about state support back in February, he was thinking of a kind of IOU to be placed in the 1987 appropriations bill. But I'm glad the Legislature realized it's better to have what Jack called CIF—cash in fist.

Thursday, 2 May 1985

Today I addressed 200–300 members of the Norfolk Ombudsmen Assembly, the women (and some male command master chiefs) who provide a link between the ships and crewmembers' families. I used the forum to announce the creation of the new position of deputy assistant secretary of the Navy for Personnel & Families. In a phrase John Lehman could love, I said the new function "is not to be a bureaucracy but to battle bureaucracy."

[Back in Washington] I attended a reception honoring Bill Lawrence given by the Association of Naval Service Officers, which speaks for Hispanics in the Navy and Marine Corps. The main address was given by Ed Hidalgo, who as SecNav in 1980 established ANSO with an assist from the then-superintendent at Annapolis, Bill Lawrence. Hidalgo said his personal interest was natural "because my name ends in a vowel." He then presented Bill with a plaque and proclaimed him "an honorary Hispanic." In his humble fashion, Bill accepted the award and noted that that his name, too, ends in a vowel.

---

10. I also showed her the model of a generic Los Angeles–class submarine on my conference table. I had attached a small plaque declaring it USS *Houston* (SSN-713), which she had christened in 1981. This enabled me to tell her that we both had christened a sub the *Houston*. Historically, the Navy gave city names to cruisers and those of fish to submarines. But Adm. Hyman Rickover started naming subs for cities. When traditionalists decried this change, the savvy Rickover simply said, "Fish don't vote."

Saturday, 4 May 1985

About 60 miles out from Jacksonville, Sam Yow, Steve Rhodes [departing domestic policy advisor to VP Bush], and I passed over the cruiser *Ticonderoga* to land on the carrier *Saratoga*. Side boys were paraded, but no officer waited on the other end of the cordon to greet me. This was odd, but after all we were just transiting to a waiting helo. I figured the captain was preoccupied with his special passenger, Congressman Charlie Wilson, who had brought along two women. We lifted off and headed astern the carrier about five miles, where "Tico" was trailing. The pilot landed expertly on the pitching helo deck.

Ticonderoga is a new Aegis cruiser whose ultra-modern electronics can spot a missile traveling at over 1000 knots popping up over the horizon only 14 miles distant. Within two seconds the Aegis system can identify and lock onto the contact, destroying it with one or two of the ship's missiles, almost literally before a human being might even notice something was happening. The ship's last line of defense is called the Close-in Weapons System (CIWS, or "sea wiz") by the Navy, Phalanx by its manufacturer, and R2D2 by the crew, after the robot in *Star Wars*. A white-domed Gatling gun, it has three long gun barrels that spin at high speed and spit out nonradioactive uranium projectiles at over 3000 rounds per minute, creating a wall of heavy metal for the missile to hit and blow up. We got a demonstration: the system shot off three bursts of 100 rounds in instants, emitting fire from the barrels and a loud sound of *zzzzblatt!*

The demonstrations done, we went aft to watch the sunset on the fantail and see the huge kick *Tico*'s four gas turbine engines give to its twin screws. It looked as if we were powered by a gigantic outboard motor. As we muscled through the healthy swells, water would occasionally wash over the lower deck, adding to the drama, excitement, and beauty.

Sunday, 5 May 1985

We flew back to Washington from Jacksonville aboard a P3 Orion subhunting aircraft. En route we exercised with the sub *James K. Polk;* a genuine Soviet sub was many miles away. The pilot and officer in tactical command had the comic book–perfect names of Bart and Rip. We took off over the St. James River and headed out to sea till we reached our op area due east of Savannah. There we descended to only 300 feet above the surface to track the sub. The two enlisted acoustic trackers picked up the sounds of the sub right away and from their training could even identify the source of the noise: a defective pump. (And our subs are quieter than the Soviets'.) I realized that the sailors' hearing is a critical national-security asset, and with trepidation I asked what kind of music they listen to. As I feared, it isn't Mozart.

Tuesday, 14 May 1985

Nine-fifteen brought an event in the works for more than two months: an open-ended meeting with SecNav on how to manage the Department's 350,000 civilian personnel, a responsibility that OpNav has hoarded. We proposed that power over civpers be moved into the Secretariat (specifically to me), that Joe Tausig be excised as DASN, and that he be replaced by a high-ranking civil servant with the title of director. The unanimous choice for this job was Dr. Jim Colvard, despite a reputation for independence and wiliness.

To give this plan the acid test, Lehman called in the VCNO [Admiral Hays]. Ron studied the org chart I had drawn on a board and said he had no problem with it but wondered whether the plan is any more efficient than the current lash-up. "It's not," Lehman admitted. "But I had a sense of unease that I have no say in civilian personnel. In my continuing lust for power, I want to have the guy in charge of civpers under our thumb. I want him to be part of *us* rather than *them*," he said to the vice-chief of *them*.

A quiet afternoon of inbox work and telephone calls was interrupted at 4:00 by a call from SecNav on the hotline. He didn't say hello or engage in chatter; he spoke as if choosing his words with extreme care. "I never used to understand why George Sawyer liked being in Crystal City," he began, "but after a year [of wrestling with Naval Materiel] I understand why. That's why I wonder if it's time to move you to the Annex, where the [Navy and Marine personnel] power is."

I was thunderstruck. John Lehman, who very well knows and appreciates the Washington axiom that where you sit is where you stand, was telling me he wants me out of the Pentagon. He continued: "I get the impression that the people on the hill [i.e., in the Annex] give us the mushroom treatment[11] if you're not there to walk the corridor and hear all the gossip." He asked what I thought of the idea. "I don't like it," I said swiftly, going on to ask if this was a gambit to give Jim Finkelstein [SecNav's public affairs officer] my office. I had heard *that* gossip right on the E-Ring. Lehman laughed, and I couldn't tell if he was laughing at paranoid nonsense or for being found out so fast. "No, no,

---

11. This is defined as "being kept in the dark and fed a lot of shit."

no," he said. "It's that increasingly personnel is the key to what we're doing around here, and I've never had a feeling that I knew what was going on."

Aha; he was coming closer to what I suspected: a lack of confidence in my stewardship and a suspicion I am too deferential to the manpower moguls of OpNav and HQMC. "If that's true," I said, "then you've got a problem deeper than location," adding that if he's in any way displeased with my performance, he should say so. I wasn't as impassioned as I have frequently gotten on this subject in these pages, despairing at Lehman's isolation and refusal to share either his thoughts or his time with me. But he got the message. "There's no problem at all," he said. "You're doing a first-rate job. That's not what I had on my mind." Yet he didn't sound convincing. Either out of failed mission or reassurance, he ended the conversation: "Right now I am ordering you to *mull* what we should do." And he rang off.

I know I have done a good job, even a fine one, as AsstSecNav. I know how to relate to people in a way John Lehman never will. But I'm not a Lehman or a Mel Paisley, and that's what he wants. I have never lost sight of the fact that on two occasions Lehman hired me strictly because George Bush asked him to. This is a form of illegitimate parentage that makes both of us uncomfortable. SecNav can't outright fire me for fear of upsetting Bush, and he doesn't like firing people in any event. So he devises clever stratagems like making them give up their office.

I took the subway home, where I spent almost two hours working on this entry. It's good therapy, and unless John Lehman also keeps a journal, it guarantees that I shall have the last word.

Wednesday, 15 May 1985

Don Hittle called on some other business, and I took the opportunity to tell him of yesterday's shocking phone call from Lehman. I see Don as a counselor I can trust, someone who wouldn't hesitate to tell Lehman he was wrong or to tell me that relocating M&RA to the Annex is a brilliant idea. I was therefore grateful when Don swiftly observed, "There are few if any pluses to your going over and getting into the same rabbit hutch with 'em. It's important that they have to get in a car and come over to see *you*." I wondered aloud if Lehman were trying to send me some "signal" about my performance. "No signal," said Don. "John must have pulled it out of left field. If you need any help on this, call me in."

Next I called Dr. Jim Colvard to discuss yesterday's decision for him to come work for me as director of Civilian Personnel Policy. With typical immodesty, he noted, "I'm good, but I'm damn sure not omnipotent." I said that the prime thing I want him to tell me is what's really going on in the civpers world. Colvard will be a management challenge, but I welcome having him on my team—or, in words attributed to LBJ on retaining J. Edgar Hoover as director of the FBI, I'd rather have him inside the tent pissing out than outside the tent pissing in.

Thursday, 16 May 1985

The most interesting event of the day was meeting with Bill Lawrence and Vice Adm. Ron Thunman, deputy CNO for Submarine Warfare, on whether female shipyard workers can embark in subs on sea trials. I have read a lot about this and concluded that the submariners are being pigheaded and fool-hardy to fight the issue, which won't go away.

Ron is a likeable, overgrown farm boy who hews to the holy word among nukes, which is *Never!* He conceded that women could be accommodated aboard subs during sea trials but that the "disruption" and aggravation to the crews would make an always-difficult period unacceptable. I simply don't believe it, but the submariners are not to be persuaded. Bill, perhaps grant-ing his colleague the courtesy of agreement, said he thinks the risk of trouble on board a sub outweighs the "equal opportunity" aspect of the issue. Not having him as an ally hurt my side of the debate.

Friday, 17 May 1985

[Exposé journalist] Jack Anderson got wind of Charlie Wilson's taking two women on board *Saratoga* two weeks ago under the pretext that they were both on his staff. Once this got out, Charlie quickly hired one of the women and reimbursed Navy for the expenses of the other.[12]

There was a lineup at 9:00, with SecNav in good spirits. When I told him I'd be going to his hometown today, he said, "Be sure to have them take you to Pat's Steak," a dive famous for the Philly specialty, cheesesteaks. Added Hugh O'Neill, also a Philadelphian, "Ask for one with extra grease." To which Ev Pyatt rejoined, "They can't *put* extra grease on it!"

Along with Cdr. Patrick Sabadie, one of my special assistants, I left the

---

12. Admiral Hays later told me with a tone of absolute disgust, "For Congressman Wilson to take two girlfriends to sea is one thing. But to have them with him in the admiral's cabin is just tacky."

building in the rain and was driven to Union Station. (Taking a train to board a ship for a weekend's cruise off the Virginia Capes: the AsstSecNavs Roosevelt would have done the same thing!) We pulled into Philadelphia's 30th Street Station at 3:00, to be met by a Navy car and an escort officer. We went all the way down Broad Street to its foot, the historic Philadelphia Navy Yard. It is a fairly beautiful place, with lots of trees, old buildings, and three mothballed cruisers of World War II vintage. *Ticonderoga* be praised, but these were *real* cruisers.

The splendid silhouette of *Wisconsin*, also buttoned up, loomed before us. (A Marine sergeant in my office, using a tape to type up a recent speech, had me saying "The battleship *Wisconsin* is in golf balls.") Already on board was Wayne Arny, in town visiting family. Fighter jock though he be, Wayne is an authority on ships, and he pointed out the size, beauty, and condition of the equipment with the reverent voice of a museum guide. What we both found particularly remarkable is the time-capsule nature of *Wisconsin*. Scattered on desks and bunks were mimeographed sheets from 1958, just before the ship was decommissioned.

Patrick and I had dinner in a restaurant on one of the narrow streets of the Italian section right outside the base. We then proceeded to the pier where *Oliver Hazard Perry* (FFG-7) was tied up. Commissioned in 1977 as lead ship of the guided-missile frigate class, it was recently converted from active to Reserve use. To the announcement "Navy arriving!" I passed briskly through the sideboys. When the bosn (saluting with his left hand) finished piping, I was greeted by the CO and taken down the ship's main passageway (called "Broadway," just as on *Wisconsin*) to the wardroom for coffee.

On a gray evening *Perry* turned down the Delaware River for the six-hour trek to open water, which the captain called "the longest sea detail in the Navy." As I write, we must be getting to the broad part of Delaware Bay, for we've picked up speed and I'm beginning to feel some rolls. It's good to be back at sea again, just a train ride away.

Saturday, 18 May 1985

The ship went through some casualty drills, which Patrick and I observed in Damage Control Central. This was made memorable by some staged realism. One of the ship's corpsmen had a sailor spring into the space screaming and holding up the bloody stump of an arm, a gorily realistic appliqué used in first-aid training. Worse, the fellow had a pump that squirted fake blood all over the place, including my jacket. The damage control officer didn't appreciate the disruption to his calm operation and instructed his people to ignore the unfortunate man and concentrate on saving the ship.

Eschewing the film (*Death Wish II*), I went up to the bridge to drink in the long and lovely sunset. The wind had died down, and the Atlantic had that orange glow which to me is the sea's way of getting comfortable after a tough day. We were then conducting close-in maneuvers with a sister ship, *Patterson*. This was a special sight for Patrick, who was XO of *Patterson* before joining my staff. The wind picked up and the temperature got colder, so I welcomed having some quartermaster-prepared coffee while talking with the XO. Then I went below to my cabin to read a biography of George Bancroft.[13]

Tuesday, 21 May 1985

Charlie Dougherty, my brand-new deputy for Reserve Affairs, asked if I had heard anything from the White House on his becoming a DASN. I hadn't and called Jane Kenny in the VP's office to find out. Jane called back to say Charlie has a genuine problem: the political office under Ed Rollins has denied Charlie clearance because of his weak support for RR in the House during 1981–82 and because he endorsed some Democrats for office in Philadelphia. Charlie had a tough district for a Republican [in North Philadelphia], and only efforts by the White House (possibly Ed himself) kept him from switching parties to save his skin in 1982. He didn't, and he went down in the Democratic sweep—no doubt because his constituents considered him *too* pro-Reagan. Marybel Batjer was furious at the White House for not giving a hint of this problem until now. We both believe that this is unbelievable treatment for a former Republican member of Congress.

The main event of the day—leading to the main event of the season— was the much-awaited OpNav report on Gulf Coast homeporting. The team leader, Capt. Jim Ridge, said: "If you want a base for the 21st century, I'd say Pascagoula. If you want a base for now, I'd say Corpus Christi." I conceded that Galveston is a less desirable home for the battleship than is Pascagoula, but there is sound demographic sense to putting the frigates there, since the Houston area has 90% of the reservists needed to man two ships.

---

13. While SecNav from 1845–46, Bancroft founded the Naval Academy, whose huge dormitory is named in his honor.

Wednesday, 22 May 1985

At the Naval Academy graduation today, I sat in the superintendent's section with the foreign military attachés, US flag officers, and political appointees. The atmosphere was infectiously festive, enlivened by the band's light airs, the Blue Angels in tight formation streaking not far overhead, and the youthful radiance of the Class of 1985.

The crowd cheered as the white-topped Marine helo bearing the Reagans landed behind the stadium. The President was announced by "Ruffles and Flourishes," "Hail to the Chief," and (due to a hang fire) a twenty-*two*-gun salute. Chuck Larson delivered a brief and fond valedictory to the class with all his South Dakota boyishness. Then SecNav introduced the President, who was making his first appearance at Annapolis.

RR praised the Navy and took pride in its buildup "under John Lehman's aggressive leadership." His speech mentioned the USNA grads in his administration: Robert (Bud) McFarlane and Vice Adm. John Poindexter at the National Security Council and "James" Webb at Defense. Reagan quoted at length a part of Jim's [novel] *A Sense of Honor,* which describes his senior year at the Academy in 1968. It was splendid and appropriate, but being singled out by the president of the United States did absolutely nothing to moderate Jim's ego. Indeed, no later than mid-afternoon there was hand-delivered to my office (and how many others in the Pentagon?) a copy of the President's graduation address with a cover note from Jim expressing the hope that "you will find President Reagan's comments useful in many ways."[14]

The President handed out the diplomas to the first 100 members of the class, as is customary, but continued to stand in the direct sun and shake hands with every other graduating midshipman—a gigantic thrill and tribute to them all, as well as an act of spectacular physical endurance by a 74-year-old man. [*Only eight weeks later, Reagan would have major surgery for colon cancer.*] This did lengthen the proceedings by about an hour. All ended with the traditional cheers "for those who are departing" and "those who are staying behind" and the famous hat toss, with a lot of after-tossing.

I had been invited to a buffet lunch at the Superintendent's House, but I skipped it so as not to be late for the scheduled 3 p.m. meeting with SecNav on Gulf Coast homeporting. Captain Ridge had barely begun his report

---

14. When Jim ran for the Senate as a Democrat almost twenty-one years later, Republicans attacked him for resigning as SecNav in a policy dispute in 1988. He responded with a TV ad that featured a clip of Reagan praising him that day in May 1985, and the issue promptly died.

when Paul Miller interrupted to tell the Secretary that "the System" had announced a politically sensitive contract that Lehman had wanted to personally notify certain members of Congress beforehand. The Secretary laughed:
"It's just like Admiral Zumwalt's kiddie car seat," he said, pretending to be
a child gaily turning a fake automobile steering wheel. "Gee, it's fun being
SecNav! You've got a lot of control!" Then he said, deadpan, "But you have
to expect this sort of thing will happen now and then. *It's only the fortieth
fucking time!*"

After Capt. Ridge went through the study, Lehman pronounced it "tremendous, great, perfect. . . . It gives us maximum variants and options." In
particular, he liked CNO's proposal to split the battleship group, [the training carrier] *Lexington,* and another carrier among four states, including Alabama. Speaking "in my role as the greasy politician," Lehman said, "I have no
support from Alabama; the Army owns it." Wayne Arny and I argued against
putting Reserve frigates in Mobile, pointing out the greater population den-
sity of the Houston-Galveston area.

Wayne came with me to my office, and we agreed that Texas must be
tied to the Navy with more than just a few minesweeps. Lehman knows he
has to take care of Texas somehow. I have some hometown prestige riding on
this. The least I can bring home is a naval station on Galveston with frigates.

Wednesday, 29 May 1985

Ten o'clock brought the farewell ceremony for Fred Davidson. An all-star
cast turned up to witness the happy event. Lehman draped the Navy's Distinguished Civilian Service Medal around Fred's white linen suit and credited
him with "revolutionary" changes in the reserves. Of course, everyone in the
room knew that it was John Lehman who pushed those reforms, and in his
response Fred duly gave him this credit. He also gave him a jeweled dagger
from Turkey and a certificate of appreciation from the National Committee for Support of the Guard and Reserve. "Fred, do you know something I
don't?" Lehman asked. "I thought *you* were leaving." Joe Taussig had the best
line: he said the SecNav Mess is naming a sandwich in Fred's memory: "It has
tongue, ham, and baloney."

Friday, 31 May 1985

Today on Bill and Diane Lawrence's recommendation I interviewed Alice
Stratton for the new position of DASN for Personnel & Families. She flew in

from Newport, where her husband, Capt. Dick Stratton, is CO of the Naval Academy Prep School. It was clear from the outset that Alice was exactly the person I wanted for the job. She would have 100% credibility as a down-to-earth Navy wife who, for the six years when Dick was a POW, experienced family strains far beyond those of today's Navy and Marine Corps spouses. She started the family service center at Annapolis and has long been a social worker among Navy families. She is therefore not the "white-gloved admiral's wife" that Marybel Batjer thinks I want.

Friday, 7 June 1985

I received a clipping from the *Galveston Daily News* sent by Mayor Jan Coggeshall. It was a letter to the editor from one Luvine Elias, who appears to be a mystic of some sort. Ms. Elias told her fellow Galvestonians how they can secure *Wisconsin* for the island: "From now on to the 4th of July, make it your chore to convince the secretary of the Navy, either by writing letters or parapsychology, psychokinetics, or skewing (*sic*). Black candle rituals are too powerful. Not for amateurs. Misapplied, they could dull or addle minds, and we don't want to dull or addle the secretary of the Navy's mind."

Monday, 10 June 1985

SecNav called me on the hotline to "shoot down here," which I duly did. I had no idea what was on his mind and accordingly was rather nervous, which I hid as Lehman asked me to pull up a chair and finished some business with Como. Paul David Miller. He waited till the EA had left the room before he began speaking with me, a rare sign that he wanted total confidentiality. Was I about to be dressed down? No, he does that only when others are present. It was on the Gulf Coast homeporting decision—not on the site selection per se but how the announcement can best help the Vice President, knowing that "Feel" Gramm will try to take total credit for any homeporting in Texas. The deal is that Gramm will make the announcement but give GB some credit; no doubt reporters will have to listen very carefully to hear it. The signal Lehman was giving me—and once again I was amused at the games he plays—was how much he is looking out for GB's interests for 1988.

From this meeting I took the feeling that I have more job security than I feared of late. If Lehman considers it helpful for his sake in a future Bush administration to let me know the crafty things he is doing for GB, then he'll want me around as a witness. It's crazy, of course: a man of Lehman's

talent, cleverness, and connections oughtn't need me to become secretary of
Defense someday.

Tuesday, 11 June 1985

Today Lehman gave lunch to members of the Naval Academy Board of Visitors to enlist them in his battle to reform USNA's admissions and curriculum policy.[15] Among those attending were GB's close friend from Houston,
C. Fred Chambers [for whom their cocker spaniel, C. Fred, was named], and
Lynn Wyatt, the Houston socialite who is a friend of Lehman through his
first cousin once-removed, the late Princess Grace of Monaco. I had never
met the fabled Lynn, currently on the cover of *Town & Country* as one of
ten "first ladies of charity" around the country. She is a bright, cheery Texas
gal rather than a snooty sort. When SecNav arrived, he kissed her on both
cheeks.

Lehman was fresh from holding a press conference with CNO on the
"very serious" damage to naval communications done over a period of almost
20 years by the spy ring led by ex–chief petty officer John Walker, some
friends, and members of his family. This story has been the rage for three
weeks, and it has cast a pall over Lehman. In this dark mood, he told his
guests a remarkable story. In the mid-1970s [when he was deputy director of
the Arms Control & Disarmament Agency], the FBI told Lehman he was just
about to hire the top East German intelligence agent in the US. The young
man, James Sattler, had ingratiated himself with the eminences of the Atlantic Council (an Eastern establishment, pro-NATO group), who wrote letters
of recommendation for him. Had Sattler not been nabbed, Lehman told us,
"I can assure you he would be *at least* an assistant secretary of State today."
The anecdote, both thrilling and frightening, had special meaning to me, for
I have been struck by Lehman's poor choices of people to work with him.
No doubt he agreed to hire Sattler to please the man's recommenders—not
unlike hiring *me* on two occasions.

After lunch, I escorted the lovely Lynn Wyatt to the Mall Entrance. She

---

15. Each service academy has a board of visitors composed of four senators, five representatives,
and six citizens appointed by the president for three-year terms. The presidential appointments
are considered "plums." The BOVs are not fiduciary boards like state university boards of re-
gents but are overseers who submit an annual report to the president (via the service chain of
command and the secretary of Defense) on their findings and conclusions. The author was appointed to the Naval Academy board by President George H. W. Bush on his last day in office,
serving from 1993–96 and as chairman in 1995.

admits to knowing nothing about the Navy and wants to learn more so she can have a better feel for what the Academy is trying to produce. I said it is no problem to get her out to the fleet, in particular the Sixth Fleet during one of her European sojourns. "I don't want [the naval officers] to think there's this girl they have to take care of," she said. I assured her that with SecNav's cachet she will be treated royally.

Thursday, 13 June 1985

Tomorrow is Col. Doc White's last day as my Marine aide. A true infantry-man, he never liked E-Ring duty, saying, "I'm not a politician." This after-noon we talked over the past year. He was plainly uncomfortable hearing himself praised. He doesn't want an office ceremony to bid him goodbye, and he specifically doesn't want the Legion of Merit. Pointing to the rows of ribbons on his chest, Doc said, "I can tell you what I did to earn each one of these. I don't think I did anything to earn the LOM." I went over to a desk drawer to get the medal and, in a light-hearted way, said that SecNav had already signed the papers and he had to accept it. For a long while, I thought he would actually refuse. Finally, I "ordered" him to accept it, and he did.

Friday, 21 June 1985

My final event at Quantico today was unscheduled. Two days ago, gunmen in San Salvador shot and killed six Americans in a restaurant, four of them Marine guards at the US embassy. Because the Marine Security Guard School is located at Quantico, I asked Colonel Walls [Doc's successor] to set up a quick stop there so I could express my sympathy and support.

We were met by the new CO, Col. Walt Boomer,[16] a tall, erect southerner who was clearly distraught at the shootings. Two of the four Marines gradu-ated from the school in February, and one of them was the honor graduate. In order to perk up morale, Colonel Boomer ordered current students to go ahead with a previously planned picnic and softball game. The great fear is that Marine guards will become targets throughout the world. They lead very vulnerable lives, sleeping in unguarded "Marine houses" apart from em-bassy compounds. In many capitals, there are perhaps only one or two decent

---

16. Walt would lead Marine forces in Kuwait and Iraq during the first Gulf War and rise to four-star rank, serving as assistant commandant.

places to eat, which the Marines are discouraged from frequenting so as not to establish a pattern on which terrorists can plan.

Tuesday, 25 June 1985

After hearing of some childish rant against the Navy by a congressman, SecNav turned to his general counsel and asked, "Walter, how can it possibly be against the law to be in contempt of Congress?"

Wednesday, 26 June 1985

SecDef Weinberger has decided to put *Missouri* on Treasure Island and the destroyers and frigates at Hunter's Point. On the Gulf Coast, Texas is the big winner. Corpus will get *Wisconsin,* a cruiser, a destroyer, and *Lexington,* the training carrier now at Pensacola. Galveston will get the two reserve frigates and two minesweepers, making for a tidy little naval station. Lehman scattered other ships in all the other competing ports: destroyers in Mobile, cruisers in Pascagoula, a conventional carrier in Pensacola, and a reserve oiler in Lake Charles. The plan has something for everyone and everything but subtlety. Later, when asked the name of the carrier to go to Pensacola, Lehman himself snorted, "The USS *Pork Barrel.*"

The fact that Texas came out so richly was due to two curious personalities, Phil Gramm and John Lehman. For Gramm, it is a huge hunk of bacon to bring home, a perfect parallel with young Congressman Lyndon Johnson's getting the naval air station for Corpus some 45 years ago. (Not for nothing does Gramm have a portrait of LBJ on the wall of his private office.)[17] For Lehman, pleasing Gramm is a means of cementing him as Navy's man on the SASC. It also serves Lehman's mid-range objective of becoming SecDef in a future Bush (or Gramm) administration.

To the extent that C. G. Untermeyer played a role in snaring ships for Texas, it was simply by being a constant reminder to John Lehman of George Bush. I amuse myself with the thought that Texas Democratic potentates like Mark White, Bill Hobby, and Kathy Whitmire may give me all the credit, simply because they don't want any of it to go to Phil Gramm. Thus will my (undeserved) reputation be made as a young Texan in Washington who copped a big public works project for the Lone Star State.

Waiting for me at home was a note that GB personally typed with in-

---

17. Gramm in fact held Johnson's old Senate seat.

structions to his staff, "send to his residence as-is—no copies." It said: "I have talked battle groups with John Lehman. I am satisfied with the [announcement] arrangements, having had a good talk with Gramm." Then he added, "Come over—lots of politics to discuss."

Tuesday, 2 July 1985

In an interview on homeporting today with Tim Carrington, Pentagon correspondent for the *Wall Street Journal,* I said, "For John Lehman, it's no trick to pull a rabbit out of a hat. When called upon, he can pull a hat out of a rabbit."

Chapter 9

Punching the Feather Bed

Saturday, 13 July 1985

President Reagan was successfully operated on today at Bethesda [Naval Hospital] for removal of a cancerous growth in his intestine. All the medical bulletins are glowing, but just in case they might not be, RR transferred the powers of the presidency until further notice to Vice President Bush under the 25th Amendment to the Constitution.

Lt. Col. Terry Mattke, a Marine aide to the VP, told me on 30 March 1988 of "the first time George Bush was president"—the eight-hour period when RR was unconscious during and after his colon cancer operation. Then–chief of staff Don Regan told the Vice President, on vacation in Maine, not to bother about coming back to Washington. Mattke said that Bush held a "council of war" at Walker's Point with his family, received medical advice from his own physician, and even consulted his houseguest, the presiding bishop of the Episcopal Church. Bush then decided to overrule Regan and return to the capital.

Monday, 15 July 1985

Lunchtime brought the conclusive meeting on civilian personnel. The Under and Don Hittle conspired to keep the wild man Mel Paisley out of it, but the first thing Lehman asked when he entered his private dining room was, "Where's Mel? Get him in here; he has some strong opinions on this." As indeed he did. Mel acts strictly out of impulse, typically without reference to the piece of business under discussion. In the same mood, the Secretary ordered all SESers [senior civil servants] who have been in their current jobs for five years or longer to be rotated in two months. This will cause pandemonium, but that's the way Lehman (and Paisley) like to operate. "The only reason I have any power over the blue-suiters [the unformed Navy] is because I personally decide every assignment of every flag officer," he told us. "Nothing will happen in the civilian world until I can do the same." He and Mel are absolutely convinced that Navy's "civil serpents" think they own their desks and can ignore secretaries and admirals alike.

Wednesday, 17 July 1985

My staff gave me some disturbing news: late last week, Vice Adm. Bill Lawrence checked himself into Bethesda with severe depression. The official word is that he went on leave, but the truth got out (probably from the hospital), inspiring rumors that he had had a seizure or a heart attack. CNO told Bill he will keep him as chief of Naval Personnel but not include him in the imminent round of "flag slatings," in which he would have picked up a fourth star and become VCNO. I feel sorry for Bill as a friend, but inasmuch as I'm not supposed to know any of this, I must hold off expressing my sympathy.

Thursday, 18 July 1985

Shortly before noon on the steps of the Mall Entrance, I welcomed Ken Starr, the 39-year-old judge of the US Court of Appeals for the DC Circuit. He was "guest Starr" at my monthly luncheon for the M&RA staff [held to expose them to interesting non-Pentagon personalities and responsibilities]. I introduced Ken by saying that he serves on the court considered second in importance only to the Supreme Court, and I predicted he will one day sit on the higher bench "because he has raw youth in his favor, and presidents of the United States over the next 25 years will have the chance to act appropriately."[1] Ken spoke like a popular law professor, tossing out witty commentaries on constitutionalism and citing regulatory cases that nonlawyers could understand. He quoted Justice Brandeis as saying that the difference between the judicial branch and the other two branches is "we do our own work." Staffed by only a few very young clerks and forbidden to consult outside "experts," appellate judges must master complex issues on their own — a challenge Ken obviously enjoys.

---

1. In 1989, Ken left the DC Circuit to become US solicitor general. Were it not for his later service as special prosecutor in the Whitewater and Monica Lewinsky cases involving President Bill Clinton, I am convinced my prediction would have come true. Indeed, Ken might have been appointed chief justice in 2005 instead of John Roberts, who had been his deputy in the Solicitor General's office. In 2010, Ken became president of Baylor University.

Saturday, 20 July 1985

I took the subway downtown, walking quickly to the East Wing entrance to the White House. Late yesterday, all political appointees in the Administration were offered tickets to attend President Reagan's homecoming from the hospital. Most of the 1000 or so who came were in their twenties. Senior appointees could be easily picked out; they were the ones gamely sweating in business suits. The AsstSecNav, however, was in khakis and a sport shirt, knowing that RR would be casually dressed.

I arrived just as the President's weekly radio address—delivered live from Bethesda—was being broadcast to the crowd on the South Lawn. He thanked the doctors and nurses who cared for him; urged his listeners with health problems to seek help right away ("Tell 'em Dr. Reagan sent you"); joked about the budget battle now on Capitol Hill ("Excuse me, but I don't have as much stomach for that sort of thing anymore"); and made a touching tribute to Nancy: "Thanks, partner. And, say, are you doing anything tonight?"

As Marine One settled onto the lawn, a Dixieland combo from the Marine Band played "When You're Smiling." The President emerged from the chopper wearing a western snap shirt and jeans, escorted by Nancy in one of her many red dresses. He walked a bit stiffly and slowly, and the crowd cheered lustily, lofting multicolored balloons and waving handmade signs. After greeting the Cabinet, the Reagans entered the White House, to walk out a few minutes later onto the Blue Room balcony to stand and wave above a printed banner that said, "Welcome home, Mr. President!"

Mitchell Stanley, an aide to Ed Meese when we both worked in the West Wing and now an appointee at Commerce, asked, "As one former White House staffer to another, do you miss it?" I replied that "I miss *this*"—the easy access to special moments in the Reagan presidency.

Thursday, 25 July 1985

Tonight I attended the "party leader dinner" of the International Democrat (*sic*) Union, an organization of conservative political parties from all over the world, including some not-so-democratic but noncommunist lands. It was put together by Dick Allen after his resignation as national security advisor. The main stars tonight were GB and Margaret Thatcher, but also at the head table were the prime ministers of Belize, Jamaica, Dominica, Denmark,

Norway, and Grenada, plus Mayor Jacques Chirac of Paris and Franz-Josef Strauss, minister-president of Bavaria.

As the foreign leaders were announced, they mounted the dais with great dignity and deliberateness. But GB acted just like the Senate candidate he was in 1964: in those JFK-influenced days, "vigah" became the standard for American politicians, who ever since have been expected to bound onto platforms. This Bush did, starting a domino-like cascade of falling flags, which the foreign leaders struggled to catch while an oblivious US vice president strode down the line, grabbing their hands.

"Mrs. T" was the undisputed favorite of the crowd. She began with a gracious, lyrical tribute to GB, RR, and the US and then picked up the tempo to pound the theme that "freedom and responsibility are linked indissolubly." She closed with a poem[2] of Kipling's:

> Keep ye the law—be swift in all obedience;
> Clear the land of evil, drive the road and bridge the ford . . .

Friday, 26 July 1985

For security reasons, the Pentagon arrival ceremony for PM Thatcher was held in the central courtyard (nicknamed "Ground Zero" by the Pentagonians who lunch there). John Lehman, anglophile supreme, chose not to attend, and with UnSec Goodrich on leave, the duty fell to me. I was of course delighted and found myself the only non-service secretary and non-JCS member in the official receiving line. Protocol put Army Secretary Jack Marsh first, me second, Air Force Secretary Verne Orr third, and General Vessey, chairman of the Joint Chiefs, fourth. I chatted with Marsh, who (unlike Lehman) loves military ceremony and seemed affronted that Navy would send a mere assistant secretary to today's big event.

SecDef Weinberger appeared and nodded to us all, making some light remarks till the PM's motorcade swung into place. Mrs. Thatcher wore a print dress and carried a handbag. With practiced aplomb, she stood at attention, handbag at the left, during the playing of the anthems. She and Weinberger trooped the line and then, back in their designated spots, watched as the Army Fife & Drum Corps, in white wigs and tricorn hats, slow-marched past, playing "The British Grenadier." Mrs. Thatcher was visibly thrilled,

---

2. "A Song of the English," ca. 1915.

causing Sec. Marsh to beam with pleasure and pride. SecDef then introduced Mrs. T to us official welcomers. She shook hands with Marsh and, on taking my hand, declared that the ceremony was "the most *mahvelous* I have *ever* seen!" I smiled and said nothing till she had passed, at which time I turned to the seething Marsh and said, "That was meant for you."

Friday, 2 August 1985

I was called by Patty Presock in the VP's office, who brightly said, "The Vice President wants to buy you a drink. Can you come by the residence at 6:30?"

Alighting at the gate of the VP's House, I walked up to find GB and Lee Atwater sitting on wicker chairs on the verandah watching the evening news. They had just come back from running together. Soon we moved indoors, up to the second-floor den, where the TV reception was better. There was a long feature on tomorrow's special election in the First Congressional District of Texas, with two segments of tape featuring Lee. It's a tight race, but Lee is nervously optimistic our candidate can win. [*The GOP lost.*]

Lee left for home, and I was invited to stay for supper, served on trays back on the verandah. GB thinks the new staff situation is going "pretty well," though he doesn't like the looseness with which Craig Fuller and his people talk to the press and how they act as if all that occurred before their arrival was disorder and amateurism. David Hoffman of the *Post* wrote an article that said when RR was in the hospital, Craig called old Reagan political sage Stu Spencer to inquire what the VP should do. Answer: take all leads from Nancy. Loyal to the old team, GB found this repugnant. "I told Craig it made it look as if I needed someone to tell me how to act. I rather think I know how to conduct myself at such times," GB said, with clear reference to 30 March 1981. All this is not to say Craig is in trouble, just that he still has a lot to learn about GB's way of doing business.

Thursday, 8 August 1985

Vice Adm. Ron Thunman, deputy CNO for submarine warfare, was waiting for me at Andrews. The tall, shambling Thunman is one of the most amiable of the barons and has long been eager to teach me about submarines. So today and tomorrow he is my personal escort on my first sub cruise. During the 2½-hour flight down to Ft. Lauderdale aboard a T39, we had a non-stop discussion on the retention, pays, sea-shore rotation, and psychological stresses of the men who serve on subs.

Friday, 9 August 1985

About 9:15, Navy cars lined up to take Ron and me the short distance to Port Everglades. There we boarded a pilot boat and lingered off the quay in the sparkling sunshine until the black hull of USS *Norfolk* (SSN-714) appeared out of the morning glare.

We approached her on the port side, where a sort of canvas ladder (with wooden staves as steps) was laid down the sloping hull. A beefy fellow tethered to the deck stood by to grab us. With what I hope was grace, I jumped from the pilot boat into his arms and was welcomed by the XO. I then went down the hatch with him to the snug wardroom. In addition to a basic introduction to the 365-foot-long ship, I was given a small device to wear on my belt. It measures radiation in millirems, and the corpsman who outfitted us said he doubted we would get even one millirem while we're on board—and that more likely from the sun up on the bridge than from the nuclear power plant.

Climbing another ladder, I arrived atop the sub's "sail," where there is a small area close by the periscopes and other retractable gear. As we headed out to sea on a glassy Atlantic, the water swept over the sub's bow in a perfect veil and the powerful screw kicked up a wide wake. The vista was wonderful, and I drank it all in, knowing that soon we would be underneath it.

I was standing in the control room—where the ship is navigated, steered, and fought—when we submerged. Just as in the World War II movies, the command is, "Dive! Dive! Dive!" followed by the sounding of an oogah horn. A TV monitor displays the view through the periscope, which was of the deck awash moments before we sank beneath its surface. According to doctrine, we went to 150 feet and leveled off, later cruising at 450 feet. Descent was rapid and at about a ten-degree angle. Except in times of vertical movement, there is almost no sensation of being underway: no roll, no pitch, and, because so much is done to dampen noise, no engine vibration.

Life aboard a sub is like being in a windowless building with limited space. I certainly prefer the surface Navy, but I don't think I would go crazy aboard a sub. According to what everyone tells me, few people ever do freak out. The corpsman told me that he looks after the mental health of the crew, sitting in on every meal to spot guys who appear tense or aren't eating well. The special isolation and close quarters in which submariners live is overcome by what the corpsman called "craziness," meaning harmless, good-natured nuttiness to reduce tensions. From my impression, the 110 sailors and 20 officers aboard *Norfolk* are bright, affable people who are more outgoing than the introverted chess players I had imagined nukes to be. I was pleased that some sailors unabashedly came by the XO's cabin (where Ron and I are bunking) to talk to me. That hasn't happened on any of the surface ships I've visited.

Saturday, 10 August 1985

Today at 5:30 I was awakened by the announcement "Prepare to surface!" followed a while later by "Surface! Surface! Surface!" After washing and dressing, I went to the wardroom for coffee and coffee cake and where I made departing remarks to a groggy audience. I then climbed to the bridge, where George Walls was already admiring the view as we passed through fishing boats and pleasure craft. Bridge duty is prized because in some ports girls on board the boats will take off their tops—or so the story is reported on the mess decks.

I leapt from the sub onto a pilot boat, which sped off toward Ft. Lauderdale three miles distant. Looking back, I saw *Norfolk* riding high and black on a silvered sea—impressive, menacing, and death dealing, though the atmosphere on board had been anything but grim.

On the flight back to Washington, Ron Thunman told some anecdotes about Admiral Rickover. So august and so fearsome was Rickover that it's only now, four years after SecNav cashiered him, that submariners dare to speak ill of him to outsiders. Even so, at over 40,000 feet in a small jet with just George nearby, the three-star admiral leaned in close to me and spoke in a whisper.

Thursday, 15 August 1985

Larry Korb hosted the "counterparts" breakfast to tell us what was already in today's paper, namely that he has resigned as AsstSecDef for manpower to become vice president for government relations at Raytheon. Only Del Spurlock [of Army] gave Larry a tribute; Ty McCoy and I were silent.

Not long after I got back to my office, Larry called. "I didn't want to embarrass you in front of your colleagues," he explained, "but I understand you are under consideration for this job." Not knowing whether Korb had heard that officially from Weinberger or Taft, I said, "I've already got the best job in military manpower." Korb, who said he has only heard rumors that I might succeed him, agreed. "You do have a great job," he said, "and I tell you as a friend and as someone who is going to go far in this town, I wouldn't touch

OSD at this time. You can't get people to focus on the issues. Weinberger may not leave, but he ought to."

Friday, 16 August 1985

The Navy surgeon general, Vice Adm. Lew Seaton, made one of his house calls this afternoon. We had a classic go-round on the quality of medical care. I said that common elements I see in all reports on medical "misadventures" are that someone failed to listen to the patient or to believe the seriousness of his/her symptoms or neglected to take certain necessary actions. In response to all such critiques, Seaton either says it wasn't true *or* it doesn't happen as often as one might think *or* that it also happens in the private sector *or* that it's inevitable in the practice of medicine. If, as FDR said, dealing with admirals is like punching a feather bed, then dealing with admirals who are also *doctors* is worse.

I agree with Dr. Bud Mayer,[3] who once said that had Lew gone into the priesthood instead of the Navy, he would today be an archbishop and a Jesuit at that. I make as much progress discussing the quality of naval medicine with Admiral Seaton as if I were debating the virgin birth with Cardinal Seaton.

Thursday, 22 August 1985

Today I attended a briefing on the problem posed to the Armed Forces by AIDS (Acquired Immune Deficiency Syndrome). It is the modern plague, incurable and infectious, and it has begun to leap out of the homosexual community into the heterosexual world, including the military. The blood trait of AIDS can at least be screened in the lab, and the Army briefer, a Colonel Tramont, said that Walter Reed [hospital] has discovered 48 cases of AIDS in just six weeks of screening. Gay groups have been screaming that DOD is using AIDS as an excuse to identify and persecute homosexuals. But Colonel Tramont persuaded them that the Armed Forces have a particular problem in that we administer live vaccines to our recruits. If any of them have AIDS, then they'll contract the disease against which they're being inoculated. Our only hope is identification and containment.

---

3. Dr. William (Bud) Mayer, the assistant secretary of Defense for Health Affairs, was a personality/political doc with white hair and red eyebrows, looking a lot like Burt Lancaster. He was in Governor Reagan's cabinet in California, and with his clear ideas, warm manner of speaking, and general appearance, it's easy to see how he would have been popular with the Reagans.

Dr. Bill Narva and I agree that Navy should change its policy of mustering out people for homosexuality if they have AIDS in order to encourage victims to give us (in confidentiality) the names of their partners, so we can contain the disease.

Monday, 26 August 1985

While speaking with Marybel Batjer, I took the opportunity to say that I don't want to succeed Larry Korb as AsstSecDef. I was reassured when she told me SecDef has already selected someone else. *Navy Times* today said it will be Chapman Cox, twice my predecessor and now DOD general counsel.

Tuesday, 27 August 1985

The first thing I did today was call Dr. Bud Mayer to propose that we start screening all recruits for the presence of the AIDS antibody. Oh, no, Bud said: we have to wait for the report of the Armed Forces Epidemiological Board (the Epi Board) in mid-September. And what are they likely to recommend? Why, screening the blood of all recruits, of course. Bud said we at Navy can take "preliminary steps" for screening so long as we don't give the impression that DOD has adopted any policy yet.

I raised this matter at the SecNav lineup and also recommended that we no longer muster out men who confess to homosexuality in the process of being treated for AIDS. Lehman agreed and asked for a policy that protects persons from "adverse action" and to deal with them strictly as medical discharge cases.

My lunch guest was Ty McCoy. He is a motor mouth, but if one is patient through all the patter, the egoism, and the obscenity, a few nuggets of wisdom can emerge. Ty thinks it's time for him, after four years in office, to quit and get a job in aerospace or consulting. "If fuckin' Korb[4] can get $150,000 [from Raytheon], I sure as shit better get $200,000 or I'm a fool," he said. Ty added that I ought to do the same while I can still trade on my ties with GB and DOD. I demurred, noting that he has four years in grade while I have less than two. That doesn't matter, he insisted: in Washington, one year is as good as five for resume purposes. As we walked down the Navy corridor after lunch, I pointed out the portrait of Thomas Gilmer, who was

---

4. This was Ty's unvarying way of referring to the Asst SecDef, as if Larry's name were the Honorable Lawrence J. Fuckinkorb.

SecNav for all of nine days before being killed in the *Princeton* disaster.[5] "See what I told you!" Ty said. "That fucker was in for only nine fuckin' days, and he gets his picture here the same as all the others!"

Wednesday, 28 August 1985

[In San Antonio to address the Fleet Reserve Association,] I was escorted down the center aisle toward the dais as the conventioneers clapped in march time. The average age of the thousand or so attendees seemed to be 65; very few looked younger than 60. Here was the World War II generation, all dear older people, Middle America incarnate, with the angel of death hovering over them and the FRA. My remarks, half prepared and half extempore, could not fail to please, since I praised them and the US Navy. At one point, I said our current crop of sailors is "the best ever, except that I see before me the faces of some sailors we were once mighty glad to have."

Afterwards I met with my former colleague State Rep. Frank Tejeda (D-San Antonio), whom I have always liked and admired. Frank is running for the Texas Senate next year. He is confident of victory but won't slacken his active pace, even this early. "In the Marine Corps [during Vietnam] I learned that the more you sweat in peacetime the less you bleed in wartime," Frank said.[6]

Tuesday, 3 September 1985

Lehman convened the topmost uniformed and civilian officials in the Department to motivate and mobilize them against the forces he sees coalescing against the Navy—specifically Army, Air Force, and the JCS. "We shouldn't lose sight of the fact we are the keystone of the national security," he said. "If we lose, then all America is endangered." A true Kissingerian, Lehman loves the drama of high intellectual and political battle against a malign conspiracy, even if he must invent it.

---

5. A new gun on the warship *Princeton* exploded during a demonstration on the Potomac for various Washington dignitaries in February 1844. In addition to Gilmer, the accident killed the secretary of State (who had been SecNav), a congressman, and a senator. It would have killed President John Tyler as well, only he went below decks minutes before the explosion.

6. Frank was elected a state senator in 1986 and six years later was elected to Congress. He would have become a major leader, especially on defense issues, except that he was tragically felled by a brain tumor in 1997 at age fifty-one.

Thursday, 5 September 1985

I sat down with Lew Seaton to hear his plans for screening the blood of all recruits for AIDS antibodies. We agreed that if a recruit comes up positive on the initial screening he should be allowed to continue training while awaiting the results of the second more thorough confirmatory test. This way we can reduce the stigmatization and worry for the guy.

Thursday, 19 September 1985

I convened a meeting on blood testing recruits for the AIDS virus. Acting at Army's insistence, OSD has directed that recruits be removed from training if their blood tests positive on the basic screen, on which there are an estimated 90% false positives. I prefer that they continue training, ignorant of the first results, until the more definitive confirmatory test comes back positive.

Given the OSD directive, should the recruit be told why he's being removed from training? The draft MedCom message flatly said no, with which I disagree, saying the kids will either figure it out or suspect the worst anyway. My opinion carried, and I emphasized that telling the person he tested positive must be done sensitively with full psychological support. The very nature of the disease will cause (and already has caused) panic among victims and the general public alike. But at least we can try to deal with the mental as well as physical well being of our people, especially those whose confirmatory test comes back negative and who can then return to training.

Friday, 20 September 1985

This evening I went to the Vice President's House for a dinner given for key contributors to his PAC [political action committee], the Fund for America's Future. Speaking to diners in a tent erected on the Observatory grounds, GB said, "what matters most to Bar and me is friendship. We can't forget those who helped us get to where are, living in this beautiful place." Cracked gagman Dick Jackman, "I didn't realize that we force the vice president of the United States to live in a tent in somebody's backyard. But when he was a boy, George Bush had two dreams: one was to be a great leader of this country, and the other was to join the circus. So, he came to Washington, where he can do both."

Friday, 27 September 1985

Today George Walls and I journeyed to Bethesda and the campus of the Uniformed Services University of the Health Sciences, the Armed Forces medical school. USUHS (pronounced "you sis") may be the only abbreviation in America in which the "US" doesn't stand for United States and the "HS" doesn't stand for high school. Its vice president and ranking military officer is Dr. Bill Narva. The walls of his relatively small office are completely covered with photos signed by CNOs, presidents, SecNavs, and numerous admirals. Bill is the naval equivalent of the civilian "society doctor," such as [my grandmother's] physician in New York, who had signed photos of stage stars in his waiting room. [My sister] Margot saw one there: "To my *dahling* Dr. Garbatt. Love, Tallulah Bankhead." A dermatologist, Bill is, appropriately, smooth of skin and thus all the more slippery. Dick Elster calls him "Dr. Nova," and I suspect that our gutsier health initiatives disappear into the self-same celestial void.

Sunday, 29 September 1985

Capt. Gene Peltier died yesterday of a viral infection on top of leukemia. He was the best thing to happen to me when I came to the Navy Department in March 1983. Gene's knowledge and calm good judgment helped me learn the world of installations and facilities as fast as I did, and his splendid humor (masked by the exterior of a Trappist monk) made annoyances such as dealing with OSD a great game. Chapman Cox and I maintain that without Gene's advice and hard work, which made both of us look good, we never would have been promoted to AsstSecNav. I shall miss him as I have Mrs. Peggy Kauffman, a loss that the passage of time will not diminish.

Monday, 30 September 1985

I got a call from the political aide to Drew Lewis, who said that the former secretary of Transportation and Pennsylvania politico is "100 percent opposed" to making Charlie Dougherty my deputy for Reserve Affairs. Oddly, it was Lewis himself who asked SecNav to hire Charlie in the first place. In any event, it's curtains for Charlie—and the start of a long process to find a politically clearable alternate, with another Fred Davidson always a threat. I called SecNav on the hotline to tell him this. Lehman said, "Let's wait it out. Time wounds all heels."

Friday, 4 October 1985

The proposed AIDS policy has sat on Paul David Miller's desk for a month, missing us the chance to be out front on the issue. As George Sawyer once said out of frustration with Lehman for failure to act on some matter, "A boss's first obligation is to answer the mail."

Saturday, 5 October 1985

[In St. Louis for the annual conference of the Association of NROTC Colleges and Universities] my staff and I gave a rundown on everything we have been doing on officer education. We tried to elicit a response from the audience of academics, but there was silence. Dwight McDonald of the University of Texas said they were all so delighted that they truly had nothing to add. He recited the *Nunc Dimittis* from the Mass: "Now lettest Thou Thy servant depart in peace."

Wednesday, 9 October 1985

Bud Mayer called a meeting to hammer out a uniform DOD policy on AIDS. Army Sec. John Marsh feels strongly that anyone with the AIDS antibody should be mustered out of the ranks. His assistant secretary for Manpower, Del Spurlock, argued Army's line, saying that if we discharge active-duty folk [for homosexuality] we should throw out recruits as well. Also, Army worries about battlefield transfusions, in which a soldier gives blood directly into the body of a wounded buddy.

I scoffed at both points: we should err on the side of retaining our active-duty personnel because we are proud to have them and have already invested a lot of money in them. As for "hot blood" transfusions, if the wounded man doesn't receive one he will die for sure, whereas the chances are minuscule that he will die receiving the AIDS virus this way. I therefore pled for a revision of DepSec Taft's memo requiring that recruits be withdrawn from training until such time as they are confirmed to have the AIDS antibody.

Dr. Mayer concurred with me, especially since severe mental health problems may result from the policy laid out in Taft's memo. Bud's redraft is now sensible and sensitive, geared for retention. If medical research and experience show that we are wrong and that the policy needs to be toughened as Army wants, then we'll do it without hesitation or apology.

Friday, 11 October 1985

[After a Lehman blast at several of us in a lineup:] Yes, working for Lehman is often aggravating, but it's also instructive, in ways both positive and negative. The trouble is that he's *too* brilliant and *too* capable; he knows each of our responsibilities and could easily do each of our jobs if he had the time. Problems arise when he does do them and fails to notify us. I would get angrier at him except I know he won't ever get really mad at me. After all, I might one day be the last person to whisper in President Bush's ear whom the next SecDef should be.[7]

Thursday, 17 October 1985

A big pending question is whether SecNav really wants to abandon CNT (certified Navy twill) in favor of mixed cotton-polyester for uniforms. Lehman wrote this instruction in his own hand after looking at a package of swatches we sent him. The textile industry—and its representatives in Congress—will howl if we drop CNT. Uniforms are a subject I have disliked since my midshipman days, largely because I looked so dumpy in them. Lehman, however, would study swatches of cloth all day. The next thing he will decide is the precise shade of brown shoe he has ordered back in the fleet for use by aviators.[8] OpNav's choice is one named Airdale, in preference to Peanut Brittle and Tropic Wine.

Friday, 18 October 1985

At the Pentagon, I changed into black tie for tonight's two very different social occasions. The first was the chief petty officers mess night at the Bethesda Hospital CPO Club. Master Chief Corpsman Jay Hood, who had welcomed me to Bethesda when I came for my recent physical, was the mess president and a stern one. The other chiefs were anything *but,* and not long after dinner began Hood was wailing, "When did we lose control?" There were offers

---

7. Jennifer Fitzgerald told me that on 23 September she had sat next to Lehman at a dinner and he praised me highly. I replied: "John Lehman looks at me and sees George Bush. I feel like the showgirl who laments, 'I wish he admired me for my mind!'"

8. Traditionally, surface officers wore black shoes and aviators wore brown shoes, which gave rise to expressions like "the black-shoe Navy" and "he's a brown shoe." In the interest of literal uniformity, some CNO had banned the brown shoe, and Lehman brought it back.

to escort female officers to the head, forced trips to "the grog bowl" (out of which plastic snakes and insects crawled), and general disarray.

I had no prepared remarks and decided to wing my talk in the spirit(s) of the evening. "I am *shocked*," I said, "to see the reckless abandonment of the high standards of taste and dignity that befit a chief petty officer of the United States Navy. Furthermore, I am appalled at something that never existed when I was in uniform, which is outright *irreverence* toward junior officers!" Glad to have an excuse to skip out, I left to a standing ovation.

The driver motored down Wisconsin and Massachusetts Avenues and into the gates of the British Embassy. The occasion was a dinner given by Sir Oliver Wright, the British ambassador, on the 180th anniversary of Admiral the Lord Nelson's victory (and death) at Trafalgar. Called Trafalgar Night, it is commemorated every year by every Royal Navy ship and station around the world. Tonight marked the first time it was observed in Lutyens's grand 1928 embassy residence. The car let me off in the carriageway, and I climbed the steps (past a portrait of George III) to the garden. There I joined guests ranged on the terrace, sipping cocktails.

A blast of trumpets called us into the ballroom, where tables were arranged with candles and masses of flowers. A small orchestra of Royal Marines in scarlet tunics performed dinner music. Two drummers and a fifer entered for the "parading of the beef," with tonight's main course held high on a platter by the chef. Later, with glasses charged with King's Tawny Port, we stood for the loyal toasts. Ambassador Wright proposed the President, and Secretary Weinberger, the guest of honor, proposed the Queen. The entertainment included all of us joining in on the choruses of sea "shanties" like "What Shall We Do with a Drunken Sailor?" as the port was passed round each table.

When the evening ended, Sir Oliver escorted SecDef to his car, and the rest of us stood and talked in enthusiastic clumps, so delighted with the occasion that we couldn't bear to leave.

Monday, 21 October 1985

Last Friday it was officially announced that Dudley Carlson will be nominated for deputy CNO for Manpower, Personnel & Training, succeeding Bill Lawrence and getting a third star. Dudley is more of a cynic and legerdemain artist than a humanist, but he is smart and has always been friendly to me. It will be crucial to establish a harmonious relationship with him. At the very least I'll need Dudley to tell me what Lehman asks him to do.

Tuesday, 22 October 1985

At a budget meeting SecNav attacked the eternal imperative to spend more and more money on research and development. He cited the case of AMRAAM, an air-to-air missile. "If we develop it," Lehman said, "the Soviets will only steal it because they can't develop one on their own. And if they get it, we'll have to have Son of AMRAAM. So aren't we better off by not developing it? We could stop the arms race all by ourselves." When the guffaws died down, Lehman said, "I'm not being facetious."

At 4:00 I had an hour-long, relaxed, friendly, and wide-ranging talk with Dudley Carlson. Although the meeting was marked by mutual regard and good humor, I have never fully trusted Dudley. He is "too clever by half," always eager to make a wisecrack and now quite full of himself. Dealing with Dudley will be alternately fun and tricky. "I'm an entirely different personality from Bill Lawrence," he correctly observed.

Friday, 25 October 1985

Tonight in black tie I drove to the Chilean residence in the heart of Embassy Row. The guest of honor was Adm. José Toríbio Merino Castro, commander of the Chilean Navy and, more importantly, the naval member of the *junta* in power since the overthrow of Salvador Allende in 1973. I entered the beautiful old mansion with Adm. and Mrs. Wes McDonald. He holds the dual titles of commander-in-chief Atlantic and supreme allied commander Atlantic. Wes will soon retire, and if it's hard enough to end a 30-year Navy career, it must be much more painful to cease being a supreme allied commander!

A strength of the American military is that a few select highly-able officers hold quite powerful positions for only four years and then retire, suddenly becoming private citizens. The joke is told of a CINC who, following his retirement ceremony, got into the family car, which didn't move. When he made this observation to his wife, she said, "That's because you're sitting in the back seat."

Saturday, 26 October 1985

[Arriving in Buffalo to represent the Navy Department at the annual observation of Theodore Roosevelt's birthday,] I was met by Les Foschio, head of the foundation that maintains the site where TR took the oath of office in 1901. Outside the airport terminal, Les spotted Sen. Daniel Patrick Moynihan (D-New York) and called "Pat!" A good politician, Moynihan dutifully climbed back out of a station wagon, into which he had just settled his long frame, to greet his constituent. Les introduced us, and the senator was inspired to say of the Gramm-Rudman deficit-reduction bill,[9] "A majority of Democrats voted to undermine the New Deal of Franklin Roosevelt, and a majority of Republicans voted to undermine the defense buildup of Ronald Reagan." It was a delight to be in the presence of the playfully dramatic Moynihan, and, with his trademark tweed hat blocking a bright sun, it was comforting to be in his shadow.

Tonight's dinner stopped just short of being a disaster. In the adjoining ballroom, across a thin partition, was a teen party with a thumping rock band. My oration steadily shrank as I realized few people would be able to hear it. In the remnant, I noted that "This observation of TR's birthday is being held a day earlier than it should, but that is perfectly all right, because TR's birthday *present* was two weeks ago. That was when the Palestinian terrorist murderers of Leon Klinghoffer [on the Mediterranean cruise ship *Achille Lauro*] were captured by jets of the US Navy off the carrier *Saratoga*. Does anyone here doubt that TR, up in heaven, smiled a grin that lit the universe and gave a cry of 'Bully!' that could be heard clean to Yasser Arafat's bedroom?"

Wednesday, 30 October 1985

[Capt.] Joe Harford [my new EA] and I left the office for our quick trip to Pensacola. Waiting below on the Mall Entrance steps, wearing a green Tyrolean hat, smoking a pipe, and talking with the Navy drivers was my special guest: ex-SecNav Edward Hidalgo. Several times he said how grateful he was for my inviting him to attend the retirement of his friend Vice Adm. Jim Sagerholm [commander of Naval Education & Training], especially under the nostalgic conditions we traveled. Waiting for us at Andrews was a 25-year-old A3 (a carrier-borne electronic intelligence-gathering plane) with the seal of the Navy Department on its tail. "It's my old A3!" Hidalgo exclaimed. "I went on 24-hours' notice to Diego Garcia in this plane, and I've never had finer meals than the ones we had on board—not even at Lion d'Or [a fancy Washington eatery]."

---

9. Finally passed that December, the bill placed across-the-board caps on federal spending. Although it had a Democratic cosponsor in Sen. Ernest Hollings of South Carolina, the law was commonly known by the names of two Republicans, Senators Phil Gramm of Texas and Warren Rudman of New Hampshire.

The A3's folded wings were lowered and locked, and we took off shortly after 5:00. Though I did a lot of work on my speech for tomorrow's ceremony, mostly I listened to Ed's nonstop anecdotes and recollections. Joe later said I deserved a medal for putting up with it all. But I said, "Someday when I'm 73 years old, I hope the assistant secretary of the Navy invites me on his plane, and when he does, I'll want him to listen to all *my* stories."

Less than two hours after leaving Andrews, we hit the ground with a jolt, as carrier planes do, and a parachute opened up aft to give us extra drag. We were met by Vice Adm. Sagerholm and members of his staff. With grand Castilian courtesy, Ed Hidalgo notified one of the officers that his fly was open.

Friday, 1 November 1985

This morning I had another round of arm wrestling with our wonderful surgeon general, this time over an outbreak of malaria aboard [the carrier] *Kitty Hawk* following a port visit to Mombasa. In the effort to get the truth, I asked Vice Admiral Seaton every conceivable question from every conceivable angle, once with the help of Joe Harford, who has the benefit of Catholic catechistic training. Lew's tactic is to confuse and deny. He refuses to be pinned down and always manages to find an escape: the problem belongs to the local CO or with the fleet or with an inattentive division officer, not with the Medical Command. In the *Kitty Hawk* case, I was surprised he didn't try to place the blame squarely on the mosquitoes. "I didn't say we don't have a problem," Lew corrected me at one point. "I said what we have is not an *unusual* problem."

At last Thursday's lineup, SecNav blasted the plea bargain arranged by the Justice Department with master spy John Walker, who got life imprisonment and a measure of leniency for his son for stealing classified documents out of the *Nimitz* burn bag. "It treats espionage just like another white-collar crime, like insider trading," Lehman said. After practicing on us, John went to a news interview, where he repeated all these things and seized the headlines on Wednesday. Needless to say, it was gutsy (or dumb) for a service secretary to attack a decision jointly made by the attorney general and the secretary of Defense. On the A3 to Pensacola on Wednesday evening, Ed Hidalgo tapped an article in the DOD clips and asked, "Did John clear all this with Cap before he said it?" The answer clearly was no, and editorial comment was divided between conservative papers that praised Lehman's courage and liberal ones that tongue clucked over his lack of "upward loyalty."

Today, SecDef put out a statement that said: "Secretary Lehman and I have reviewed completely the facts and circumstances which resulted in the plea-bargain in the Walker case. Secretary Lehman now understands that he did not have all the facts before he made several injudicious and incorrect statements with regard to that agreement. Secretary Lehman now has all the facts and is in complete agreement with the Government's decision." The incident is over, and John is safe. But, perhaps significantly, he made an unscheduled trip to [the naval air weapons station at] China Lake [Calif.], no doubt to blast away at a different kind of target and be "unavailable for comment."

My ex-boss, George Sawyer, has been indicted for accepting free trips to St. Louis to discuss a job with General Dynamics without informing the Navy general counsel while he still had authority over GD's Navy contracts. This matter has been under investigation for two years.

Wednesday, 6 November 1985

SecNav, apparently all on his own, cancelled the instruction on civilian personnel policy he himself signed in August and substituted one that doesn't allow me to delegate any authority for civpers. He thought I "gave away everything" to [senior Navy civil servant] Jim Colvard. As a matter of practical organization, civpers can't be handled any other way. Despite his constant talk about "decentralization," Lehman wants to maintain complete control in the Secretariat. So by his revision I now must execute an uncalculated amount of routine paperwork. I suppose the blow could have been worse: he could have taken me out of civpers altogether. What an odd fellow; what an odd way to do business.

Tuesday, 19 November 1985

Col. Mike Mulqueen, SecNav's Marine aide, came by my office to show me a handwritten, two-page memorandum-for-the-record from Lt. Col. Doug Berry, one of my lawyers. Doug's memo stated that at the Navy-Syracuse game at Annapolis on 9 November, he twice ran into Joe Harford, who was on a euphoric high and freely told of "smoking a reefer" in his car in the parking lot. This news was stunning, enervating, and sad. That Joe would use marijuana is one thing; but why would he brazenly talk about it to an officer known for his hardline views on disciplinary cases? Joe has been a superb EA; ideal, actually, but he does have a freestyle private life.

Clearly I must take decisive action. To look the other way or simply give Joe a talking-to would be inadequate and improper. The Navy expects more from its officers and gives them no second chance in drug cases; we have enforced that policy numerous times. Mike said that Capt. Mac Williams [the JAG officer who succeeded Ted Gordon as SecNav's lawyer] would be an excellent counselor.

Wednesday, 20 November 1985

Mac Williams told me that the Berry statement serves as sufficient cause for a urinalysis test with possible polygraph follow-up. Accordingly, I called Joe over the intercom and asked him to come see me. I told him the "disturbing" allegation from Doug Berry. Joe responded evenly and maturely, though he was undoubtedly stunned. It was all a "miscommunication," he said. "What I said [at the game] was I had been out to the reefer [i.e., an ice chest in his car] to do something illegal because you can't drink at the games." Good, I said, because I couldn't imagine anyone saying something as blatant as what Doug thought he heard. "But we do have an allegation here," I continued, "and we have a duty to dispose of it—not only to settle this matter but also because of the work we do here," ruling on hundreds of disciplinary cases. I said that a Chief Ford would be in Mac's office at 2:30. Without hesitation, Joe said he'd be glad to take the test. But as he left he made one of the wisecracks that worried Doug so much: "I've got an hour to go flush out my system."

After Alice Stratton's weekly meeting, I returned a call from Mac Williams with word that Joe's urinalysis came up negative. "I would pat you on the back for the way you handled this," Mac said. "Your reaction was exemplary." Though I am embarrassed to have the incident arise, I am pleased with the promptness and decisiveness with which I dealt with it. I called Joe on the phone to express relief over the news, which he had already heard from Mac. Joe said he told Doug Berry, "The only thing I would have done differently, if I had been in your situation, is that I wouldn't have agonized over it."

Thursday, 21 November 1985

I received a personal, two-page note from Jim Webb in response to a personal, two-page note I wrote him this morning regarding his no-show at Tuesday's scheduled breakfast with me and my service counterparts concerned with reserve affairs. Jim's reply was practically insulting. He said he deals only with service secretaries and uniformed reserve chiefs. It isn't "efficient" to meet with "the middle guys," he wrote. If I want to find out what OSD (Reserve Affairs) is doing, Jim wrote, I am welcome to come by for a briefing. Not even Larry Korb was this disdainful of the service assistant secretaries.

I intend to be as distant from Jim as he is to me; for example, I won't be a prop at any more of his luncheons for foreign generals. Notwithstanding this, I'd support Jim as Lehman's successor someday, either him or Rich Armitage.[10] Both have the potential to be "another Lehman" and aggressively help the Navy, meanwhile keeping the admirals and generals in line.

Friday, 22 November 1985

Jim Webb called this morning. It was a positive gesture, though Jim didn't say anything by voice that he didn't say in writing. I took the opportunity to remark, "Maybe it's because I'm a politician, but I believe that inclusion is always a better policy than exclusion." Jim took offense and got even more aggressive. It was *my* fault if we don't see each other, he said, because his "door is always open." There was no use in arguing with the man. In time we can both fight back in the pages of our novels.

Monday, 25 November 1985

I stayed after the lineup to give Lehman an abbreviated report on my "polite clash" with Jim Webb last week. He smiled and promised to "deflect Jim over to you on reserve affairs." Webb is a social friend, Lehman continued, whose behavior can partly be explained by the fact that "he's bored with his job and is looking for something else." I concluded the conversation by saying I recognize Webb is "a temperamental genius—and we know what it's like to live with one of *those*."

Wednesday, 27 November 1985

On a drizzly, dreary afternoon, I left for Quantico to speak at the graduation exercises at the Marine Security Guard School. It was a tough assignment, saying the right things to a group of Marines (and their families) when some of the graduates may be dead within a year from terrorist action. In the entire

---

10. Like Webb a Naval Academy graduate, Armitage was then assistant secretary of Defense for International Security Affairs. In the George W. Bush Administration, he would be deputy secretary of State.

US Armed Forces today, there may be nothing closer to sending young men off to war than to assign them as embassy guards.

In my talk, I took note of the last line of the "Marines' Hymn"—"We are proud to claim the title of United States Marine"—and said that it now has a double meaning for them. To the people they encounter overseas, they will be not only Marines but the United States as well. I praised Foreign Service Officers for their skills and knowledge but said that most are apart from the American mainstream. "You will be the real ambassadors of America," I said, "or, to put it another way, the ambassadors of the real America, representing the races, faces, and places of our country."

Tuesday, 3 December 1985

Tonight brought the 1985 edition of Roy Pfautch's annual "dinner in honor of Father Christmas," the party that people genuinely and joyfully look forward to attending. I correctly predicted who this year's mystery Santa would be: Energy Secretary John Herrington. Assisting him, an "elf" (the wife of a Cabinet secretary or senator) would call out the name of someone like Interior Secretary Don Hodel or Ambassador Wachtmeister of Sweden, who with red face would come forward to sit on Santa's knee.

There was a hilarious exchange between John and Bob Tuttle, who succeeded him as director of Presidential Personnel. Santa gave Bob a resume, saying he would like to head the World Bank. "Think how much I could give away then!" Bob warned, "If you weren't in the 1976 campaign, you're outta luck." No doubt repeating words he often heard from jobseekers, Santa/John protested, "But some of us had professional responsibilities that kept us from participating in politics."

The final "good little boy" was P. X. Kelley. John (a proud former Marine) was incapable of having the commandant sit on his knee, so he rose to greet P. X., who accepted the evening's gifts for USMC's Toys for Tots program. House Republican Leader Bob Michel, a fine baritone, then led us all in "White Christmas."

Friday, 6 December 1985

Today, at the end of one of our usual cordial, productive tours d'horizon on manpower issues, Dick Elster said he had "a personal note" to raise: due to family concerns, "I'd like to clear out of here in about two months." This was a major blow, for Dick will be hard to replace, personally, professionally, and politically. The only reason why Dick, a careerist, was permitted to be a DASN was because John Herrington knew and liked him. Presidential Personnel today is much tougher, and the whole process could take months.

At 2:30 I arrived in Jim Webb's office for a briefing on what OSD (Reserve Affairs) is doing these days. This was his way of making up for our recent clash. I would have been pleased with a private chat or a meal, for despite his towering ego I like and admire that brainy tough guy. The briefing was so elemental as to presume I knew nothing about the reserves. On balance it was a plus, though Jim will probably resume ignoring me and the others.

Wednesday, 18 December 1985

I am concerned about an incident late last week at Norfolk in which a Marine sentry shot and killed a sailor who created a disturbance at the main gate. The Marine claims the guy had taken his buddy's pistol and was about to shoot one of them. The matter is under investigation, but I wonder if Col. Tim Geraghty, CO of the Marine Barracks at Norfolk, had drummed into his gate guards the need to be ready to use their weapons to deter hostile folk. When I met with Tim in October, I was struck by the fervor with which he told me he had armed the guards—as if to say it was a lesson learned from the bombing of the Beirut barracks in 1983. If there is a connection, then the sailor may have been the latest victim of the Islamic Jihad suicide bomber that October morn.

A federal jury today acquitted George Sawyer of false swearing after a two-day trial in Alexandria. The government's sole witness was John Lehman, who praised George fulsomely. I wrote George a note expressing my happiness but saying, "It somehow doesn't seem right to *congratulate* someone whose innocence has been established by a court of law."

Thursday, 19 December 1985

I reached the Pentagon earlier than normal to attend a meeting of the Department of the Navy Civilian Executive Resources Board, chaired by UnSec Goodrich and attended by the vice chiefs of Navy and Marine Corps. Mel Paisley couldn't resist the fun of shooting off his mouth and announcing that SecNav didn't like the way I originally proposed reorganizing responsibility for civilian personnel. I didn't get mad, even though the Secretary (and Mel) charged off stupidly on the issue out of a conviction that the Navy's civil servants are all out to gut them. I said with firmness and finality that the important thing isn't structure but that we start managing our 350,000 civilian workers better.

This quieted Mel for the moment, but he leapt in again later to propose his own candidate to replace Jim Colvard as ranking civil servant in the Department. I shut off this discussion by saying that I would remember his suggestion when *I* choose the person for *my* staff. This got general endorsement from all except Mel, perhaps as a way of telling him to shut up. The VCNO [Adm. Jim Busey] later phoned to say I did "damn well," and the Under commended me for standing up to Mel, saying, "You showed him you know what you're talking about."

At 1630 there was a special meeting in the Blue Room to devise the budget strategy Lehman will use with OSD and later with the Congress. I can't imagine Jack Marsh doing this sort of thing at Army. In the unwritten social contract that Lehman has with the "blue suiters," he gets them the money they want and they acquiesce in his running the Navy. And of course Lehman loves fighting and winning budget battles, as if they were sport.

Sunday, 22 December 1985

I spent four hours in the Pentagon working on personnel cases. The stack included the first parole on which I could rule, using a brand-new SecNav instruction I put through after "the System" paroled a fellow who tried to sell classified documents to the Soviets. Today's case concerned the mastermind of a brutal premeditated murder. After serving just 10½ years of a 90-year sentence, he was recommended for parole by the Navy board that reports to me. I said no.

Determined to get some enjoyment out of this cold, overcast day, I went to the Smithsonian Museum of Natural History to see its wonderful exhibit on the Navy Exploratory Expedition of 1838–42. Led by Lt. Charles Wilkes, the "Ex.Ex." sailed through the Pacific and around the world, even touching Antarctica. The specimens brought back by the flotilla's complement of "scientifics" formed the heart of the original Smithsonian collection. These artifacts, flora, and fauna are still enchanting and evoke the call of the "South Seas" that drew Melville in the same era. I learned from the exhibit that the strong-minded Wilkes appended to himself the rank of commander even though SecNav James K. Paulding had specifically told him not to do so. Did Paulding spend a wintry Sunday afternoon in the 1840s reading the file on the Wilkes case?

Tuesday, 24 December 1985

For an hour and a half, Joe and I discussed where M&RA should go in the new year. He said that relations with "the front office" improved measurably after a couple of frank confrontations I had with SecNav. "I think the Secretary likes it when people stand up to him," Joe said. Perhaps that was his way of saying I should be more aggressive more often. Though I want to be candid with Joe, I held back from saying that my stern counterthrusts to John Lehman worked not so much because I was tough but because I may have shocked him into thinking I might not be on his side someday in the Bush Administration.

Betty Thompson gave me the *Merck Manual on General Medicine* for Christmas, saying it is "for your little talks with the Surgeon General."

This indeed would prove a useful gift, for in addition to astonishing the SG whenever I would casually mention some obscure disease, the Merck Manual *enabled me to read up on the afflictions for which sailors and Marines sought higher disability ratings.*

Thursday, 2 January 1986

In 1985, after several years of striving, I was at last able to *be* and to *do*. It was a year dominated by my boss, John Lehman, and all he had me do. One of the biggest tasks was overseeing the process by which he selected homeports for the battleships *Missouri* and *Wisconsin* and several escort ships. Though he never said so, this was handled near-flawlessly, the only leaks and glitches being entirely and eminently John Lehman's.

Because Lehman's energy and creativity gave rise to most of what my staff and I did this year, rare were the times I could take the lead on issues. Developing and promulgating a rational, humane policy on AIDS was the one in which I take the most pride, for it showed what I might do if left to my own devices. And I took the first steps into managing the Navy's 340,000 civilian employees.

I expect 1986 to be much like 1985. I shall contentedly cruise onward, gaining in confidence, knowledge, and, yes, Lehmanism, in readiness for a time when I shall truly need it all.

Friday, 3 January 1986

Although I meet privately with the other flag officers with whom I deal most closely, I always have Joe Harford present as a note taker and interlocutor whenever Vice Admiral Seaton comes to my office. The Surgeon General has a special trick—I used to think it Jesuitical, but it's really more rabbinical—of hearing a simple question, looking puzzled, and asking that it be rephrased, whereupon the question naturally becomes more complicated.

Tonight the oceanographer of the Navy gave a little reception at the Naval Observatory to let his guests see Halley's Comet. Alas, this generation can get only a poor look at Halley's (rhymes with "valleys"), unlike those around in 1910 or 2061, when earth passed or passes through the comet's tail, lighting up the heavens. Tonight we had about as good a viewing as anyone in the Northern Hemisphere will have this year, and all we could see was the comet's misty halo. Through a telescope's lens, Halley's Comet resembled a blue porch light seen a block away on a very foggy night.

Monday, 6 January 1986

Shortly after 6:00, I left the Pentagon for the Spanish-style residence of the Swedish ambassador, Count Willy Wachtmeister, and his wife Countess Ulla, who are *the* social swells of the DC diplomatic set. Tonight, with full connivance of the Vice President, the Wachtmeisters hosted a surprise party for Barbara Bush on the occasion of her and GB's 41st wedding anniversary. Waiters passed drinks and little horns. When the Bushes arrived at the door, we all tooted and sang, "Happy anniversary to you . . . ." We then went in to the ballroom for a five-course dinner and entertainment by some of the guests. Bill and Phyllis Draper[11] sang takeoffs on some Yale songs, such as "Bar, Bar, Bar" (to the tune of "The Whiffenpoof Song") and, in tribute to the hostess, "Ulla Ulla" (to "Boola Boola").

The fun, typically Bushian affair ended at 9:30 with the departure of the vice presidential motorcade. Inside the limo, GB picked up the microphone to broadcast to all of Ward Circle: "Good night, Willy! Good night, Erik! Good night, Christina! And good night to *you,* Ulla Ulla! Ulla Ulla. . . ." It was so funny that the Secret Service agents in the follow-up cars were all laughing.

---

11. William H. Draper III was a successful venture capitalist who at the time was chairman of the US Export-Import Bank. He later headed the United Nations Development Program.

Wednesday, 8 January 1986

Today SecNav gave a lunch for William F. Bennett, PhD, who before becoming secretary of Education last year was director of the National Endowment for the Humanities. Bennett has both taught and proselytized the humanities, which is what brought him to Lehman's attention. He has also gained no small amount of notoriety with the liberal press for stoutly maintaining that patriotism, morality, and ethics should be taught in the public schools (at least by example) and that teachers should be held to a minimum level of competency.

Bennett arrived with his special assistant Bill Kristol,[12] son of "neo-conservative" writer Irving Kristol, a young fellow with a bright manner who teaches ethics at the Kennedy School [at Harvard]. We chatted briefly in SecNav's office before proceeding to the small private dining room for lunch. There Bill and I witnessed a conversation between two impressive men with a zeal for results.

Looking rumpled and acting the tough Gonzaga High[13] kid with brains, Bennett cited statistics and anecdotes on the decline of public education, over which the rest of us clucked our tongues. Bennett would like DOD to expand on a Navy pilot project in Florida in which our personnel (especially those nearing retirement) teach math and science in the schools, with the possibility of their becoming teachers in a second career. Lehman strongly endorsed this and told Bennett how to circumvent the Pentagon bureaucracy by going straight to his Cabinet colleague Cap Weinberger.

In turn, Lehman would like the Department of Education to audit the selection process for Naval ROTC scholarships and for Bennett to spend a day at the Naval Academy to see to what extent the folks there have embraced his new emphasis on the humanities. "I've got them by the balls," Lehman said. "What I'd like is for you to see whether their hearts and minds have followed."

The two young rulers thanked each other and then returned to their happy wars with the numbskulls.

---

12. Later chief of staff to Vice President Dan Quayle and founding editor of *The Weekly Standard*.

13. A Jesuit school in Washington that Bennett attended.

Friday, 10 January 1986

The bulk of Dudley Carlson's and my conversation today was about Cdr. Jay Foley, my outstanding special assistant for naval personnel. Earlier today, Jay asked to have his orders changed from commanding USS *Stark,* a frigate out of Mayport [Florida], to any ship out of Norfolk. The reason is that Jay's family doesn't want to leave Washington, and Norfolk is close enough for him to commute on weekends. I grilled Jay closely on whether it's a risk to his career to use higher authority to change a set of orders. Since this is the first time in a 16-year career that he's asked to do this, Jay thinks not.

So I raised the matter with the chief of Naval Personnel, who swiftly said he'll get Jay's orders changed (at what later price, I wonder?). But there followed a long exposition on why it isn't good for a ship's captain to be a "geographic bachelor": the skipper becomes a clock-watcher on Friday afternoons; if he lives on board to save money, he becomes a curse to every after-hours duty section; and if he lives in an apartment or at the BOQ [bachelor officers quarters], he either is very lonely or, the opposite, tempted into an affair. Navy wives today don't want to give up careers in order to lead a ship's family support group when the vessel is deployed, and yet that is not only strong Navy tradition, it's better for the ship. Said Dudley: "Someone should tell these things to Foley," meaning me, if none of his "sea daddies" have done so yet. Right after Dudley left I spoke with Jay, who clearly is caught between duty and family.

The final event of the day was the reporting-out of the selection board for major general in the Marine Corps. The president of the board was the dynamic Lt. Gen. Al Gray, commanding general of FMFLant [Fleet Marine Force Atlantic]. Not on the list was Lehman's former Marine aide. Al explained that another brigadier edged out the Secretary's man because the successful one-star had been working in his specialty while John's favorite had been working in the Secretariat. Lehman smiled, nodded, said "A very good group," signed the report, and shook hands with Al.

The general departed, and Lehman turned to a JAG officer in the office to request a "memorandum for the record" on what Al had just said. Lehman wants this memo when he talks with the Commandant about the Marines' notion that it's death to the career of an officer to spend time in the Pentagon. Lehman also asked me for a similar memo, adding, "Do it tonight."

I took the incident as a sign of something I've never heard anyone say: that from the outset John Lehman has kept hands off the USMC, recognizing that the Corps (and especially the popular, well-connected P. X. Kelley) has the ability to pound him into powder on the Hill and even in the White House. No doubt this causes him considerable anguish. So if the memos can score a point with the Commandant, Lehman might count that a victory.

Tuesday, 21 January 1986

At 4:30, I left the Pentagon for Quantico with Alice Stratton and her husband Dick, director of the Naval Academy Prep School in Newport. Dick said he bears no ill will against the people who incarcerated, tortured, and "bent" (not broke) him during six years as a POW in North Vietnam. "One advantage of being in prison is you have a lot of time to think," he said. "And great leaders like Jim Stockdale and Robbie Risner helped us go back to basics, back to what our parents taught us. And that was that hatred is a very self-destructive force." As with other POWs, he felt pity for the Vietnamese upon his release, "because we were going home and they had to stay, the poor bastards."

After dinner with a brigadier, we proceeded to the Amphibious Warfare School, where waited captains and majors in crew cuts and sport coats. I was introduced but was happy just to be a fascinated and admiring listener like everyone else. Alice began with a very low-key description of her experiences as a POW wife, advising the couples present to talk with each other about "what if" the Marine is killed or captured; to seek, or give, company for the spouses whose husbands are gone; and not to hesitate getting outside professional help.

Dick's presentation was masterful, polished, and riveting from the first sentence. With his hulking size, ugly-handsome looks, and gravelly South Boston voice, he personifies the "tough love" of the Jesuits who taught him before he went to the Naval Academy. He credited Marines for understanding moral courage more than most groups he addresses, though he, like Alice, urged them always to think about it. Dick's fiercest words weren't against American "wimps" or Vietnamese goons but against the man whose name he delighted in saying in full: Robert Strange McNamara.[14] "The politicians operating in the basement of the White House" chose targets and devised rules of engagement that tied the hands and endangered the lives of the loyal fighting men they sent to Indochina to wage war, he believes. Dick also hit at flag officers who privately chafed at those restrictions but never dared resign in protest.

---

14. Secretary of Defense, 1961–67.

Wednesday, 22 January 1986

I was briefed by Dottie Meletske, director of the Naval Civilian Personnel Command, on the effect of the civpers reorganization. Quite simply, it means my staff will expand by a numbing 407 people, some 250 of whom are in offices from Honolulu to London, working away on EEO, reclassifications, and the like. If Lehman becomes incensed on why the Secretariat staff has doubled, it's due to the instruction he himself issued.

Thursday, 23 January 1986

Today I gave a lunch for the Washington lobbyists of the major reserve associations. Their main concern was that Gramm-Rudman will mean an "erosion of benefits" for their members. Over dessert I said no one knows at this point the law's impact on DOD. As for whether it is sound budgetary policy, I quoted "that great philosopher, Mae West, who said that when faced with a choice between two evils, she always chose the evil she hadn't tried before."

Dudley Carlson has offered Jay Foley a frigate in the Naval Reserve Fleet out of Jay's hometown of Philadelphia, which is actually closer to DC than is Norfolk. I called Jay to tell him he got his wish, but he remains torn between being with his family and getting a ship that won't be considered as "real" as the one for which he was originally slated.

The tragic benefit to Jay Foley's career from this switch in orders was that he was not in command of USS Stark on 17 May 1987 when it was hit by an Iraqi air-to-surface missile and almost sunk in the Persian Gulf, at the cost of 37 lives. Stark's captain was removed from command for not firing on the plane before it launched its missile. I like to think Jay would have defended his ship and been upheld by the Navy, as was the CO of the cruiser Vincennes a year later when it shot down an Iranian airliner thinking it might be another "hostile."

Thursday, 30 January 1986

SecNav led off the third Boston Conference by announcing, "For those who were not here last time,[15] Chase Untermeyer will now give us a history of this house." I was surprised but not unprepared, having yesterday reread the chapter on Longlea in Robert Caro's first volume on LBJ, *The Path to Power.*

---

15. See 13 December 1984.

I pretended to remember all the luscious anecdotes from legend rather than from notes I had reviewed in the car on the trip down from Washington.

When the agenda reached the rotation of the Senior Executive Service, I said the major accomplishment was not the number of executives with new assignments but the fact that for the first time the Navy Department is truly managing its senior civilians. Mel Paisley was a seconder to all I said, the first sign of relief from the tension I had about the meeting. Indeed, Mel was not a problem all day, not for me or for others. "I have just one question," P. X. Kelley asked with Gaelic playfulness. "Does the five-year rotation rule apply to the secretary of the Navy as well?" When the laughter died down, a blushing Lehman (in office now for five years) said, "Give me the $20,000 bonus that SESers get, and I'll move!"

The conference ended at 1730, having been a success in mood as well as matter. Lehman and others went to dinner at The Inn at Little Washington, which I escaped for two reasons: one is that I didn't want to go to the hugely expensive eatery to hear Mel echo Lehman's praise of the sauces. And another was that I had an important dinner of my own back in Big Washington.

In a private room at the Madison Hotel gathered Bush political operatives and sages handpicked by Rich Bond at the request of Lee Atwater, the head of Bush's PAC. It was primarily an effort to elicit thoughts and suggestions from those not involved in the nascent campaign. I was the only government official present, and among "Bush intimates" I am the only one in assistant-secretarial ranks. This is amazing for the candidate of the Administration but speaks to the freeze out of Bush people in the early part of the first term and to the fact that the VP has never tried to infiltrate his supporters into the bureaucracy.

Our main focus was on the criticism that Bush is trying to pander to right-wing groups, an impression echoed this very morning in a column written by George Will. Among other slams, Will wrote: "The unpleasant sound Bush is emitting as he traipses from one conservative gathering to another is a thin, tiny 'arf'—the sound of a lapdog. He is panting along Mondale's path to the presidency." Knowing that Lee is behind Bush's opening to the right, I said, "When George Bush tries to be what he isn't, he becomes shrill, which has the opposite effect of seeming tough. I think he should talk from his strengths and be warm, wise, and pensive. I wish he could throw red meat to the conservatives, but he can't. If he could, he'd have been elected senator from Texas and been president already."

Monday, 3 February 1986

Under Sec. Jim Goodrich and I left by Navy car for the White House and a pep session for the principal appointees of the Administration. We went up to the State Dining Room for juice, coffee, and pastries until military aides herded us toward the East Room. There we sat closely packed together on the little golden chairs. Chief of staff Donald Regan, that most arrogant of men, felt he had to tell us, "President Reagan is in full control; I am not running the White House." Then with a nod he said, "I see a cousin approaching," at which time RR was announced. The President received a prolonged and fond standing ovation. When it quieted, he looked around and asked, "Who's minding the store?" Official Washington may be wringing its hands over Gramm-Rudman, but Ronald Reagan is practically joyful over it. He came to power after years of decrying federal deficit spending, only to preside over the worst flood of red ink in peacetime history. But now that he can turn his full attention to slashing federal spending, he is a happy man.

Wednesday, 26 February 1986

There was a special social event after work for all living former secretaries of the Navy: Fred Korth (1961–63), Paul Nitze (1963–67), Paul Ignatius (1968–69), John Chafee (1969–72), John Warner (1972–74), Bill Middendorf (1974–77), Graham Claytor (1977–79), and Ed Hidalgo (1979–81). It was a distinguished group, for their service not just to the Navy but also in later years: Nitze and Claytor were DepSecDef, Nitze and Middendorf were ambassadors, and Chafee and Warner are senators.

After champagne and hors d'oeuvres in his office, Lehman summoned us all out into the corridor for the official dedication of the SecNav portraits recently hung there. He gave an amusing spiel on several secretaries, including Thomas Gilmer, who perished in the *Princeton* disaster.[16] Looking straight at Senators Chafee and Warner, Lehman deadpanned, "We honor Secretary Gilmer, even though he only served nine days, because he died in a good cause: he took two congressmen with him."

---

16. See footnote on 27 August 1985.

Friday, 28 February 1986

I left at noon for a unique Washington experience: the weekly luncheon of the Alibi Club. The club is located in an old red brick building at 1806 I Street, to which commuters leaving the Farragut West Metro station across the street might not pay much notice. On a heavy wooden door the brass plate reading ALIBI has been shined almost to the point of obliteration. The door made a horrendous squeaking and clucking sound as I opened it. When I did, I stepped into the late 19th century. I first found myself in a narrow entry hall whose walls are thickly covered with old prints, maps, and drawings. After hanging my overcoat on a hook, I walked into the parlor, its wooden floors laid with well-worn oriental rugs and its walls encrusted with additional memorabilia, caricatures of old members, and miscellaneous bric-a-brac. It was an ancient, upper-class (and senior-citizen) version of a boys' tree house.

A tall fellow of about 50 broke from a group of men to introduce himself. I'm glad he did, for he was my host: Nicholas (Nick) Brown, whom I had not seen in more than 16 years. Nick was flag lieutenant [naval aide] to Admiral McCain when I was aide to Rear Admiral Kauffman. Among the first and biggest things I had to face in that job was a visit by CINCPAC to Sangley Point. In that tense time, nothing was as comforting as Nick's help and sympathy. That a mighty commander could act so kindly toward a mere JG was impressive enough; that he was also scion of one of America's noblest families [the Browns of Providence] was even more so. Nick is the son of John Nicholas Brown, who was AsstSecNav in 1946–49; his mother was a noted military historian, and his brother Carter is director of the National Gallery of Art. Retired as a captain, Nick himself is the director of the National Aquarium in Baltimore.

The other members present were all striking in the way that confident and established older men can be, with white hair, florid complexions, and hearty personalities. Many were of the small and seldom-seen Washington social (as opposed to political) elite called "cave dwellers." Among the more celebrated names were William McChesney Martin, longtime chairman of the Federal Reserve Board, and Graham Claytor, who today heads Amtrak. Without hesitation, Claytor agreed to supply a private car for Alibi members to travel to Baltimore and be Nick's guests at the aquarium—fish not on the menu.

An old waiter entered the parlor, reached up, and began rattling a set of loud, unmusical temple bells to announce lunch. We then walked into the refectory (dining room), over whose entrance is the club's motto, "He who enters here leaves rank and precedence behind." The overall look to the room is medieval, with a winter sun streaming in through tinted leaded windows to cast a yellow light on tankards, flatware, and mugs displayed on the walls.

The single table was of a rough-hewn wood that has been brushed to a blond color and made velvety to the touch. At each end was a cauldron of clam chowder, and the most substantive responsibility of the club's proctor (president) and bulldog (vice president) is to serve the soup. Fellows sitting next to them sprinkled on the parsley. A bottle was passed for lacing the chowder with sherry. To my considerable surprise, the bread taken with the chowder was matzo, buttered and salted. The rest of the meal was very Eastern: a chicken potpie, salad, and a fruit compote spikable with Kirsch.

When he had something to say, the proctor—W. John Kenney, AsstSecNav and UnSecNav in the Roosevelt-Truman era—used a mallet to thwack what might have been a wooden Philippine carabao bell. Kenney introduced Nick, who introduced me, pointing out how in 1969 he considerably outranked me and now I considerably outrank him. He also noted that I had worked for a veteran member of the Alibi, Vice President Bush. (There are two cartoon caricatures of the VP in a gallery of such drawings located between the refectory and the parlor.) The rest of the meal contained general banter, mostly about fixing the roof.

Members began drifting away around 2:00, and Nick and I were among the last to rise. With SecNav in Munich,[17] I could fully enjoy a lazy and most memorable Friday afternoon.

Tuesday, 4 March 1986

Tonight at the Madison I attended a dinner that was small only by Pfautchian standards: four tables of eight persons each. Roy hosted the affair in honor of Attorney General Meese and a federal district judge from St. Louis he wanted the AG to meet. Meese leaves soon on a trip to Asia on drug-related matters. His funny, moleish principal aide, Ken Cribb, was at my table. "We South Carolinians have much in common with Asians," he announced. "We both eat rice and worship our ancestors."

I sat next to Kathy Osborne, RR's personal secretary. She is very circum-

---

17. Lehman was a regular at the Munich Security Conference, a must-make annual event for all former and future defense ministers. Attendees like to call it *Wehrkunde*, invariably adding for the benefit of the ignorant and lowly, "That means 'defense studies' in German."

spect, recoiling when I innocently asked how someone phones the President. (She screens all calls.) Kathy did allow that the power of the presidency—or at least of the president's secretary—does not extend to getting the GSA to fix the thermostat in the Oval Office.

Friday, 7 March 1986

[On a visit to the Bremerton Naval Shipyard in Washington State] I met for the first time with union representatives at one of our major industrial activities. This became an important mission after gaining responsibility for the civilian bureaucracy and, with it, labor relations. I was consciously copying what FDR did during the Wilson Administration, which was to become acquainted with the labor movement.[18] I met with the heads of the unions represented in the yard—metal workers, machinists, operating engineers, and others—around a horseshoe table in a conference room with no one from management present.

Under the law, unions in federal installations can't negotiate with management over wages, but they can bargain over the vast area of "work rules." I particularly wanted their views on mandatory urinalysis testing for drugs. The leaders responded candidly and without rancor. They don't object to urinalysis, just as they don't object when a worker is taken off the job for drunkenness. But they want the test to be for *impairment,* not just for off-duty recreational use of drugs. This is the important distinction between civilian and military personnel: the latter are deemed on duty and under our control for 24 hours a day. When the hour-long session ended, the union leaders expressed their gratitude that "someone from your level would want to talk with us."

Saturday, 8 March 1986

[At the submarine base at Bangor, Washington] the highpoint of the day came when we went down to the waterfront and beheld a classic Northwest vista of still, dark-green and blue waters, fir forests, and snow-capped mountains. The sub piers are triangular and set out from the shore so that salmon fingerlings can swim in relative safety, away from predators in deeper water.

---

18. "Few of the lessons Roosevelt learned in Washington were of more lasting value than those that came out of his supervision of the shore establishment of the Navy with its thousands of civilian workers." *Franklin D. Roosevelt: The Apprenticeship* (1952) by Frank Friedel, p. 192.

Moored alongside one such pier is *Alabama,* the newest Trident [interconti-
nental ballistic missile-firing sub] in commission. At 560 feet, she is five feet
longer than the Washington Monument.

I was chiefly impressed by the ship's spaciousness, especially considering
that its middle third contains 24 thick missile tubes. A group of officers on
board must concur in a decision to launch; even so, the skipper has far greater
power over war and peace than does the commander of an Air Force missile base. Everywhere we went on board, the captain introduced me to crew
members by name. One of them, a Petty Officer Mahoney, was the model
for the statue *The Lone Sailor* that will stand watch at the Navy Memorial on
Pennsylvania Avenue.

Later I visited with some of the Marines, just out of boot camp, who are
charged with the security of "special weapons" at Bangor. They are locally famous for being on duty last November when an Alaska bush pilot, trying to
make Seattle, ran out of gas and landed right in the middle of the ultra-secure
missile-stowage area. The young Marines did their job so convincingly that
the pilot didn't want to come back the next day to claim his plane.

Chapter 10

The Tongue of the Ocean

Thursday, 20 March 1986

Joe Harford and I speculated on who will become CNO when Jim Watkins retires in July. The choice is SecDef's and ultimately the President's, but Lehman no doubt is in the thick of the process. Recently, he was with Vice Adm. Frank Kelso (commander of the Sixth Fleet) in the Med, bringing his name into the speculation. It is interesting to imagine a situation in which Weinberger rejects Lehman's choice and picks a CNO who fights his management of the Navy. Would SecNav then quit in protest? In all likelihood nothing that dramatic will happen, but one thing is for sure: the next CNO will outlast the Secretary, unlike his two predecessors.

Monday, 24 March 1986

The final event of the workday was a meeting in my office with lawyers Hugh O'Neill and Capt. Mac Williams on the case of Midshipman 1/c Jeff Bellistri, a champion lacrosse player at Annapolis accused of taking cocaine. The drug showed up in his urine, but Bellistri denies the allegation and got a private polygraph affirming his innocence. Navy's own polygraph was "inconclusive"; the operator thinks Bellistri tried to alter his breathing rate and move his feet to foil the machine. SecNav will have the final say on the case, which has drawn a lot of local publicity.

Tuesday, 25 March 1986

CNO came to the Secretary's office for a meeting on the Bellistri case. Hugh, Mac, and I believe him to be guilty; Lehman called us "the hanging jury." But Lehman and Watkins are uneasy that Bellistri's two polygraphs show different results. Lehman may not have full faith in polygraphs, but he has even less in drug urinalysis. In the interest of fairness, SecNav and CNO want a tie-breaking third polygraph administered by an impartial agency such as

FBI. I remarked that no one could doubt our fairness if, on the morning after a major naval confrontation in the Mediterranean,[1] the secretary of the Navy and the chief of Naval Operations spent an hour dealing with the case of one midshipman.

Wednesday, 26 March 1986

The star of tonight's Navy League banquet was of course John Lehman. Wearing a batwing collar and a smug smile, he spoke without a text. Last year he blasted his contractor audience, but this time he praised them for bringing down the unit price of every major weapons system Navy buys. "I am not averse, humble though I am, to taking some credit for this," he said to knowing chuckles. Lehman said there is as yet no second source for the HARM missile, used so effectively off Libya two days ago, "but *I* have taken the place of competition by keeping the pressure on to bring the price down."

Thursday, 27 March 1986

After Dudley Carlson and I had discussed recruit advertising with him, Lehman suddenly said we should talk about women in the Navy. Simply put, he doesn't favor increased roles for women at sea. In this, he and Dudley are precisely in synch. He will allow (as Dudley and I recommend) more women to serve aboard Military Sealift Command ships but not (as I favor but Dudley fervently opposes) aboard Mobile Logistics Support Force ships. The ever-clever Dudley wants to change the name of the MLSF to "battle force ships," since this would make them sound like combatants, from which women by law are excluded. The session ended with Lehman and Carlson trying to one-up each other with puns about women's "positions." I'm beginning to wish SecNav had given me another of his buddies as chief of Naval Personnel.

Friday, 28 March 1986

In the afternoon I left for Bath, Maine, and the long-awaited launching of the frigate *Kauffman*. Because Joe Harford has to hoist a sword in a friend's

---

1. Libyan leader Muammar Qaddafi had warned the US not to go below what he called "the line of death" in the Gulf of Sidra. Viewing the Gulf as international waters, the Navy ignored Qaddafi's warning and steamed south. Soviet-built missiles were fired on Navy aircraft, after which elements of the Sixth Fleet proceeded to destroy the missile sites and some patrol boats.

wedding, Cdr. Dale Bosley is wearing the four-strand "chicken gut" aiguillettes as naval aide this weekend. I'm very glad this worked out the way it did, for Dale has earned the right to do something enjoyable, and in the time he's been on staff we haven't done anything as friends—the odd artificiality of rank intervening. Dale is anxious to do the aide job right, to the extent of grabbing all the luggage or running around to open the car door for me. This is bad enough when a full Marine colonel does it; it's worse when a friend does it. There is no small irony in all this, inasmuch as I'm on a pilgrimage to pay honor to a man whom I served as an aide.

Saturday, 29 March 1986

Dale and I left Brunswick Naval Air Station for Bath Iron Works, where an officer gave us hardhats and led us to *Kauffman*. She is the last *Perry*-class frigate to be built at Bath, which pioneered the design. For this reason, the yard invited all present and former workers to today's launching ceremony.

We arrived in time for the last two "rallies" by which a ship is readied for launching in the traditional method "down the ways." In order to transfer the weight of the frigate from its "cradle" onto greased blocks, workmen drove wedges into the cradle's seams with long iron poles, three men on each pole, working for three minutes and resting for ten. When the buzzer sounded after "the final rally," a cheer went up from the husky, whiskered men, one of whom said as he sauntered past, "She's all yaws naow!"

Vice President and Mrs. Bush arrived from Kennebunkport for the pre-launch reception given by Bath and attended by several members of the Bush-Kauffman family and a full complement of Maine politicians. The presence of the VP, a man Mainers are proud to claim as one of their own, brought out the state's top political leadership: Senators Bill Cohen[2] (R) and George Mitchell[3] (D), Gov. Joe Brennan (D), and Congressman Jock McKernan (R).[4] All of these VIPs, each of whom expected a role in the ceremony, presented the day's toughest challenge to shipyard CEO Bill Hargett. This is because Bath launches ships "on the tide," which meant that *Kauffman* was going down the ways at 3:19 whether or not the dignitaries had finished

---

2. Congressman, 1973–79; senator, 1979–97; and secretary of Defense, 1997–2001.

3. Senator, 1980–95; Senate majority leader, 1989–95.

4. Brennan and McKernan swapped jobs in that fall's election. McKernan later married Olympia Snowe, who succeeded Mitchell in the Senate.

speaking. Happily, no one gave a lengthy oration, but praise of the Navy's performance in the Gulf of Sidra was the order of the day.

Hargett's introduction of me closed with words no doubt given to him by his predecessor at Bath, UnSecNav Jim Goodrich: "Chase Untermeyer is regarded in Washington as a young man of great ability and with a great future." Barbara Bush, next to whom I sat, leaned over and asked, "Did you write that?"

I rose to deliver remarks that began, "This day is particularly poignant for me, for I once served as aide to Rear Adm. Draper Kauffman — rather badly, I fear. Often, when some fresh disaster had occurred at my hands, Admiral Kauffman would say in exasperation that I was an aide who *needed* an aide." There was a tension-breaking laugh. "So, Admiral, I know you're up there watching us today, and I want to reassure you that the Navy Department is in good hands. For I *do* have an aide, and he is a SEAL officer, one of that outstanding group you helped found."

Shifting moods, I removed from my pocket a quotation from Herman Melville, "a man who was familiar with these coasts and who knew the business we are all in, namely the way of the sea." It was a passage from *Moby Dick:*

> However baby man may brag of his science and skill, and however much, in a flattering future, that science and skill may augment; yet for ever and for ever, to the crack of doom, the sea will insult and murder him and pulverize the stateliest frigate he can make.

Kauffman, I said, was indeed a stately frigate, and what will make the difference in how she fares against her enemy — "whether that enemy be the Soviets, the new Tripolitan pirates, or the sea" — will be the men who sail aboard her. I thanked the men and women of Bath for building her strong and said that when she is commissioned next year we shall outfit her with the quality of sailors that the Admirals Kauffman would have wanted and — in a phrase that suddenly came to me as a perfect peroration — "send her forth with the best of God's good intentions."

There was a comfortable margin of minutes before 3:19, and Beth Bush[5] took her place at the bow, with the VP, BPB, and Cary Kauffman standing

---

5. The daughter and sister of the ship's namesakes, she was married to the VP's brother, Prescott Bush Jr.

nearby. Speaking into a microphone, Beth proclaimed, "In the names of Vice Adm. James Laurence Kauffman and Rear Adm. Draper Laurence Kauffman, I christen thee *Kauffman!*" Then, with a look of deep concentration, she raised the red, white, and blue–covered bottle of champagne, gave the bow one clunking blow without effect, and then took another swing, at which the bottle spewed up a stream of bubbly, cracking more than breaking. Meanwhile, under the keel, Linda (Mrs. John) Dranchak, the wife of *Kauffman's* prospective skipper, "pulled the trigger," engaging a lever that shifted the last of the ship's weight onto the greased skids.[6]

The ship started slipping down the ways. Balloons rose, a band played "Anchors Aweigh," and workers on the focsl yanked up the remains of the champagne bottle for later presentation to Beth. *Kauffman* was arrested by a couple of tugs, brought about, and towed to a nearby pier for another 11 months of outfitting. It was a beautiful, emotional sight, something that one can never tire of seeing.

Alas, one cannot see ships launched in this fine old fashion anymore. Modern vessels are built in modules in graving docks that are subsequently flooded long before the christening ceremony. When my wife Diana christened the fleet replenishment oiler Guadalupe *at Avondale Shipyard at New Orleans on 6 October 1991 (our first anniversary), the ship was already in the water some distance from the viewing platform. Given a small hatchet, Diana pronounced the name of the ship and chopped a short length of cord. This let loose a long rope, at the other end of which was a metal arm that smashed a champagne bottle against the hull—no whacking required, with a 100 percent guarantee of first-time success.*

Monday, 31 March 1986

I received a note from Nancy Bush Ellis, written before we saw each other at Bath. She closed by asking, "Do things go well for GB? I hate all this conservative courting—oh, Lord. But I suppose it must be done."

---

6. Also down there was my future wife, Diana Kendrick, who had "advanced" the Vice President's visit to Bath. We would not meet for nearly three years, at which time we realized we had both been at the launch. Diana said she did not remember my speech, only how cold it was that day.

Friday, 4 April 1986

The *San Diego Union* is saying that Frank Kelso will be the new CNO. It also said that SecNav's first choice was the combative Adm. Ace Lyons (CINCPACFLT), whom he supposedly likens to Adm. Horatio Nelson. Unfortunately for both Lehman and Lyons, SecDef doesn't fear an imminent conflict at sea with the French. I wonder if the guileful Lehman tried Ace's name on Weinberger just to make Frank, a very junior three-star, seem more desirable.

Thursday, 10 April 1986

I joined SecNav and Rear Adm. Ron Marryott (president of the Naval War College) at the end of their lunch. Lehman had invited me in order to impress upon the next superintendent of the Naval Academy that I am the one to whom he will directly report. Alas, John didn't quite say this, only that I would be Ron's "intermediary with the bureaucracy." Ron is an agreeable fellow with whom I worked well on Outer Continental Shelf issues. So I expect a much warmer relationship with him than with "Admiral America," Chuck Larson, who's leaving USNA to command the Second Fleet.

Later, Lehman and his lawyers, Capt. Mac Williams and Hugh O'Neill, gave me the news that Midshipman Bellistri passed his third (FBI-administered) polygraph test and would therefore be readmitted to Annapolis. I was to "tell the supe" [superintendent] after a press release was prepared.

My office soon swarmed with lawyers working on the statement. We discussed when Bellistri should return to the Academy. To me the answer was clear: he was found innocent by the secretary of the Navy and thus must be "made whole"; if Bellistri wants to return to the Yard tomorrow and play lacrosse, he can do so. This view was backed up by the quick opinion Hugh got from Larry Garrett, the new OSD general counsel.

I then phoned Chuck Larson at home, where he was dressing for a Naval Institute dinner. In all our conversations these past two years, Chuck and I never had a genuinely friendly talk. Mostly our exchanges have had an undertone of tension. This one was by far the tensest. Never raising his voice but obviously distraught, Chuck said the Secretary's decision will have "a devastating effect" on the Academy, and he doesn't want the kid returned this spring at all. We wrangled over that for half our talk. Ever up to his tricks, Chuck threatened to "board [Bellistri] out" academically on the pretext that the midshipman would of course flunk his exams since he's missed 14 weeks of classes. By law, SecNav has no power to restore a midshipman discharged on academic grounds, and USNA always tries to do this if it can't remove a guy on a conduct charge. I told Chuck that wouldn't work because we already agreed that Bellistri will take makeup classes this summer and fall.

Then, just as predictably, Chuck swung his other fist. He revealed that in his safe is a statement by a midshipman saying that Bellistri had told him he had used cocaine on several occasions. It was the same old over-the-transom information that Larson has consistently used against mids whom we in the Secretariat want to pardon. Larson said, baldly, that this anonymous middie promised to come forward "if you [Larson] get rolled by the Secretary." I said that of course we wouldn't entertain such a proceeding. The conversation soon ended.

In one of the grimmer ironies of my life, Admiral Larson and I were thrown together again in 1994 when, after a big cheating scandal, he was recalled from retirement to serve again as superintendent. I was then a member of the Naval Academy Board of Visitors and soon would become its chairman. Seated at Larson's table at a Board dinner, I overheard him tell his dinner partner how "they" forced him to take back a midshipman who used cocaine. I think Chuck spoke extra loudly, just so I would know he had never forgotten the Bellistri case.

Monday, 21 April 1986

Nineteen eighty-six was the 150th anniversary of the independence of the Republic of Texas. Because many Texans still thought of George Bush as a Yankee, I pressed the VP's office hard to make sure he attended the crowning event of "the Sesquicentennial," a ceremony on the battleground at San Jacinto, where Sam Houston had defeated the Mexican army under Gen. Antonio López de Santa Anna.

Three old-looking CH 47 (Chinook) Army helos from Ft. Hood were neatly lined up on the polo field at the Bayou Club [in Houston]. In the shade of some nearby pines I talked with Congressman Bill Archer[7] and with the Bushes' close friend C. Fred Chambers. When the vice-presidential motorcade arrived, we boarded the lead chopper, styled "Army II." The ride was noisy and smoky, and we sat on rack benches along the bulkheads, able to

---

7. Archer succeeded Bush in the US House in 1971 and from 1995 until his retirement in 2001 was chairman of the Ways & Means Committee.

see out the front hatch and the tail. The city and its refinery belt glistened below us.

The Chinooks put down in a field about a mile away from the San Jacinto Monument, scaring the horses of the mounted Houston policemen who secured the site. We were driven to the monument, to be greeted by Gov. Mark White. I was accorded a seat on the dais with the principal dignitaries and introduced as "under secretary of the Navy." The Ross Volunteers of Texas A&M formed an archway with their sabers, the official welcome for the Whites and the Bushes, who arrived to "Texas, Our Texas" and "Hail Columbia," respectively.

The first major speaker was ex-Congresswoman Barbara Jordan (D-Houston), now a professor at the LBJ School in Austin. She was introduced as "the greatest orator in the world," and while that may have been Texan overstatement, Ms. Jordan richly proved she has a strong claim to the title. Speaking from her wheelchair, she thundered, "Freedom! Freedom! That was what it was all about." Then she proceeded to describe the day of the battle, on which "even the frogs were hushed, as if waiting, waiting." Her message was that Texas and Mexico were not separated on 21 April 1836, only Texas from the dictatorial rule of Santa Anna.

It was hard for GB to follow such a speech, but he read his text as well as I have ever heard him. It was optimistic and full of Texas pride, and (in a paragraph I had written) it announced that an Aegis cruiser will be named *San Jacinto,* just like the small carrier on which Bush served during World War II. The crowd applauded this and the mention of Navy's recent role in the Med. As soon as the VP finished, the chairman said, "We know you have an exacting schedule to meet," and excused him and the rest of us from further attendance at the proceedings, which meant listening to Mark's speech.

Tuesday, 29 April 1986

Edmund Morris called, apologizing for the short notice, with an invitation to dinner in Clare Boothe Luce's apartment in the Watergate. I arrived a bit after 7:30 to find Edmund and his wife Sylvia (Clare's biographer) talking with Mrs. Luce and playing with a woolly Himalayan cat. Out the windows a sunset was painting the Potomac a brilliant golden orange. The apartment at first glance cannot compare with Clare's breathtakingly beautiful house on Kahala Beach [near Honolulu], but it does have its points. There are, for example, several small paintings by Magritte, two of them "portraits" of Clare. One is of a feather holding up the Leaning Tower of Pisa, and the other is of a dagger caressing a rose. The hostess wore a circular necklace of golden zigzags, with either diamonds or emeralds in the interstices. Dinner was served by a Castilian maid in proper black dress and white apron.

Conversation at first dwelt on the stunning explosion three days ago in a Soviet nuclear power plant north of Kiev [at Chernobyl]. The accident provided a powerful jolt of doubt in the ability of Soviet scientists and technicians to make anything work—reactors and missiles alike. We moved off this dread subject and on to the lighter ones at which Clare has no equal: reminiscences about the stingy Duke and Duchess of Windsor,[8] how Clare got a bit part in a silent film, how Noël Coward frankly discussed his homosexuality, and how she gave [film producer] Otto Preminger his first break as an actor in her anti-Nazi play *Margin for Error*. As these stories rolled out, Sylvia madly took notes for use in the bio.[9]

To bring the evening to a close, Clare asked her guests if they would like anything. Edmund drawled, "Yes, I'd like the sunset back again. You can do it, Clare. You have contacts."

Tuesday, 6 May 1986

SecNav seemed distracted at this morning's lineup. His attention was briefly seized by word that the Senate will take up tax reform before it does DOD reorganization ("Great! Perfect!") and by general counsel Walter Skallerup's report of dueling with the wife of Gov. John Ashcroft (R-Missouri) for the return of the silver service of the battleship *Missouri*, due to be recommissioned on Saturday.

The officers' wardrooms of old battleships and cruisers boasted fine sets of silver donated by the states and cities for which the ships were named. Even if the vessel was subsequently retired, the Navy retained ownership of the silver. Sometimes it was lent back to the donor, and Missouri's silver was actively used in the governor's mansion in Jefferson City. When Mrs. Ashcroft staunchly resisted giving the set back, Lehman directed Skallerup to sue the State of Missouri for repossession. Attorney General Meese reminded the Navy of the constitutional provision that when the federal government sues a state, the court of original jurisdiction is the US Supreme Court, and he was not going to trouble the justices on such a trivial mat-

---

8. The former Wallis Warfield of Baltimore had died five days earlier.

9. *Rage for Fame: The Ascent of Clare Boothe Luce* was published in 1997, ten years after its subject's death.

ter. Lehman neatly solved the problem by informing the Ashcrofts that they would not be allowed on board Missouri for the ceremony unless they surrendered the silver, which they did. John Ashcroft was later US senator and US attorney general.

Wednesday, 7 May 1986

In a meeting in Lehman's office, the Surgeon General spoke of the need to move ob/gyn specialists out of populated areas (where civilian doctors are available) and send them to remote places like Subic Bay [in the Philippines]. The trickiest place is Orlando, where all women recruits are trained and where there are almost always some 2900 women service members present, not to mention female dependents and retirees. I said the problem with Orlando is political, with Sen. Paula Hawkins seeking reelection. "I am under orders from the White House not to do anything to upset Paula Hawkins," Lehman said,[10] prompting Lew Seaton to suggest that he could "restudy" the matter and report back in December. Political considerations also govern the announced reduction of surgical services at Millington Naval Air Station near Memphis, which Sen. Albert Gore Jr. has attacked. Capt. Joe Prueher,[11] SecNav's affable EA (and a Tennessean), leaned over and said to me with a tone of sympathetic sarcasm, "Your job sure involves all the neat shit."

The Secretary leaves tomorrow for festivities in Pensacola for the 75th anniversary of naval aviation, followed by the recommissioning of Missouri in San Francisco on Saturday. It will take his mind away from the deadening 95–0 vote in the Senate for the DOD reorganization bill.[12] Seldom, if ever, has John Lehman lost so heavily on a matter in which he was intensely interested and involved.

Tuesday, 13 May 1986

Back in the Pentagon, SecNav was in an expansive mood and had no items to fling at us in the lineup. What has become of the Lehman who liked to chew on assistant secretaries in 1984 and 1985? Have I grown more confident

---

10. After a drought of twenty-six years, Republicans won the Senate in the Reagan landslide of 1980 and held it in the next two "election cycles." Because controlling one house of Congress was critical to the success of Reagan's legislative programs, the White House was desperate to keep the Senate in the 1986 election.

11. Later VCNO, commander of the Pacific Command, and US ambassador to China.

12. The law, which became known as Goldwater-Nichols, strengthened the Joint Chiefs of Staff (and especially its chairman) at the expense of the services.

or has he grown more mellow? The only flash of secretarial anger came against an unlikely target: Mel Paisley. Lehman's best buddy left last night on an extended trip to WestPac. Nettled over some R&D problem, the Secretary said, "This is a hell of a time for him to be away! And he won't be back till June! We have an ironclad rule: no travel over two weeks. If you can be gone more than that, who needs you?" Turning to UnSec Goodrich, Lehman said sternly, "I thought you were in charge of approving travel." Replied Sunny Jim, "I assumed you approved it" — and he was right.

Wednesday, 14 May 1986

At 4:00 there was a truly unusual event: a visit to my office by Jim Webb. All he wanted to do was chat, warmly explaining his scarceness by saying "the Navy's reserve programs are in such good shape I never have to bother with them." When I told Jim about Los Angeles banker Leonard McRoskey, whom Lehman has decided to appoint as DASN for Reserve Affairs, he laughed and said, "A Fred Davidson without the Panama hat!"

Friday, 16 May 1986

SecNav is eagerly anticipating the premiere of *Top Gun*, a feature film about young Navy pilots at Miramar. Navy gave its producers full cooperation on the presumption that if it proves a summer blockbuster we'll reap a lot of recruits. My enthusiasm is low, for *Top Gun* conjoins two strong prejudices of mine, those against Hollywood and against aviators. I'll probably go see it, but first I need to see *An Officer and a Gentleman*.[13]

Friday, 23 May 1986

There was an item in the Navy news clips from the Norfolk *Virginian Pilot* headlined "Navy Changes Pharmacy Policy." It said that starting 1 June, dependents and retirees would no longer receive free over-the-counter drugs like aspirin and cough medicine. In a time when sailors and Marines think they are being abused by the entire system, especially on health care, this

---

13. Navy did not cooperate in filming *An Officer and a Gentleman*, starring Richard Gere and Debra Winger, and as a result the script got many things wrong. Even so, the 1982 drama led to a huge jump in recruitment, encouraging Lehman on *Top Gun*.

little money saver (netting only $1.6 million for the balance of the fiscal year) would be devastating to morale.

I called our beloved surgeon general and demanded to know what was going on. He calmly explained that the drug cutoff was merely one of a dozen actions he took to trim $16 million in Gramm-Rudman hits on MedCom's budget. The reason he hadn't checked it out with me, Lew said, was that it had been approved up through the Financial Management chain of command. I guess Lew never will understand how something like this is different from, say, reducing janitorial services or not hiring more record clerks.

I called SecNav on the hotline and proposed canceling the cutoff. Lehman instantly said, "Revoke it! Get me a piece of paper down here in five minutes and I'll sign it!" This was done, and the crisis ended. Perhaps best of all, CHINFO [chief of information] was able to stop the presses at *Navy Times.* The original story was pulled and one was substituted with the headline "Lehman Saves Free Over-the-Counter Drugs." As long as Lew & Co. prove incapable of foreseeing the human and political dimensions of their actions, I shall always be jumping on them.

All this activity occurred when Gen. J. K. Davis, the ACMC [assistant commandant], was being retired in a ceremony at the Barracks. I wanted to go but cancelled in order to deal with the issue at hand. This is why I haven't taken a WestPac or Med trip: the work to be done in the Pentagon every day outweighs the benefit, real or symbolic, of being with troops abroad. SecNav was at J. K.'s retirement, something he could do because I was back in the shop working his will.

Monday, 26 May 1986

This evening I overcame my prejudices and saw *Top Gun.* It has superb aerial footage and excellent scenes of the deck action on a carrier. The plot, however, was so juvenile as to be an irritating interrupter of the sequences at sea. The star, Tom Cruise, looked too young to be a pilot; he would have been better cast as a sailor. The credits thanked John Lehman and CHINFO Jack Garrow for being (as I can attest) enthusiastic supporters of the film. In fact, I'm surprised that Jack, upon his recent retirement, went to work for Newport News Shipbuilding; I was sure he'd wind up with the sunglasses and exposed-navel set in Hollywood.

Wednesday, 28 May 1986

During the M&RA staff meeting, Betty brought Joe Harford a slip of paper that prompted him to announce, "Now we know why SecDef is back in the building: his choice for CNO won." The choice is Adm. Carl Trost, CINCLANTFLT. The admiralty, in the person of Dudley Carlson, is very happy over the news.

Thursday, 29 May 1986

The American Film Institute at the Kennedy Center has a series of movies commemorating the 75th anniversary of naval aviation. Tonight I saw *Hell Divers* (1931) with Wallace Beery and Clark Gable. It was far better than *Top Gun,* with much more of a plot and so many scenes of the Navy of 55 years ago as almost to be a documentary: San Diego from the air, twin-seater bi-planes, flight operations aboard the beautiful old carrier *Saratoga,* the Navy dirigible *Los Angeles* landing on the carrier's deck, a line of battleships creating an inferno with their guns, and the *Sara* going through the Panama Canal. The movie credits thanked the Navy Department for its cooperation but, unlike *Top Gun,* didn't name the SecNav of the day, my officemate Charles Francis Adams III.

Friday, 30 May 1986

Dudley Carlson thinks Carl Trost is going to be even more sympathetic on manpower and personnel issues than Jim Watkins, which is saying a lot given that Watkins once had Dudley's job as chief of Naval Personnel. Perhaps significantly, SecNav said nothing about the new CNO in the lineup today, and of course no one dared raise the matter. Some newspapers have given the choice an unflattering twist. The *Baltimore Sun*'s story was headlined, "Reagan Overrules Lehman on Naming Top Admiral."

Thursday, 24 June 1986

[In Norfolk,] Alice Stratton and I went aboard USS *Yellowstone,* a destroyer tender whose crew of 1300 has 340 women, ten percent of whom are currently pregnant. We met with about three dozen sailors, all of them single parents and all but five or so of them women. (One woman complained about being told to attend the meeting. Before then, none of her shipmates knew she has a child.) Several eager and voluble women carried the discussion, which easily filled an entire hour. They spoke of the great difficulty of finding daycare or babysitters when they must be on duty at any time of day. Some keep their kids with parents in other cities. One young woman told of visiting her son in New Jersey and discovering that to him "Mother" was *her* mother and that she was simply "Annette." Interestingly, the men spoke not at all; they seem to bear single-parenthood with intense sadness and perhaps other emotions, such as personal failure. One guy I encouraged to speak almost cried.

Wednesday, 25 June 1986

Accompanied by Col. George Walls and retired Col. Gerry Turley USMC, a deputy assistant secretary in Jim Webb's office, I went aboard USS *Iowa* (BB-61), lead ship in the class of battlewagons built during World War II. We were escorted to the captain's in-port cabin, a comfortable space that was FDR's stateroom when he went to the Cairo and Teheran conferences in November 1943. For the President's use, the head contains the only bathtub ever installed in a US naval vessel.

We were given "poopy suits" and taken into the #2 gun turret—the second aft of three, each with three 16-inch guns. We went down, down, down through seven decks to see the powder magazine, the projectiles, and the gear that raises and lowers the guns and turns the turret. It was a world straight from the 1940s. There was a generous use of brass, even for the table and seats where sailors prepare the powder charges to push into the magazine. The trip was not for the claustrophobe or for one with a fear of falling, because we went up and down narrow rungs with shoes made slick from decks made oily, the easier to slide projectiles.[14]

As on the carriers, there is a Marine detachment aboard *Iowa* to guard "special (= nuclear) weapons." But long gone are the days, bitterly recounted in *White Jacket,* when Marines enforced discipline over the sailors and protected the officers from the crew. There is friendly joshing and competition between the crew and the 50-man "MarDet" but none of the hatred of old.

At sea after dinner, I went up on the focsl to stand on the bulbous bow, far from the noise of stacks and engines. Here the day's best time was spent, as a broad splash of orange filled the sky toward Virginia. Looking aft, I beheld *Iowa* as a mighty, dark triangle, her two forward gun mounts at "bristle."

---

14. On 19 April 1989, this turret exploded, killing forty-seven sailors.

Thursday, 26 June 1986

The grand finale of my visit to *Iowa* was the firing of her 16-inch guns. Nothing on sea, and very little on land, can compare with the awesomeness of those guns. Their merely being pointed over the side or elevated or lowered commands total attention and respect. For the first shot, from Turret #1, there was a one-minute standby and then a 10-second countdown, followed by the command "Shoot!"

Then came a flash of yellow and burnt orange, a sudden hot wind, and a concussion that blew my hair, restrained though it was by a ball cap and hard earmuffs. It was, in fact, the *feel* of the report more than the sound that remains my primary impression of the day's shoot. A fellow with a Polaroid camera caught the fireball erupting from the gun barrel, something our winced eyes failed to see. On a couple of occasions, I could see the 1100-pound projectile lofting into the sky, a black speck against the clouds, en route to an altitude of 37,000 feet before splashing into the sea 10 miles to port. With every shot I could hear for several seconds the whiffling sound of this projectile in flight.

We fired about 20 rounds altogether, all but a few from Turrets #1 and #2. The master chief gunner's mate in charge of the shoot, who still remembers with relish salvos fired by the cruiser *St. Paul* against the Chinese in Korea, beamed in delight. "Now, doncha think this would get Qaddafi's attention?" he asked.

Later, I asked to see some of *Iowa*'s engineering spaces, the realm of the snipes, where few battleship visitors ever go. The massiveness and quadruple redundancy of the machinery is impressive, and like the guns, it is a working relic of the 1940s. A delighted captain personally led me on the tour, introduced me to the sailors on duty ("Meet the assistant secretary of the Navy!"), and had them tell me what they do. For over 20 years now on a wide variety of vessels, people have yelled at me in the din of an engine room, trying to explain the steam cycle. I sort of understand it now, but my main aim in going below today was to meet and show solidarity with the guys who work in the heat and muck.

Wednesday, 2 July 1986

The highlight of the day was having Edmund and Sylvia Morris to lunch. I suggested to SecNav that he make the lunch his own, and he eagerly agreed. With Edmund chronicling the Reagan presidency, exposing him to one of the Administration's stars would literally help John's place in history.[15] I let John play gracious and witty host. Among the things Lehman said:

★ After firing Admiral Rickover in 1981, SecNav thought it would be a sincere and appropriate gesture if President Reagan personally thanked Rickover for his 60 years of service in the Navy. On the appointed day, Lehman, Rickover, and SecDef Weinberger were ushered into the Oval Office. The photographers had their minute, and the instant the door closed behind them, Rickover exploded at Reagan, shouting, "What kind of a son-of-a-bitch president of the United States are you to let a little pissant secretary of the Navy fire me?" Reagan looked shocked, and Weinberger's eyes poured daggers into an equally astonished Lehman. Rickover asked to speak privately with the President if "these clerks" could be sent from the room. The President ("who's such a nice guy") granted this request, with Lehman and Weinberger straining to listen through the wall. His time over, a recomposed admiral coolly asked Lehman if he could give him a ride back to the Pentagon. "Underneath that gruff exterior was a pretty mean little guy," Lehman said. "He was totally schizophrenic, just like Henry Kissinger, with two completely formed personalities."

★ Speaking directly to Edmund, Lehman noted that it's been the civilian leadership of the Navy, not the admiralty, who saved the fleet in times of national neglect—in 1981 just as in the 1890s, "when, as you pointed out in your book [*The Rise of Theodore Roosevelt*], it was Teddy Roosevelt[16] who gave his theories to [Capt. Alfred Thayer] Mahan and not the other way around."

★ The villain in the recent struggle over the new CNO was Vice Adm. John Poindexter, the President's national security advisor, and not Weinberger. "That job [NSC director] needs a gut fighter," Lehman said. "That's why Henry was so perfect in it. He was slitting throats faster than others could slit his."

Back in my office, Edmund inscribed my copy of *The Rise*, "To Chase Untermeyer, a worthy successor to the 'Hot Weather Secretary' mentioned in these pages."[17]

---

15. For better or worse, Lehman got only a cursory mention in *Dutch*, Edmund's controversial, novelized biography of Reagan, published in 1999.

16. Rooseveltians know that their hero hated the nickname "Teddy" and preferred to be known as "TR."

17. As AsstSecNav when that was the number-two job in a Cabinet department, TR was only too happy to run the Navy when his boss, John Davis Long, spent the summer of 1897 back home in Massachusetts rather than in steamy Washington.

Thursday, 3 July 1986

Dudley Carlson was typically caustic when I raised some of the things I learned aboard *Yellowstone* last week. "I'm glad you go out and see our ships and learn so much!" he said. When I replied that if I didn't visit ships he'd accuse me of not knowing what's really happening in the fleet, he laughed.

Friday, 4 July 1986

On this day, the restored Statue of Liberty was rededicated by President Reagan in a gala event that featured an in-gathering of naval vessels from around the world, many of them full-rigged "tall ships." I could have gone but jumped at the chance to do something that in an ordinary year John Lehman or Jim Goodrich always did: represent the Navy Department on the annual "turnaround cruise" of USS Constitution ("Old Ironsides") in Boston Harbor. Then and still today, Old Ironsides remains a fully commissioned vessel of the US Navy with a commanding officer and crew. Every year on Independence Day, the ship (built in 1797) is hauled by tugs to a point in mid-harbor, turned around, and returned to the dock the other way around so that she will weather evenly.

A *Constitution* crew member, wearing a naval uniform from 1812 with a tasseled straw sombrero, picked me up at the hotel and drove me the short distance to the Charlestown Navy Yard. In the headquarters building I met my fellow special guests, most notably the consul general of Japan. We were then led on board in reverse rank, passing through a double line of gents in Revolutionary War uniforms, dipping colonial flags, and past a line of sailors who held their broad-brimmed hats at arm's length—a salute called the "hoozah"—and on board ship.

A tug pushed us out into the harbor, where we picked up an escort of Coast Guard, police, fire, and pleasure craft. I was below, touring the gun and berthing decks, when *Constitution* started firing a 21-gun salute to the flag, answered by an old fort on one of the harbor islands. Sailors in old-style dungarees and new-style goggles and earmuffs fired the shells in what an officer called "the world's only breech-loading muzzle loaders"—iron guns cast in the 1920s to resemble the ship's original armament.

When we returned to the pier, I stopped at the foot of the brow to receive a 17-gun salute. The battery caused the crowd to jump and squeal, and the smoke from the black powder made the air as thick and gray as fog. When the firing ended, I stumbled blindly off, waving the cloud away.

Saturday, 12 July 1986

While eating breakfast, I read a front-page story in the *Post* ("Pentagon Pressure Forces Out Company Official") saying that Mel Paisley and Ev Pyatt complained to Raytheon when Larry Korb (now a lobbyist for the firm) testified against the Reagan defense budget as a member of some sort of DOD-watch committee. Raytheon, a major Navy contractor, got the message and canned Korb, who now will be what he should have been all along, a dean at the University of Pittsburgh. My guess is that Raytheon wasn't pleased with the arrogant, acerbic Korb to begin with.

Monday, 21 July 1986

At the lineup I said that the Army and Air Force academies immediately discharge any cadet who tests positive for the AIDS antibody. Navy's more humane policy is to keep someone on duty until such time as he/she becomes sick. OSD wants a consistent policy, as is always its wont, and Lehman concurs. He will ask SecDef to make *our* policy the standard. Listening to this discussion, Ev Pyatt said to me, "I'm sure glad I don't have to deal with tough issues like that. Mine are simpler: they're all about greed."

Monday, 4 August 1986

This morning there was another of the periodic briefings at the White House for political appointees below Cabinet rank. Chief of Staff Don Regan introduced "the other fellow—the one who doesn't know how to spell his name." The President sauntered in wearing his famous brown suit and his even more famous glowing smile. "It's time for a finale the world will never forget," he said. "We have 2½ years to crown our achievements. As I look around this room, I don't see a single individual who looks like a lame duck. And I certainly don't feel like a lame duck."

Tuesday, 5 August 1986

Today the *New York Times* reported a leaked SecNav memo directing CNO to commence design for fast-track construction of a square-rigged, iron-hulled sailing vessel to be called *United States*. No doubt inspired by the glories of sail seen in New York harbor a month ago, Lehman said in the memo that the tall ship will symbolize America's naval heritage, teach seamanship, aid recruiting, and be "a suitable gift to the nation on the 200th anniversary of the Constitution's ratification" [in 1988].

I may be like those who considered Shah Jahan's plan to build an elaborate tomb at Agra in memory of his departed wife a needless expense. But the tall ship proposal is literally ridiculous, in that it begged for (and promptly received) ridicule. *United States* was aborted at conception: the DOD press spokesman said, "It is not approved and would not be approved." Right when both houses are debating the DOD authorization bill and are poised to cut combatants from Navy's budget, proposing such a folly is crazy—as a master of the congressional process like John Lehman should instinctively know. On the heels of trying to make Frank Kelso CNO and pushing Paul David Miller for the Seventh Fleet, this gambit raises new questions about John. As the ancients said, those whom the gods would destroy they first make mad.

It is odd that the Coast Guard has a tall ship (Eagle) and the US Navy does not. But the Naval Academy has a first-rate fleet of sailboats on which midshipman learn at close range the ways of the sea and gain experience as both deckhands and skippers.

Thursday, 7 August 1986

Before the morning budget strategy session began, Carl Trost (former chief Navy budgeteer) had a jovial exchange with the Assistant Commandant over some trick the Marines tried to play. Carl boomed, "Don't forget that I *understand* this bullshit!" When SecNav entered the room, it was in a mood of triumph: the Senate had defeated (34–65) an amendment to strike funding for the new homeports at Everett and Staten Island. "It reflects the consensus that Navy has in the Senate," Lehman said. "The gauntlet was thrown by Goldwater and Nunn, and we won." He said the 600-ship goal requires a steady rate of not less than 20 ships a year. "Once we ever go below that level," he warned, "the unraveling and the slide will begin. This building is so loaded against the Navy Department that the only reason we have done as well as we have is that Senate consensus." He added that the ship numbers are far more important than the date we reach them.

The highest number of battle-force ships reached was 566 in 1988. After that, the end of the Cold War and the loss of élan for naval shipbuilding caused the number to drop precipitously, as Lehman had predicted. As of 2013, there were just 286 vessels in the fleet, many of them built or authorized during the Lehman secretaryship.

Tuesday, 12 August 1986

As I was heading out to a meeting, the Marine receptionist called, "Sir: you've got a call from France!" It was from Lynn Wyatt, the remarkably down-to-earth jetsetter from Houston. She's now at their villa in Villefranche [on the Riviera], from the terrace of which she spied a USN vessel coming into port. Loyal to the service on whose academy's board she sits, Lynn called me to invite the captain and his officers to dinner tonight chez Wyatt. This I passed to staff, who passed it to the Naval Command Center, who by now have passed it to USS *Whatever*, whose skipper is in for a surprise and a treat.

Wednesday, 13 August 1986

This morning I represented Navy at the Pentagon arrival ceremony for the defense minister of El Salvador, a General Casanova. He looked the part: a husky, swarthy fellow of the sort with many mistresses and few favorite civil liberties. The Marine Band played the national anthems, that of El Salvador being almost ludicrously long. Complained Vice Adm. Cec Kempf afterwards, "I hope the General appreciates that holding that salute as long as I did will be hell on my golf swing."

Thursday, 14 August 1986

In his lunge to tie down a majority in the House on homeporting, SecNav has offered to place two more Naval Reserve frigates in Philadelphia as a lure for the vote of Congressman Bill Gray. Philadelphia can barely support the four frigates they already have. A few days ago, when informed that Rep. Vic Fazio (D-California) expects an NROTC unit at Sacramento State, Lehman mockingly admonished, "We are not selling indulgences." But of course he is; who knows what the real cost of homeporting will be?

Tuesday, 26 August 1986

At 2:00, I was in the Blue Room for the big meeting on next year's Navy budget. The most significant part of the session—indeed, it could prove historic—came when budgeteer Charlie Nemfakos[18] got Lehman to focus for

---

18. Charlie's brilliance, professionalism, and loyalty made him a senior civil servant whom Lehman and Paisley liked.

the first time on successors to *George Washington,* the last Nimitz-class carrier currently planned. Charlie and his gnomes found some $700 million in various accounts to fund the initial year of a two-carrier buy. His argument was political: unless DOD commits to pursuing the carriers next year, the chance may be lost, for Congress probably would take no action in a presidential election year, and there may be a hostile administration in office in 1989. Furthermore, Charlie said, prices may never be cheaper, thanks to various Lehman initiatives on procurement, and Navy's budget may never be higher.

"I'm not trying to flatter you, Mr. Secretary," he said, "but if you don't do this, no one else will be able to pull it off."

There's no question Lehman wants the ships, but he fears that if he goes to Weinberger and Taft saying he has $700 million set aside to start construction on two carriers, they will turn him down and take the money away. That's the gamble, Charlie said firmly. "Let's see," Lehman said at the end of the discussion, still not appearing to be sold on the deal. "Which one will be the *Cap Weinberger* and which the *Ronald Reagan?*"[19]

Tuesday, 9 September 1986

A Navy car took me to the officers club at Bethesda for a dinner for the department heads of all naval hospitals. In my remarks, I spoke of Cadwallader Cuticle, the sawbones surgeon aboard USS *Neversink* in Melville's *White Jacket:*

> Surrounded by moans and shrieks, by features distorted with anguish inflicted by himself, he yet maintained a countenance almost supernaturally calm. . . . Indeed, long habituation to the dissecting-room and amputation table had made him seemingly impervious to the ordinary emotions of humanity. . . . Yet you could not say that Cuticle was essentially a cruel-hearted man. His apparent heartlessness [was] of a purely scientific origin. It is not to be imagined [he] would have harmed a fly, unless he could procure a microscope powerful enough to assist him in experimenting on the minute vitals of the creature.

19. Although there would eventually be a carrier named for Reagan, these two ships were named *John C. Stennis* and *Harry S Truman.* In 1983, then-DepSecDef Paul Thayer thought he had killed Navy's request for two new carriers. But Lehman won a famous victory by getting the White House to announce that President Reagan had endorsed his Navy secretary's recommendation to name the fleet's next two aircraft carriers *Abraham Lincoln* and *George Washington.*

I'm certain the shade of old Herman smiled contentedly to have his words read at a dinner of Navy doctors, including Cuticle's spiritual descendant, the Surgeon General.

Thursday, 9 October 1986

SecNav called in a playful mood, recounting the laugh "everyone" in SecDef's staff meeting this morning had at SecArmy Marsh's expense when he showed the fancy certificates they give soldiers who receive dishonorable discharges. "Surely we don't do the same," he half-asked. I said we surely do — or did until Lehman ordered them destroyed. Actually, the certificates we issue are rather plain. As a joke I sent him a sample that I further embellished with curlicues and mock legends: "Give up the ship!" "We have met the enemy, and I am his!" "Damn! Torpedoes! Full speed *ahead?*" and "Sighted sub; sank self."

Thursday, 16 October 1986

Lynn Wyatt's appointment to a full term on the Naval Academy Board of Visitors is being held up by Phil Gramm because [her husband] Oscar attacked the senator for opposing an oil import fee.[20] SecNav asked me to contact Gramm's office and "probe discreetly" into whether he will allow Lynn's appointment to go through in time for her to attend tomorrow's Board meeting. I called Al Ptak, Gramm's assistant for military affairs, who was just about to go see the senator on other matters. Ten or fifteen minutes later, back came the reply: "Over my dead body!" When I reported this to Lynn, she said she had asked Oscar why an appointment to the Naval Academy board should be affected by an oil issue, and he said, "Honey, you've just had your first lesson in politics."[21]

Later I returned a call from Congressman Dick Armey (R-Texas), who has been pushing us to discharge his perfectly healthy, well-performing sister-in-law from the Navy so she can go to college. I told Armey that this does not qualify her for a hardship discharge. He then asked whether it isn't a hardship

---

20. Appointees to the service academy boards of visitors do not require Senate confirmation, but as a courtesy the White House routinely clears prospective members with their home state senators.

21. On 5 May 1987, Gramm asked me why Navy pushed the wife of his archenemy for the Annapolis board. When I told him of the Lynn-Lehman-Princess Grace connection, Gramm paid me the ominous compliment of saying, "I thought you had done it because you come from Houston."

"to have a congressman mad at you." I offered a compromise that Armey accepted (but that my staff didn't much like), which is to transfer the woman to a duty station near where she wants to go to school. If Armey were important to Navy, such as being on one of the committees we constantly court, I would have granted the discharge.

Armey was not then important, but he would father the Base Realignment and Closure (BRAC) process that eventually would claim Lehman's cherished new homeports in New York and Texas, and he would be majority leader of the House of Representatives from 1995–2003.

Friday, 17 October 1986

Joe Harford came into the office with the best news in a long while: that Dick Elster wants to return east, the family problems that forced him back to Monterey last winter apparently resolved. This is wonderful, for it means that after months of searching we can fill Dick's vacancy with the original article.

Friday, 24 October 1986

I dropped in to brief SecNav on DACOWITS, which he'll address on Sunday. I said he can announce the opening of the boiler tech, machinist's mate, and ops specialist (radar-watcher) ratings to women. Lehman laughed at the mental picture of a female BT [boiler tech]. But the prime topic before the group is whether women should serve in Mobile Logistics Support Force ships. Lehman still resists doing this because of the tensions in the families of men aboard such ships. "It's wives who make Navy men leave the Navy," he told me (and won't tell DACOWITS).

Monday, 27 October 1986

At the lineup I asked SecNav about his appearance yesterday before DACO-WITS. With great despair he said there is no way to prevent legislation to open the MLSF to women. "We don't have a very impressive argument," he said. But then he went on to his main argument, which is very Father McGehee-from-the-parish: "How can you put a few women aboard a ship with a lot of men, send them to sea for six months, and keep peace of mind at home? Every time we throw another baby off the sled [to appease DACO-

WITS] it just increases the appetite for more. If we lose the MLSF, then that will open up the issue of women on combatants. Our divorce rate is double the national average. Wives and husbands have enough tensions without this."

I think Lehman is wrong, or mostly wrong. In the new year I shall make a major effort to get him to think through the whole women-in-the-Navy issue.

Tuesday, 28 October 1986

The final event of today's visit to the Naval Academy was meeting with members of the Brigade Honor Committee. Like the last time I did this, some were astonished to learn that their recommendations to discharge fellow midshipmen for honor offenses are not final with the superintendent but go on to my desk and sometimes SecNav's. I spelled out the US constitutional system in which civilians supervise the military and added: "The test of our society is not whether we have a great naval academy or a great navy. The test, as we have defined it for ourselves, is whether we protect the rights of the individual." The task of my listeners, both now and in the fleet, I said, is to balance those rights against the needs and mission of the institution.

When the mids raised the Bellistri case, I explained the Secretary's desire to be fair to the accused. There was no argument, though no one looked particularly persuaded, either.

Wednesday, 29 October 1986

"Boston IV" [the fourth Boston conference] commenced with a long monologue by the Secretary, something he called a preamble, on what he hoped would be the tone of the meeting. It would be focused on "midcourse corrections" in order to "solidify in the next two years those major improvements we have made in the way we do business."

Reading from notes with half-glasses halfway down his nose, Adm. Kin McKee [head of Naval Reactors] told the Secretary that his "well-intentioned" pushes for competition and low cost are threatening quality. "Even though you think things are going well, I can tell you that poor-quality work is increasing in the shipyards because the shipyard commanders' attention has been diverted" from quality to competition. "This is not a midcourse correction," he warned the Secretary. "You're on final."

Lehman didn't lash back at this criticism. He endorsed McKee's concern for quality and said he "assumed that the customer [e.g., McKee] doesn't accept shoddy work. . . . I don't ever want to hear you happy and content with cost pressures on the yards. You should keep raising issues of quality control, for if you have a defect on one of your subs it's the end of the Navy."

Returning to his "preamble," Lehman said that in order to protect Navy and Marine Corps on the Hill and elsewhere, the Department's civilian officials need full access to information and participation in policy making. Our civilian predecessors were neither fools nor incompetents, Lehman said, but they were cut out of this process. "In my first year in this job it was like pulling friggin' teeth to find out what was happening," he said with a trace of choler. CNO didn't dispute him: "When I was EA in the office you now occupy [serving then-SecNav Warner]," Carl Trost said, "I know very well that CNO [Bud Zumwalt] made every effort to keep the secretary in the dark."

We were then subjected to a long, confused chart talk by Mel Paisley on why acquisition should be centralized under him. Only John Lehman really likes Mel; the rest of us heard his muddled spiel with almost comical looks of boredom, puzzlement, or gastric attack. P. X. Kelley reacted fiercely to Mel's proposal. Later, when his chopper passed over HQMC to land at the Pentagon, the Commandant looked out and bellowed, "That damn Paisley's got his flag flying from *my* goddamned flagpole!"

Thursday, 30 October 1986

This afternoon brought the reporting-out of the major general selection board, chaired by the affable, pipe-smoking Texan, Lt. Gen. D'Wayne Gray, CG of FMFPAC [commanding general of Fleet Marine Force Pacific]. D'Wayne gave SecNav the list of the eight selectees; Lehman studied it and frowned. He was disappointed, he said, not to see the name of Brig. Gen. Jim Mead (CG at Cherry Point) among the aviators chosen for promotion. Lehman said he would reconvene the panel with another "letter of guidance" saying that the needs of the Marine Corps are such that it needs another two-star aviator. In that event, D'Wayne said, "Large James" will be selected. It was an interesting glimpse into how Lehman manipulates flag selections.

Friday, 31 October 1986

Shortly after the reporting-out of the brigadier general selection board, D'Wayne Gray returned with the revised major generals list. "They got the message," D'Wayne said laconically. Seeing Jim Mead's name on the report, Lehman said, "This is *much* better" and signed it.

Tuesday, 4 November 1986

I got to the VP's house in a drizzle, appropriate for the general Republican mood. Inside, however, everything had the usual Bushian glow. The VP and Barbara's election watch party would draw almost all the top Bush political friends and plotters, including Treasury Secretary Jim Baker, Nick Brady, Craig Fuller, Lee Atwater, Dean Burch, Jennifer Fitzgerald, and press secretary Marlin Fitzwater.

Also present was ex-national security advisor Bud McFarlane. He and I had arrived before the other guests and watched the evening news together. There was a crazy story out of Beirut that Bud had gone to Tehran to try to free the Americans held in Lebanon, bringing a cake in the shape of a key (as in the key to their cell). I laughed out loud at the ridiculousness of the report, and GB, looking bemused, drew Bud aside to talk about it.

Quite early in the evening, the networks called Democratic Senate victories in Florida, Maryland, and North Carolina. With the GOP margin in the Senate now only 53–47, we could only afford to lose three seats to maintain control (using the tiebreaking vote of our host). The best news of the night was winning the governorships of Texas and Florida.

Wednesday, 5 November 1986

Today the "morning after" was rainy, cold, and bleak. The Dems will control the new Senate 55–45. Though this is of course a setback for the President, every one of his Republican predecessors since 1954 also endured a Congress completely in Democratic hands.

Last night Marvin Bush confirmed that his brother George has sold his business (doing quite well) and will come east this spring to help his dad's campaign. Marvin has the same doubts that Jennifer, Thadd Garrett, and I do about Craig and Lee. Nodding in the direction of both men, Marvin said, "They're out for themselves, not to see my dad elected president." We both agreed that George will lay into that crowd.

The Under invited me to join him at lunch with his special guest, Rear Adm. John Bulkeley, the 76-year-old president of the Insurv (Inspection & Survey) Board.[22] So splendidly tough and energetic is Bulkeley that CNOs, SecNavs, and the Congress have happily kept him on active duty well beyond his retirement date. Bulkeley loves doing his act, speaking at high speed,

---

22. See 3 June 1983.

putting his half-glasses on and off, and making gruff jokes that use his audience as straight men. For example, he condemned the Phalanx or CIWS[23] antimissile Gatling gun as unreliable. "What does CIWS stand for?" he asked, pointing at me.

"Close-In Weapon System," I replied.

"Wrong! It stands for 'Christ, It Won't Shoot!'"

Monday, 10 November 1986

In the late afternoon I went to the State Department for the swearing-in of Jim Lilley as ambassador to Korea. The large and eminent crowd included Barbara Bush and Cap Weinberger. A protocolary administered the oath to Jim, who then made elegant and moving remarks. He paid special tribute to Sally and to her father, a fellow CIA operative who was killed on a mission to North Korea. As Sally teared up, BPB squared her padded shoulders as if to say, "Oh dear; ambassadors' wives don't cry."

There was a long receiving line that I skipped, since I'd be seeing the Lilleys at a celebratory dinner and farewell this evening. Plucking a glass of champagne off a tray, I walked out onto the 8th floor terrace to take in one of the most glorious views in all of Washington. I had the clear presentiment that one day on the premises I'd be taking the oath as an ambassador myself.[24]

Tuesday, 18 November 1986

Tonight brought a big black-tie dinner benefiting the conservative Ethics & Public Policy Center. I was the guest of Federal Trade Commission chairman Dan Oliver and his wife Louise.[25] The master of ceremonies was the aging actor Charlton Heston, who in a rich, resonant voice introduced his predecessor as president of the Screen Actors Guild, Ronald Reagan. The President was in fine form, though his wattles seemed rouged. The past few weeks have

---

23. See 4 May 1985.

24. And so I did, a little under 18 years later.

25. As members of the New York Knickerbocker elite, the Olivers brought old-shoe elegance to the conservative movement. Dan liked to say, "I'm everything Ronald Reagan wanted in an FTC chairman—and less." Louise became US ambassador to the United Nations Educational, Scientific & Cultural Organization (UNESCO) during the second Bush administration.

been among the roughest of his administration, with the loss of the Senate, the disclosure of the foolish arms-for-friendship gambit in Iran, and the known opposition of his own secretaries of State and Defense to the plan. Perhaps for this reason RR gave one of the strongest speeches I've ever heard from him, reaffirming his conservative faith with several references to a day when the citizens of the USSR might have liberty.

Wednesday, 19 November 1986

Susan Porter Rose, Mrs. Bush's chief of staff, was my guest for lunch in the private dining room. We both agree that the Bush campaign needs a senior, respected figure who can tame Lee Atwater and command the respect of GB—like Jim Baker if not Jim Baker. We disagreed on the desirability of George W. Bush's arrival on the scene next spring. I think George will make and express some fast opinions about the organization that GB needs to hear. Susan fears that George "wants to be another Lee Atwater."

Thursday, 20 November 1986

In five years at the Navy Department, I never once went overseas, highly unusual if not bizarre behavior in the Pentagon. But I had had enough official travel jetting all over the globe with Vice President Bush. I realized quite early that while it was enjoyable and informative to visit the troops, there were plenty of them to visit along the 750-mile axis from Washington to Orlando, doing everything the Navy and Marine Corps did anywhere in the world. The only foreign country to which I ever traveled on business was not very far: The Bahamas, on whose Andros Island was AUTEC, the Atlantic Undersea Test & Evaluation Center.

Leaving overcoats behind, George Walls and I departed the Pentagon for Andrews with our escort, Capt. Anson Burlingame. The tall, sandy-haired Kentuckian is in charge of readiness and tactics for SSNs (attack submarines). He holds that "there are two kinds of ships—submarines and targets."

We banked over the Everglades and landed at the Tamiami Airport to pick up my special guest: Jeb Bush. My aim in inviting him was twofold: to see him again, Jeb being the young Bush I admire most; and to introduce him to the Navy, since he has never had any exposure to the military. Jeb will resign as Dade County GOP chairman next month (after ensuring his successor is pro-GB) to support his father overtly. Earlier this month, gubernatorial candidate Bob Martinez carried the county, something only two Republicans have done in modern times: Richard Nixon in 1972 and RR in 1984. So, Jeb can resign with a record of success.[26]

The plane took off on the 45-minute hop to Andros Island, the largest of the Bahamas. From the air we could clearly see the division between the deep blue of the Tongue of the Ocean (TOTO) containing the AUTEC range and the light green of the Great Bahama Bank. As a saltwater environment protected against general ocean noise, TOTO is a unique feature perfect for submarine exercises and tests. Andros itself is scrubby and swampy, with some sections thick with trees. The US has leased land for AUTEC since the 1950s, and about 1500 Americans live and work there.

Jeb came to my room in the BOQ for a beer, full of questions about how the Navy is organized and how I fit in. (He likes to call me "Admiral.") When we then joined the others in the bar, one of our hosts boomed, "Let me buy the Vice President's son an 80-cent drink!"

After dinner we were taken to "the blockhouse," a large building filled with computers tied to submerged sound detectors out on TOTO. These machines monitor and record what happens on the range. We were asked to sign the guest book, its most prominent signature being that of "Elizabeth R." in October 1985. Jeb experienced his baptismal military briefing, complete with an endless number of viewgraphs filled with incomprehensible, even laughable acronyms. On a big screen in another room we sat down to watch the absorbing "mini-war" exercise that had just started.

What we saw was this: the sub *Atlanta* (SSN-712), which we'll ride tomorrow, was stalking the destroyer *Kidd*, commanded by Dan Murphy Jr. *Kidd* and air assets were stalking the sub, too, but the sub got in a torpedo shot before it was "killed" by one of its hunters. We watched a replay of the torpedo heading for *Kidd*, which went to max speed to outrun it, and the torpedo ran out of fuel within 1000 feet of its prey.

Friday, 21 November 1986

In the clear pre-dawn a chopper flew us down Andros to an AUTEC outpost where we boarded a small cabin cruiser, our taxi out to the sub. We headed for a point on the horizon that showed as little more than a pillar—

---

26. On 10 December, Martinez would announce Jeb's selection as state secretary of commerce. Jeb would be governor himself from 1999–2007.

the conning tower of USS *Atlanta*. Elsewhere on the horizon were USS *Kidd* and several helos dipping their sonars into the water, looking for another sub in today's exercise. The purpose of the mini-war is to give real-time training to PCOs (prospective commanding officers) just out of a six-week course on submarine tactics. It was a tense time for these future skippers, for although they weren't being graded, their quickness and command authority were under close and immediate review by their peers and everyone else in the crowded control room of a real sub.

Atlanta lay on the calm surface like a big buoyant shark. A deck party was standing on the ship's narrow spine to receive us as we jumped from the boat. I immediately went down the hatch, a tricky maneuver in a Mae West lifejacket and sunglasses, as the bosn of the watch rang a bell eight times and announced "Navy, arriving!" on the speaker system. After a breakfast of hotcakes we went on a quick tour. This was primarily for Jeb's benefit, but because he doesn't hold a Top Secret clearance he couldn't go into the reactor compartment. We ended up in the control room—a sub's equivalent of the bridge—for the dive. This was on a gentle slope, but almost immediately there were exciting sharp-angled rises and falls at high speed to engage surface contacts and to avoid the pesky, swarming helos.

At first it looked as if Cdr. Ralph Stoll, PCO of *Albany,* had done poorly, for the helos knew where we were, losing us the element of surprise. Stoll evaded to the east at flank speed and then took some quick looks through the periscope—quick so that the scope's tiny wake would not be observed from the helos. What he saw was the cruiser *Ticonderoga;* by lucky stroke we had fled from the helos to the very place *Tico* had gone to evade *us.* We fired a Mark 48 torpedo, which left the sub with a loud whoosh and a sudden decompression in the atmosphere. The Mark 48 homed in on the cruiser, which never knew it was under attack, and we scored a bull's-eye. Later, we had another chance to sink *Tico,* and we did. Stoll was thus the star of the class.

In between these two attacks, I left the control room to do what I usually do on board a ship, which is to visit with the crew. Their biggest gripe was about when they get paid, which is always acute for submariners. On deployment they don't get regular paychecks, causing severe problems at home.

Atlanta soon set course for the main base, sparing us the chopper ride back. I went up on the sail to join the captain and a blissful Jeb. When the pilot boat approached, we said our goodbyes and went down one hatch and up another, departing the ship with all the PCOs. I chatted with one of them,

Cdr. Ed Giambastiani,[27] on the run into port. Meanwhile, *Atlanta* stole away, back to war.

Tuesday, 25 November 1986

When I returned from the Pentagon Concourse to buy a few items, Betty told me people were gathered in Joe's office to watch TV. The President, in the White House briefing room, announced that his national security advisor, Vice Adm. John Poindexter, had resigned and that Poindexter's assistant, Lt. Col. Oliver North USMC, had been relieved. Attorney General Meese followed to explain that the crazy arms-to-Iran deal was even crazier than we imagined: North had apparently taken the money the Iranians paid for the weapons and passed it on to the Contras in Nicaragua. This has the makings of the biggest national scandal since (I dread to say it) Watergate.

Thursday, 27 November 1986

I drove to Baltimore for another wonderful Thanksgiving with John and Eve Hilgenberg.[28] Fellow guests were their family friends Janek and Jolanda Osmanczyk. He is a 74-year-old, white-haired, bowtie-wearing senior Polish journalist, and she is also a writer. Their stories of censorship and official boobery in a communist state are what every American should hear on Thanksgiving. (Of course, official boobery is not a Polish monopoly, as events of the last three weeks have shamefully shown.) Only Party members get luxury goods, but everything is available to those with influential friends, which the Osmanczyks have. A steward on Aeroflot obtained for them a half-kilo tin of genuine Caspian caviar, which we enjoyed before heading to the Maryland Club for the traditional turkey dinner. (Man cannot live by caviar alone.)

---

27. Twenty years later, Giambastiani would be a four-star admiral and vice-chairman of the Joint Chiefs of Staff.

28. I had met John while an admiral's aide in the Philippines. A Navy supply officer, he was second in charge of the R&R (rest and recreation) center in Singapore, which was under Rear Admiral Kauffman's purview. This duty required John to oversee the hotels in which US troops spent their five-day leaves. These hotels were in effect US Navy–sanctioned bordellos, an amusing but potentially explosive circumstance that never became public but that figured into the plot of Paul Theroux's 1972 novel *Saint Jack*.

Friday, 28 November 1986

The Evans & Novak column in today's *Post* said that RR was intrigued with the notion of making John Lehman his national security advisor but that Ed Meese and Don Regan shot it down. The Iran arms affair has provided handy cover for Lehman: a few days ago, SecDef censured him, Mel Paisley, and Ev Pyatt for pressuring Raytheon to fire Larry Korb last spring. Ordinarily, that would have received a great deal of play.

Saturday, 6 December 1986

The star of stars in Navy's hospitality room at the Army-Navy Game in Philadelphia was Lt. Col. Oliver North himself. The CNO, Carl Trost, was telling people, "With the Army and Navy both here, the Air Force is back in Washington scraping up all the budget." Other celebrities on hand were Lynn and Oscar Wyatt, OMB [Office of Management and Budget] director Jim Miller, John and Lois Herrington, FBI director William Webster, Amtrak chief (and ex-SecNav) Graham Claytor, ex–NSC director Bud McFarlane, and Bob Ballard, discoverer of the *Titanic*. I most enjoyed talking with Sen.-elect John McCain III (R-Arizona). I told of hosting his mother at lunch at the Pentagon recently, and he thanked me for being so kind to her. "As far as I'm concerned," I replied, "the Navy can never repay the debt it owes the McCain family." The middies ended a miserable season by losing miserably to Army, 27–7.

Monday, 8 December 1986

[GOP operative and Bush supporter] Ron Kaufman and I both are ticked off at how Lee Atwater, Craig Fuller, and others rushed to take credit for GB's successful speech last week at the American Enterprise Institute (AEI) on Iran/Contra. Ron read me an item from the *New York Times,* obviously planted by [vice presidential deputy chief of staff] Fred Khedouri, who recently resigned. The story bewailed the loss to Bush, since he [Fred] had played such a major role in shaping the AEI speech. The leak is worthy of refusing Fred's letter of resignation—and then firing his ass.

Tuesday, 9 December 1986

Today the top Navy and Marine Corps leadership traveled back to the Longlea manor for "Boston IV Alpha" to finish what wasn't covered on 29 October. The Secretary spoke of how well things work now that he and CNO have direct access by telephone hotline to the three-star systems commanders (for air, sea, and space) and vice versa. I leaned over to observe to UnSec Goodrich, "It works well because John Lehman is secretary." I can easily imagine his successor walking into the office, gaping at the telephone, and asking his EA, "What are all these buttons on the phone? Get rid of 'em. All I need is a hotline to CNO."

When we completed the agenda, a tray of bottles and a crumbly cheese ball were brought out. The standup talk was all about Ollie North and the NSC. Lehman, an NSC staffer in the Nixon years, said people who work there get subsumed in its power and "the really neat stuff" that comes in the cable traffic. They also spend long hours at work, which Lehman rejects: "The only way to have an impact in Washington is to stay around long enough, and the only way to do that is to keep having fun."

Wednesday, 10 December 1986

At noon I took a Navy car to the Senate side of the Capitol, arriving simultaneously with Lee Atwater, Rich Bond, Pete Teeley,[29] and Ron Kaufman. We had been invited to lunch with the VP and the Bond Group of present and former Bush political operatives. When GB arrived in the private dining room he was escorted by his well-dressed walrus of a chief of staff, Craig Fuller. When we sat down, I positioned myself in clear and close line of sight across the table from the VP.

The table talk inevitably centered on the Iran arms controversy. GB bluntly said his fortunes will rise and fall with the Administration, as they have since 1980. He does want to seek some forum wherein he can put to rest any concern that he and RR have been untruthful to the American people. I am glad GB is thinking about a more complete disclosure than he gave in his carefully-phrased AEI speech last week [in which he acknowledged "mistakes were made"]. Vic Gold[30] was in prime form, seething and salivating on any subject. When he condemned his old friend Pat Buchanan as "out of control" for giving speeches disclaimed by the White House, Vic provided the opening for a little speech I had devised and practiced since the morning.

---

29. Teeley had been press secretary to George Bush during the 1979–80 campaigns and the first half of his vice presidency. He would be ambassador to Canada from 1992–93.

30. Bush's tempestuous ex-speechwriter and co-author with him of *Looking Forward: An Autobiography* (1987).

"I'd like to raise a matter about control that's a little closer to home," I began. "You gave a fine speech last week, and it was well received. But I was offended to read in the *Washington Post* a fat paragraph of movie credits of all the people supposedly working for you, at least one of whom made sure those names were in the story—all with the effect of not giving you the credit for that speech." There was silence, even from Vic; the VP looked at me with a benign smile. I continued: "I remember before the '81 inauguration how Dan Murphy told the staff, 'There is only one star in this office, and that is George Bush.' That's why I see all these self-advertisements as disloyal to you. And I promise to make a public recantation when, after you make a *disastrous* speech or a catastrophic appearance, these same people rush forward to tell their friends in the press, 'I wrote that speech' or 'I advised him to make that trip.'"

GB nodded in response and said with a soft voice, "That's been taken care of." After lunch he said, "I appreciate your comments." Both statements were general, and yet I sensed some deep sincerity in his gratitude for what I had said.[31] Surely it deserved to be aired, especially with Atwater and Fuller listening. I may have sown the seeds of danger with those two, but I'm happier for having been honest, forthright, and concerned strictly for GB.

Ron Kaufman called me tonight to say, "You made me proud to be a friend of Chase Untermeyer today. You said something that everybody in that room—save two—felt but didn't have the balls to say." I asked Ron how he felt those two took my words. He laughingly quoted his wife as saying, "Lee is just egotistical enough to think you weren't talking about him." Craig is another matter: "He is unforgiving and unrelenting, with no sense of humor about him. You're either a friend or an enemy."

This evening I attended a Christmas party given by the Christian Embassy, which runs a number of Bible studies for people in the Executive Branch, Congress, the Pentagon, and wives thereof. Someone handed out a hilarious list that I shall relabel "OSD/JCS Christmas Carols" and give SecNav. Among them are "We, a Triumvirate of Near Eastern Heads of State," "Embellish the Interior Passageways," "Listen, the Celestial Messengers Produce Harmonious Sounds," and "Tintinnabulation of Vacillating Pendulums in Inverted, Metallic, Resonant Cups."

---

31. The next day, the Vice President handwrote a note saying "Chase—Magnifico, my friend. George."

Sunday, 14 December 1986

I was in the motorcade from the VP's House to the Shiloh Baptist Church at 9th and P Streets in Northwest Washington, a prominent congregation of middle- and upper-middle-class blacks. Inside the church we were met by its pastor, Rev. Henry Gregory, and today's guest preacher, Thadd Garrett. Shiloh is famous for its music, which today was a splendid assortment of gospel, blues, spirituals, and traditional European hymns. As I learned to do a decade ago in black Baptist churches in Houston, I nodded and tapped my hand on my knee in time with the music, mouthing words I didn't know.[32] When Reverend Gregory asked God to "shower Thy grace upon the vice president of the United States," a man in the congregation shouted, "Do it, Lord; do it!"

Thadd sat on the dais, looking imperiously up toward the balconies and exclaiming "My, my, my!" to a favorite hymn. When he took the pulpit, Thadd told the congregation, "I'm a preacher and a politician. I can't help it; I was born that way." His sermon was on sacrifice, and he said: "Christ did for us what none of us would do for each other; he *died* for us! ["Amen!"] How many people would *you* die for? Don't answer that question just yet." Compared with other sermons I've seen and heard Thadd give, today's preachment was shorter and less athletic, but it was a good show nonetheless.

Monday, 15 December 1986

Today I was the designated representative of the Navy Secretariat at a meeting of SecDef's regular Monday staff meeting, grandly known as the Armed Forces Policy Group (AFPG). It was held in the secretary's private dining/conference room adjoining his office. Secretary Weinberger entered, accompanied by his protégé, Will Taft. As Cdr. Dale Bosley [formerly of my staff and now of Weinberger's] had warned, the AFPG is significantly lacking in depth. Conversation consisted of such jovial froth as this:

Weinberger: We've had a number of foreign visitors lately. Will, you met with a Cambodian?

Taft: Yes, Prince Somebody. He's a law professor.

Admiral Crowe [chairman of the JCS]: They've got the same problem we do.

---

32. This technique came from observing Diana Poteat Hobby, a North Carolina aristocrat married to Texas Lt. Gov. Bill Hobby.

Audience, knowing both Weinberger and Taft are lawyers: [Chuckles].

The CNO, Carl Trost, asked to walk with me so he could confide that collections for Navy Relief are up. That's the sort of thing John Lehman's successor can expect to hear from Trost all the time.

Wednesday, 17 December 1986

In a budget-driven drill, Secretary Lehman asked for proposals to reduce his own staff, the civilian Secretariat.

Lehman rails against "the System" [the uniformed Navy], but if he slashes the Secretariat he would make it impossible for a successor without his gifts to stand up to the admiralty. To presume the Navy Department will always be led by Lehmans is as risky as it would have been for the framers of the Constitution to presume we would always be led by Jeffersons, Hamiltons, and Madisons.

Sunday, 4 January 1987

Everything I did this past year was of course under the imperial crown of John Lehman. Yet I never forgot that I was really working for the men and women of the Navy and Marine Corps and for Ronald Reagan. Especially after Lehman was so roughly rebuffed in the choice of a new CNO, I thought his days as SecNav were numbered. This wasn't the case, and unless something dramatically good or bad happens to him in 1987, I think he'll hang on a full eight years, the first since Josephus Daniels to do so. Indeed, during the few days in November-December when Lehman's name was mentioned for national security advisor, I feared that his regime would end too suddenly, without his telling his colleagues (or successor) where the keys to the office are.

Nineteen eighty-seven will see more of the 1985–86 pattern. A year hence I may be writing another essay despairing of another year working for John Lehman. I make this sound tedious, but I recognize that I am fortunate to hold a superb job in an exciting place and time. I rejoice that I have been in Washington in this administration, and when back in the land of enchiladas and barbecue I shall be doubly glad.

Chapter 11

Change of Command

Monday, 5 January 1987

At his luncheon today with the assistant secretaries, Lehman did something astonishing and unprecedented. He opened a loose-leaf notebook with pocket pages, each one containing a slip of paper. "The CNO and I have to put together a flag slate. So, let's talk slating. Who should we get to head the Supply Corps?" My colleagues and I were speechless with surprise. John Lehman, who wrenched the power of the slate away from CNO in 1981 and has used it ever since as his principal tool of control over the Navy, has never before sought our opinion. Even Ev Pyatt, who works with more flags than any of us, was unprepared to give considered answers to the rare questions we were being asked. Jim Goodrich and I had no hesitation, however, in recommending a new surgeon general.

John was strangely self-critical when he said he has "done the worst job in choosing people" as chief of the Office of Legislative Affairs (OLA). "The problem in being your OLA," I said, "is that it's like being Caruso's voice teacher." The fascinating discussion closed with Lehman observing what "thin gruel" there is among aviator flags. Jim Busey[1] [the VCNO] is the shining exception in a community that once seemed to be taking over the Navy but now is edged by the submarine community in talent.

Tuesday, 6 January 1987

Today upon my arrival in the office, George Walls reported that Jim Webb has resigned as AsstSecDef for Reserve Affairs. I don't know the reason, though I guess it was frustration, boredom, or (I hope) the desire to write a novel

---

1. Adm. Jim Busey was an extremely able man of commanding calm. He would retire in the joint position of US naval commander for Europe and NATO commander for southern Europe. It was my pleasure as director of Presidential Personnel in the first Bush administration to support his becoming administrator of the Federal Aviation Administration and later deputy secretary of Transportation.

about the Pentagon. Ty McCoy [my Air Force counterpart] and I invited each other to succeed Webb, without success. It is a horrible job, a world of purple[2] and gray.

At 11:00 there was a meeting in SecNav's office billed deceptively as a discussion of "accession policy." It was in truth to decide what to do about 7'1"-tall Naval Academy basketball player David Robinson. It's been known all along that he's too tall to have a normal career as an unrestricted line officer. The question is how to permit him to play ball while still getting some useful service from him.

Lehman, scuffed a bit last year when he decided to let USNA's Napoleon McCallum play pro football while an ensign, announced to the group that it's politically impossible just to let Robinson "walk" or be discharged from the Navy as physically unqualified. I agreed, saying that Robinson's future shouldn't appear "contrived" (as was McCallum's). It was decided that Robinson should be offered a program by which he'll serve two years on active duty as a staff corps officer followed by four years (Lehman wanted six) in the Reserves. Robinson and his family may object to the decision, since it would mean the loss of a lot of money, but Lehman would be positioned on the correct side of the controversy.

Next, attention turned to McCallum, who wants to change from being a supply officer so he can avoid deployments and keep playing football. This time Lehman was his old self: no change of job for McCallum—but he will deploy off-season!

Monday, 12 January 1987

SecNav is holding the captains selection board hostage till he gets from OpNav what he has repeatedly sought: a plan giving aviators a crack at command equal to those in the surface and submarine communities. He feels that rising in an air squadron is competitive enough. "I'm tired of being ignored on this," he told his pal Dudley. "Do you have a proposal, or do you want me to do it?" Probably no previous secretary has cared to get into such an issue, but then no previous secretary has hung out in the back bar at the Oceana [Virginia] officers club with disaffected aviators. The test of wills illustrates his basic rule of civilian leadership: "When the System doesn't automatically use common sense, we have to help it do so."

---

2. In the Pentagon, "purple" is contemptuous slang for a joint-service activity, arising from the image of mixing all uniform colors into one blob.

Friday, 6 February 1987

Both Commander Lehman and Captain Prueher were in khakis, as they would later leave for Joe's old command, Strike U [the Naval Strike and Air Warfare Center], in Fallon, Nevada. On their feet were the brown shoes that Lehman recently returned to an aviator's "sea bag," along with the leather flight jacket. Lehman's own shoes were personally given to him by non-aviator Dudley Carlson. Typical for Dudley, right after telling me of his gift he groused that Lehman should spend more time visiting surface units instead of "flying over them." I assured the chief of Naval Personnel that "with Vice Admiral Carlson and Lieutenant (junior grade) Untermeyer (retired), the surface community is well represented."

Monday, 9 February 1987

Defense Week—not an entirely reliable or respected journal—has an item labeled "Where's John?" It says that SecNav "seems to have disappeared," apparently referring to his recent trips to Wehrkunde, the Sixth Fleet, Strike U, and Sun Valley. The article suggests that Lehman is about to leave office, but I doubt John will quit.

Thursday, 12 February 1987

Just before noon, Betty said that Dennis Kenneally (deputy assistant secretary of the Air Force for Reserve Affairs) was on the line, asking about a report on CNN that SecNav is resigning. I took the call and said I didn't know of any such thing, unless it was the gossip item in *Defense Week*. But when I finished the call, Betty told me she had called down to Ruth, SecNav's social secretary, to ask about the report. Instead of getting a denial, Betty was put on hold and then instructed to direct all inquiries to Public Affairs. Joe Harford grinned and said, "It's February, sir"—a reminder of his longstanding prediction that Lehman would resign this month.

Before leaving the Cosmos Club after lunch, I called back to the office to check on the rumor. "It's true," Betty said. Bob Sims, the AsstSecDef for public affairs, announced at the regular press briefing that "Secretary Lehman met with Secretary Weinberger last Friday and told him it was his desire to return to private life." Betty said that the Under wanted to see me when I got back.

Beaming and imperturbable as always, Jim Goodrich said Lehman probably will leave in April, perhaps to do some sort of consulting in league with Mel Paisley, whose departure is taken for granted. I suggested that we survivors get together soon to discuss the immediate post-Lehman era, in which the admiralty and HQMC will try to assert leadership "absent another John Lehman." As I departed, I said, "It's going to be a new world, and I'm glad I'll be around to see it."

Dudley Carlson and I then had our weekly meeting. He had an ashen look, and for good reason: in two short years he went from captain to vice admiral under John Lehman's patronage, and now the run may very well be over. Dudley dropped a heavy hint that he intends to assert his leadership in the manpower area. He will testify before the HASC [House Armed Services Committee] two days before I do. Dudley said, "It's important that you follow the line" he sets in his testimony. This may have only been a clumsy way of saying we should be consistent, but it more than indicates he's rapidly going to align himself with CNO in the great power shift to come.

I was just about to put on my overcoat to leave for an evening event when I was moved to return to my desk and place a totally gratuitous phone call. And when I did, Jim Webb came on the line.

"For some time when I've thought who should succeed John Lehman," I began, "I've thought it should be Jim Webb. It's clear that the admirals and generals are rubbing their hands tonight in happy contemplation of rushing in to recover lost territory. What the Navy needs is someone to maintain civilian control of the military. And so, for what it's worth, I hope you'll consider going for this."

Jim chuckled and then, doing what he didn't have to, made me party to some stupendous news: this afternoon, perhaps within just the previous hour or two, SecDef called him in and said, "I know we've offered you things to get you to stay and you've turned them down. But how would you like to be secretary of the Navy?" Jim said he couldn't refuse such an opportunity, "though what I've always wanted to be is secretary of the Army so I could kick some ass around there." While Jim and I haven't been close friends, we have been friends, and it was an act of friendship and of trust to tell me his news.

The irony of this wish come true is that Jim Webb is an even moodier person than John Lehman, with a fiery temper of the sort that John suppressed. His work habits and accessibility may be just as chaotic as Lehman's. And as time passes he may lose confidence in my ability. If so, I hope we can part as friends, for I consider Jim Webb the preeminent member of my generation of Americans and I am fortunate to know him.

Tuesday, 17 February 1987

There was high attendance at the SecNav lineup at 9:00, the first since last Thursday's dramatic news. Lehman played with the expectant atmosphere by asking offhandedly, "Anything new since I left?" There were laughs, punctuated by Ev Pyatt saying, "Yeah—good news!" followed by more laughs. Lehman then brought us up to date: the nomination of Jim Webb as his successor would be announced today by the White House. "I won't go till he's sworn in," Lehman said, recalling with a wry smile how during the Hidalgo-to-Lehman interregnum in 1981, then-CNO Tom Hayward annexed ten feet of the SecNav office suite. Of Webb, Lehman said, "I am unaware of anything in which his thinking differs from my own." I noted that Webb is even more opposed to women in the services than he is, predicting that "DACO-WITS will soon long for the good old days of John Lehman."

Lehman closed the discussion by saying, "Chase, I will count on you to see I get back my pay billet [in the Reserves] the day after I leave." I said, "Well, we'll see about that. You'll have to submit your form in triplicate; then we'll see if you have any special skills and that you're not over the age limit." Still more laughs.

I left the lineup for my weekly meeting with the Under. I gave him my rundown on the Webb personality and mystique. Like Lehman, Webb loves a fight, I said, "but whereas with John fighting and beating your enemies is sport, with Jim it's a *blood* sport."

Lehman held a lunch with the Under and us assistant secretaries at 1:00. He said that the idea of leaving came last May when he was overruled by the White House on the choice of CNO. When a threat to resign failed to alter the choice, he realized his effectiveness was at an end. "It had nothing to do with Carl [Trost], whom I like and think is honest and smart." But, he said, "The Navy is too important to be left in the hands of the blue-suiters. And if the secretary isn't completely on top of procurement, he can't be secretary of the Navy. He can be *head of state*, like Bill Middendorf [at Navy] or like Jack Marsh at Army."

Wednesday, 18 February 1987

At this afternoon's medal-pinning ceremony for Jim Webb in the SecDef dining room, Cap Weinberger said, "Usually we hold these events to say goodbye to someone who's leaving and to welcome those who are coming. But I can't recall an occasion on which we've done both at the same time." Speaking of the President's nomination of Jim as the 66th secretary of the Navy, Weinberger said, "I'll bet that's something you never dreamed would happen when you were a midshipman at the Naval Academy."

Jim's remarks in response were for him quite modest. Only he could face an audience of that power and say most casually, "I thought this would be a tearful occasion. I cry easily—at weddings, at funerals, at squirrels being run over in the road. Maybe it's the redneck in me: you either cry about something or you fight over it."

In the receiving line, Jim gave my hand a smack-and-squeeze shake and in his soft baritone said with conspiratorial urgency, "We've got to talk *soon!*"

Thursday, 19 February 1987

I went to the Naval Observatory prior to the dinner the Bushes gave tonight at the State Department for PM Yitzhak Shamir of Israel. In the foyer of the residence was the VP's son George, whom I hadn't seen in several years. He has jogged himself into wiriness, and the bearish oil business in West Texas may have made him less cocky. Tonight he was in black tie to stand in for his father at the Conservative PAC dinner. Laura came with us. She said they will move up here in April and are now in the grim business of finding affordable housing in the DC area, having taken a loss on their home in Midland.

Friday, 20 February 1987

Tonight's dinner/dance for Jim Webb was organized before this week's news, which is why it was composed just of Pentagonians, reserve association leaders, and old Webb buddies, with nary a contractor in sight. Among those with whom I talked was Lt. Gen. Al Gray. I can easily see him as Jim's choice to be the next commandant. But Al is reportedly opposed by P. X. Kelley, perhaps because Al is so gloriously a grunt and lacks P. X.'s inner-Beltway classiness. I also talked with Frederick (Rick) Hart, the sculptor of the trio of soldiers at the Vietnam Veterans Memorial. An outgoing fellow with a personality geared to charming arts commissions and other patrons, Hart confirmed that he used Jim's combat boots and dog tag as models for the ones on the central figure in the sculpture.

Saturday, 28 February 1987

I returned to Bath, Maine, for the commissioning of USS Kauffman, whose launching I had attended on 29 March 1986. The ship was named for my former boss, the late Rear Adm. Draper Kauffman, and his father, also an admiral. Rear Admiral Kauffman's last act as superintendent of the Naval Academy before going out to the Philippines was to preside over the graduation of the USNA Class of 1968. This remarkable group included two future CNOs (Jay Johnson and Mike Mullen), a future chairman of the Joint Chiefs of Staff (Mullen), a future commandant of the Marine Corps (Mike Hagee), a future director of National Intelligence (Dennis Blair), a future astronaut and NASA administrator (Chuck Bolden), a future conservative icon (Oliver North), and a future SecNav, senator, and best-selling novelist—Jim Webb.

Arrival honors for me were rendered pierside next to a crowd estimated at 1200. When I crossed the brow, I received a salute from the ship's skipper, Cdr. John Dranchak. "Welcome aboard, Mr. Secretary!" he said, and I replied, TR-like, "Delighted!" There were preliminary welcomes and remarks, after which I was introduced.

"Draper Laurence Kauffman was an admiral of the old school," I began, "someone who could inspire you with a word or scorch you with a glare. I had both inspiration and scorching when I was his aide in the Philippines, and the experience served me well. Today, as an assistant secretary of the Navy, I am more glare resistant than when I was a JG [lieutenant junior grade]. Rank *may* have something to do with it, but the specialized training with Admiral Kauffman certainly helped."

I went on to speak of Rear Admiral Kauffman's tenure at Annapolis and how he viewed the brigade as his bequest to the nation. "But we can only imagine the mixture of astonishment and pride he would have felt to know that one of his midshipmen, in the very month in which we commission this ship, would be named by the president of the United States as secretary of the Navy."

I gave a fond tribute to Peggy Kauffman ("Mrs. K") and closed with a verbal salute to all Navy and Marine wives: "They have been strong and resourceful, because the demands of seagoing life have made them so. They and their children have always risen to meet the test, forming the unbeatable second echelon of the Navy–Marine Corps team."

Kauffman then "came alive" as its first crew marched through the crowd and up the gangplank to take stations along the rail. The ship's radars twirled, there were blasts of the horn and the torpedo tubes, balloons rose, and a band played "Anchors Aweigh." Kelsey Kauffman called it all "a three-hanky affair," and I admit the sight was so splendid that tears came to my eyes as well. (In the Webb regime, tears may become regulation.)

Monday, 2 March 1987

Because another meeting ran overtime, Jim Webb and I only had ten minutes to talk before we went into John Lehman's regular lineup. Webb was in shirtsleeves and smoking a cigar, the Marine officer/young lawyer touch. He asked what lineups are like, and I told of having to seize them as opportunities to transact business with Lehman, since seeing him privately was often impossible. Webb furrowed his brow and said how amazed he is at the disorganized way in which Lehman conducts his office.

This horror at Lehman's way of operating increased during the meeting to follow, when SecNav railed against the continued trade status of New Zealand as a "most-favored nation" when it denies port visits to US nuclear-powered vessels. Lehman is encouraging efforts on the Hill by dairy-state senators and representatives to yank this status, over the protests of State Department and OSD. "We have to make it clear that no nation can kick the Navy in the teeth without its affecting the larger relationship," he said. "It's a virus that has and will spread. For socialist governments, it's irresistible and cost-free. Every time I say this, State issues a statement saying I don't speak for the Administration, and the ambassador [in Wellington] sends a cable saying, 'Please do something about this maniac!' Every time I see the New Zealand ambassador, I say, 'We're gonna git ya!'"

When Jim and I reconvened after the lineup, he sputtered, "The Navy has no business conducting its own foreign policy!" Shifting the subject to something closer than New Zealand, namely M&RA, I began, "My appointment says I serve at the pleasure of the president, but as a practical matter I serve at the pleasure of the secretary of the Navy. If you don't like what I'm doing, tell me so. I've been here three years, and I still can't tell you whether John Lehman thinks I'm doing a fantastic job or otherwise." Jim reacted with an elaborate blink of his eyes and a snap of his head, and all he said was, "That'll be no problem. You'll always know what I want and what I think."

Wednesday, 4 March 1987

The SecNav "read file" contained a very interesting passel of letters. In them, Lehman asked the wives of several admirals and other buddies to sponsor (launch) various ships[3] from now till late 1988. In other words, John has denied his successor the opportunity to invite any lady of his choosing to launch any ship. This was a highly unfriendly and grabby act. He did ask JoAnne Webb to christen [the carrier] *Abraham Lincoln*.

Thursday, 5 March 1987

Although testifying before Congress is considered one of the awful duties of Washington life, I rather enjoyed it and chafed at the preference of the House and Senate armed services committees to hear from the uniformed manpower chiefs instead of the civilians responsible for personnel policy. A rare exception came in 1987, when my counterparts and I were invited to testify before the Personnel & Compensation subcommittee of the House Armed Services Committee. The panel was chaired by Rep. Beverly Byron (D-Maryland), a friend of the Navy whose father had been naval aide to General Eisenhower during World War II. She and I would later serve together on the Naval Academy Board of Visitors.

"I'm glad you are here today," Mrs. Byron began, "though you may not feel that way after I ask the following questions." Actually, they were softballs on manning the 600-ship Navy and on the fracas over the captains selection board.[4] On the latter I said that although I wasn't a participant in the secretary's actions (indeed, I wasn't even invited to the meetings), "it is emphatically the prerogative of a service secretary to establish the relative strengths of warfare communities." The actual selections were made by senior military officers serving on the board, and in his press conference on the controversy Lehman said he didn't even inquire into the names of those chosen. There was no follow-up question, and the hearing soon ended.

---

3. This is a dual honor, for just before the woman cracks the traditional champagne bottle, her husband delivers the occasion's main address.

4. A few days earlier, Lehman had sought and received the resignation of Vice Adm. Bruce DeMars (deputy CNO for Submarine Warfare) as president of the selection board for captains because the board promoted a greater number of submariners than SecNav specifically authorized. This evoked a stinging rebuke from senior members of both parties on the Senate Armed Services Committee, who accused Lehman of interference in the promotion process.

Tuesday, 10 March 1987

SecNav and I had a one-on-one meeting to talk about the M&RA issues on which I'd like him to act before he leaves office. First, though, Lehman wanted to know whether Jim Webb and I had talked about "your future." With the same put-on tone of voice he used four years ago when faced with an edict from the White House to hire me, Lehman said, "I told Webb you had done a first-rate job and that it would be crazy to bring in a new guy." Those words will have to stand as John Lehman's tribute to my service to him; I doubt I'll get more than an "also present was" mention in his memoirs.[5] But that's all right: Henry Kissinger only mentioned Lehman in passing in *his* memoirs.

Wednesday, 11 March 1987

I am interviewing candidates for EA to succeed Joe Harford when he leaves to take command of the Belle Chasse Naval Air Station in New Orleans. Today I spoke with Capt. Louise Wilmot, chief recruiter in the Midwest region. She is a very strong-willed and incisive officer, and I'm grateful that she wasn't interviewing *me* for a job. I was very impressed with her; she may be one of the very few women line officers selected for flag in the next five years. But I shall continue searching in the ringknocker[6]/aviator world because I need a resource in those areas more than I do one in recruiting. Betty and the staff liked Captain Wilmot, who made a point of meeting all of them and asking about their jobs.

Monday, 16 March 1987

Under Secretary Goodrich and I met with the SecNav-designate to discuss who should be the next surgeon general. When the meeting ended, Webb asked me to stay behind. He wanted my advice on how to handle a most sensitive matter: he would like to replace Jim Goodrich with Larry Garrett, currently the DOD general counsel and a former Navy JAG officer.[7]

---

5. True: see Lehman's *Command of the Seas* (1988), page 238.

6. Military slang for graduates of one of the service academies, who all proudly wear their class rings.

7. In the Reagan Administration, no one rose faster or higher on sheer merit than did Larry Garrett. A former enlisted man in the Navy, he was in turn a member of the White House

I know that a Webb decision is pretty final, but out of loyalty and conviction I hailed the Under's expertise in procurement and shipbuilding. I also
said he served the useful role of leavening Lehman's brashness with soothing
grandfatherliness—"something you might also have need of," evoking a smile
from Webb. He didn't need this advice; only how to break the word to Jim.
I said that of course it should be given in person—and predicted that Jim
will happily trek back to the retirement house on Maui from which Lehman
plucked him in 1981.

Back in my office, I was interviewing another candidate for EA when
Betty buzzed to say that Larry Garrett was calling: "He says it's pretty important." I thought Larry was calling in connection with what Webb had just
told me, but not so. With a concerned tone of voice, he said he needed to
talk to me right away in his office. When I got there, Larry asked me to take a
seat at the foot of a conference table; he himself remained afoot. "Something
has come up," he said, showing me a memo from SecDef directing him to in-
vestigate allegations of impropriety with the Marine major generals selection
board last October. Pacing like a courtroom lawyer, Larry asked about my
role in the matter. I said I was a witness to Lehman telling Lt. Gen. D'Wayne
Gray he would reconvene the board and giving clear indication he hoped Jim
Mead would be selected.

Larry stood, puffing and deflating his cheeks rapidly. He asked some
questions about the incident under review but then asked me some broader
questions: What do I think of John Lehman, and was he good for the Navy?
I suspect these questions came not from special-investigator Garrett but from
future UnSecNav Garrett. My reply was a mixture of admiration for Lehman's
skill and accomplishments but also my befuddlement over the uneven quality
of his protégés: for every warrior pushed upward, men like Ace Lyons and
Jim Mead (or like Joe Metcalf, protected from a silly scandal involving war
souvenirs from Grenada), there are henchmen like Dudley Carlson and Paul
David Miller. I was somewhat nervous, just as I might have been on the witness stand, so I left Larry's office not knowing how well I came across.

I finished the EA interview, had a brief swim at the POAC, and went
to the Navy Yard for a farewell reception for Jim Busey, who is off to Italy as
NATO's southern commander. Each of the three-star barons gave a little jab-
bing tribute to the departing vice chief. Dudley climaxed his patter by removing his coat, sweater, tie, and shirt to reveal a T-shirt on which was "MP" with

counsel's staff, general counsel of DOD, UnSecNav, and finally SecNav in the first Bush administration.

a red slash through it—a jocular attack on the Materiel Professional program invented by Lehman and Paisley and spearheaded by Busey.

Wednesday, 18 March 1987

Ten o'clock brought Vice Adm. Cec Kempf's fourth and final chance to get SecNav to approve his proposed reorganization of the surface Reserve force. We entered the secretary's office to see a strange scene: on the desk was a standard Navy soup bowl filled with water. To one side stood Capt. Joe Prueher with a towel folded over an arm. "Gentlemen, behold!" proclaimed Lehman as he dipped his fingers into the bowl, reached over to dry them on the towel, and then walked forward to remove from a stunned Cec his armful of documents. These he dramatically handed to Joe, saying, "I am turning these over to the scribes and the Pharisees." All of this meant (as I had predicted to Cec) that Lehman was letting Jim Webb decide the issue. Cec was downcast, but at least he got to witness a classic Lehman performance.

Friday, 20 March 1987

"Word has filtered out that your conversation with Larry Garrett wasn't helpful," Joe Prueher said over the phone. I replied brightly, "I told him what happened. Whether that's helpful or not depends on how one defines help." Speaking slowly with a tone that said "uh-oh, better watch out!" Joe said I should talk with Lehman. "It's a matter of utmost concern with him at this time."

Undoubtedly this conversation will be unpleasant. I can imagine Lehman looking on me as a traitor or as one more of those pursuing him with whips as he leaves office. Does he think I should have lied or otherwise covered up what he did last October? That would be foolish enough if Larry were merely the general counsel of the Department of Defense. But what Lehman may not know is that Larry is also Jim Webb's choice to be UnSecNav. The problem, I should tell Lehman, is not disloyalty but his wide-and-fancy way of doing business, that excess of cleverness that has brought him great triumphs but also carries the seeds of his eventual destruction.

Tuesday, 24 March 1987

To my surprise and relief—but not, till many years pass, total relief—Lehman was calm, serene, and even a tad fraternal on the phone from Key West. He merely said he wanted to "get an idea about how your conversation with Gar-rett went, since he'll be here tomorrow night." I told him what I had said, and Lehman replied, "That's about the way I remember it. It was pretty cut and dried. I told [D'Wayne Gray] to make sure Mead got a fair shake. He didn't, so I added another number [for an aviator]." I said Larry had asked why I thought he (Lehman) had done it, and I speculated it was because John has always advanced "warrior types" in both the Navy and Marine Corps. "Pre-cisely!" Lehman interjected. When I asked if I could be of further help, he replied, "No; this is just part of the overall Nunn effort to get at me," referring to Sen. Sam Nunn (D-Georgia), chairman of the SASC.

Monday, 6 April 1987

In addition to finding a new naval aide, I have to find a Marine aide to suc-ceed George Walls. Today I interviewed a real star: Colonel-selectee Manfred Rietsch, an F18 pilot and former Top Gun instructor who's currently at the Air War College in Alabama. Born in West Prussia in 1942, Rietsch emigrated to America a decade or so later. He looks the part—square jawed, graying hair, blue eyes, and white-white teeth—and when we shook hands he gave a quick bow from the shoulder. All that was missing was a click of the heels. Rietsch (whose airborne nickname is Fokker) must do a tour in DC, which he accepts as inevitable. What he really wants to do is fly, keeping his skills up so he can be an effective leader of the younger guys if and when he gets his dream, an air group (equivalent to a Navy air wing) two years from now.

The colorful and able Manfred was picked, and in 1991 he would lead the Marine air group in the Gulf War.

Tuesday, 7 April 1987

Today brought the Under's farewell luncheon for John Lehman, held in the City Tavern Club in Georgetown. There was a "class photo," an OK meal, many amusing recollections, and a sobering discussion of the penetration by the KGB of the Marine Security Guard detachment in Moscow. Lehman thinks that if the Marines could be compromised, the penetration of the Foreign Service must be far worse. He then told again the story of how in the Ford Administration he hired a man named James Sattler[8] to be an arms

---

8. See 11 June 1985.

negotiator, only to be informed by the FBI that Sattler's name was on a list of agents found with an East German spy they had nabbed. Lehman cooperated with the Bureau in an attempt to "turn" Sattler, but something happened and he disappeared. Deadpan, Lehman swirled his wine and said, "The last I heard, he went to East Berlin, had plastic surgery, and is back in Washington as an assistant secretary of the Navy."

Jim Goodrich started a round of informal tributes by saying, "It's been fun—more fun than I've ever had in my life." Mel said of his close pal, "I just wish I had met you several years earlier." When my turn came, I noted that one can be a success in Washington by merely giving a good press conference or by getting a bill passed. A few operate on a broader level, seeking goals and changes that take years. Both of these John mastered, I said, but he also operated on a third level, seeing far beyond the years to "make America Navy-minded, creating a permanent constituency for the Navy as in Britain, where it's the senior service." All of Lehman's controversial actions—on homeporting, supporting *Top Gun,* letting Napoleon McCallum play football and David Robinson play basketball—can best be understood on that level. I closed by saying that I now know what it must have been like to be a contemporary and coworker of the young Theodore Roosevelt and the young Winston Churchill.

Lehman concurred with my interpretation and amended it. His aim, he said, was not so much to give the American people faith in the Navy but to help the Navy keep faith in itself. He sees the Navy as the "vessel" for the enduring values of American life since the courageous days of the Revolution. In fact, he said, he first resolved to become SecNav at an issues conference at the Naval War College in June 1979, where a Carter Administration official lambasted the Navy as outmoded and ineffective. That wasn't so shocking, given the speaker, he said. What shocked Lehman was that the hundreds of naval officers present merely mumbled agreement and hung their heads.

"Nothing is permanent," Lehman told us, "but at least now there's a new frame of reference as to what's right." He then raised his glass to toast us, saying, "We'll be together again in the decades to come!" I joined in the toast, the only man present who could chronologically aspire to be with John Lehman in such an age of further glories—if he wants me.

Friday, 10 April 1987

Noontime brought the full-honors ceremony at which DOD officially said goodbye to John Lehman. It was a beautiful early-spring day. As the Navy band played marches, I chatted with flag officers and civilian officials. Among the latter was Larry Garrett, who is normally friendly. I told him that I am "interested in knowing what's happened since our last conversation." But Larry said in so many (or so few) words that it was none of my business. This made it seem as if he considers me a guilty party.

A few minutes later, Jim Webb arrived solo. Shaking his hand, I asked, "Confirmed?" and he said yes. Out in California, RR signed the appointment, and late this afternoon Jim was sworn in as SecNav in a very private ceremony in SecDef's office.

A fanfare announced the arrival of Weinberger and Lehman, the latter jauntily wearing a red tie and matching red breast-pocket handkerchief. There was a 17-gun salute, after which the two men trooped the line. Lehman seemed to be enjoying it all immensely. SecDef and the three under secretaries of the services pinned medals on John's lapel till he looked like a Bolivian general and a sloppy one at that. Then Weinberger took the rostrum.

SecDef may have had his furies against Lehman's independent style of operating, but today he was full of praise for "the father of the 600-ship Navy." He said, "One man *can* make a difference, but such a man must have the qualities of a John Lehman."[9] In his remarks, Lehman called secretary of the Navy "the best job in the world." He spoke of the fun and satisfaction of visiting the fleet. He lavished praise on his former Pentagon colleagues, saying, "I have not been known as an admirer of the growth of bureaucracy, but never have I said anything about bureaucrats, among whom I count myself." There was no flyover of A6s and not even the playing of "Anchors Aweigh" and the "Marines' Hymn." But it was to applause that Lehman left the field—sure to return, I've no doubt, as SecDef himself.

If any proof was needed of the impermanence of Dudley Carlson's loyalty, it came through clearly in our meeting after lunch. When I pressed him on something SecNav had requested at a recent lineup, Dudley demanded to know, "Who's interested in this?" He then answered his own question. "John Lehman? He's gone!"

---

9. Weinberger gave no such tribute to Lehman in his 1990 memoir, *Fighting for Peace: Seven Critical Years in the Pentagon*. In fact, he mentioned Lehman just three times and then only briefly.

Chapter 12

Plebe Spring, Plebe Summer

Tuesday, 14 April 1987

The DOD auditorium on the top floor of the Pentagon was filled with flag and general officers, political appointees, and senior civil servants for an 8 a.m. "officers call" with the new secretary. From the rear came a shout, "Attention on deck!" and a galaxy of stars jumped to their feet. Down a side aisle came SecNav, CNO, and the Commandant. They took seats onstage, we took ours, and Carl Trost gave Webb a brief and warm welcome. Speaking in a sepulchral voice that Seth Cropsey later called "ominous," Webb then proceeded to tell his audience "where I'm coming from."

First of all, he said, "The policies in place are Reagan Administration policies, not those of any one man, and they will remain for the next two—or six—years." Throughout his talk, Webb made clear again and again that he is not John Lehman—the invisible fourth man on stage this morning. He began by saying with emphasis, "There is a Defense Department, and Navy is part of it. There is, for example, no Navy policy on New Zealand." Of allowing USNA grads to play professional sports, Webb said, "Here is the clearest example of letting the public relations aspect of an issue overcome a principle." There was more: Webb said he would not involve himself in promotion boards after the boards go into session. As SecNav, he intends to reward courage, including moral courage. And he closed by saying he would review all of his predecessor's last-minute SecNavInsts [secretary of the Navy instructions]: "Some will stay, and some will go."

When he finished, Webb asked if there were any questions. No one wanted to expose himself, so the meeting ended, to prolonged applause.

In our regular meeting at 10:00, Jim Goodrich and I discussed Webb's speech. After a pause he gave a brave smile and said, "Now, let me tell you about me—though perhaps you already know." He then said that yesterday Jim Webb asked if he would step aside so that Larry Garrett can become the new UnSecNav. Jim seemed a bit hurt by the suddenness of his removal, which will become effective about 1 July. He said he hoped I would remain, adding, "Y'know, you weren't John Lehman's choice for that job; he had to take you. And I felt sorry for you the first year or so because he never let you talk with him. But by the end I think he admired the way you handled things. I bet he didn't say so, though." I told Jim that I shall miss him, especially since he, alone among my colleagues, was someone with whom I felt I *could* talk.

Thursday, 16 April 1987

I asked Joe and George, What if I were to choose Capt. Louise Wilmot, the hard-charging recruiter, as my EA? They liked the idea and felt she would get along well with SecNav's new EA, Capt. Tom Daly, who would appreciate her brainpower. The major question is whether Jim Webb would view the selection of an activist woman naval officer as a threat or insult.

I didn't have to wait long to find out. After Webb's first lineup, I walked back into his office. It now contains the Jim Webb artifacts: the bronze casting of his boot by Rick Hart; his Emmy statuette; and strange little trinkets from Vietnam, each with its story. When I asked about Captain Wilmot, Jim had no objection at all. He called it "a great idea," perhaps seeing the selection of the first woman officer in a major E-Ring assignment as a political plus. But he said Louise should not be hired if she has ever said or written anything critical of him. He said this with clenched teeth; then he unclenched and added I shouldn't be "McCarthyite" in making my inquiry.

I reached Captain Wilmot in St. Louis. When I asked if she were willing to take the job, Louise's immediate response was to give a sort of warning: "I hope you understand that I have some real strong opinions on some things, and I will give them to you." I said that is what I want to hear. Next I asked the sensitive question about any statements she may have made about the Secretary, adding that I know "he isn't exactly a pinup for the Women Officers Professional Association." She swiftly said, "I have never said one word about Mr. Webb." Then she added, with an interesting choice of words, "The two of us could ease his problems by doing something smart like putting a woman in there [as an EA]!" The conversation closed with Louise brightly calling me "boss." I was left with a sense of relief and moderate joy over my principal staff starting this summer.

Friday, 24 April 1987

My meeting with SecNav on M&RA issues was (enjoyably) lengthened by stories he told from the Webb vita. One of these was how, home on Christmas leave as a midshipman, he got into a fight with a ponytailed biker who gave him the finger. "I had him by the hair and was beating his head on the sidewalk when he suddenly went limp on me," Webb recalled. "Then it came to me: I had *killed* the fucking son of a bitch, and I would be put on report back at the Academy! So I revived him—whereupon he came to and kicked me in the head about ten times till I was able to grab his leg."

"Moral: show no mercy in a fight."

"Absolutely!"

Webb suddenly asked, "What do you think of [Lt. Gen.] Ernie Cheatham?" I said I have found the Marine manpower chief candid, friendly, and helpful, though inclined to keep canceling our weekly meetings. The reason Webb asked is that he's told SecDef that he wants Ernie as the new commandant! It's an excellent choice and understandable for two reasons alone: Ernie (like Jim) received the Navy Cross for valor in Vietnam, and he is hated by P. X. Kelley, whom Jim considers a destroyer of combat careers. In fact, Jim expects P. X. will try to block Ernie's selection all the way to the President. If Kelley balks at Cheatham, Jim said with a grin, he will then propose Al Gray, whom P. X. hates even more.

Saturday, 25 April 1987

In proper Navy-Marine fashion, the 150 or guests at John Lehman's farewell party at the Naval Observatory pretty much arrived simultaneously at 7:00. John had wanted "only the just and the righteous," which meant very few flag officers and a maximum number of Lehman friends and staffers. Among them was the celebrated/notorious Ollie North, with whom I spoke briefly. He has Naval Investigative Service protection, guarding against some death threats. The agents have also helped sweep away the phalanx of news reporters camped on his lawn. George and Barbara Bush walked over from the VP's house, to be greeted by Lehman. I introduced them to some attendees until BPB said they were old hands at doing the job themselves. Yes, ma'am.

Tabbed by Joe Prueher as official party organizer, I was also the MC. With John and Barbara Lehman standing nearby, I commenced my patter:

★ "When John called Barbara to tell her he was resigning, she sighed contentedly and said 'There certainly will be five very happy people out here in McLean.' John then asked in alarm, 'Really? What are the Joint Chiefs of Staff doing at our place?'"

★ The job offers since John retired haven't been particularly good. One came from the Juicyfruit Corp., which wanted someone classy to promote their new gourmet product line, something called Top Gum. (There were great groans over that one.)

★ "So, John decided to write a book. The papers last week reported that he got an advance from Scribner's for $200,000, which is relatively modest for a celebrity memoir. But he received this letter: 'Dear Secretary Lehman: Don't feel distressed over the low amount of money they gave you for your book. In life we must, after all, always think of the future instead of the greedy present. Besides, 200 grand is a hell of a lot more than I'm going to make right now. (Signed) David Robinson, midshipman, US Navy.'"

★ "People have asked me, what's the difference between Jim Webb and John Lehman? And I've said that the thing to remember is that Jim is a former Marine officer. Tell him to take a hill, and he'll take the hill. But with John it's a little different. Tell him to take a hill, and the first thing he'll do is get together with Mel Paisley for a few drinks to concoct the plan. (Paisley will think it's a wonderful idea.) Then John will start a competition among real estate agents over the purchase price of the hill. Next he'll go to the senator in whose state the hill is located and make a deal: the Navy will build the chrome bumper-guard assembly for the Trident sub in his hometown if the senator will slip an amendment into the Wild & Scenic Areas Act to purchase the hill. Then, with the money saved from the competition, John buys another Aegis cruiser."

Tuesday, 28 April 1987

The *Atlanta Constitution* has a story based on an interview with Carl Trost, who with uncharacteristic intemperance called John Lehman "not a balanced person." It seems that CNO considers John's last-minute SecNavInsts a personal insult.

Wednesday, 29 April 1987

As I was walking away from the Mess, Jim Webb asked to speak with me privately in his office. "I wasn't taken with your remarks at the Lehman party," he said. "That business about taking the hill—me just going at the hill and Lehman doing all sorts of things like getting an Aegis cruiser." I flushed with the sheer surprise of this statement. In a calm, friendly fashion I replied that Lehman was the object of the jokes, not him, and I thought Jim would enjoy them—which was precisely why I sent him a copy. Our conversation ended quickly.

I walked down the corridor in a state of mixed wonder and disappointment. Someone with a secure sense of himself usually has the freedom to laugh. And yet it was the self-confident Webb who took offense and the insecure Lehman who laughed. This may be the difference between being Irish and Scots-Irish. There are two possible reasons for what Jim said. One is his sensitivity to any comparison with Lehman. The other is that Jim has so apotheosized his life as an epic of American courage and spirit that any criticism (or perceived criticism) is akin to sacrilege or even treason. I was bothered by the incident for the rest of the day.

Toward 6:30, while I was waiting for a meeting with the Secretary that was 45 minutes overdue (shades of the *ancien régime!*), Jim came out and motioned me in "for 15 seconds." He then said: "I want to apologize if I seemed thin-skinned this morning." It had clearly troubled him all day, too, and it's the mark of a strong man to make the apology—and the mark of a friend to want to. In burying the incident, Webb gave an indication why he objected to the "hill" anecdote: "In time people will come to know my style. It's not always take the hill. Yeah, when the time comes, you do it. But other things can be done, too. Maybe not getting a cruiser—more like a frigate." So it seems that what wounded him was the implication that he isn't capable of the sly plots that were a Lehman trademark.

Friday, 1 May 1987

I rode to Annapolis with Ev Pyatt and [his principal deputy] Keith Eastin for SecNav's formal swearing-in, held outdoors on a glorious day of bright spring sunshine. The brigade of midshipmen stood in ranks on the fringes of Tecumseh Court, which was filled with 2000 military and civilian dignitaries. The principals emerged from Bancroft Hall. Showing his obvious fondness and regard for today's honoree, Secretary Weinberger said, "Jim Webb will be noted as the only official in the Department of Defense who wrote his books *before* he came to the Pentagon." He then administered the oath, after which came full honors, including the distant booms of a 19-gun salute.

It was a moment Jim clearly had looked forward to, and he savored it totally. He first saluted "classmates and fellow Marines," getting a vigorous *oorah!* from somewhere in the crowd. "It is great to be back at the Naval Academy," he said, "though it may have something to do with my more improved position." (Webb was banned from his alma mater after writing his controversial 1979 article against having women in combat, "Women Can't Fight," and his 1981 novel *A Sense of Honor*.) Referring to a *Washington Post* story that he ordered a big ceremony at Annapolis three weeks after officially taking the oath as SecNav, Jim said, "I am not confusing the second taking of the oath with the second coming of any other being."

Very swiftly Webb moved to a favorite theme, the mood of his first-class [senior] year in the late winter and spring of 1968 and in the decade of military neglect to follow. He said he is proud to be serving once again with people who are dedicated to duty and to sacrifice. And he repeated something he likes to say: "In peacetime, sons bury their fathers. In wartime, fathers bury their sons."

The extraordinarily moving climax of the ceremony came when country singer Lee Greenwood took a handheld mike and, to a recorded backup, sang the "God Bless the USA" anthem that he wrote for President Reagan in 1984 and that has become this decade's equivalent of Irving Berlin's "God Bless America."[1]

When Greenwood finished, we all rose to our feet, and Jim came forward to give him a long embrace, as Vietnam combat vets are wont to do. Partly out of a feeling of triumph for the Good Guys of '68 and partly because sunscreen stung my eyes, tears rolled down my cheeks, and I waited till the benediction of the Naval Academy chaplain to wipe them away.

Monday, 4 May 1987

Having lunch with a delegation from Corpus Christi kept me from hearing Dudley Carlson's speech to DACOWITS, in which he unsuccessfully argued that Navy can bar women from serving aboard Mobile Logistics Support Force on the grounds that these ships may be involved in combat. As I know from many private sessions with him, Dudley gets incendiary on this subject, and, true to form, he reportedly flailed his arms and used deck plate jargon like "lounge lizards." DACOWITS members assailed him for the transparent silliness of changing the ships' name to the *Combat* Logistics Force. When I saw Dudley tonight, I said, "I understand that the job of chief of Naval Personnel is being changed to that of a combatant." He laughed, but I think he realized how much of a bomb his presentation was. I don't feel too sorry for him because he deserved the hit.

---

1. The song became such a standard at Republican/conservative/patriotic events, often with Greenwood himself doing the vocal, that I gave it the shorthand name "Goblusa."

Tuesday, 5 May 1987

The lineup at 9:00 proved a shocker. SecNav bluntly announced, "Yesterday the chief of Naval Personnel gave a speech in which he misrepresented the [Defense] Department's position on women to the acute embarrassment of Secretary Weinberger. It's obviously also an area where I have a lot of sensitivity." Later Jim told me that he and Carl Trost met yesterday on flag slating *before* Dudley spoke to DACOWITS and that he told the CNO "Carlson has to go." CNO was noncommittal but not opposed. In my year-end essay, I expressed that my dearest hope for 1987 was "either a fourth star or a hanging for Dudley Carlson." It looks like I will get that wish, courtesy of Dudley and the coils of rope he wrapped around his own neck yesterday.

Thursday, 7 May 1987

I hurried back to the office from a meeting to find George and Laura Bush. The voluble "George W." had already been wisecracking with my staff, who were puzzled over how to react. He has a brittle form of humor that exceeds the gentle gibing the Bush family enjoys inflicting on each other and friends. Laura by contrast was typically composed and gracious.

We went to the private dining room and the weekly Mexican plate lunch.[2] Without my asking, George gave me a rundown on what's happening in the Bush for President campaign. Most of his ire was directed at Craig Fuller, whom he sees as a plastic-headed Southern Californian "bureaucrat" without any prior campaign experience. "This is among family," George said, "but Mother walked in while I was telling Dad something that Craig had done, and she said, 'Don't worry; Craig will never be White House chief of staff.'" George will continue to perform his role as Fuller-watcher, with his superior ability to reach the VP to complain and pester.

Tuesday, 19 May 1987

Today's senior staff meeting (no longer "lineup") was dominated by the Iraqi attack on *Stark* in the Persian Gulf on Sunday. Whereas John Lehman would have fulminated about the rules of engagement, about a constipated chain of

---

2. This meal, like the one served in the White House Mess, was not Tex-Mex but (I told guests) "Cal-Mex as prepared by Filipinos."

command, or about defects in weapons systems, Webb was focused on family notification and press coverage.

I make this contrast—which of course I wouldn't dare make with Jim himself—to underscore the difference between the two secretaries. A little Lehmanism could help both Jim and the Navy right now. For example, if Jim were to seize the day and use the national emotional need to do *something*, he might demand that Congress fully fund the new *Burke*-class destroyer, whose Aegis combat system and greater firepower makes it the right sort of ship to station in a war zone, not a poor little *Perry*-class frigate. Webb's declaring it a national priority might just carry the day. Lehman used the shooting down of two attack jets over Lebanon in December 1983 to found Strike U and revolutionize bombing tactics.

Wednesday, 20 May 1987

With a check to see if anyone was nearby, Col. George Walls whispered that the next commandant will be Al Gray. Apparently SecNav ran into problems with Ernie Cheatham. Either P. X. Kelley campaigned against him or SecDef had his own favorite (reportedly Gen. George Crist, the CENTCOM commander). So, Al is chosen by compromise. For whatever reason, it is an excellent selection.

Thursday, 21 May 1987

I found Webb reeling from interviews, congressional brushfires, and a lot of scurrying in OSD, all over the attack on *Stark*. That was the subject of my visit. I urged him to use the incident to "gain some ground for Navy" by pressuring or embarrassing Congress into funding *Burke*. Now is the time, when Democrats are wailing about the inadequacy of *Stark*'s defenses, to lock them into supporting a state-of-the-art vessel like DDG-21 [the *Burke* class]. If not this, I suggested using the admiralty's current confusion and anguish to push through some internal reform, as Lehman did with Strike U. I should have expected that even this tiny recollection of the Lehman regime would nettle Jim, who said that Strike U "didn't have as much impact on [the April 1986 raid on] Libya as Lehman said it did."

My mission was a failure. Webb's response to *Stark* is twofold. One is to work with OSD to press the Iraqis into cooperating fully with the investigation and paying compensation to the families, as well as raising the question of whether we should maintain forces in hostile areas solely for "presence."

His other response is to fly next week to Bahrain to give a Meritorious Unit Citation to *Stark* and hang other medals on some sailors.

I didn't press my message any further, having had my say. I suppose it's better to be seen as aggressive rather than inert. But I am disappointed that Jim seems more focused on the symbolism and solidarity aspect of *Stark* than on its fresh opportunity for unabashed parochial gain.

Tuesday, 26 May 1987

When I arrived in the office, Betty said, "You're going to have an interesting day today." George quickly explained that I might be asked to represent the civilian Navy Department leadership at today's ceremony at Dover AFB for the return of the caskets of the men killed aboard *Stark* last week. A few minutes later, SecNav called to say I *would* go. He himself has been in the air a lot this past week, and he leaves soon for Bahrain. "I'm also afraid of overkill; that's why I recommended that the President only go to Mayport. Besides," he added, "what do we do when the next ship goes down?"[3]

At 1:00, I walked to the so-called helo entrance of the Pentagon. Waiting on the landing pad was a green Marine H53 helo with the complete VIP interior and my flag inserted in the holder at the front. On board were Vice Adms. Dudley Carlson and Joe Metcalf; Rear Adm. John McNamara, the chief of chaplains,[4] and Bill Plackett, the master chief petty officer of the Navy. They were all in dress whites with the choker collar. Not expecting to do funereal duty today, I had worn a light blue suit, a poor choice that would have been worse had the others been in blues.

Once I was aboard, the helo lifted off and headed east. We passed alongside the Mall and shortly were above Annapolis and Chesapeake Bay. The rest of the journey was over the neat farmland of the Eastern Shore and southern Delaware. Dover is the East Coast home of the giant C5 Starlifter transport planes. The Air Force has about 70 in inventory, fully half of which were lined up on the field today, an impressive sight.

A motorcade formed, and we went to the six-story-high hangar known as Memorial Hall, where the bodies of servicemen killed in Vietnam, Beirut, and other conflicts have been officially received. (At other times, the hangar is used for washing the C5s.) A sadly familiar sight greeted us: a huge American flag hung from the rafters, creating the backdrop for 35 flag-draped cas-

---

3. *Stark* was badly damaged but not sunk in the attack.

4. Later bishop of the Merrimack Region and auxiliary bishop of the Archdiocese of Boston.

kets, each with a sailor in ceremonial whites standing alongside it. (Thirty-seven died on *Stark,* but the remains of one victim have not been recovered, and the family of another sailor asked that his casket be sent directly home.) We entered the hall through a long cordon of airmen and took seats in a section that included the families. I sat between Joe Metcalf and Sen. Bill Roth (R-Delaware).

The ceremony was simple: a band played the National Anthem, after which John McNamara said a few words and gave a prayer; he is always most eloquent. Then CNO spoke, saying how a ship's crew are like a family and how joyous homecoming is—except when homecoming is a day like today. There followed a benediction and the playing of the Navy Hymn ("Eternal Father").

The Navy principals (minus CNO) proceeded to the fellowship hall of the base chapel. There was a long table of cookies, cakes, and sandwiches provided by the people of Dover. About ten minutes after we arrived, the families came. The admirals automatically formed a sort of receiving line, which proved somewhat awkward because of the slow rate of speed by which we met and talked with people, keeping others waiting outside. It would have been better just to circulate and meet people informally. What was the most difficult part of the event, finding the right words to say, was made easier by the strongly positive attitude on the part of the families, most of whom voluntarily said how much they appreciate what the Navy did to help them. Last in line, I asked where people had come from and whether they had been in the Navy, too. We didn't stay long, instinctively recognizing that the families needed time with each other and their Navy escorts before returning to homes across America. So without notice we withdrew, returning to the airfield and a somewhat muted flight back to the Pentagon.

Wednesday, 3 June 1987

A week later, I was tasked with attending a quite different ceremony, this one a short distance from the Pentagon at Arlington National Cemetery (which Dudley Carlson called "the F-Ring").

At the far end of the property is a globular monument marking the grave of Rear Adm. Robert Peary, the Navy civil engineer who reached the North Pole on 6 April 1909. Today there was a ceremony with some very special guests: Karree Peary and Ahnaukag Henson, the sons of Peary and his black compatriot Matthew Henson, born of Eskimo women in northern Greenland. They had been located by Dr. Allen Counter of Harvard and brought (with several relatives) to the US. The proud Eskimos, dressed simply, were seated with black American relatives of Henson.

I brought a message from President Reagan and then made remarks of my own. It was a challenge to find words to celebrate a dalliance by two lonely American men in an igloo long ago. I began by recounting the Navy's long involvement in scientific exploration, from Charles Wilkes in the 1840s to Rear Adm. Richard Byrd to naval-aviator astronauts to Bob Ballard of *Titanic* fame. Then I said: "Beyond exploring our earth, the heavens, and the seas; beyond defending democracy, the Navy has also tried to make friends around the world. And we're happy to honor today Mr. Peary and Mr. Henson, proof of friendships forged in Greenland many years ago."

The ceremony concluded with the laying of two wreaths: one a traditional floral offering and the other a small circlet of tundra flowers made by the Eskimos. When the color guard retired, I gave "presentos" to the two men, their sons, and a female interpreter: ASN (M&RA) cigarette lighters, found in the bottom drawer of a filing cabinet in George's office. Since few people smoke these days, I don't normally hand them out, but today the Eskimos were most grateful.

Monday, 8 June 1987

There was diversion in midafternoon because the willowy blonde Fawn Hall, ex-secretary to Ollie North, was testifying before the joint congressional investigative committee on Iran/Contra. "I can type," she said with a smile in her opening statement.

Ms. Hall was the daughter of a longtime secretary in the West Wing office of the national security advisor. When Fawn also went to work at NSC, she did so as a "seconded" employee of the Navy Department. She lost her security clearance for disposing of documents relevant to the scandal, and Navy suddenly had to find a job for her. At first this was in the office of Vice Adm. Tom Hughes, the DCNO for Logistics. Tom's office was on the E-Ring, and numerous officers would peek in, hoping to spot the new celebrity. This irritated Tom's aide, who one day discovered a sign in a Pentagon corridor that he hauled to the entrance to their suite. It read: "We regret that the exhibit has been removed."

Wednesday, 17 June 1987

On the drive from San Francisco to the Naval Postgraduate School in Monterey, Dick Elster and I were entertained by Manfred Rietsch. He told nonstop flying stories in his offhand, raspy voice. The more excited he got, the thicker his accent got. One memorable tale was "How I almost started World War III": in September 1969 in Vietnam, ground controllers ordered Manfred to target a certain plane. It was going too slow to be a fighter, so he didn't shoot at it—which was wise, since on board was Soviet premier Alexei Kosygin, leaving Hanoi after the funeral of Ho Chi Minh.

Monday, 22 June 1987

Today, before he gave Louise Wilmot the lead and the loops (aiguillettes) as my EA, Joe Harford reported on last Friday's senior staff meeting. His Academy classmate Secretary Webb was highly exercised over an M&RA reply to OSD that was 11 days overdue. Navy is notorious for being late with its paper, in part because we lack the hordes of Pentagon staffies that Army and Air Force have. Of course, promptly responding to OSD "taskers" was definitely *not* a priority during the Lehman regime, which is why Navy's normal sloth has endured as long as it has.[5] Now it is a priority. Perhaps my greatest surprise and disappointment of Jim's tenure is his passion for bureaucratic paperwork. I simply did not expect it out of a self-defined man of action.

Thursday, 25 June 1987

Betty nervously passed the word that SecNav is "making the rounds to meet with the worker bees." About a half hour later, SecNav buzzed into the suite. He spoke briefly with Louise Wilmot and then, with his stiff-legged cowboy strut, came into my office. In a pleasant, non-accusatory but obviously intent fashion, he asked, "What's this inability to get the right numbers [for a "matrix" of naval medical needs] out of the System?" To Jim, who takes great pride and pleasure in winning major battles in OSD on the strength of airtight staff work, the lack of rigor in Navy paperwork is appalling. There

---

5. One of the many endearing eccentricities of my former deputy for civilian personnel, Joe Taussig, was his delight in stuffing OSD taskers into a small refrigerator in his office. This permitted him the fun weeks later, when an OSD official would angrily ask where was the such-and-such paper, to feign momentary mystification and then brightly announce, "Oh, that! It's in the icebox."

was nothing I could say, for short of digging up the numbers for the matrix myself, I have to rely on the library-research skills of my staff and MedCom.

At this point I decided to surge forth and tell Jim some of what's been on my mind for a while. "The best possible matrix isn't going to tell you very much more about naval medicine than what I can tell you right now." But Webb, who has called naval medicine his "number one priority," doesn't want to take any actions until after the new surgeon general, Jim Zimble, completes a 60-day review. "We don't need 60 days," I said. "We need 60 *minutes,*" a session to tell what we already know and what needs to be done. But Webb, shaking his head with a trace of a smile that indicated he thought he was talking to a babbling fool, considers such knowledge to be "anecdotal" and therefore worthless. He prefers the computer-generated tools of those whom John Lehman dismissed as "anal-ysts."

Friday, 26 June 1987

The most amusing incident in a busy day came when [my assistant for Marine personnel] Maj. Frank Stephens asked to see me. Their Navy yeoman is being transferred to Florida, and for 45 days Ollie Ashe [the Secretariat's administrative chief] will assign to us a Summer 1987 superstar: Fawn Hall. "I hope you don't mind, sir," Frank said, to which I replied, "I don't mind. The question is, will Linda [his wife] mind?" Frank's office is tucked away on the fifth floor, far from curious crowds. But this will make me famous in Houston.

At 4:00 in SecNav's office, Al Gray was "frocked" to full general, in advance of his becoming commandant. A thick cluster of men in green surrounded the short, round-headed, round-toothed, and pink-cheeked Al. When I greeted him and his perky wife Jan, Al rasped in his New Jersey accent, "Watch out fer her, Mr. Seckatary. She's not as young as she looks!"

Jim helped Jan pin the row of four chrome stars on the epaulettes of Al's uniform, and then in the soldierly tradition he gave him a hard punch on the upper arm. This is something Gray himself does on promotions. But, unable to punch back the secretary of the Navy, Al played along with the gag, reeling one step to the side and blushing as applause rose.

Two days later, upon becoming the 29th commandant of the Marine Corps in a ceremony at the Marine Barracks, Al said, "America loves its corps of Marines, but the nation demands that we, you and I, be a little bit special—that we teach nothing but winning, in combat and in life." P. X. Kelley, whose four-year tenure was troubled by the Beirut bombing, the Moscow spy scandal, and the high jinks of Ollie

North, said in his valedictory, "I ask that you simply say, there goes a Marine who tried. And, with God as my witness, I did."

Tuesday, 30 June 1987

When my turn came at the senior staff meeting, I handed Webb a folder, saying only "Matrix." Had I been friskier—and riskier—I would have said, "Holy matrix, mother of goddamns." Jim's reply was, "As I live and breathe!"

Tuesday, 7 July 1987

Match the individual described in the column at left with his performance as secretary of the Navy in the column at right:

A. A scrappy military brat, he was a furious boxer at the Naval Academy; received the Navy Cross in Vietnam for falling on a grenade to save the life of one of his Marines; wrote three novels exalting the military man of action.

1. Rammed the authorization for a 600-ship navy through Congress; cuffed and cowed the admiralty; thumbed his nose at superiors in DOD; won seemingly impossible political battles by sheer gall.

B. Educated by Jesuits, he earned a PhD in international relations; was a lower-level staffer for Henry Kissinger and an official of the Arms Control & Disarmament Agency; before returning to government, had a consulting firm.

2. Insisted on thorough analysis before acting on what he called his #1 priority; devoted the opening months of his tenure to getting his staff to move paper better and faster.

In the corridors I encountered Capt. Dennis Blair, a USNA classmate of Joe Harford, Jim Webb, and Ollie North. He's now EA to Vice Adm. Dave Jeremiah.[6] We talked a little about North, who today began his testimony before the Iran/Contra committee: "Everybody's always known that Ollie needed

6. Blair would become commander of the Pacific Command and the director of National Intelligence. Jeremiah became commander of the Pacific Fleet and vice chairman of the Joint Chiefs of Staff.

adult supervision," Dennis said. "He had it at the Academy, and he had it in the Marine Corps. But apparently he didn't have it in the White House."

I watched some of the colonel's televised testimony, which he delivered in uniform. Figuring, I suppose, he has nothing to lose and a nation to win, North was vigorous, confident, and extremely articulate—an all-American up against the cretins of the Congress. I can easily see how he charmed, bamboozled, or bludgeoned people into doing what he wanted at NSC.

Thursday, 9 July 1987

Today I joined Wayne Arny (now deputy director of OMB for international and defense matters) for breakfast in the White House Mess. "From what I hear about things at Navy now," Wayne said, "the German army is grinding to a halt in the mud before Moscow." He referred to the paper-constipation that has afflicted the Secretariat since Jim Webb's arrival. We are both amazed that Jim hasn't been the equally aggressive heir to John Lehman we thought he'd be. Maybe this shouldn't be such a surprise. Webb has been quoted as saying he thinks of himself as a writer rather than a government official, and writing, after all, is a very contemplative, paper-centered existence.

When talk turned to congressional relations, a comparison between the two secretaries was inevitable. Lehman had a very gritty, very cynical, and very pragmatic attitude toward the Congress: they were all hogs eager to be slopped. The only variable was the kind and quantity of slop, and sometimes he gave them a whole new trough. Webb, by contrast, sees the Congress as he sees humanity as a whole, divided between good guys and bad guys. The good guys get fraternal admiration and deep respect; the bad guys get contempt.

In midafternoon, the new surgeon general, Vice Adm. Jim Zimble, came to my office to talk before we went down to the Blue Room to meet with the Secretary. Webb entered, carrying the pre-doomed matrix prepared by my staff on what ails naval medicine. With a trace of sarcasm, he said, "This shouldn't take long." Holding up the folder, he said, "It's incredible to me how bad the data is. The first step is the database. Otherwise you fall into anecdotal situations." By the time he returns from WestPac in two weeks, he wants us to fill gaps in the matrix, and he thought of more items to put in it. Unfortunately, Zimble didn't say to Webb what he said to me [on 26 June]: "When you've got a starving man, you don't do a complete nutritional analysis before giving him a bowl of chicken soup."

There was nothing Webb specifically said, but I read in his expression and eloquent body language that he thinks I let him down on the matrix project, either through antagonism, inattention, or incompetence. With such a man, a notion can quickly become a conviction. I may not be fired, but why let matters get to that point? I doubt I can either change my ways or change Jim's opinion of me.

So, tonight for the first time I am thinking I should resign. My departure needn't be bitter or aggravated. I am not flushed with the willful spirit of "think I'll go eat worms." I don't want to spite Jim Webb but to regain my freedom and self-esteem, refreshing my spirit on a long trip to South America before joining the Bush campaign. In this book on 2 January 1985, I wrote that being AsstSecNav "is a wonderful job, and if ever it gets boring or no longer fun or challenging, then I should just quit and go home." My only amendment to those words is to strike "home" and insert "to Buenos Aires, Montevideo, and Santiago."

Jim Webb likes to say how much he admires "moral courage." Resigning as assistant secretary doesn't quite qualify, but the direct opposite—clinging to the office for reasons of income, prestige, and perks—would certainly be morally *un*courageous. I rather wish I could resign in protest on a matter of principle, in the British style. No such pretext exists, and in any such circumstance the man who would be most directly hurt would be Jim Webb, and I don't aim to do that. Unlike his predecessor, he doesn't deserve it.

Saturday, 11 July 1987

There was at least one small ray of sunlight in this increasingly gloomy "plebe[7] summer": along with Mary Jane Shackelford of Midland, a high-spirited young woman who was good friends since girlhood with the former Laura Welch, I introduced the 43rd president and first lady of the United States to Washington.

Shortly before 6:00, I arrived at the Marine Barracks and walked into Center House, the handsomely appointed officers club, for the reception that Mary Jane and I had long planned to welcome George and Laura Bush to town. The three of them were already there, George in his usual saucy spirit, stuffing a wad of Red Man into his lip when he felt like it.

Though a furious electrical storm flooded the parking lot, guests kept ar-

---

7. At the service academies, freshmen are called *plebes*—derived from *plebeian*, a member of the Roman lower class. Plebes arrive in early July and are subjected to intense mental and physical pressures to test whether they can survive the four years to follow.

riving for what would be a merry and successful affair. Some 60 or so came, including Congressman Bill Archer of Houston, Congressman Joe Barton of Ennis, Judge Ken Starr, White House congressional liaison Will Ball, Jim Cicconi, deputy assistant SecDef Mike Huffington and his tall, glamorous wife Arianna, party-giver Roy Pfautch, and the ever-funny Mitchell Stanley. "This is an amazing party!" Mitchell declared. "All those guns and knives on the wall, all these Texans, and nobody got killed!"

George invited Lee and Sally Atwater "to let him know he's really part of the Bush crowd." It was an odd and interesting motivation, especially since the party wasn't a Bush campaign event. Indeed, some of the guests—Bill Archer, Joe Barton, and federal highway administrator Ray Barnhart—have not declared for GB for president, to George's irritation.

Wednesday, 15 July 1987

The "Personalities" column in the *Washington Post*'s "Style" section today carried this item: "Pentagon tour guides say that visitors are asking, 'Where's Fawn Hall? Can we see her?' Unknown to the tour groups, they pass within 50 yards of where she works. She is on the fourth floor in Room 4E788, where she is secretary to Chase Untermeyer, assistant Navy secretary for manpower and reserve affairs. Who knows? One tour group may see her running for a cup of coffee." The false item [*which yielded my greatest national publicity as AsstSecNav*] brought forth a number of calls, most of them from friends of Betty Thompson, concerned that she had lost her job.

Tuesday, 21 July 1987

On a very hot evening I walked to Edmund and Sylvia Morris's Capitol Hill townhouse. We sat and talked awhile—I denied the reports that Fawn Hall is now my secretary—and Edmund played some Schubert on the piano. Then we rode in their Jaguar to Georgetown for a dinner party that proved even more remarkable than I thought it would be. The occasion celebrated the birth five weeks ago of a girl to Joanna Sturm, granddaughter of Alice Roosevelt Longworth. It was held in Joanna's sizable house at the corner of 29th and P Streets. Once owned by artist William Walton, the place is crammed with paintings, antiques, and such relics as a signed portrait of the Emperor Taisho, father of Hirohito. John F. Kennedy spent the night there before his inauguration in 1961.

When we entered the house, we were first met by Joanna's cousin Alexandra Roosevelt, a photographer in New York [and granddaughter of Theodore Roosevelt Jr., brother of the late Mrs. Longworth.] Inside the parlor were more Roosevelts: Kermit and Alexandra's sister Susan, a specialist on Chinese literature who is married to William (Bill) Weld. Bill is a tall, strawberry blond Boston lawyer who is assistant attorney general for the Criminal Division. He was US attorney for Massachusetts before coming to DC, and tonight he hinted he'll return to the Bay State to run for attorney general in 1990.[8] The hostess, Joanna, likes to say provocative and outrageous things in a low, matter-of-fact fashion and then watch how her companion reacts. For example, when I asked if there are tape recordings of her grandmother, Joanna said there are hours of them, "but they're not of any historic value." It's inconceivable that hours of interviews with one of 20th-century America's greatest wits could be uninteresting to historians, but Joanna verbally toyed with the notion that one day she might just heave them out.

We proceeded into a dining room with high-backed embroidered chairs and two portraits of Mrs. Longworth. I sat next to Alexandra, who was tonight's chef, producing an "all-green" supper of jalapeño soup, chunks of chicken with a verde sauce, and a salad. I mentioned my father's ability to dismiss from mind any relatives he didn't like. That was an utterly impossible concept for a Roosevelt. Alexandra said she likes *all* her kin, including the outlanders they went off and married.

I was rescued by Edmund's typically graceful toast: "People think that I have written about Theodore Roosevelt because I admire him. The real reason is that I was fascinated by, truly smitten by, the one true love of his life, a gentle girl from Boston named Alice Lee. She died in February 1884 giving birth to Joanna's grandmother, who of course was also named Alice. And now Joanna has given us a new Alice, of whom we are all so pleased. So, I ask you to raise your glasses. . . ."

There followed what seemed another round in an ancient game of tease among the cousins, Joanna declaring that Edmund verified that TR indeed "loved *my* great-grandmother" and only later "fell back on *your* great-grandmother."[9] Apparently the business of being a Roosevelt is a fulltime, life-long preoccupation. "They talk of it constantly," Edmund told me. The Roosevelts are an artistic and intellectually bracing bunch, ever eager to contest another in repartee, a quotation of poetry, or cooking. I am grateful to

---

8. Weld in fact ran for and was elected governor, serving until 1997.

9. Edith Kermit Carow, whom TR married in 1886.

Edmund and Sylvia for letting me glimpse their special world in this hidden Washington.

Friday, 24 July 1987

Waiting for me in the office was Gerry Turley, the 70-ish retired Marine colonel who was one of Webb's deputies in OSD Reserve Affairs and now is a sort of elder counselor to him. He gave me some advice based on his experience and observations: Webb drives his people hard and expects a lot from them, especially loyalty. When they do well, he is not particularly good at telling them so. I described the struggle over the medical matrix and asked Gerry at what point I would know when to stand aside. He was quick to say, "Don't do it. He needs you. He's just grouchy. He's a *boxer,* for God's sake!" So, tonight I think I will soldier on a while longer.

In the late afternoon, Manfred and I went to the main side of Andrews AFB. Lounging in the Distinguished Visitors Lounge were State Department security agents watching a television as their protectee, Secretary Shultz, testified before the Iran/Contra committee. The Secretary and Mrs. Shultz later boarded the C9 for a hop to their summer place in the Berkshires of western Massachusetts. On board I introduced Shultz to Manfred, the secretary having been a Marine during World War II. He looked drained, so I didn't engage him in further talk.

After we dropped off the Shultzes and their companions, we flew on to Pease AFB on the New Hampshire–Maine border. There an Air Force-enlisted man waited to drive us the rest of the way to Kennebunkport. The town was filled with sailors in whites off the cruiser *Yorktown.* The ship itself, trimmed in light like an ocean liner, is anchored off Walker's Point. I piloted us toward Ocean Avenue and out along the belt of grand old cottages. Too bad it was nighttime, for the full effect of the Point can't be appreciated when it is just a broken series of bright lights in the inky dark. We stopped at the gate, on which a paper plate sign said, "Blow horn." We did, and the gate slid open. "Just like in the movies!" Manfred marveled. We were not stopped by anyone from the Secret Service, not did we see any agents. I pointed the way to the big house, which was totally dark, causing me some concern. Quite soon a car with t-shirted agents pulled up, and they jumped out to politely ask our business. Paula Rendón, the Bushes' longtime housekeeper, appeared, greeted me and told the guys I was OK.

The Bushes were en route from an engagement in Tennessee and didn't arrive till 1:15 a.m. Lulled by the sound of an incoming tide surging against the rocks, I fell asleep in an armchair. I was awakened by their arrival and ordered to bed.

Saturday, 25 July 1987

While Manfred and I were having a proper Maine breakfast of blueberry muffins, GB appeared in his swim trunks. I introduced him to Manfred, afterwards saying, "You saw more of the Vice President than you expected."

The plan was for me to get out to *Yorktown* ahead of the VP so I could officially welcome him on behalf of SecNav. At Kennebunkport's so-called Government Wharf idled a souped-up speed boat seized from drug runners; Secret Service agents use it to chase after the VP in his Cigarette boat. At the wheel was Jeff Vasey, who has been on the VP's detail since my days on staff. "When they told me to take the assistant secretary of the Navy out to the ship," Jeff said, "I didn't know it was going to be *you*." He opened up the throttle and sent us smacking along the tops of the low swells. *Yorktown* was at anchor in 90 feet of water. Already the crew, in whites, was manning the rail, as glorious a backdrop as could be imagined. For an instant I could imagine what it was like for TR to join a ship in Oyster Bay.

With agility I leapt from the boat onto a floating pontoon and then shot up the accommodation ladder to be greeted by Capt. Phil Dur, the CO. He commanded the destroyer *Comte de Grasse* when the VP (and I) came aboard in October 1981, at the time of the bicentennial of the Battle of Yorktown. On that day, Dur told the VP that his wife's family has always summered at K'port, prompting Bush to say, "You should bring your ship up there someday." Remembering this invitation, Dur all on his own arranged *Yorktown*'s port call. In fact, he confessed to me, he doesn't think CINCLANTFLT knows why the ship is here.[10]

About 15 minutes later, the blue hull of *Fidelity,* the VP's boat, came skipping our way. With practiced helmsmanship, GB brought the boat alongside the pontoon and was soon aboard for a tour. He was escorted by the head of his detail and my friend Ralph Basham.[11] When time came to leave, GB in-

---

10. The commander-in-chief of the Atlantic Fleet did not, in fact, know. My service to Captain Dur's career was drafting for the VP's signature a note to the admiral, profusely thanking him and praising him for the inspired idea of sending *Yorktown* to Maine.

11. Director of the Secret Service, 2003–2006, and commissioner for US Customs and Border Protection, 2006–2009.

vited me to go fishing with him. I, of course, accepted and clambered aboard *Fidelity*. Once we had cast off lines, GB said, "Let's give 'em a thrill" and roared away from the ship. We returned to cruising speed en route to a sea buoy that's a favorite spot when "the blues [bluefish] are running." He and I both caught some of the wily blues. On the trip back to the Point, Ralph motioned for me to hold on with both hands, for GB likes to come into the cove at full speed, make a sharp right turn, and then kill the engine, sliding neatly alongside the pier.

This evening I left Walker's Point with the Bushes in the limo, riding in the jump seat and helping with the waving. We boarded *Fidelity* at the Government Pier and slowly cruised down the Kennebunk River, past the massive yacht of country singer Jimmy Dean, whose wife comes from this area. (The boat is named *Big Bad John*, after his 1961 hit single.) The VP went to flank speed in the open water, headed for *Yorktown*. With "Columbia, The Gem of the Ocean" playing triumphantly in my head, we approached the ship, whereupon GB did a 90° fast turn and throttled down to come alongside the pontoon. Despite wearing heels, BPB made it off the boat and up the accommodation ladder with no trouble.

Captain Dur held a reception on the helo deck for the Bushes, their extended family, Jimmy and Sue Dean, and selected locals. At sundown there was a brief ceremony to retire the colors, after which I joined Nancy Ellis. She passed on news that immediately cast a pall over the party: Secretary of Commerce Mac Baldrige, a great personal friend of the Bushes, was killed today in one of the rodeo events he loved. GB left immediately for Walker's Point to call Midge Baldrige and Jim Baker. Mac was a delightful soul and an impressive man. I envisioned him as chief of staff to a President Bush; maybe GB did, too. At the very least, his death robs Bush of a valued advisor over the course of the next year.

Sunday, 26 July 1987

I accompanied the Bushes to services at St. Ann's Episcopal Church, the quaint seaside chapel sustained over the decades by the Walker family. One of the readings was from Psalm 49, which condemns "the dull and stupid [who] perish and leave their wealth to those who come after them." Surely this is not a popular passage in Kennebunkport, at least not during the summer.

Afterwards, the Bushes gave a picnic lunch on Walker's Point for the officers and crew of *Yorktown* and their families. Jimmy Dean kept saying how impressed he was with the ship and her crew. "Back when I was in military service," he drawled, "the guys I served with were so stupid that probably 90 percent of them thought *Moby Dick* was a social disease!" In saying goodbye, Phil Dur sonorously declared, "I told the Vice President he should consider *Yorktown* his personal flagship—and you should, too." The offer was both preposterous and delightful.

Tuesday, 28 July 1987

In our meeting today, SecNav suddenly said with the hint of a smile, "Dudley [Carlson] will be going home—soon." Webb said the chief of Naval Personnel had "no excuse floating a new [sea/shore rotation] policy about women in the *Navy Times* without checking with me," especially after the DACOWITS disaster in May. CNO agreed but asked the Secretary to allow Dudley to remain on active duty till January so he can retire in the grade of vice admiral. Webb said that is fine so long as Dudley vacates the job of personnel chief sooner than that.

I put in a plea that Dudley's successor be a "people person" like his predecessor, Bill Lawrence. The man Webb is considering is Rear Adm. Bud Edney, currently director of the Office of Program Appraisal for SecNav. I gave Bud my hearty blessing; he has the brains and sensitivity to be an excellent chief of Naval Personnel, and I would definitely enjoy working with him, as I have in the past year he's headed OPA.

Thursday, 30 July 1987

Just before leaving for work, I was called by "G. W." [Bush] with an invitation to dinner tomorrow night. He quoted his father as saying that last Saturday aboard *Yorktown* was one of the three most exciting days of his life. What were the other two? "Marvin and I figured it must have been our births, but we don't know where that left Jeb, Neil, and Doro."

Friday, 31 July 1987

I stayed in the office till 6:30, when I drove to George and Laura Bush's townhouse in Westover Place on Massachusetts Avenue, close to where it crosses Nebraska Avenue. Their old and close friends from Midland, Don and Susie

Evans,[12] are in town. Over very tender medallions of beef, George freely gave candid descriptions of the internal goings-on in the Bush campaign.

Of his nemesis, Craig Fuller, George said, "I don't think Dad respects him, and I think Fuller's scared of the old man. I know he's sure scared of *me*." Notwithstanding this staff issue, George thinks the campaign is in strong shape, and he has about three-quarters confidence that his father will score a shutout in Iowa, Michigan, and maybe New Hampshire before clinching the nomination in the South. I don't think it will be that easy. GB will win the nomination but only after a second-stage struggle, like Mondale in 1984.

Then George sprang a question at me: Who should be the vice-presidential running mate? I said the best ticket balancer would be Gov. George Deuk-mejian of California, a sound (if dull) choice. But the lieutenant governor of California is a Democrat, and surrendering Sacramento on the eve of congressional redistricting would be tragic. George thinks a geographic balance isn't required, given his father's unique national rather than local powerbase. GB is therefore free to choose someone with whom he would feel comfortable serving. George's favorite right now is Sen. Alan Simpson of Wyoming. No doubt GB would be comfortable with Simpson, but I wondered if the senator's reputation as a western humorist might make him seem frivolous to some voters. So I countered with a more serious fellow from the same state: Congressman Dick Cheney, a respected legislator and former White House chief of staff. George was struck with the idea.

I had completely forgotten this suggestion until preparing this book and do not claim or even imagine it had any influence on a vice-presidential selection 13 years later. Al Simpson, whom I was blessed to know in later years when I married a Wyoming-ite, is both funny and wise. He would take himself out of consideration for the vice presidency because he was pro-choice on abortion.

Tuesday, 11 August 1987

At the end of the senior staff meeting, Webb announced a series of SPRs (Secretarial Performance Reviews) like those held by SecDef, and he rather pointedly said the first will be M&RA. The formal tasker, which we got later in the day, seeks all kinds of Webbian operational analysis on accession stan-

---

12. A high school classmate of mine, Don would be secretary of Commerce during George W. Bush's first term as president (2001–2005).

dards, recruiting, Naval ROTC quality compared with other officer sources, a breakdown on honorable and dishonorable discharges, and so forth. He wants to hold the SPR in early October. It will take almost all the time till then to assemble the data (and draw some pretty charts to go with it). Already I have dark images of Webb dismissing our numbers as insufficient.

Monday, 17 August 1987

Louise briefed me on the gathering clouds that await SecNav's return this afternoon from Europe. The most astounding concerns the Naval Postgraduate School. CNO sent Webb a memo saying he is "holding in abeyance" John Lehman's reforms of the curriculum in Monterey "as you and I were not a party" to them. Clearly CNO is trying to strengthen his power position by playing on Webb's antipathy to anything done by Lehman. If CNO can "hold in abeyance" anything he doesn't like, where does this leave the writ of the secretary? I always predicted the jungle would grow back fast once Lehman left office; I suspect Carl Trost is using Jim's emotions as the fertilizer.

Maybe I am more of a Lehmanite than I realized when John was around, but I like a SecNav with a clear vision of where he wants the Navy and Marine Corps to go and then strides forth to get us there. In the present atmosphere, I smell the mustiness of academia and not the black powder of the battlefield. And in such an atmosphere, it will be a wily fellow like Carl Trost, with a budgeteer's mastery of all things naval, who does the striding forth.

It's a bit premature to characterize the Webb secretaryship, but it seems to be dominated by three things: (1) an absolute fetish for prompt and flawless paperwork; (2) an absorption with studies, ideally resulting in a matrix of some kind; and (3) a resurgent OpNav.

Chapter 13

The Evolution of Authority

Tuesday, 18 August 1987

In the late afternoon, as I was working on some packages of paper, SecNav entered the suite, accompanied by two Marine aides. "I'm just seein' if everybody's workin,'" he said as he moved around the office to say hello to people. At 6:15, as I was about to head out for an evening engagement, the SecNav hotline rang. Webb said he was calling on "a minor matter": while in Louise's office he had seen a cartoon on the wall called "The Evolution of Authority." It shows an ape's footprint, then a man's shoeprint, and then the distinctive imprint of a high-heeled shoe. It was a feminist joke and a mild one at that.

"We should be applying the same standard we would to a male," Webb declared. "That [cartoon] was inappropriate and unnecessarily inflammatory. If a man had put something like that against women on his wall, we would be stuck with an EEO [Equal Employment Opportunity] complaint. If Captain Wilmot were 25 years old and in law school, maybe she could get away with that. But she's an EA, charged with implementing policy across the board, and she shouldn't have that sort of thing." I paused before asking if there was anything else he picked up on his walk around that I should know or do, and he laughed and said no. That ended the call.

Carrying my portfolio as if saying goodnight, I walked into Louise's office, where she was being visited by a female Air Force officer. Obviously I couldn't tell her about my call from the Secretary just then. But I saw that the infamous cartoon was not on Louise's wall but on the bulletin board of her secretary, Barbara Berry. Blithely unaware of how much the drawing had provoked him, Louise happily recounted showing it to the Secretary and asking if he wanted a copy. I didn't tell her that the cartoon not only struck Webb as offensive but that he obviously seethed about it for half an hour before hitting the phone to tell me so. For Webb's own good I didn't tell Louise about the episode, for it would eventually get out, at the very least confirming Louise's doubts about Webb's commitment to naval women.

I don't know whether to look on this incident as amusing or appalling. They say you can tell the size of a man by the size of what makes him mad, and of my twin feelings about Jim Webb—admiration and disappointment—I have to say that this evening's phone call reinforced the latter.

Wednesday, 19 August 1987

In a cheery tone of voice—the only one appropriate for a boss who's raised a crazy issue—I called Webb this evening to tell him that I had investigated the matter and found that the offending cartoon is not on Captain Wilmot's wall but on that of her secretary. Webb sounded a bit embarrassed to be reminded of his reaction yesterday. "Thanks for the clarification," he mumbled before asking, "It *is* gone?" I told him that it would be. Fortunately, at that hour everyone had left the office, so I could walk to Barbara's desk and quickly take down the drawing, which is now in my naval archives.

Also today, Seth Cropsey analyzed the Webb secretaryship: "It's clear from what he's written that Jim doesn't believe civilians should get into the military's knickers." Seth has a less conspiratorial notion of Carl Trost's role in all this. He doesn't think CNO is raising issues decided by Lehman in the clever expectation that Webb will revoke them on that basis alone. Rather, Seth thinks that Trost simply wants to run the Navy, as did his predecessors Bud Zumwalt and Jim Holloway. Carl is happy to let a SecNav play in his own blue and gold sandbox while he (the CNO) takes care of the myriad dull matters involving money. For John Warner the sandbox was dressing up in a flight suit and visiting the fleet; for Bill Middendorf it was leading the Navy Band in selections of his own music; and for Jim Webb it's studies and paper handling.

Monday, 24 August 1987

The shrewd and outspoken senior civil servant Charlie Nemfakos had some choice words on the new crew in the Secretariat: "It's the craziest damn thing I've ever seen. I mean, I really have to wonder how we managed to build a 600-ship navy, make some significant management reforms, and save billions of dollars when we were as screwed up as we were."

Thursday, 27 August 1987

Louise entered the office to say a group of my deputies wanted to see me on the women-in-the-Navy issue. She gave me a copy of the long report by

Dr. Jacquelyn Davis, chairman of DACOWITS, on her trip through West-Pac to look at Navy and Marine activities. It was a scathing chronicle of poor morale, sexual harassment, and a sense that Navy (more than USMC) really wishes it didn't have women in its ranks. The group feels it's inevitable that the Davis report will leak to *Navy Times* and that before then SecNav should aggressively try to make the women's issue his own. I fully concur, though I passed on Rear Admiral Edney's warning that Webb is as rigid as John Lehman on the subject of letting women serve on Combat Logistics Support Force ships.

Friday, 28 August 1987

It wasn't until 6:00 p.m. that Webb was in a mood to talk about women. I called Dr. Davis's report on her WestPac trip a "time bomb" that prompted me to make "a public relations proposal as much as a policy proposal, one that will help Navy's image, and—if I may say so—your image. And that is to make this issue *your* issue." In short strokes (seeing that I had pushed several buttons in Webb and had a limited amount of time before he surged), I suggested that he make a clear pronouncement on the need to utilize and accommodate women in the Navy and Marine Corps, accompanied by some specific points: a condemnation of sexual harassment, a pledge to fill all available billets on ships to which women can be legally assigned, opening more military specialties to women, and the convening of a joint Navy/Marine task force to come up with specific recommendations on such things as career advancement.

Happily for policy purposes and happily for Untermeyer after a couple of bad weeks, Webb immediately seized on the idea and directed that we work up a statement for him. He had a few disagreements with my list but on the whole adopted the initiative. It was the first time in the Webb tenure, at least in my realm, that SecNav has acted decisively to *do* something rather than request further data on it.

Thursday, 3 September 1987

As I was walking back to the office from the head, I saw Bud Edney with a distressed look on his face. "The Secretary wasn't happy with the package [on women]," Bud said, his achingly polite way of saying Webb tossed it on the deck and stomped all over it. The paper was too specific in its directives to CNO and the Commandant; also, Webb wants a "historical review" of women in the fleet. Even the dutiful Edney could not keep from observing, "He always seems to want something like this." Though Bud denies it, I suspect Webb has gotten nervous about championing the women's issue, probably because he is truly against women in the military and detests those who keep pushing the matter.

I abandoned a pile of signature folders to go swim in the POAC and work off my reaction to Bud's report. Then I went to Georgetown for the swank dinner party that Arianna Huffington gave [husband] Mike on the occasion of his 40th birthday. Not unexpected, given the social swath Arianna has cut since moving to Washington less than a year ago, the event brought out a number of big names, such as Abe Rosenthal, executive editor of the *New York Times;* columnist William Safire; Chris Wallace, NBC's White House correspondent; columnist Rowland Evans; chief of protocol Lucky and Archie Roosevelt; Democratic fundraiser Esther Coopersmith; Edmund and Sylvia Morris; and Mike's boss, Under Secretary of Defense Fred Iklé.

We dined exquisitely while a string quartet performed. Then came champagne and various toasts, led by the witty, erudite Arianna. She amply demonstrated how she became the first woman, the first non-Briton, and the first non-native English speaker to head the Cambridge Union. Arianna began by citing the extensive, even mystical use of the number 40 in the Bible, and she said Mike's previous years were but a chrysalis stage before he burgeons into something even more splendid. There followed toasts by others who tried but failed to be as clever as the hostess. The passing of liqueurs provided a chance to say hello to the Morrises and melt away.[1]

In 1992, Michael Huffington was elected as a Republican to Congress from a district surrounding Santa Barbara, California. He sought a U.S. Senate seat only two years later, spending $28 million of his personal fortune but losing to Dianne Feinstein. He and Arianna divorced in 1997, after which she became a celebrated author, columnist, and founder of the liberal news website the Huffington Post.

Tuesday, 8 September 1987

Dick Rumpf, acting AsstSecNav for Research Engineering & Systems [Mel Paisley's old job], is back from a three-week senior management course at

---

1. A few days later, I received a note from Edmund, written in an elegant hand in black fountain pen ink: "I had no idea you were one of Arianna's former lovers. Does Fawn know?"

the Kennedy School. Harvard is one of Webb's special hates, and his way of welcoming Dick back was to ask, "Are you an asshole yet?" Another primal antipathy came out when I mentioned the call by Congressman Tom McMillan (D-Maryland) for higher faculty pay at USNA. (McMillan represents Annapolis and serves on the Academy's Board of Visitors.) "He's a nonvet," said Webb dismissively.

[*The one thing that always stood me in good stead with Jim Webb was that I was a Harvard College graduate who served in the Vietnam War. He never failed to note how many Harvard men served in the world wars but how few in Vietnam.*]

Another copy of the "footprints" cartoon returned to Barbara Berry's enclosure, and I found myself fretting what would happen if SecNav staged another raid to check for it. To ask Barbara to take it down risked telling why, and I have resisted telling anyone (though it's a fantastic story) out of consideration for Jim. So, I devised another plan. This evening, after everyone had gone home, I took out a sheet of paper and, free-hand, did my own version of "The Evolution of Authority." Instead of footprints I drew coffee containers: first a "Pentagon Cafeteria" Styrofoam cup, then a "SecNav Mess" coffee cup and saucer, and finally an elaborate silver coffee pot inscribed, "To Barbara Berry, Secretary of Defense, 1989–93." I signed and dated the drawing and replaced "footprints" with it.

[*Just as I hoped, Barbara was so delighted to have a personalized cartoon from the boss that it remained on her bulletin board and the other never came back. Crisis solved.*]

The Secretary was on the "McNeil-Lehrer Report" on public television tonight. Over the weekend, the papers reported he had sent an eyes-only memo to SecDef, objecting to the Administration's policy of having the Navy escort Kuwaiti tankers through the Persian Gulf ["reflagging" them as American to provide the fig leaf of a rationale for the mission]. And, the reports said, Weinberger told him to get with the program. Jim Lehrer (a friend of Webb's) pressed him on the memo, and Webb refused to comment. If he couldn't support the policy, he said, "I'll resign. I don't need this job."

Wednesday, 9 September 1987

Bud Edney and I slipped into the rear of the fifth-deck auditorium to hear SecNav's address to the Women Officers Professional Association (WOPA). Someone called, "Attention on deck!" and everyone sprang to her/his feet. The president of WOPA read from Jim's official bio, giving him the chance to say, "She left out that I'm a noted misogynist, the man women love to hate." That got a laugh, though tension remained in the room for the next 45 minutes.

Webb strung on a neck mike so he could walk away from the lectern and make full use of gestures and his special angular grace. I don't doubt that for many of the women present, the hated/feared SecNav was a damn sexy animal; this may have occurred to him, too. There were flashes of defensiveness on the matter of women in the military, but fortunately these didn't dominate his presentation. "I hope that women in the Navy will listen to what people [meaning himself] are saying. When I say something, it's serious—I'll back it up. And if I say something you don't like, at least it's on the table."

Webb then laid out the various things that he has said and done regarding women since his nomination as SecNav (and that he felt naval women weren't listening to or believing), such as the decision to let women shipyard workers go on submarine sea trials and the sacking of Dudley Carlson. "When the new policy on sea/shore rotation was announced without my knowledge," he declared, "I decided to get a new chief of Naval Personnel." He then announced that he is directing CNO and the Commandant to conduct "an intense, flag-level review involving females [the word he used in preference to "women"], with a 60-day turnaround," on such things as job assignments, sexual harassment, and fraternization. There was no applause for the announcement, but it served its purpose. Webb himself said he should be judged on the results, and that's what the women will wait to see.

What Webb announced was the heart of the M&RA proposal, using the speech to WOPA in the spirit of getting out front on the women's issue, as I had urged last Friday. But I don't feel any particular sense of triumph this evening. For one thing, it was so obviously what he should have done and so typically what he likes—a study—that Webb might have said exactly the same thing today had my office remained silent. And I suspect that any compliments to M&RA would to him be a salute to Louise Wilmot, which he doesn't want to give.

Bud Edney was disturbed about the reference to Dudley's being cashiered. "We announced it as a retirement," he reminded SecNav's EA, Capt. Tom Daly.

Thursday, 10 September 1987

After a big briefing on officer manning, all staff withdrew, leaving Dudley Carlson and me alone. "My happiness quotient is pretty low today," he said, gazing at me. "You know that, don't you?" He was of course referring to yesterday's extraordinarily uncalled-for remark by SecNav to WOPA. There wasn't much I could say to Dudley, except that I was shocked. The comments were not only out of keeping with good leadership but also out of character: Jim Webb trying to score points with a feminist crowd. My anguish for Dudley—whom I never liked as chief of Naval Personnel but who has been a colleague for three years—was partly over his obvious pain and partly out of grim recognition that a Webb who can be so mean and thoughtless to a vice admiral can be the same to an AsstSecNav.

Friday, 11 September 1987

It was announced today that Adm. Ace Lyons is resigning as CINCPACFLT and retiring, supposedly because he lost a bureaucratic battle to have operational control of forces in the Persian Gulf. But everyone knew his days were numbered: as a prime protégé of John Lehman's, Ace was probably high on both Jim Webb's and Carl Trost's execution lists.[2] When I talked to Dudley Carlson today I attempted to give him some grim comfort by suggesting that the news makes his departure seem the result of a general purge.

Tuesday, 15 September 1987

I attended the luncheon of the Reserve Forces Policy Board (RFPB) to hear the speaker Ken Bergquist, nominated by the President as the first AsstSecDef for "low-intensity conflict," or special warfare. Bergquist is a good friend of Webb's from their days on the minority staff of the House Veterans Affairs Committee. It's easy to see why he's Jim's sort of guy: physically impressive, a Silver Star combat soldier in Vietnam, an Army reservist (in special warfare),

---

2. The *Washington Post* on 12 September quoted Lehman as calling Ace's ouster "the revenge of the nerds."

and a lover of conflict with political and bureaucratic foes. "Isn't this unadulterated bullshit?" he asked, speaking of one such fight. "And isn't it wonderful?" I wouldn't be surprised that if Ken doesn't get confirmed, Webb might want him at Navy—such as AsstSecNav (M&RA).

Wednesday, 16 September 1987

I invited Manfred to come with me to hear the Commandant speak to RFPB. Relishing the stage, Al Gray spoke with feigned disgust of "people on my staff who start off at 0930 in their silk shorts and Adidases [running shoes] and run to the University of Maryland or the Eastern Shore or wherever the hell they go, coming back at 1530. I swear, we're gonna be the best-lookin' outfit that ever got run off a hill."

At 3:00, Tony DiTrapani [my deputy for Civilian Personnel Policy] and I went to the offices of the Equal Employment Opportunity Commission to meet with the chairman, Clarence Thomas. He is an assertive young conservative black who has infuriated liberal Democrats for not being one of them. On the TV set in his office, with the sound off, ran the confirmation hearings of Judge Robert Bork to be a justice of the Supreme Court. Thomas knows and admires Bork, calling his "the finest legal mind in America." He shook his head at Bork's treatment by Democrats on the Senate Judiciary Committee, calling it a travesty.

Bork's nomination was eventually defeated by the Senate, and the brutal treatment he received in the hearings was a rehearsal for what Clarence himself would endure and triumphantly surmount four years later when he was nominated for the Court.

Wednesday, 23 September 1987

This evening I read the biography of Gideon Welles by John Niven, acquired in a book sale last weekend. Welles was of course the great Civil War secretary of the Navy, but I didn't know until tonight that in the Polk Administration, when he was about 40, he held a political appointment in the Navy Department. The only non-naval officer to be a bureau chief, he was in charge of what today would be called logistics. I was highly amused that Welles, a Connecticut newspaperman, had great difficulty with his famous boss, the historian George Bancroft.[3] According to the book, Welles "was irritated at

---

3. SecNav, 1845–46. See footnote for 18 May 1985.

Bancroft's ceremonial, condescending air, his tendency to find fault where no fault existed, [and] his temperamental outbursts. . . . Eventually, the Secretary came to appreciate Welles's honesty and competence, but their association was never really harmonious."

Ah, Brother Gideon, I know exactly how you felt!

Monday, 28 September 1987

Bud Edney, about to become chief of Naval Personnel, came by my office for general advice, saying, "You've been around a long time and know the program." It's somewhat amusing that I am so relatively senior in the Navy Department after just 3½ years on the job. That's of course because senior military people change their jobs frequently and because four principal civilians have left the Secretariat in just the last six months.

I told Bud that his greatest service would be to master the ponderous bureaucracy in the Navy Annex. Unlike OSD, which has civil servants who remain forever, trotting out favorite old schemes in hopes a new appointee will accept them, "the Bureau" is staffed by naval officers who are constantly coming and going. This leads to what I called "the tyranny of the filing cabinets" in which old policies and methods are always served up in briefing papers and proposals. If Bud can get the Annex to think anew and act anew, this would be "one of the greatest achievements in peacetime naval history." In Bud Edney and Jim Zimble [the surgeon general] I have what I so painfully lacked in 1985–87, two solid doers and cooperative friends. With time and patience (and some influence on the personnel system), such counterparts can eventually come to be.

Friday, 2 October 1987

"Tell 'em about the teddy bears," Capt. Tom Daly prompted Webb, knowing it was one of his favorite anecdotes. Though aware he had to choose his words carefully, Webb told of visiting the women's berthing spaces on a sub tender at Holy Loch [Scotland] and discovering that "a sizable majority of racks had something to hug at night." I suppose the moral to him was a pathetic one: that you can call a woman a sailor, but within those dungarees is a vulnerable little girl.

"I would laugh except it's not funny," observed a steely Dr. Mary Murphy, his consultant on women's issues. I suspect Webb took this as an endorsement of his belief, but I think she was amazed that a secretary of the

Navy would consider stuffed animals not only worthy of comment but deeply significant. (Ah, if only she knew about the "footprints" cartoon!) I chuckled to myself, recalling the (male) sailors aboard *Benner* who had ingenious little rubber statuettes, bought in places like Olongapo, that they carried with them and probably examined in their bunks at night, too.

"Tell me honestly," Seth Cropsey asked later in the day. "Which one [of the two SecNavs with whom we've served] do you prefer?" Despite the many blows of the summertime, I still have to say I prefer Webb to Lehman on personal grounds, for I feel closer to him. But insofar as the Navy is concerned, Lehman was of course the better boss. After only six months it now seems almost legendary that once there was a secretary who gave us all a sense of drive, of direction, of being on a winning team. He also gave us some dutifully dumb-assed foes who were easy to beat, that fact not diminishing by one whit the joy of victory. Enemy #1 was OSD, and now our masters are three veterans of that outfit — Messrs. Webb, Garrett, and [Webb's top staffer Denny] Shaw — who want Navy to do what OSD tells us. Oh well, it was fun while it lasted.

Saturday, 10 October 1987

Despite his quirks and shortcomings, Jim Webb remains in my estimation a great man with enormous potential for further service to his country or at the very least to American literature. As I have struggled with the question of when and how to leave my job, the hardest aspect has been how to remain his friend.

What is worrisome is the way Webb has either tacitly or explicitly given the lead in military matters to the CNO and Commandant. Lehman clearly went to excess in his management of the Navy, which may have arisen from sheer love of power and of the game. But he had a solid philosophical base to his acts, and that was civilian control of the military. He considered such control absolute, and his reading of history persuaded him that the admiralty, if left to itself, will do short-sighted and stupid things to the detriment of the fleet. Webb comes from a proud military tradition, and he honors those who have worn the uniform of the country, no matter how briefly or unspectacularly. In Carl Trost and Al Gray he is fortunate to have two smart and capable men who may serve him precisely right. The danger that Lehman always saw in "the System" is that even strong CNOs and commandants can't fully control their bureaucracies, which is why Lehman frequently did their work for them.

The law, after all, gives all power to the civilian secretary of the Navy.

Lehman chose not to surrender this authority, particularly on those things that he cared about, which were many. If the faculty of the Naval Postgraduate School thinks of itself as a cloistered brotherhood and its two-star superintendent thinks of Monterey as a cozy spot to play world-class golf, then you reach in and tell the PG School what to teach and whom to hire. If the Naval sea and air systems commands like dealing with familiar old suppliers that turn out a decent product but at high cost, then you force competition on them. And so on.

Webb bridles at this "day-to-day control" and refuses to engage in it, giving CNO and CMC rein to handle their services and report back to him in the classic military fashion. This they are only too happy to do. The Navy and Marine Corps will survive and do well in this period, but they will also settle back into the sloth of "the System," with all of its long-term dangers.

Wednesday, 14 October 1987

George W. Bush confided that he's intrigued with the idea of running for governor of Texas in 1990. He thinks the opportunity for the GOP is ripe, especially if liberal Atty. Gen. Jim Mattox is the Democratic nominee. "I'm spending a lot of time these days in Texas campaigning for George Bush," he told me. "Only I'm not tellin' 'em *which* George Bush."

George would not make the race in 1990, when state treasurer Ann Richards bested Mattox in the Democratic primary and went on to defeat Republican Clayton Williams in the fall. Instead he waited until 1994 to run, scoring an upset victory over Governor Richards.

Tuesday, 20 October 1987

Webb seems generally happy and more enthusiastic about his job nowadays. The trip to the Persian Gulf a month or so ago might have been an emotional turning point for him. And my relations with the Secretary are practically pleasant, boosted by an SPR of M&RA that Webb declared "very helpful." It's clear we passed our test of competence in his eyes.

Friday, 13 November 1987

In the reporting-out of the selection board for rear admiral, [Adm.] Hunt Hardisty [the VCNO] was talking about the attack pilots who had been selected when Webb got up from the conference table and pulled a snapshot out of his desk. It showed a 250-pound [American] bomb dropped but not detonated in the middle of Webb's platoon in the Arizona Valley in Vietnam. The VCNO (an ex–fighter pilot) exclaimed that that was sure some bomb all right and passed the picture around. "I'm just a grunt," Webb said. It was unnecessary autobiography, and I think he said it to declare that, unlike his predecessor, he isn't crazy about airplanes and what they do.

Thursday, 19 November 1987

The highlight of the morning was Manfred's being "frocked" to full colonel, for which he was selected almost a year ago.[4] The new deputy chief of staff for Manpower, Maj. Gen. John Hudson (an aviator who is Manfred's "sea daddy"), came to re-administer the oath of office, a Marine tradition. In my remarks I joked that we were having this event "in order to help Manfred's self-esteem. As you know, Marines in general and aviators in particular have such a poor opinion of themselves that we have to do special things like this from time to time to buck them up." Then Connie Rietsch and I removed the silver oak leaves from Manfred's epaulettes and installed the eagles. They were supposed to be "beak out," which I got 90° wrong, providing extra merriment.

Later, the new Colonel Rietsch and I took a T39 from Andrews to Monmouth County Airport in New Jersey. There we were met by my second cousin, Barbara U. Carton, who hosted us in the area[5] and at 7:00 p.m. delivered us to NWS [Naval Weapons Station] Earle. A port security vehicle led us down Earle's famous 3½-mile-long pier, at the end of which ships load and unload ammunition. As we drove, we had a glorious view of Manhattan at night.

We pulled alongside USS *Estocin* [a guided-missile frigate], to be met by its skipper, Cdr. Jay Foley, formerly of my staff and one of the finest people I have known in my recent life. *Estocin* has just been at AUTEC,[6] where she

---

4. The military lets officers hold a rank to which they've been promoted, even if they still must wait to be paid at that grade. The act of putting on the insignia of their new rank is called "frocking." I had successfully made the case to HQMC that Marine aides should rank with their Navy counterparts, and as a captain Louise Wilmot was equivalent in rank to a full colonel.

5. I was born in nearby Long Branch and lived in Rumson until my family moved to Texas in 1948.

6. See 20–21 November 1986.

had a very successful time, taking only four torpedoes and evading ten. As part of the Naval Reserve Fleet, the ship does not deploy overseas but has more steaming time than most active-force ships do. In commanding an NRF ship, Jay has one problem that other captains do not: he had to wait to get underway tonight until a bus arrived from Philadelphia carrying 41 reservists to fill out his crew. Time was critical because with the winds expected to increase later tonight, Jay needed to get *Estocin* out of the narrow (125-foot) Earle channel and past Sandy Hook into open water, a difficult transit even without stiff winds.

The wind was already biting cold and whipping up the bay when, helped by two tugs, we cast off from the pier and headed out to sea. As I write now (at 12:45 A.M.), there is a discernible pitch to the ship but nothing violent. *Estocin* has fin stabilizers that counteract the effect of roll. I welcome the weather as a real at-sea experience, unlike the stately progress of a carrier.

Saturday, 21 November 1987

I had a good night's sleep in the odd way I do at sea: awake, I tell myself how wonderfully relaxing it all is. After breakfast I went up to the bridge to behold the white-capped, slate-gray seas of the Narragansett operating area off Long Island. The sky had dramatic patterns of light streaming through cloudbanks with clear sectors in between. At that moment we were taking station behind three ships with which we exercised today. Seas caused one of the ships to break away from the oiler while refueling, snapping the hose line. That meant we wouldn't refuel, so we came about and headed down to the Cape Henlopen–Cape May entrance to Delaware Bay, where easterly swells gave us a rough ride.

At 1500, dressed in jacket and tie, I was the prime actor in an all-purpose ceremony on the mess decks, pinning on medals and reenlisting one sailor. I managed to twirl pin clasps and say cheery words to awardees while maintaining my balance on the deck. I'm glad to say certain things never change: a bosnsmate looked like a bosnsmate (chunky) and a gunner's mate looked like a gunner's mate (spare). In my remarks I quoted Melville in *White Jacket,* who said it is better, in both ships and life, to confront adversity head-on rather than scud, or be blown along by it.

I changed into khakis, a thick Navy sweater, and an *Estocin* foul-weather jacket and went up to the bridge. ("Mr. Untermeyer on the bridge!" the bosnsmate of the watch sang out.) Manfred was there, and he said things were worse than about an hour before, meaning very rough. Waves were 15 to 20 feet high, and when we plowed through them there would be a great splash of water against the windshield and the ship would shudder and wallow. A very worried Jay Foley was proceeding at slow speed toward a point some 20 miles off the central Jersey coast, where he hopes the lee of the land and the shallowness of the water will reduce the sea state. Then we can turn south down the coast at higher speed. The wind howled over the bow at 55 mph.

Dinner in the wardroom was served on paper plates and accident free. Back in the XO's cabin, I sat down to read on the couch, propping my legs against the coffee table. This made the ship's rolls feel like sitting in a room-sized rocking chair. I returned to the bridge, and until my eyes adjusted to the dark it was just a collection of glowing dials and shadowy figures. Jay said, "I've seen some things today I never thought I'd see: a total breakaway from an unrep [underway replenishment] and 60 knots of wind over the bow for hours." As we talked, the ship took some of its deepest bobs and rolls. With assurance that we would indeed find smoother water as we turned southward, I went off to bed.

Sunday, 22 November 1987

When I awoke, sea conditions had become a good deal gentler. We headed into Delaware Bay for the six-hour transit to Philadelphia. By 1:00 p.m., *Estocin* was maneuvering toward the pier in the Navy Yard. This took longer than usual because tugboat workers are on strike, and the scab crews on two tugs handling us didn't quite know what to do. Though the day was beautiful, sailors were removing ice from the port side, which got the worst accumulation last night. Up on the mast, my wind-shredded flag had only three stars: two full ones and two half ones.

When we docked, there was a brief farewell at which I was given a framed picture of the ship, and I gave the wardroom a British book on the history of naval warfare. When the signal came, Jay Foley escorted me out to the quarterdeck, where side boys in dress blues and peacoats were paraded. I thanked him personally for this weekend and then briskly strode ashore. A Navy car took Manfred and me to the 30th Street Station, and the Metroliner took us back to DC.

Two weeks later, Captain Foley sent the tattered remnants of my flag along with a letter attesting that it had been ripped by 65-knot winds and that the AsstSecNav "suffered no discernible ill effects from 18-foot seas." Betty Thompson pinned this note up for the staff to see. Unfortunately, one night it came off the wall and fluttered into the trash. Valuing it for my archives, I apologetically asked Jay to send another copy, which he did. This was better for the historical record, for in the second letter the seas rose to 20 feet and the winds to 70 knots!

Wednesday, 25 November 1987

The DOD Women's Task Force met for two hours on the question of combat exclusion. Dr. Dave Armor, acting AsstSecDef for manpower, asked us to examine "inconsistencies" among the services in the assignments women can take. There's no doubt the group will recommend telling Navy to put women on unrep ships. I'm not a clone of Jim Webb on this issue, and yet I think he's right to raise the question of wartime readiness of military units in which women are assigned. The Task Force seems to view the women's issue as only one of peacetime job opportunities and career progression. Unless we consider the wartime aspect, I said, "some other group will have to sit around this table in a few years." Dick Carver, my counterpart at Air Force and ever the smooth politician,[7] said he concurred with my analysis that "we're only nibbling around the edges of this thing, but that's all we can do now." Armor ruled that the Task Force won't do as I proposed.

Thursday, 4 December 1987

With CNO's internal study of women in the Navy just about complete, Bud Edney floated the idea of allowing women aboard stores and ammo ships, which shuttle to and from the battle group but are not part of it. He then asked SecNav whether "this is within your toleration."

Because of his respect for Bud, the idea was something Webb had to take seriously, rather than dismiss it as caving in to the feminists. He paused and said, "My greatest concern about women aboard ship is—." At that moment he turned to me and said, "Chase, stop taking notes." I instantly dropped my pen. "If I'm going to think this thing out loud," Webb said, "I have to concentrate." I introduced the fact that opening Combat Logistics Force ships to women is an officer issue, and it's women officers who have been pushing DACOWITS. It's not an issue for women sailors, who for the most part are concerned over quality-of-life and general job matters.

Webb at last was able to speak his mind (and emotions): "What I'm con-

---

7. He was mayor of Peoria, Illinois, from 1973–84.

cerned about is what having women on ships will do to the *focus* of the ship."
By this he meant that, especially after many days away from port, the sailors,
male and female, will be thinking more about having sex than being ready
for combat. "That's what we can't talk about, which is why [turning to me]
I asked you not to take notes." The new SecDef, Frank Carlucci, "will be a
problem," Webb predicts, because his wife Marcia is a feminist who served on
DACOWITS. "He wants me to challenge the law, and I'm not going to do it.
He's going to have to get Ronald Reagan to tell me to do it."

For now, Webb isn't ready to embrace the Edney proposal. And as the
long meeting concluded, Webb looked at me and said, "This conversation
didn't occur. Your EA [Louise Wilmot] is a conduit to every woman in the
Navy." Webb wasn't directly accusing me of disloyalty, but he certainly sus-
pects Louise of it, and there's nothing I can do to alter his opinion. There's
nothing Louise can do, either, which is why I've never told her that SecNav
considers her a fifth columnist in the E-Ring. If I did, she would probably be
more thrilled than stunned. My response today was to say that there would
be no leak out of my office; the likeliest source of leakage would be the Navy
task force, and Bud agreed.

Monday, 7 December 1987

The brand-new secretary of Defense, Frank Carlucci, entered the Reserve
Forces Policy Board meeting right on time and shook hands with everyone.
He is a small, dapper fellow in taut good shape. Carlucci is also an accomplished super-bureaucrat who can sound tough while espousing an accom-
modationist line. On a day of "summit fever," with USSR General Secretary
Mikhail Gorbachev only hours from touching down at Andrews, Carlucci
stoutly defended arms talks with the Russians.

Tuesday, 8 December 1987

After the senior staff meeting, I briefed Webb on Dave Armor's task force on
women and the direction he's taking it. Jim had a truly Webbian interpretation of Armor's motivation: he is typical of "men of our generation" who did
not serve in uniform during Vietnam and who are now trying to "emasculate"
military service to cover their guilt or sense of inadequacy. But Webb has
greater concern for Carlucci, who told him last week, "I have none of Cap's
hang-ups over women in combat." Jim wonders "what Carlucci does stand

for," calling him "a good Number Two man who becomes Number One," more interested in process than in leadership.

Thursday, 10 December 1987

The VCNO, Hunt Hardisty, told me tonight that the report on women is acceptable (or at least non–gag inducing) to the "warfare sponsors" [surface, air, and sub forces]. This begs believing; more likely CNO simply let them know it was a closed issue. "Time's come to change," Hunt said matter-of-factly.

Friday, 11 December 1987

At 8:30 in the Blue Room, the CNO's recommendations on women were briefed to SecNav Webb. Toying with a long, unlit cigar, Webb was inclined to be testy. For example, when he got a too-simplistic answer from a briefer, he snapped, "I understand that. I've been working this [issue] for 15 years." But, testiness aside, Webb had no apparent objection to the possibly historic policy initiatives proposed by the task force and endorsed by the OpNav three- and four-stars: assigning women to oilers, ammo, and stores ships; letting them fly in reconnaissance aircraft; recruiting them into "nontraditional" ratings like boiler tech; and making stronger top-down efforts against sexual harassment and fraternization.

After lighting his cigar, Webb said he will work on the definition of combat and a combat mission on his own, "as an old committee counsel" in the Congress. My sense is that, in an unpressured environment, Webb will approve much, and possibly all, of the Navy report and reap deserved praise for his leadership. But if there's pressure, the thing could fall apart.

Wednesday, 16 December 1987

Today I scratched down some thoughts on what I might do for VP Bush after leaving Navy and returning from South America, and that would be to serve as his transition planner. Working very quietly, and perhaps alone, I could draft the agenda and timetable for a smooth Reagan-Bush turnover, ready for presentation on the morning of Wednesday, 9 November 1988. I may propose this to GB on Sunday, perhaps with a test on George W.

Sunday, 20 December 1987

A few days ago, I called Debbie Romash in George W.'s office to say I wanted to speak with him and could do so today at his parents' friends-and-family holiday brunch. Instantly upon seeing each other this afternoon at the VP's house, George said, "You want to talk? Let's do it." The talk didn't take too many words on either side. I said I had reached the conclusion that I should leave Navy, after which I'd be ready for a special assignment in the Bush world. What I proposed is to map out the presidential transition. Said George: "Perfect! That's it. You've got it." I said I realize that such an assignment might be greeted with wariness and even hostility by Craig Fuller, whereupon George said flatly, "Forget about Fuller. He's out. You know that, don't you?" Craig will remain as chief of staff to the VP through 1988 but won't have a role in the Bush presidency.

George told me he'd talk with "the old man" and said I should call him (G. W.) after he returns from Midland on 4 January. But not too many minutes later, George came back in sight and beckoned me into another corner of the dining room. "I've already talked with Dad, and he thinks it's a great idea." And that, in so many (or so few) words, was that.

Monday, 21 December 1987

Today upon my arrival in the office I saw a copy of the AlNav [all-Navy message] issued Friday in which SecNav announced his policy changes with regard to women—notably opening up 26 of 37 ships of the Combat Logistics Force. On the message Louise had appended a note, "In *my* lifetime!"

Louise, Manfred, and I went together to SecNav's 11:00 press conference. Webb announced the opening of AEs (ammo ships), AOs (oilers), and AFSs (stores ships) to women but said "the most important thing we have done isn't the number of ships" but in more closely defining a combat mission so "we can now apply logic when we're looking at units and ships." He added: "This represents to me in naval terms as far as you can go."

In the DOD task force meeting at 2:00, Dave Armor took note of SecNav's announcement and called it "a tremendous step." But clearly he and a majority of other members want to open the entire Combat Logistics Force to women. I expressed astonishment: "I seem to remember hearing people say that this task force couldn't possibly tackle the entire question of women in the military, that we could only 'nibble around the edges.' I submit that this is a major *chomp*."

This exchange inspired me, during an Army briefing that followed, to scribble lyrics to what I called "The Navy Combat Exclusion Song," to be sung to the melody of "Old McDonald Had a Farm":

> Be glad Navy changed its tune.
> AE, I.O.U.
> Women will be sailing soon.
> AE, I.O.U.
> With a nibble here, and a chomp-chomp there,
> Here a ship, there a ship,
> Everywhere a major nip.
> And still the Task Force wants the moon!
> AE, I.O.U.

Thursday, 31 December 1987

Webb was in a fine year-end mood, quite happy that Congress nicked Navy only $126 million in the appropriations bill, versus billions cut from the Army and Air Force. Showing that he still feels constantly compared to his predecessor, Webb crowed that this turned out exactly as he knew it would, not requiring emergency action on the Hill. "Lehman would have been camped out over there to see every senator," he said. "But I've worked over there, and I know how the place works."

Webb once again gave a broad hint that he's spoiling for a showdown with SecDef Carlucci over a service secretary's prerogative under the law to determine personnel policy. But, as if to reassure me that he's not going to do something rash, he quoted the warning of SecDef's naval aide "not to hang your hat on the statue"—a reference to a bust of John Paul Jones in Mahan Hall at USNA where midshipmen deposit their headgear when they quit the Academy.

The Evolution of Authority.

Chapter 14

The Second Death of Lieutenant Hodges

Sunday, 3 January 1988

I was reading the paper this morning when the telephone rang. "Chahlie m'boy!" said the familiar voice. "You have two options: a spaghetti lunch or coming over this evening about 6:30." It was GB calling to set a time to talk about my proposed transition project. Given the options, I chose the latter so I could log a full day's work in the office.

On an evening of powdery snow, the gate guards at the Naval Observatory admitted me to the grounds of the Vice President's House. GB was in a red sweater and fixing popcorn in the pantry. We had the popcorn and some beers, half-watching the Oilers-Seahawks game, which Houston won in overtime, 23–20. There was peripheral talk about Iowa, where he is slightly behind Dole in the polls. Bush said he feels "*pretty* good," but this was said without his usual buoyancy.

We also talked about John Lehman, who I said should be SecDef because he has the knowledge and the élan to break up the Pentagon in ways it needs to be broken. There would be tumult with him as SecDef, "but it would be healthy tumult." The trouble, I warned, "is that with Lehman you get Lehmanism," which is playing the game for its own sake or, worse, for power's sake. But I imagine Bush favors John Tower for Defense.

Soon GB turned to my transition proposal. He has only a sketchy recollection of the transition in which he was involved only seven years ago, remembering "some bureaucracy set up in a building somewhere, filled with people all looking to get jobs for themselves." I began by saying that if the Republicans are victorious this year, it will be the first time in 60 years [since Hoover followed Coolidge] that a party will have succeeded itself [after an election]. This allows for a very smooth transition if past lessons are learned and a "roadmap" is created before the election. I said that among the things on which the project should concentrate are Presidential Personnel, the White House staff, and whether there should be high-level, policy-oriented "transition teams" in the departments and agencies, as in 1980–81.

GB liked everything I said. "It's something I want to do, and you're the perfect guy to do it," he said. But for now we agreed to keep things quiet and quiescent till I return from South America. In the meantime, he will get into (and hopefully past) the primaries.

Monday, 4 January 1988

Toward noon I left for the Army & Navy Club and lunch with Don Hittle. I used the opportunity to reveal my plan to leave the job he once occupied himself. Don endorsed the decision: "When you think your time has come to go, it's time to go." He then laughed and said, "The word around the E-Ring is that the only reason you didn't go the way of Jim Goodrich was because of your relationship with Bush." I said that was truer under Lehman than under Webb. Don quickly said, "Oh, no. John was very fond of you."

Thursday, 7 January 1988

I was debriefing Louise and Manfred on a meeting when the hotline rang. It was the Secretary, responding to my request to talk, inviting me down to his office. Webb was at his desk, and because the doors were open I stood near him and spoke in a low voice, telling him of my decision to resign. He reacted with a mild backward snap of his neck and a little smile. His words were also soft. He said I am welcome to stay to the end of the term, but he didn't plead with me to reconsider. Indeed, he accepted my logic that now is the best time to leave, with men like Bud Edney and Jim Zimble in places recently held by Dudley Carlson and Lew Seaton. He said I should do what I want and depart when I want. The conversation was manful and friendly; I can leave office with Jim Webb's friendship and perhaps even his admiration. I felt good, even mildly relieved, about what I had done.

Back in my office, I continued the meeting with my chief sides. Louise had a certain feminine look in her eye that seemed to say, "You aren't going to hurt me, are you?" It may have been my imagination, but it was not the sort of look an assistant gives the boss while hearing a semi-boring report. I do want to tell Louise, Manfred, and Betty of my resignation as soon as possible but will first let SecNav try to line up my successor before word gets out. Manfred and Betty will do well, but I am concerned about Louise. I will ask Bud Edney to get her orders out of the E-Ring before she is eliminated by SecNav, unless she wants to stay and take her chances.

Tuesday, 12 January 1988

The day's main event was an assembly of flag officers and senior civilians to hear SecNav review his first nine months in office. The almost-stated theme was: we're doing just as well as under Lehman, but we're doing things better. "The most important thing we've done," he declared, "is reestablish open and direct communication with the senior Navy and Marine leadership based on the age-old principles of mutual respect" — unlike That Other Guy. Webb said "all this will culminate in a very difficult year, difficult because it's a year divisible by four in which there is no clear frontrunner, to be frank." At the same time there is a new SecDef and a call from OSD staffers for Navy to give up force structure in order to meet budgetary reductions. CNO followed Webb and spoke more optimistically of "a glass that's 96% full."

Tuesday, 19 January 1988

Today brought the seventh annual "executive forum" for political appointees, or what I call the pep rally. Former Sen. Howard Baker, now White House chief of staff, gave a good stump speech, saying, "Ronald Reagan was elected president of the United States for eight years and not seven. He has made the political lame duck an anachronism because of his personality. His eighth year in office will be his most successful."

There was a musical interlude, followed by the Army's Herald Trumpets blowing "Ruffles and Flourishes." Ronald Reagan was announced and sauntered on stage to "Hail to the Chief" and the yips and hoots of his strongest fans in Washington. Early in his remarks he did something interesting: he asked everyone who has been in the Administration since 1981 to stand. I did, looking not at the President but at the crowd; about a fifth of the thousand or so present were on their feet. We were all applauded. I appreciate being considered one of the "old warriors," but the scene struck me as odd: a hallful of committed conservatives hailing those who have been on the federal payroll for seven years.

Saturday, 23 January 1988

One my last official acts as AsstSecNav was to attend the commissioning of the cruiser San Jacinto, named after the site of Sam Houston's victory over Santa Ana in 1836. An earlier San Jacinto was the "jeep" carrier on which young Lt. George

Bush served during World War II. The ceremony was held at the Port of Houston, just a few miles up-channel from the battleground.

A motorcade was formed, and Houston police led us "platform guests" on a circuitous route to the north side of the ship channel. I was announced and strode aft on the starboard side to take my seat in the front row. There were something like ten speakers, including Vice President Bush, Governor Clements, Senator Gramm, and me. My three minutes were very important for me as the local boy made good. Before an audience of thousands in seats ashore, I said in part: "We are in a period in which some commentators back in Washington think our main adversary, the Soviet Union, has changed its behavior just because its maximum leader wears better-fitting suits than the burlap bags worn by his predecessors. But we know differently. The Russians never change, only their words and symbols do. In the USSR, it's always just a short step from Gucci to the Gulag." (This was the line of the day.) "So when these worriers ask what it will take to convince the Soviet Union of our sincere desire for peace, we know what it will take: *this ship* is what it will take, she and many more like her."

I took my seat to applause to enjoy the rest of the program and the ship's "coming alive." The VP left for Atlanta, and I went down into the crowd to greet friends. "Gucci to the Gulag!" several of them called.

Wednesday, 27 January 1988

At the senior staff meeting at 9:00, SecNav said yesterday there was a "bloody brawl" over unresolved budget issues in which DOD programmer-in-chief David Chu called for the retirement of the 16 older frigates and destroyers Navy proposed putting in the Reserve fleet. Chu was seconded by Steve Duncan, the AsstSecDef for Reserve Affair, who said the Reserves can't fully man the ships. He may be right, but Webb felt undercut by his own successor and fellow USNA alumnus.

Friday, 29 January 1988

In by far the hardest thing I had to do all week, I used today's travel meeting to tell Louise, Manfred, and Betty of my resignation. I began, "I don't know a better way to do it than just say it. . . ." forgoing a clever or dramatic lead-in. My tone was positive, warm, and fluid, in contrast to the ashen reaction of my key staffers. I related my meetings with the Secretary and Under three weeks ago to tell them of my decision. "I have to tell you that neither of them fell on the floor to pull at my trouser leg and beg me to stay."

The normally high-strung Betty took the news very well. Manfred, good Prussian that he is, said with a wry smile that I can have a career as an actor for hiding the secret for so long and so well. The one who had a hard time was Louise, who actually broke into tears; I offered and she accepted my pocket handkerchief. Twice I said, struggling to find the proper thing to say to an outwardly fierce and strong woman officer, that I was "complimented by your reaction." I maintained my composure, which was easy because I'm the lucky one who's getting out, who will go to South America, and who might come back into government in a much higher position. They have to remain — and so, for that matter, must Larry Garrett, Dennis Shaw & Co.

Because she was still teary eyed and would have to face other eyes, I asked Louise to stay, partially so she could regain her composure and partially to tell her I stand ready to ask Vice Admiral Edney to arrange another assignment for her if she feels she will be persecuted in the Webb Secretariat. Louise said she hadn't thought of that, which was something of a surprise, for I interpreted her reaction to my news as arising from sudden fear of an unknown future.

Monday, 1 February 1988

Today I embarked on telling my colleagues of my plans to leave. Bob Conn smiled and said, "The same for me, only it'll be the first of May." Ev Pyatt said, "I don't know how much longer I'm going to be around." After tying down the purchase of the two new carriers, "there's no future here. I've done more than most civil servants ever do." When I observed that Navy can survive losing me but not him, Ev said, "I'm not sure they [in the SecNav and UnSecNav suites] are in touch with reality." It does strike me as odd how calmly Webb is taking the loss of his three oldest hands. A mass exit will make my own departure seem less dramatic — or more so, if the gossipy defense trade magazines interpret it as a vote of no-confidence in Webb or of him in us.

Thursday, 4 February 1988

Rear Adm. Ron Marryott, superintendent of USNA, returned my call, and I told him of my departure. He gave an effusive expression of regret for losing an AsstSecNav who "stayed close" to the Academy and "was always there to help." But I imagine Ron is relieved to have me gone. Winning and maintaining popularity at Annapolis was never my aim or my duty, and with two superintendents in a row I was never popular.

Monday, 8 February 1988

Seth Cropsey, back from a week of leave, came by to say, "I've heard the good news." He also aims to quit. Seth said he admires "how well you put up with everything that went on around here," presumably meaning post-Lehman. Adm. Paul Yost, commandant of the Coast Guard, called to say I had always been a friend at Navy, a place where USCG always needs friends. Perhaps the most surprising word came from Dick Elster, who met this morning with SecNav on his future at M&RA. Webb was in a positive froth over word received Friday that SecDef Carlucci wants his longtime protégée, Marybel Batjer, to succeed me. Jim can probably fend off Marybel, but Dick said the Secretary spent most of their time together fulminating against Carlucci, who he thinks wants to "get him."

When I got home, I turned on the radio to get the bad news: GB finished *third* in Iowa, behind Sen. Bob Dole and Rev. Pat Robertson. "We got whipped" is how George the younger put matters. In simple terms, Bush ran as the legatee of Ronald Reagan in Iowa, which doesn't like the Administration's domestic and foreign policies. New Hampshire is a week from tomorrow; GB must win there to get back on track.

Tuesday, 9 February 1988

There was a small senior staff meeting in which our group photo was taken for posterity. When the photographer left, a grim-faced Webb, speaking in a low, controlled voice, said he wants us all to know that ill times attend Navy at the hands of SecDef and his budgeteers. As Webb told it, Carlucci et al. have a particular desire to cut Navy force structure and make the 600-ship Navy just a nostalgic slogan of the 1980s. By ordering 16 older ships decommissioned and possibly sold to poor allies, OSD has shoved us farther away from that goal. In a theme I've heard from him before, Webb said he is most disgusted that Carlucci "has no strategy" and is "a fixer" who cares more about his congressional relations and press notices than about giving America a "balanced" national defense.

Ev Pyatt cautioned everyone—but primarily SecNav—not to bemoan our ill treatment because OSD will just clamp down on us. With a set jaw, Webb said "the confrontation [with Carlucci] has already begun. I have already been put in a box." He refused to elaborate, but I know my man: Jim Webb is a romantic 19th-century warrior who loves battles to the death, and the fact that it may be his own death only makes the battle more noble.

I was thinking of passages like these from Fields of Fire, *spoken by or to its hero, Marine Lt. Robert E. Lee Hodges Jr.: "I fight because we have always fought. It didn't matter who. . . . It was the fight, not the cause that mattered. . . . Oh, you got to be proud of your daddy. He died standing up and fighting back. . . . And will I, in the end, meet your fate, Father? I'm not afraid. You and the others taught me that."*

Sensing that Webb may be yearning for a chance to resign in protest or to invite his own sacking, I interrupted the quiet that came at the end of the meeting to say, "I'm not sure what you mean by 'confrontation' with SecDef, but I hope it doesn't mean what I think I hear you saying. Whatever happens this year, we've got to have you there fighting for Navy. If you're not, God knows what Carlucci will give us [as SecNav]." Webb nodded silently. He may have taken what I said as loyalty, which it was, but only in part. It was also a means of puncturing Webb's rapidly inflating balloon.

Speaking with Ev and Tom Faught[1] outside the office, I spun my theory of Webb as the "American samurai," to use Chris Buckley's term. Tom, the newcomer, worried aloud that Webb may indeed be setting himself up for (self-)execution. He also asked the right question: Why did Webb convene the meeting with us? My answer was that he wanted to create dramatic tension, a normal enough thing for a novelist to do.

Wednesday, 10 February 1988

Seth Cropsey came in to talk about yesterday's remarkable meeting. We both agree that Webb may be dreaming of a fiery finish to a short tour as SecNav. Cdr. Mark Neuhart, SecNav's public affairs officer and a very businesslike, ungossipy fellow, told me that "the word in OSD is that Webb is spoiling for a fight" and that, after losing it, he will "punch out." He didn't mean that Webb, ex-Academy boxer, will take a swing at Carlucci. It was the aviator's term for engaging the ejector seat before a crash.

---

1. Assistant secretary of the Navy for Research, Engineering & Systems, 1987–89.

Thursday, 11 February 1988

Before noon I met with Vice Adm. Jim Zimble, the surgeon general, and said I expect him to ensure that nurses, dentists, and Medical Service Corps officers have an equal shot with MDs in becoming commanding officers and XOs of naval hospitals. Jim strongly believes doctors should be COs of at least certain hospitals; the question is how many. Though Jim (whom I like a lot) seemed hurt that I would question his good faith, it's not my job or my experience to ascribe the purest intentions to admirals.

Dick Elster stayed behind to say SecNav had called him with "good news and bad news": the good news was that Marybel Batjer will not become AsstSecNav (M&RA). The bad news is that Dick won't, either. The actual Carlucci choice, highly acceptable to Webb, is Ken Bergquist, the Army Ranger who recently withdrew his controversial nomination as AsstSecDef for special ops.

Tuesday, 16 February 1988

The ship's clock in my office struck five bells (6:30), and as I pretended to listen intently to Bud Edney's explanation of a sea/shore rotation issue, I was nervously thinking instead that the polls in New Hampshire would close in only half an hour. Bud left just before 7:00, and I immediately turned on the TV in Louise's office. Dan Rather of CBS was saying, ". . . here in New Hampshire, where the voters have given George Bush a big win." I raised my arms in a whoop of joy. Down in the POAC, I saw the numbers on CNN: the VP won by a full 10 points over Dole, almost as if Iowa hadn't occurred. What saved him was the superior organization built by Gov. John Sununu, Andy Card, and Ron Kaufman. For Bushites it was probably the greatest news since 16 July 1980, when Reagan chose GB as his running mate.

Wednesday, 17 February 1988

It was a pleasure this morning to open the apartment door and pick up the *Washington Post* with its big headline, "Bush Rebounds." I had breakfast with my designated successor, Ken Bergquist. In describing the issues M&RA handles and the hundreds of personnel cases that must be decided every year, I kept praising my deputies and special assistants. I proudly bequeath to Ken a first-rate staff, in contrast to the woebegone crew I inherited four years ago.

I have told my Marine aides that before leaving I want to grant Col. Doc White's petition for a higher disability rating. Lieutenant Colonel Hertel doesn't think this would be the least bit out of line; it's a proper exercise of the plenary authority I have over personnel matters by delegation of SecNav. And I don't think Jim Webb would fault me for favoring a Marine badly wounded in combat in Vietnam.

Friday, 19 February 1988

I stayed behind the senior staff meeting to ask Webb whether SecDef had called Senators Nunn and Warner about Ken Bergquist's nomination. He didn't find out because Carlucci canceled his meeting with the service secretaries. Then he said, "Because you're a friend—a friend longer than we've worked together—I've got to tell you: I've about had it with Carlucci." According to Webb, Carlucci won't meet with him or give him clear guidance, but if Webb says or does something boldly in Navy's interest, Carlucci is quick to slap him down. "We just don't understand each other," Webb said, clenching his pipe. "He's a civil servant and I'm not." I repeated what I said ten days ago, that Jim should hold on and not let Carlucci & Co. get to him. Maybe they are actively trying to force him out, seizing on his oft-uttered comment that he "doesn't have to be" in government. But, as with that last impassioned plea, Jim pointedly declined to respond.

Monday, 22 February 1988

I welcomed Col. George Walls, the wonderful guy who was my Marine aide in 1985–87. He's been "penciled in" for command of the small base at Mt. Fuji, and he had come to say goodbye. Shortly after we started talking (ca. 11:05), the hotline from SecNav rang. A somber Jim Webb said, "Chase, I want you to know that I've just sent my letter over to the President." I needed no more explanation than those few words to know exactly what he meant: the clash with Carlucci had reached the dramatic climax in *Young Secretary Webb*, the novel that Jim has been writing with his life the past tumultuous year. "I can't have followed my instincts and followed [the budget] over to the Hill, too," he said.

In his letter to RR, copies of which soon flew around naval Washington, Webb stated that three times he and CNO tried to preserve the 600-ship navy in the budget reductions, and "since recommendations to that effect were rejected by your secretary of Defense, I am unable to support him personally or to defend this amended budget during budget deliberations. Consequently, I find it necessary to resign from my position as secretary of the Navy." It was all as I had forecast to my colleagues on 9 February: a resignation in protest in the British fashion, a noble and morally courageous act — but one that has devastated the Navy Department.[2]

For the rest of the day, I winced whenever I thought of what Webb did. As with so much else, I found myself cursing and admiring him simultaneously. He is the finest person of my generation I have ever known; he is also arrogant, melodramatic, bullying, and moody. I foresee a future for Jim Webb as a celebrated novelist and essayist, perhaps the president of a small mountain college, and always the spokesman for those who fought — really fought — in Vietnam. But will he ever again be appointed to high office? No. And will he ever run for office? Not likely. People will note his moodiness and volatility and count both more than his greatness.

Where does today's stunning news leave me? Part of my confidence in leaving office at this time was that in Jim Webb naval manpower and medicine had the best possible advocate. Now that bedrock is gone. So there's a chance I won't be going out the door next week after all.

A radio report tonight said that Carlucci wants Will Ball to succeed Webb as SecNav. Will is now the White House legislative liaison and a friend since he served on Senator Tower's staff.

Tuesday, 23 February 1988

Today I awoke with the conviction that I should extend the effective date of my resignation for the sake of continuity in Navy Department manpower during the Webb-Ball transition. My subsequent call to Betty Karabatsos, the assistant for political personnel in SecDef's office, came at the right time: my resignation letter had not progressed beyond her desk due to something procedurally wrong with it.

Retired Brig. Gen. Don Hittle called to find out what was happening in the wake of Webb's resignation. A staunch Lehmanite, he was never too impressed with his fellow Marine. When I told Don of my plan to stick around a bit longer, he said it was absolutely the right thing: "Power's for the grabbing in an interregnum. This is when [the uniformed military] moves in, grabs thing, and doesn't let go. With all his experience in government, it will

---

2. In his diary entry for this day, President Reagan wrote: "I don't think Navy was sorry to see him go."

still take [Will Ball] some time to find out where the shells are and which one the pea is under."

Maj. Gen. Jake Moore, deputy chief of staff for Reserve Affairs, had me to lunch in the generals' mess at HQMC to say goodbye and thanks. I said, "The best thing in the world is to be a Marine. I can't claim that distinction. But the next best thing is to work with Marines and to be liked by them."[3] I do think I acted just right in my dealings with the Corps, about as well as any non-Marine could: I was on their side without fawning; I always made sure they were considered in my deliberations and official acts; I attended the events that mattered to them, like Marine birthday cake cuttings; and in my personal grooming and fitness I reflected the sort of image they like.

Wednesday, 24 February 1988

Today a very sunburned Larry Garrett, acting SecNav, returned from West-Pac. To the senior staff, he said, "I am deeply saddened by Jim's decision. I'm sorry I wasn't here; I like to think I could have had an impact on him. We've all been affected by his character, by his integrity, and by his principles. All he did will remain in place until I change them or Mr. Ball changes them. That's the best way to reduce turmoil." Someone asked to speak with Larry after the meeting because "the wheels have come off the wagon" on some matter. Larry quickly rejoined, "We don't *have* a wagon!"

It was an apt description of the desolation that hangs over the Navy Department at this time. Only a year ago under John Lehman all was lusty and radiant. Despite the glumness, I privately rejoice that I have witnessed at close range the tumultuous secretaryships of both John Lehman and Jim Webb. Both will live in legend, each for a different reason.

Ev Pyatt later noted that Webb blasted Carlucci for a lack of leadership, and yet Jim provided no leadership of his own on procurement issues, the heart of what the Navy Secretariat does. But, Ev added, without question Webb's was the most remarkable tenure of any of the SecNavs he's known in his long career in the department.

At noon there was an office pizza party with an air of celebration that I'm not (yet) leaving. I said it was like being "a corpse who could enjoy his own funeral." The special assistants presented me with a pizza-sized chocolate chip cookie and recited in unison:

---

3. In all the years that followed, I noted Al Gray's standard salutation to "Marines and friends of Marines" and said I was solidly in the second category.

> We're glad you're back;
> We're happy you'll stay.
> So keep this cookie anyway.

Bud Edney came in at 2:00 for our regular meeting. He is among the flag officers who feel Webb overreacted in his fight with Carlucci. "You can't make things personal in this town," he said.

Rear Adm. J. D. Williams and I later watched a replay of Webb's interview Monday night on "The McNeill-Lehrer Report." Though he was in friendly hands and had an ideal forum in which to explain to an educated and influential audience what he had done, Jim was uncharacteristically rambling and bureaucratic. (He spoke at one point of "the Marine Corps aviation procurement accounts.") Asked what he accomplished as SecNav, Webb had to fish around before replying that he had "restored integrity to the officer corps"—meaning, I suppose, that he didn't try to influence selection boards the way John Lehman did. Lehrer asked if Webb had "had it" with government service. Webb replied, "I never say never, but I have probably fulfilled all my expectations of government service." Being SecNav, he reflected, is "a good job; with the right sort of support it's probably the best job in government." When Lehrer asked, "Is there a novel in all this?" Jim said, "I might write about American government in some way, but it wouldn't be autobiographical"—unlike his three existing novels, of course.

Said J. D., "When he sets that jaw—watch out!"

Friday, 26 February 1988

Charlie Nemfakos and I walked back from a meeting together. He said Navy will probably take a budgetary beating in the wake of Jim Webb's fiery departure. We had been winning nearly everything for too long, anyway, Charlie said, but Webb's defiant manner guarantees that our foes will have greater opportunity to prevail against us this year. Then he added: "The first thing we learn as kids is that if you're not chosen team captain you don't take your ball and go home."

At three I met with the man who will be Ronald Reagan's third secretary of the Navy. Until he's confirmed, Will Ball is operating out of the general counsel's office. Before the meeting I talked with his escort and briefing arranger, Cdr. Gary Roughead[4] of OPA. When Will appeared, he greeted me

---

4. Roughead would become CNO, serving from 2007–11. A regret I have about not return-

warmly. Easygoing and unhurried in the South Carolina manner, he said he was hoping to come to my office "and meet your folks," so that is where we went.

Will told of the sudden and amusingly casual way in which he was chosen secretary of the Navy. After a legislative strategy luncheon with the President on Monday, he and Howard Baker were walking back to the chief of staff's office when an aide handed Baker a copy of Jim Webb's resignation. Baker expressed surprise, showed the letter to Will, and asked if he had any ideas about who should replace Webb. Will, who served six years on active duty as a naval officer, grinned and said, yes, he had a name—his own—saying, "I had always thought it would be great to be secretary of the Navy, but more like in the year 2010." In the Cabinet meeting that met soon afterward, Baker conferred with Carlucci. The two of them later told Will it was all settled: they had gotten the President's blessing, and he would be the new SecNav.

Ever since deciding to remain at my post during the transition, I have become firmer in my desire to leave and see South America while I can. Will may prove the sort of boss/friend I hoped to have in Jim Webb, and he certainly will be the easiest SecNav to work with, far above Lehman and Webb. But I am not drawn to seeing how the Ball secretaryship plays out. I rather imagine it will be (to twist Hobbes) pleasant, placid, and short. But I wouldn't have missed the Webb secretaryship for anything.

Sunday, 28 February 1988

Shortly before 4:00 I arrived at the Marine Barracks for the cocktail party given in my honor by Lt. Gen. and Mrs. John Hudson. The standing joke was how the party was unnecessary since I'm staying around awhile, but we decided to have a good time anyway. The event drew the Commandant and Jan Gray. In talking quietly with Al about last week's stunning event, he said, "We didn't need that." By this and a few other words he used, the Commandant strongly hinted that he thinks ex-Captain Webb overreacted. But at least Jim left the USMC a fine legacy in Al Gray.

---

ing to Defense during a later administration was that I didn't get to serve again with men and women I had known in younger years.

Monday, 29 February 1988

Shortly before 11:30 I was in SecDef's office for a hail-and-farewell photo with Carlucci. He came out from behind the great desk, a gray man wearing a gray suit. He's an inch or so shorter than I, and he has a weary, toothy smile that invites distrust. We had a few moments chat about my future while a photographer snapped away. Then, as we walked to the door, I raised the sensitive subject of Jim Webb's sudden departure a week ago. Carlucci shrugged and said, "I haven't said one bad word about him. He attacked me, but. . . ." And he shrugged again.

Friday, 4 March 1988

Before Lieutenant General Hudson came in this morning, a distressed Manfred told me he (Manfred) is "in deep kimchi" at HQMC for not warning them that we recommended that Acting SecNav send back the USMC women's study for rewrite, which he did. (This incident proves, as if proof is necessary, that HQMC views our Marine aides as its agents more than ours.) So when John rather preposterously said he had nothing in the way of an agenda today, I raised the women's study myself. John frowned, shifted in his seat, and said, "I was going to shoot [Manfred] in both knees." I suggested he use one bullet on Manfred and another on me for not telling Headquarters either. But I didn't apologize for sending the study back. It's a terrible jumble, reflecting the lack of care and intensity that USMC gave the women's tasker [directive], in contrast to what Navy did.

Despite the discomfort this caused Manfred, it was a useful exercise, showing HQMC that it can't treat the women's issue lightly. I know of course that in the end the Marines will do exactly what they want. Even the great John Lehman didn't fight them, largely because he knew he couldn't win.

Tuesday, 8 March 1988

Tonight, for the third year in a row, I put on black tie and went to the concluding banquet of the Veterans of Foreign Wars' annual conference. On one side of me on the dais sat 80-year-old Sen. Quentin Burdick, "the first Democratic anything" elected from North Dakota. When the organist played the opening notes of each state song, vets from that state would jump to their feet to cheer and wave their napkins. The hard-of-hearing Burdick with mounting anxiety asked me to let him know when North Dakota came up.

On the other side sat Sen. Strom Thurmond (R-South Carolina). He's supporting Bob Dole over GB for president because "I think he'd be stronger—stronger ag'inst Gorbycheff and the commanists; stronger ag'inst the Cawngriss, and stronger ag'inst the boorockacy." I noted that this is the 40th anniversary of his own run for the presidency. Thurmond liked the reminder and loosed some statistics on how well he did that year against Truman and Dewey, winning the third-highest vote ever attained by a third party. "I stood against federal domination and for states' authority," he said proudly, for some reason not using the phrase "states' rights," which was the very name of his party.

Too bad for old Strom's candidate: on this "Super Tuesday," GB won every one of the 17 primaries. Soon his nomination will be deemed inevitable.

Friday, 11 March 1988

This morning I placed a call to a New York financier named John Lehman. I alerted him that the admiralty is making a big push to get Will Ball to revoke Lehman's reforms at the Naval Academy and Postgraduate School. I suggested that John speak with Will about it, and he said he would. John then said, "Pretty soon you'll be free at last, free at last! It took a little longer than I hoped to take care of that little problem of yours," referring to Jim Webb. He promised a Metropolitan Club lunch soon for "a feast of recrimination."

According to GB, John has a guaranteed million dollars a year from Paine Webber. When I asked whether this might preclude service in a Bush administration, John swiftly said, "My attitude is an Augustinian one: 'Not just yet, Lord!' But I do want to come back."

Tuesday, 15 March 1988

This evening brought the big reception at the Navy Museum for Jim and JoAnn Webb. Above our heads was a constantly running sideshow of Jim visiting the fleet, laying wreaths, chatting with the mighty, working on official papers aloft, and so forth. Seeing this, one might easily believe that there is a young man with a glorious future ahead of him. But that's not what Jim wants people to think; he wants them to admire his glorious *past*. It's what I called his way of "moving ahead while facing backwards." When Webb spoke, I was standing so far in the rear that I couldn't see him—only the slideshow, which his words seemed unintentionally to narrate.

"I'm not going to talk about the circumstances which led to my resignation," he said three times before proceeding to do so. He said that since he resigned he has received hundreds of letters of support from fellow combat vets of Vietnam, and "to a man they knew why I did what I did. The politics of pragmatism has no place in the Department of Defense. We who watched such politics in Vietnam want no part of it. Lemmings are great team players. But they don't solve the problem when they jump over the cliff." Yet Jim solved no problem other than Frank Carlucci's when he jumped, solo, off his cliff.

Jim concluded by saying, "I hope you don't think that I in any way violated the trust of the people I led." It was a tantalizing hint that maybe he has those doubts himself.

Friday, 18 March 1988

Maj. Frank Stephens came in to tell me that Lt. Col. Oliver North would hold a press conference at 4:30 to announce his retirement from the Marine Corps. I can understand that HQMC wouldn't want him standing trial in uniform, but I don't know why Ollie would voluntarily give up that uniform, which served him so well in last year's congressional testimony. In any event, the colonel's paperwork came over, reaching my desk right at the time of the press conference. Ordinarily I would never see an officer's retirement request; they are so routine that my pen-signed signature goes on the forms. But Ollie's was of course an extraordinary case. It was a low-grade historic moment in the annals of the USMC, so I signed the "Approved" block with Louise, Betty, and receptionist Sgt. Traci Smith watching. Then, in presidential style, I gave the pen to Traci. The occasion is truly sad for North, the overzealous patriot, for the Corps, and for the Reagan Administration.

Chapter 15

Bound for Valparaiso

Wednesday, 30 March 1988

I rode a Navy car past flowering trees to the Old Executive Office Building. There I went up to the old SecNav/VP's office for the ceremonial swearing-in of Will Ball. Eleven months ago, Jim Webb staged a gargantuan ceremony on the steps of Bancroft Hall that drew thousands. What today's event lacked in mass it made up for in class: the President spoke; Howard Baker administered the oath; Will's former and present bosses, the secretaries of State and Defense, attended; and numerous members of Congress, the CIA director, former SecNavs, and CNOs were in the audience.

RR said "the 600-ship navy remains our goal" and that Will's "biggest challenge will be in keeping up enlistments and recruit quality." He predicted that the 67th secretary of the Navy will give Congress "a dose of the old-time religion" as the son of a Southern Baptist preacher. In his response, Will said he spent Monday on board *Coral Sea,* the carrier built at the end of World War II and still on active duty. He said he thought of the President when he was told that the ship's nickname is "The Ageless Warrior."

Terry Mattke, the Marine colonel selectee who has been one of the VP's military assistants since 1985, rode with me back to the Pentagon. He said many of his cohorts in the Corps saw Jim Webb as "a company-grade officer who happened to be secretary of the Navy." The CO of a rifle platoon has a simple mission: to use and preserve his men. He doesn't have to worry about logistics, strategy, budgeting, etc., and those who do are the despised "Them" in air-conditioned headquarters in "the rear" or back in DC. "All of us start out thinking that way," Terry said. What changes them is responsibility, and Webb never changed.

Thursday, 31 March 1988

At tonight's $1000-a-head fundraiser for GB at Eddie and Belinda Hidalgo's house in McLean, I talked with P. X. Kelley. He said he, too, thought about the contrast between yesterday's swearing-in of Will Ball and the one for Jim Webb at Annapolis last May. A few days before the Webb spectacular, P. X. was at the Academy and a Marine-option midshipman pleaded with him to get "the coronation of King James" switched from exam week. When P. X. carried this message to Webb, Jim's eyes narrowed, and he said, "Those bastards kept me off the campus of my own alma mater for three years, and I'm going to make them suffer." The "bastards" in question were long-gone villains named Bill Lawrence and Bud Edney [the Academy's superintendent and commandant, respectively, in 1979], and the sufferers were the poor middies who had to participate in the ceremony. Barbara Kelley said succinctly, "The jackass."

Friday, 1 April 1988

Dick Elster and I had an 11:00 appointment with SecNav Ball, whose office now has only one decorative touch: a model of the Confederate ironclad *Virginia* (ex-*Merrimack*). I introduced Dick to Will and said that he is the right choice as my successor ad interim. In his courtly, slow, southern way, Will said that was just fine. Just then one of many hotlines on the secretarial phone rang, and a grumbling Will walked over to answer it. He came back to the table vowing to get rid of those lines. This prompted me to say that they are the only means an assistant secretary has to break through "the palace guard" and speak with him. Without the hotlines, I said, there must be some other means (such as regular one-on-one meetings) to talk privately. Will said he hadn't thought of that.

The evening brought an informal dinner with George and Laura Bush in their townhouse off Massachusetts Avenue. Fellow guests were Neil and Sharon Bush, just in from Denver. In the springtime of joy for the Bush family and Bush supporters, when victory, that only occasional commodity in our lives, is now routine and the White House within touching distance, ours was a zesty time.

George was in top form, both verbally and physically, entertaining us all with recollected conversations and encounters in the campaign. He is still very interested in running for governor in 1990. With an early primary and a voting public that doesn't much care to learn anything about the candidates, having a name that recently took 64% of the vote in a big GOP primary [in Texas] is a valuable asset. "I went from being a four-pound gorilla to a forty-pound gorilla," said George.

The brothers asked each other whether BPB is enjoying the campaign.

Neil said yes; she hasn't said anything sharp or critical to him. "That's because she's using your brother George as the lighting rod, buddy," a battle-scarred GWB responded. I think there's long been an elaborate act that mother and eldest son like to put on for the other: George as uncouth West Texas oilman (who tonight kept pulling strands of chewing tobacco out of his sports coat to drop in his mouth) and "Bar" as disdainful grande dame.

As the evening ended, I told George that his father last night indicated he wants to talk with me this weekend about the transition project. "A good sign!" said George. "Congratulations!" said Neil.

Saturday, 2 April 1988

Right at 9:30, I called White House Signal, identified myself, and asked to speak with the Vice President. Within a minute, GB was on the line.

"Hey, Chase," he cheerily said. "At some appropriate time I want to talk about all this transition stuff. I don't want our campaign people worrying about it. And you'd be the ideal guy." We agreed to get together after I return from South America in late May or early June. This will give me something to ponder on bus and boat rides in Chile.

Tuesday, 5 April 1988

At today's senior staff meeting, SecNav Ball announced that he has selected Capt. Phil Dur to be his EA. Phil is CO of *Yorktown* and the naval super-pol I got to know last summer when the cruiser was off Kennebunkport. I later gave Will my theory on why EAs often ignore the lowly likes of AsstSecNavs: right next to their desk is a wall covered with photos of their predecessors, men who have gone on to become CNOs, CINCS, and other four-star jobs. The tendency is for the EA to gaze at that wall and think, "That's where I'm going!" and dismiss the paltry personalities of the present. If I were SecNav, I'd take the photos off the wall, put them in a handsome binder, and place it on the shelf for occasional reference by the EA.

Wednesday, 6 April 1988

At my official farewell event, held in his office, SecNav affixed the Navy Distinguished Public Service award on my lapel. He also read the citation himself. Because this is normally the Marine aide's job, Will's doing so made the occasion much more personal. The award is one I always knew I'd get upon departure—which is why John Lehman's little insult of giving me only the #2 award when he left (while giving all my colleagues the #1) was something I welcomed: it meant I would eventually have *two* medals to wear on my tuxedo. Actually, my lapel will sport four medals, the other two received in 1968 for service in Vietnam.

In my response I quoted JFK at Annapolis in 1963: "Any man who may be asked in this century what he did to make his life worthwhile can respond with a good deal of pride and satisfaction, 'I served in the United States Navy.'" I said I would amend that by saying, "I served in the Department of the Navy in the time of John Lehman, Jim Webb, and Will Ball." That five-year segment covered the most titanic (wrong word?) events of a historic era for the Navy and Marine Corps. I gave praise to those who had really done the work: Dick Elster on manpower, Alice Stratton on family issues, Tony DiTrapani on civilian personnel, and the special assistants on personnel cases. I closed by saying, "I figure the Navy and Marine Corps got on for about 215 years before I arrived, and they probably can get on at least as long without me." But, I said, we are all keepers of the traditions of those institutions and can be grateful for that honor and opportunity.

Tonight, almost as a perfect curtain-ringer to my tenure, the Marine Band gave a concert at the DAR Constitution Hall. Beforehand, I had John and Eve Hilgenberg[1] to dinner at the Army & Navy Club. John told a delightful anecdote of his Navy days: he was a check sight observer inside the gun mount during a gunfire exercise his ship was conducting. Bored by repeatedly looking through the sight and seeing nothing, John just radioed that the check sight was clear and went back to reading *Moby Dick*. The gun then fired a round that shot across the bow of the squadron flagship. Back came a signal: "The next time you fire at your commodore, you'd better not miss."

I had a VIP box for the concert, and when we arrived we found an elderly couple sitting there. They were in the wrong box, but I welcomed them, for they were retired Gen. and Mrs. Leonard F. Chapman, commandant of the Marine Corps from 1968–72. The Band performed splendidly, of course, and my mood was enhanced by excited thoughts: the "ruffles and flourishes" of the past, prospectively greater times to come, my foreign trips, my writing, and the transition project for GB. The concert concluded with "The Stars and Stripes Forever" and the dropping of the big flag from the ceiling.

---

1. See 27 November 1987.

Thursday, 7 April 1988

In a little ceremony organized by Louise, I was "piped over the side" by my deputies. Then Yeoman 2/c Levi Andrews and Corporal Shawn Flinn, a symbolic Navy-Marine team, helped load boxes in my car. Military officers like to say that the best view of the Pentagon is the one "in the rearview mirror when you're leaving." I left with only positive feelings about the place and my five years in the Navy Department. But I did remember to look at the building in the rearview mirror as I drove away.

Sunday, 1 January 1989

On my South America trip I never got around to writing my thoughts on the years as AsstSecNav. Here they are:

It was an excellent job, and I believe I served ably in it; at least my reputation is that I did. I can take a measure of credit for what was done to maintain adequate recruiting, to improve health care, to increase career opportunities for women, and especially to keep a focus on family programs. From the outset I recognized my limitations and challenges as a political appointee (and in particular as the protégé of the Vice President), and so I set about learning the M&RA business, keeping my head down, and refraining from all but basic orientational travel. I never flaunted my four-star status, and I never wanted to be regarded as a lightweight on a lark. Like my models TR and FDR, I richly gained from service in the Navy Department, and I feel I can handle any other responsibility in government with confidence.

And yet I must look back on those four years with no small amount of bitterness, too. This was born with my arrival on the job in 1984, imposed on John Lehman—a man not ever to be imposed upon—by political force majeure. Especially that first year, I was treated by him with indifference and even scorn, such as not being invited to ride with my fellow AsstSecNavs in his rail coach to the Army-Navy Game. I would have become Lehman's complete devotee had he done such simple things as invite me in to talk or just acknowledge my notes. Even as things were, I became an admirer of the remarkable Mr. Lehman. By attaining a fairly good mastery of my area, I was able to impress others (such as the kindly under secretary, Jim Goodrich) if not Lehman himself.

When Lehman resigned in February 1987 and my quixotic friend Jim Webb was named to succeed him, I had great hopes for a cooperative, even close, working relationship with SecNav. But Jim proved even trickier and pricklier than Lehman, and I had a bad summer that year. My standing had just about returned to where it had been when Jim became secretary when I informed him I wanted to leave. Then came his own resignation a month later. In what would have seemed deeply ironic to a browbeaten Untermeyer the previous August, Webb was gone before I was. I remain Jim's staunch defender, regarding his ten months as SecNav as quite rich. But while he resigned on a matter of true principle, he is regarded today, even by his fellow Marines, as merely a hothead.

Remarkably, I thought little about Pentagonia when I finally got to Patagonia.

Afterword

Lessons Learned

After returning from South America, I threw myself into the transition-planning project for Vice President Bush. One of several interviews I conducted that summer and fall was with Oliver (Buck) Revell, then associate deputy director of the FBI with responsibility for investigations. I needed an understanding of how the Bureau investigated and cleared potential presidential appointees. Buck told me about the clearance process and then gave a friendly warning: don't consider John Lehman for an appointment; he was under investigation in connection with the so-called Operation Illwind criminal case, a result of his close friendship and working association with the principal target, Mel Paisley.

In his memoir, *A G-Man's Journal* (Pocket Books, 1998), Revell recounted what happened in March 1989, immediately after then–President Bush's nomination of John Tower to be secretary of Defense was rejected by the Senate. Boyden Gray, counsel to the President, contacted Revell to say the President wanted to send the Senate a new nominee immediately. Recognizing that this would not allow the FBI to do even a cursory background check on this person, Boyden gave Buck a list of three names the President was considering.

"When I heard one of them," Revel wrote, "I blanched. Before commenting to Gray, I told him we would conduct a records check, and I'd get back to him as soon as possible. . . . As feared, the first name on the list had serious complications with the Illwind fraud case. If he wasn't actually indicted, he would likely be named an unindicted coconspirator in the prosecutions. This obviously wouldn't pass muster with the Senate, nor with the President."

Lehman (whom Revell did not mention in his book) was neither indicted nor declared an unindicted coconspirator in Illwind, but at that moment he lost his best chance to become secretary of Defense. Instead, Bush chose the noncontroversial congressman-at-large from Wyoming, Dick Cheney. Illwind did capture Mel, who in 1991 pled guilty to several counts of bribery and conspiracy to commit theft. For this he was fined $50,000 and sentenced to a four-year term in a federal prison in Nevada. Released in 1995, Mel achieved a degree of rehabilitation by collecting films on World War II aviation and by serving as a consultant on a television documentary on the same theme. He died in 2001.

Lehman's only further federal service came as a member of the National Commission on Terrorist Attacks upon the United States (the so-called 9/11 Commission) from 2002–2004. His last chance to become secretary of Defense died with the 2012 defeat of Mitt Romney for president. Lehman had led Romney's defense policy group, with which I was affiliated.

Aside from his historic role in rebuilding the Navy as a powerful instrument of national security, John Lehman had another kind of impact on the Pentagon: no subsequent secretary of any of the military departments has been allowed to be the independent operator Lehman was, even if possessing the skill and harboring the ambition to be one. It is as if the mantra of all secretaries of Defense since Caspar Weinberger has been, "No new Lehmans!"

And what of the other major players whose names dominate the previous pages of this book?

After his resignation as SecNav, Jim Webb returned to writing and making films. He wrote two more novels (*Something to Die For* and *The Emperor's General*), a work of nonfiction (*Born Fighting*), and frequent guest editorials. His opposition to both wars in Iraq ensured he would not be appointed to any national security–related office in the next two Republican administrations. Then in 2006 he was recruited by the Democratic Senatorial Campaign Committee to oppose Sen. George Allen (R-Virginia). Given Webb's abiding hostility to members of his own "baby boom" generation who opposed the Vietnam War and who found their political home in the Democratic Party, this was something of a surprise. But it was a deft move by the DSCC to get a conservative veteran of Scots-Irish stock to run in the strongly pro-military Old Dominion. Allen's verbal stumbles during the campaign dragged him down to defeat in a national tide against George W. Bush's Republicans. Webb beat him by 9000 votes out of almost 2.4 million cast.

After his election, I sent Jim a note of sincere congratulations but opined that the Senate didn't quite seem his kind of place. "You have too much of your Uncle Tommy in you," I said. This was a reference to something he wrote in *Born Fighting:* "When I was in my teens, I asked Uncle Tommy what he considered to be his proudest accomplishment. He thought about it for a moment, and then he grinned: 'I never kissed the ass of any man.'" True enough, though he did good work there, one term in the Senate was all that Jim Webb could take.

As I predicted (26 February 1988), Will Ball's tenure as secretary of the Navy would prove just as brief as Webb's: ten months. Had his mentor, John Tower, been confirmed as SecDef in 1989, Will undoubtedly would have remained SecNav and been a fine one. But the new secretary of Defense, Dick Cheney, chose to elevate Larry Garrett instead. Larry's tenure suffered from following so closely behind the dramatic Lehman years and the tumult caused by Webb's sudden departure. Even worse, Garrett drew the principal blame for not squarely addressing the Tailhook scandal, the major sexual excesses on the sidelines of naval aviation's annual Tailhook conference in Las Vegas in 1991. Despite Garrett's resignation as SecNav, the scandal fueled the Democrats' attack on the Bush Administration in 1992, which they labeled "the year of the woman."

Tailhook not only contributed to the defeat of George Bush; it closed a historic decade of growth and pride for the Navy on a tawdry and squalid note. More infuriating, it gave John Lehman's old enemies cause to hoot, gloat, and congratulate themselves for being right all along.

★   ★   ★

My own experience at Navy was valuable for exactly the reason I went there in 1983: to learn how the Pentagon (and bureaucracy in general) really work, how to motivate and mobilize career staff, and how to promote the president's programs.

I began applying the lessons of those years immediately after the election of 1988 when, as director of Presidential Personnel, I advised the first President Bush on filling hundreds of political appointments such as the one I had held. It helped greatly that I had been in an agency myself and knew the pressures—from the boss, colleagues, bureaucrats, other agencies, the press, Congress, and interest groups—the new appointees would face. I always considered a particular appointee's "ability" to be more important than his or her "qualifications," for the first speaks to their likelihood of success whereas the second is merely an expression of their resume.

I was especially sensitive to force-filling jobs in departments and agencies where a Cabinet secretary or agency administrator wanted someone other than my choice. As the avatar of the President in matters of personnel, I was charged with entrusting the execution of his policies to his proven supporters and not simply to some hot-shot K Street or Wall Street lawyer who hadn't help elect George Bush but whom the secretary very much wanted. This often involved a struggle, because many a Cabinet secretary equated President Bush's success with his or her personal success, and this, they stoutly insisted, required "their" people. I fought these fights again and again—Dick Cheney was by far my toughest customer—but I never forgot what it was like to arrive in an agency in which its head wanted someone other than the White House choice.

Among other "lessons learned":

Dealing with the boss: Regardless of my personal problems or disagreements with John Lehman and Jim Webb, I confined my criticism to the pages of my journal and unapologetically worked with subordinates and associates to carry out their directives. I also never forgot that, while I definitely and directly worked for the secretary of the Navy, my primary loyalty was to the president who appointed me. This, I strongly believed, required me to give the secretary my candid opinions and to give the men and women of the Navy and Marine Corps, plus civilian employees, my full attention and labor.

Dealing with other grandees: Although my position gave me rank equivalent to that of a four-star admiral or general, I accepted this simply as a means to doing my job. I respected those people who had stayed in uniform, doing hard jobs, facing danger, and rising in the ranks when I had chosen to get out of uniform and seek advancement through politics. At the same time, I took very seriously my role as "appeals judge" of the Navy and Marine Corps on disciplinary and personnel cases, relying on my judgment rather than automatically adopting that of the chain of command. The law puts civilians at the top of that chain, and when I ruled on a case I could almost feel the mandate of the American people rising out of the elections of Ronald Reagan and of one hundred senators to surge down to the tip of my pen.

Dealing with senior civil servants and "experts" in general: My attitude, acquired from George H. W. Bush, was to presume loyalty and competence from career staff and to work cooperatively with them. With rare exceptions, I found these people to be helpful and instructive, not the "civil serpents" of John Lehman and Mel Paisley's imagining. Their attitude is self-fulfilling: treat people as untrustworthy, and they will definitely prove so. But the senior official retains ultimate responsibility, and, as Margaret Thatcher learned early in her career, "Bureaucratic logic is no substitute for ministerial judgment."[1]

Choosing my staff: I paid a great deal of attention to the selection and, as required, replacement, of my civilian staff. This, too, proved useful in my next life as director of Presidential Personnel, balancing the needs of the job with the requirement of political clearance. For my military staff, I wanted (and could pick from) truly outstanding officers, and I wanted the experience of serving on my staff to be a boost on their way toward flag rank. I always made sure to give my staff time to see me, often on short notice. After all, I suffered from an inability to see John Lehman (especially at the crucial outset of my time as AsstSecNav), and while I couldn't dictate his schedule, I could dictate mine. An executive, in or out of government, who lets his outer-office staff "protect" his time to the exclusion of his principal deputies should not be surprised when unexpected and unpleasant things happen.

The critical importance of congressional relations: Despite the growth of the executive branch in the last century, Congress retains the central role in American government, simply because it dispenses the money. I always enjoyed my excursions up to Capitol Hill, even to testify before congressional committees. As an assistant secretary, I could not count on the Navy Department's legislative liaisons (all military officers) to give me the same information and attention they gave SecNav, the CNO, and the commandant. And as a former political practitioner, I definitely had a better touch in dealing with senators, representatives, and Hill staff than they.

The crucial importance of budgets: One of John Lehman's many lapidary expressions was that "Policy follows the dollars." No program or initiative means anything until it has a place in the budget. As trying and as interminable as budget meetings may be, they are mandatory for the political executive, especially in a place like DOD. (Once, when some pipes burst, a journalist reported that "water ran through the corridors of the Pentagon like money.") At any given time, *three* budgets are under consideration: the one being executed, the one pending on Capitol Hill, and the one being prepared for submission to Congress the following year.

---

1. Margaret Thatcher, *The Path to Power* (1995).

The value of relationships: Personal ties help lubricate action in Washington as much as in the Harris County (Texas) courthouse, scene of my first full-time government service. This was true both within and without the walls of the Pentagon. Having meals and other regular meetings with my principal military and civilian counterparts occupied a major part of my calendar every week, but they were essential for exchanging information, establishing ties of trust, and working out problems.

The value of reading: This final item may seem surprising, but reading history, biography, and also literature was of enormous value to me. *Dossier* magazine once said I constantly quoted Herman Melville and C. S. Forester to my staff and other naval audiences. This was a calumny: I have never read any of Forester's "Horatio Hornblower" books and don't intend to. But I did read (and quote) a lot of Melville and found particular reward in his *White Jacket.* I truly felt that in Melville's pleading with the civilian leadership of the Navy in the mid-1850s to think of the welfare of the men before the mast, he was talking directly to me 130 years later. Also, as related in my journal on 23 September 1987, I found considerable solace in reading of the problems young Gideon Welles had with his difficult boss, George Bancroft, in the Navy Department of the 1840s. This discovery greatly encouraged me in my stormy relations with a latter-day literary SecNav, Jim Webb.

About this time I also read a biography of Admiral the Lord Louis Mountbatten,[2] whose father, Prince Louis of Battenberg, was also first sea lord of the Royal Navy. When the heir to the throne suddenly died, the future King George V despaired of his ability to rule Great Britain, since the only thing he had been was a naval officer. Prince Louis said, "George, you're wrong. There is no more fitting preparation for a king than to have been trained in the navy."

Not as a king, but as an assistant to the president, as director of the Voice of America, and as an ambassador, I was also well prepared by my times in naval service, all three of them.

---

2. Philip Ziegler, *Mountbatten* (1985).

Abbreviations and Acronyms

AA: Administrative assistant
ACLU: American Civil Liberties Union
ACMC: Assistant commandant of the Marine Corps
Adm.: Admiral
AE: Ammunition ship
AEI: American Enterprise Institute
AFB: Air Force base
AFPG: Armed Forces Policy Group
AFS: Stores ship
AG: Attorney general
AIDS: Acquired Immune Deficiency Syndrome
AO: Oiler
ASD: Assistant secretary of Defense
ASN: Assistant secretary of the Navy
AsstSecDef: Assistant secretary of Defense
AsstSecNav: Assistant secretary of the Navy
AUTEC: Atlantic Undersea Test & Evaluation Center
BCNR: Board for Correction of Naval Records
BOQ: Bachelor officers quarters
BPB: Barbara Pierce (Mrs. George) Bush
BRAC: Base Realignment and Closure
Brig. Gen.: Brigadier general
BT: Boiler technician
Capt.: Captain
Cdr.: Commander
CEC: Civil Engineering Command
CENTCOM: Central Command
CG: Commanding general
CHINFO: Chief of information
CIA: Central Intelligence Agency
CINC: Commander-in-chief
CINCLANTFLT: Commander-in-Chief Atlantic Fleet
CINCPAC: Commander-in-Chief Pacific
CINCPACFLT: Commander-in-Chief Pacific Fleet
Civpers: Civilian personnel
CMC: Commandant of the Marine Corps
CNO: Chief of Naval Operations
CNT: Certified Navy twill
CO: Commanding officer
COD: Carrier onboard delivery (aircraft)

Col.: Colonel
Como.: Commodore
Cpl.: Corporal
CPO: Chief petty officer
CU: Chase Untermeyer
D: Democrat
DACOWITS: Defense Advisory Committee on Women in the Services
DAR: Daughters of the American Revolution
DASN: Deputy assistant secretary of the Navy
DASNIF: Deputy assistant secretary of the Navy (Installations & Facilities)
DC: District of Columbia/Washington
DD: Destroyer
DepSec: Deputy secretary
DepSecDef: Deputy secretary of Defense
DI: Drill instructor
DOD: Department of Defense
DV: Distinguished visitors
EA: Executive assistant
Ens.: Ensign
FDR: Franklin Delano Roosevelt
FMF: Fleet Marine Force
FMFLANT: Fleet Marine Force Atlantic
FMFPAC: Fleet Marine Force Pacific
GB: George Bush
GD: General Dynamics Corporation
Gen.: General
GOP: Republican Party
GSA: General Services Administration
HAC: House Appropriations Committee
HASC: House Armed Services Committee
HHS: Department of Health and Human Services
HQMC: Headquarters Marine Corps
HUD: Department of Housing and Urban Development
I&F: Installations & Facilities
Insurv: Inspection & Survey
JAG: Judge Advocate General
JCS: Joint Chiefs of Staff
JFK: John Fitzgerald Kennedy
JG: Lieutenant (junior grade)
JIMFOG: Joint Installations Management Flag Officer Group
LA: Legislative assistant; Los Angeles
LAV: Light armored vehicle
LBJ: Lyndon Baines Johnson
LCUs: Landing craft utilities
LHA: Landing helicopter assault (ship)

LST: Landing ship tank
Lt.: Lieutenant
Lt. (j.g.): Lieutenant (junior grade)
Lt. Cdr.: Lieutenant commander
Lt. Col.: Lieutenant colonel
Lt. Gen.: Lieutenant general
LVT: Landing vehicle, tracked
M&RA: Manpower & Reserve Affairs
MA: Marine aide
Maj.: Major
Maj. Gen.: Major general
MarDet: Marine detachment
MCAB: Marine Corps air base
MCAS: Marine Corps air station
MCRD: Marine Corps recruiting depot
MedCom: Medical Command
MIA: Missing in action
Midn.: Midshipman
Milcon: Military construction
MLSF: Mobile Logistics Support Force
MMS: Minerals Management Service
MOU: Memorandum of understanding
MSC: Military Sealift Command
NAS: Naval air station
NATO: North Atlantic Treaty Organization
NAVFAC: Naval Facilities Engineering Command
NavSea: Naval Sea Systems Command
NRF: Naval Reserve Fleet
NROTC: Naval Reserve Officers Training Corps
NSC: National Security Council
NWS: Naval Weapons Station
OLA: Office of Legislative Affairs
OMB: Office of Management & Budget
OPA: Office of Program Appraisal
OpNav: Staff of the chief of Naval Operations
OSD: Office of the Secretary of Defense
PAC: Political action committee
PAO: Public affairs officer
PCO: Prospective commanding officer
PDASN: Principal deputy assistant secretary of the Navy
P.I.: Parris Island
PM: Prime minister
POAC: Pentagon Officers Athletic Center
POW: Prisoner of war
PRIMUS: Physician Reservists in Medical Universities

R: Republican
RE&S: Research, Engineering & Systems
RFPB: Reserve Forces Policy Board
ROTC: Reserve Officers Training Corps
RR: Ronald Reagan
S&L: Shipbuilding & Logistics
SASC: Senate Armed Services Committee
SEC: Securities and Exchange Commission
SecAF: Secretary of the Air Force
SecArmy: Secretary of the Army
SecDef: Secretary of Defense
SecNav: Secretary of the Navy
SecNavInst: Secretary of the Navy instruction
SES: Senior Executive Service
SESers: Senior civil servants
SG: Surgeon general
Sgt.: Sergeant
SPR: Secretarial Performance Review
SSN: *Los Angeles*–class nuclear submarine
Strike U: Naval Strike and Air Warfare Center
TBS: The Basic School
TOTO: Tongue of the Ocean
TR: Theodore Roosevelt
Under (The): Under secretary of the Navy
UnSecDef: Under secretary of Defense
UnSecNav: Under secretary of the Navy
USIA: US Information Agency
USMC: US Marine Corps
USN: US Navy
USNA: US Naval Academy
USNR: US Naval Reserve
USUHS: Uniformed Services University of the Health Sciences
VCNO: Vice chief of Naval Operations
VP: Vice President
WASP: White Anglo-Saxon Protestant
WestPac: Western Pacific
WM: Woman Marine
WOPA: Women Officers Professional Association
XO: Executive officer

Notes on Sources

The primary source materials for this book are the journals of Chase Untermeyer, volumes 118 through 142 (covering 1 March 1983 through 4 July 1988, inclusive).

Consulted for occasional facts and quotation:

Coletta, Paolo E., ed. *American Secretaries of the Navy.* 2 vols., 1775–1972. Annapolis: Naval Institute Press, 1980.

Department of the Navy. *The Navy Secretariat, 1798–1996.* Washington, 1996.

Lehman, John F. Jr. *Command of the Seas.* New York: Charles Scribner's Sons, 1988.

Melville, Herman. *White Jacket: Or the World in a Man-of-War.* New York: New American Library (Signet Classics), 1981.

Pasztor, Andy. *When the Pentagon Was for Sale: Inside America's Biggest Defense Scandal.* New York: Scribner, 1995.

Reagan, Ronald. *The Reagan Diaries.* Edited by Douglas Brinkley. New York: HarperCollins, 2007.

Revell, Oliver "Buck." *A G-Man's Journal.* New York: Pocket Books, 1998.

Thatcher, Margaret. *The Path to Power.* New York: HarperCollins, 1995.

Timberg, Robert. *The Nightingale's Song.* New York: Simon & Schuster, 1995.

Vistica, Gregory L. *Fall from Glory: The Men Who Sank the US Navy.* New York: Simon & Schuster, 1995.

Webb, James. *Born Fighting: How the Scots-Irish Shaped America.* New York: Broadway Books, 2004.

Webb, James. *Fields of Fire.* New York: Prentice-Hall, 1978.

Websites:

Biographical Directory of the United States Congress, 1774–Present (bioguide.congress.gov)

United States Navy (navy.mil)

Wikipedia.org

About the Author

Chase Untermeyer has held both elected and appointed office at all four levels of government—local, state, national, and international. A diarist since the age of nine, he went to Washington two weeks before the inauguration of Ronald Reagan in January 1981 to work for the new vice president, George Bush. He remained over the next 12 years, closely observing two presidencies. This he did as executive assistant to the Vice President, as an assistant secretary of the Navy, as director of Presidential Personnel for the first President Bush, and as director of the Voice of America. He would later serve the second President Bush as United States ambassador to Qatar.

Untermeyer is a 1968 graduate of Harvard College with honors in government. During the Vietnam War he served as an officer in the United States Navy aboard a destroyer in the Western Pacific and as aide to the commander of US naval forces in the Philippines.

Upon his return to Texas, Ambassador Untermeyer was a political reporter for the *Houston Chronicle* for three years before becoming executive assistant to the county judge (chief administrative official) of Harris County, Texas, the jurisdiction surrounding Houston. In 1976, he was elected to the first of two terms as a member of the Texas House of Representatives, resigning to go to Washington.

He is married to the former Diana Cumming Kendrick of Sheridan, Wyoming, whom he met when they were both on the White House staff of the first President Bush. Their daughter, Elly, is a student at Stanford University. The Untermeyers live in Houston, where he is an international business consultant and a member of the Texas Ethics Commission.

Index